Atlas ROAD

Contents

MAP LEGEND

ROADS/HIGHWAYS
- INTERSTATE
- CONTROLLED ACCESS
- CONTROLLED ACCESS TOLL
- TOLL ROAD
- PRIMARY DIVIDED
- PRIMARY UNDIVIDED
- SECONDARY DIVIDED
- SECONDARY UNDIVIDED
- LOCAL DIVIDED
- LOCAL UNDIVIDED
- UNPAVED ROAD
- UNDER CONSTRUCTION
- TUNNEL
- PEDESTRIAN ONLY
- AUTO FERRY
- PASSENGER FERRY
- SCENIC BYWAY
- 10 DISTANCE BETWEEN MARKERS
- 25 EXIT NUMBER-FREE/TOLL
- INTERCHANGE FULL/PARTIAL
- ? WELCOME/INFORMATION CENTER
- REST AREA/ SERVICE CENTER

BOUNDARIES
- INTERNATIONAL
- STATE
- COUNTY
- TIME ZONE
- > > > > > > CONTINENTAL DIVIDE

ROAD SHIELDS
- 95 / 95 INTERSTATE/BUSINESS
- 22 / 22 / 22 U.S./STATE/COUNTY
- 227 / 227 FOREST/INDIAN
- TRANS- CANADA
- 1 PROVINCIAL AUTOROUTE
- 1 MEXICO
- 66 HISTORIC ROUTE 66
- VT 41 REFERENCE PAGE INDICATOR

AREAS OF INTEREST
- INDIAN
- MILITARY
- PARK
- FOREST
- GRASSLANDS
- HISTORIC
- INT'L/REGIONAL AIRPORT
- INCORPORATED CITY

POINTS OF INTEREST
- ○ TOWN
- NATIONAL CAPITAL
- STATE/PROVINCIAL CAPITAL
- AAA/CAA CLUB LOCATION
- FEATURE OF INTEREST
- COLLEGE/UNIVERSITY
- CAMPGROUND INFORMATION PROVIDED BY WOODALL'S®
- CUSTOMS STATION
- HISTORIC
- LIGHTHOUSE
- MONUMENT/MEMORIAL
- STATE/PROVINCIAL PARK
- NATIONAL WILDLIFE REFUGE
- SKI AREA
- SPORTS COMPLEX
- DAM

CITIES/TOWNS are color-coded by size, showing where to find AAA Approved and Diamond rated lodgings or restaurants listed in the AAA TourBook guides and on AAA.com:
- ● Red - major destinations and capitals; many listings
- ● Black - destinations; some listings
- ● Grey - no listings

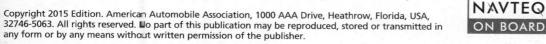

COPYRIGHT 2014 NAVTEQ

United States population figures - U.S. Census Bureau; Census 2010
Canadian population figures - Statistics Canada's 2011 GeoSuite, by permission of Canadian Minister of Industry.

Printed in the United States
Library of Congress 85-117512

This atlas was printed on third-party certified sustainably forested paper.

The routes used to determine these mileages are not necessarily the shortest distance between cities, but represent the route considered the easiest drive for general travel. Distances are shown in miles.

Main

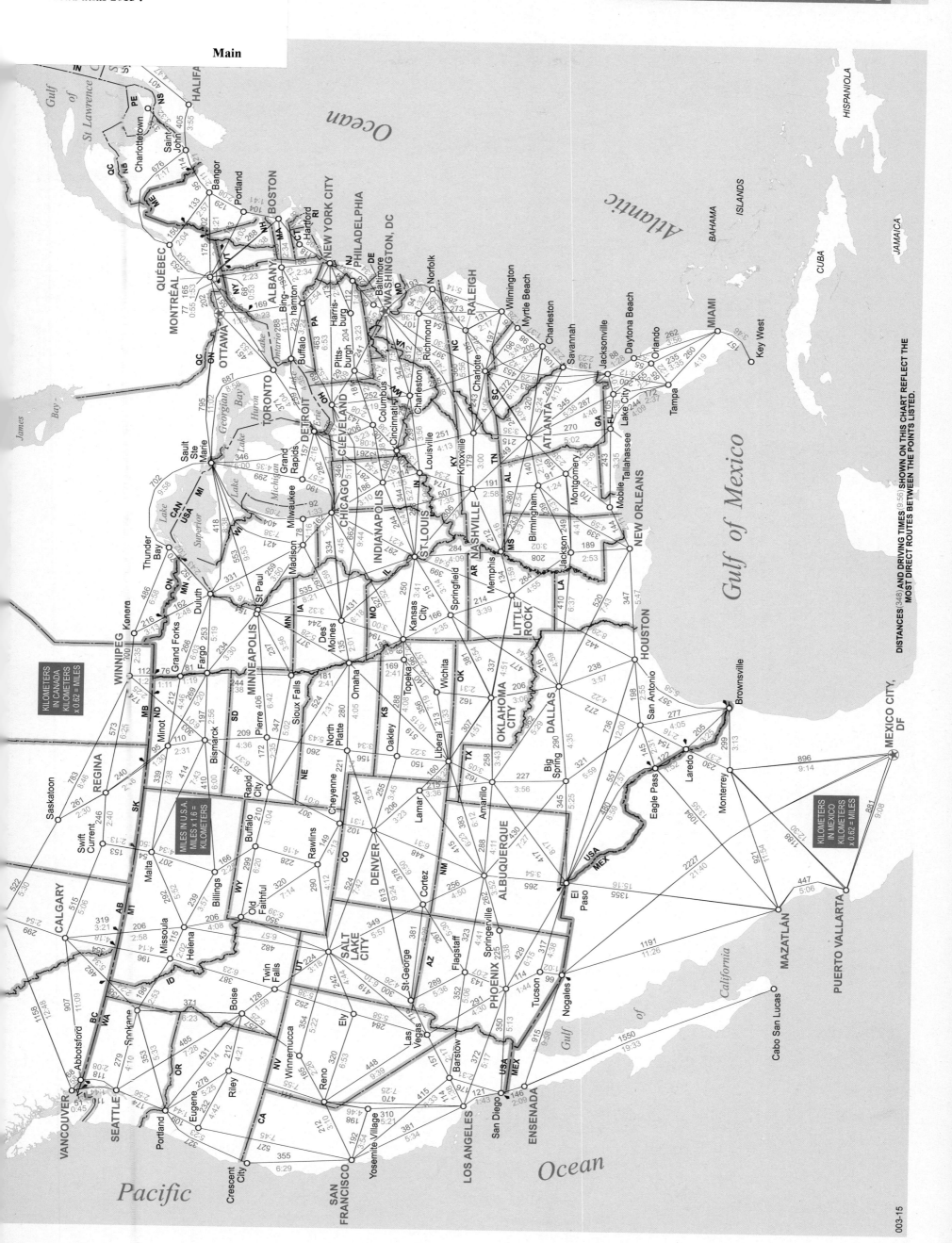

DISTANCES (348) AND DRIVING TIMES (9:56) SHOWN ON THIS CHART REFLECT THE MOST DIRECT ROUTES BETWEEN THE POINTS LISTED.

003-15

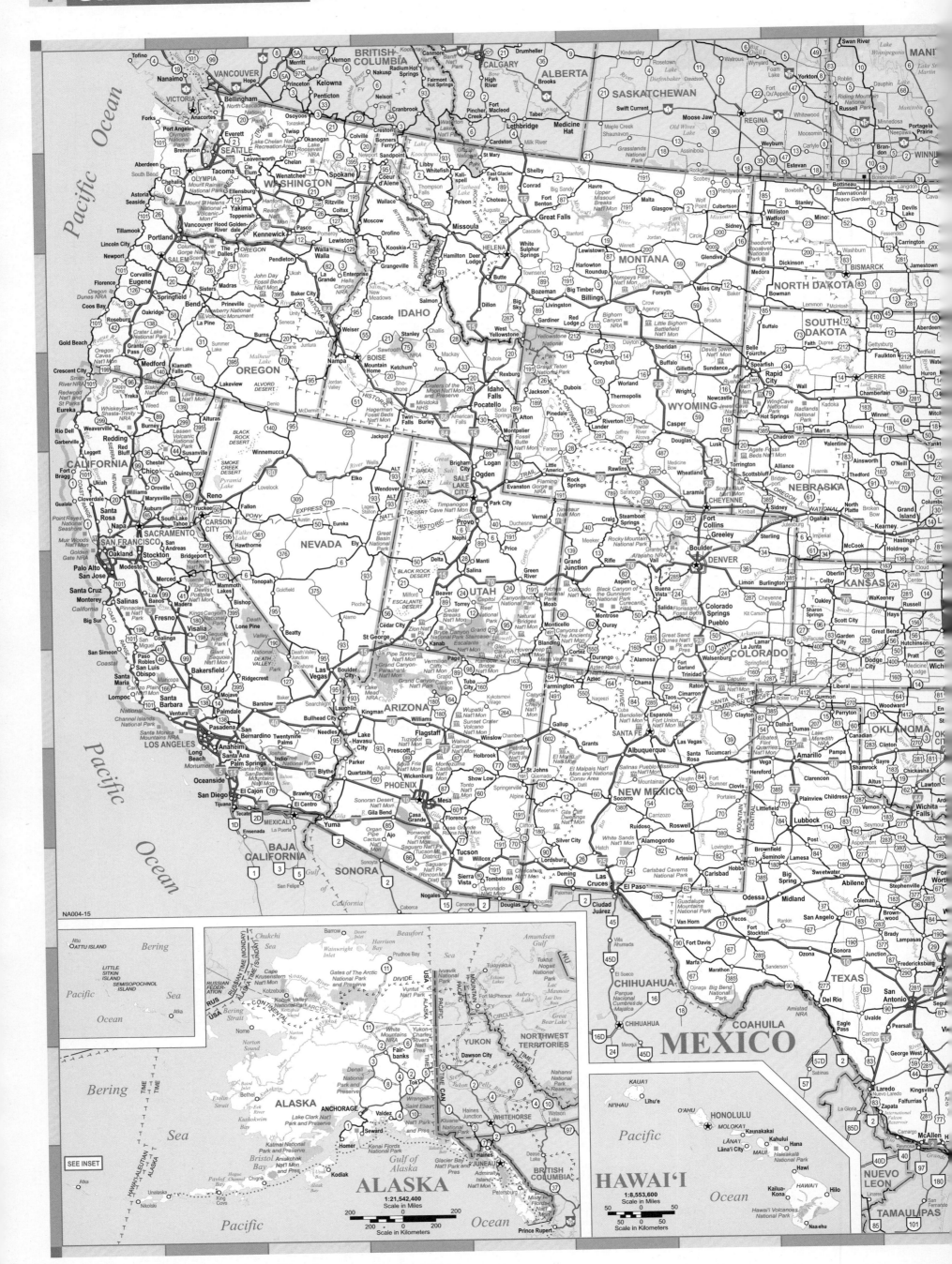

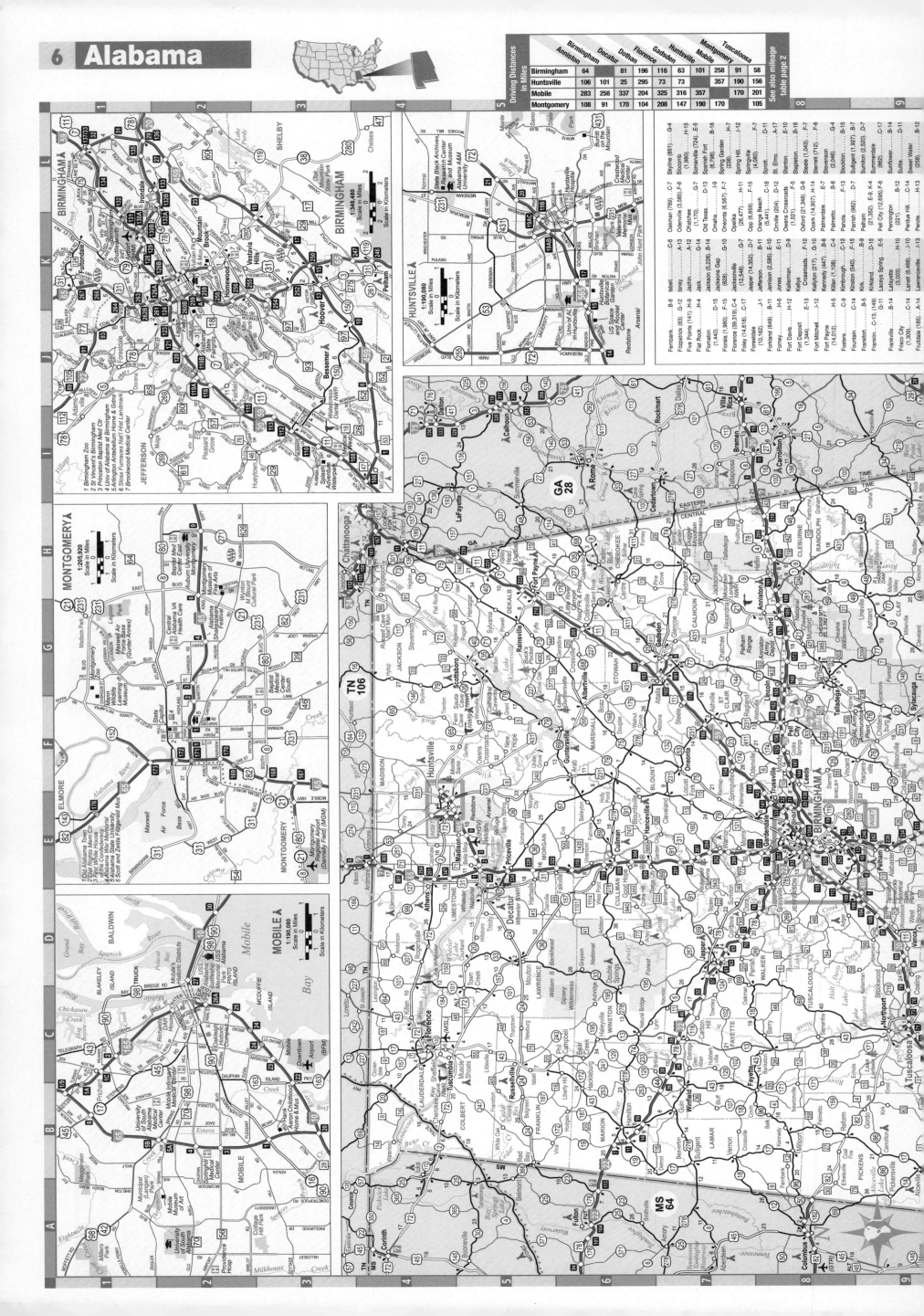

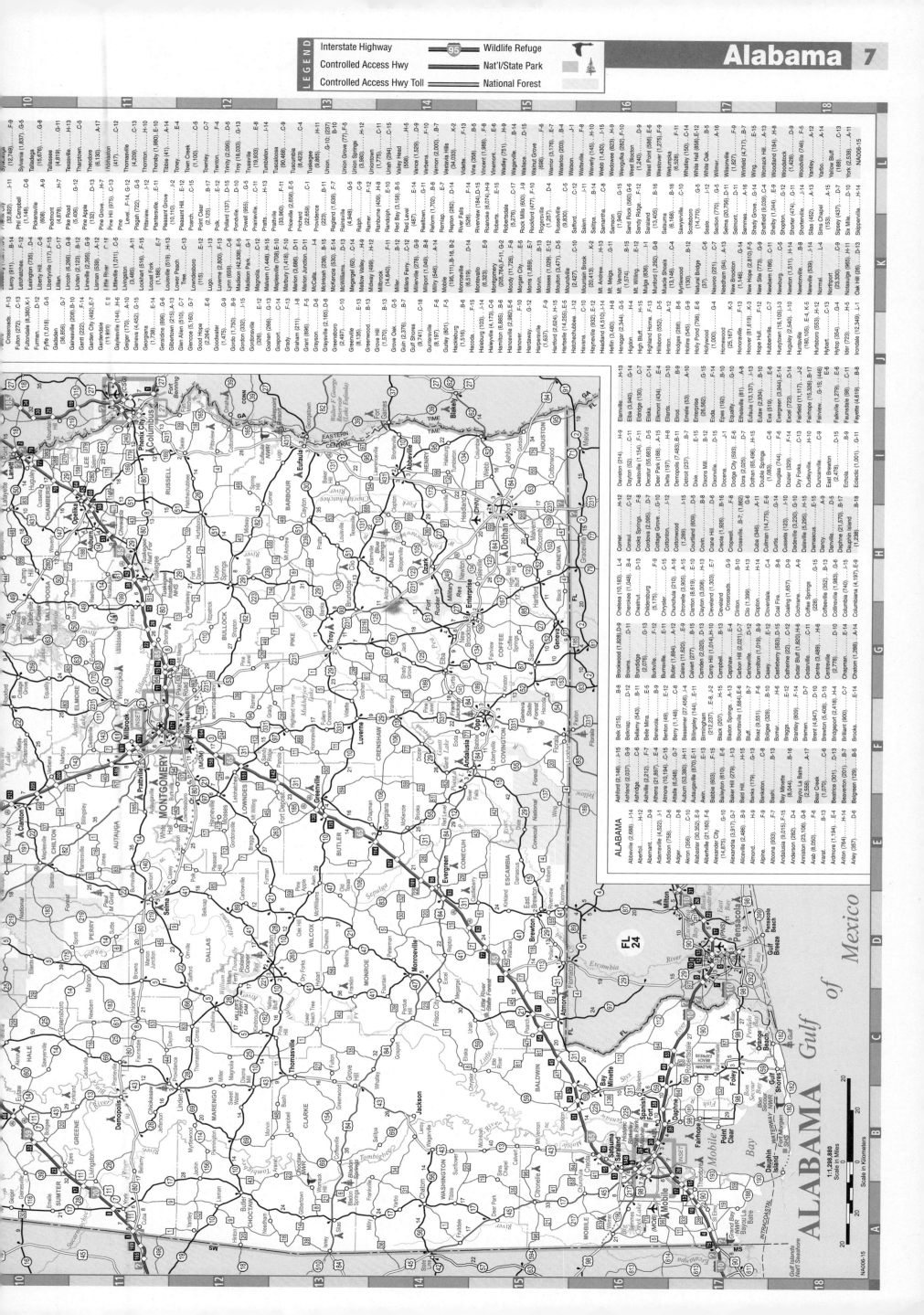

Driving Distances In Kilometers	Dawson City, YT	Fort Simpson, NT	Fort Liard, NT	Haines Jct., YT	Watson Lake, NT	Inuvik, NT	Whitehorse, YT	Yellowknife, NT
Dawson City, YT		1633	1187	659	774	969	533	2413
Whitehorse, YT	533	1103	1379	155	1227	438		1895
Yellowknife, NT	2413	795	632	2035	3112	1449	1895	

See also mileage table page 2

ALASKA

Akiak (326)....L-3
Akhiok (71)....J-5
Akutan (1,027)....L-5
Alakanuk (677)....F-2
Aleknagik (219)....H-3
Allakaket (105)....D-5
Ambler (258)....C-4
Anaktuvuk Pass
(52)....C-7
Anchor Point
(1,930)....H-6
Anchorage
(291,826)..G-6, K-17
Anderson (246)....E-6
Aniak (459)....J-11
Aniak (85)....F-3
Arctic Village
(152)....C-7
Atka (61)....L-3
Atqasuk (233)....A-5
Attu....K-1
Barrow (4,212)....A-5
Beaver (84)....D-7
Bethel (6,080)....G-2
Bettles (12)....D-6
Brevig Mission
(388)....D-2

Buckland (416)....D-3
Cantwell (219)....F-6
Cape Yakataga....E-8;
(105)
Central (96)....D-7
Chalkyitsik (69)....D-8
Chandalar....D-6
Chefornak (418)....G-2
Chena Hot
Springs....E-7
Chevak (938)....F-1
Chickaloon (272)....G-7
Chicken (7)....E-8
Chignik (91)....J-3, K-6
Chitina (126)....G-8
Chuathbaluk (118)....H-9
Circle (104)....D-8
Clam Gulch (176)....H-6
Coffman Cove
(176)....J-12
Cold Bay (108)....L-6
Coldfoot (10)....D-6
College (12,964)..H-15
Cooper Landing
(289)....H-6
Copper Center
(328)....G-8
Cordova (2,239)....H-7
Council....D-2

Craig (1,201)....J-12
Crooked Creek....E-8;
Deadhorse....A-6
Deering (122)....D-3
Delta Junction
(958)....E-7
Denali....F-6
Dillingham
(2,329)....H-3, K-7
Dot Lake (13)....E-8
Douglas....H-11
Eagle (86)....E-9
Eagle River....G-6
Edna Bay (42)....J-12
Eek (296)....G-2
Egegik (109)....J-4
Ekwok (130)....H-3
Elim (330)....E-3
Emmonak (762)....F-2
Ester (2,422)....E-7
Eureka....E-8
Fairbanks
(31,535)..E-7, I-16
False Pass (35)....L-5
Fort Yukon (583)....D-7
Fritz Creek
(1,932)....H-6
Gakona (218)....F-8
Galena (470)....E-4
Girdwood....G-6
Glennallen (483)..G-7

Golovin (156)....E-3
Goodnews Bay
(243)....H-2
Grayling (194)....F-3
Gulkana (88)....F-7
Gustavus (442)..H-11
Haines (1,713)..H-11
Holy Cross (178)...F-3
Homer (5,003)....H-6
Hoonah (760)...H-11
Hooper Bay
(1,093)....F-1
Hope (192)....G-6
Hughes (77)....D-5
Huslia (275)....D-4
Hydaburg (376)..J-12
Hyder (87)....I-13
Iliamna (114)....J-12
Juneau
(31,275)..H-11, K-11
Kake (557)....I-12
Kaktovik (239)....A-8
Kalskag (190)....E-4
Kantishna....E-6
Kasilof (549)....H-6
Kenai (7,100)....H-6
Kennicott....G-8

Kenny Lake (355)..G-8
Ketchikan
(8,050)....J-13
Kiana (361)....C-4
King Cove (938)...L-6
King Salmon
(374)....J-4, K-7
Kipnuk (639)....H-2
Kivalina (374)....C-3
Klawock (755)....J-12
Kobuk (151)....C-4
Kodiak
(6,130)....J-5, K-8
Kokhanok (170)...H-4
Koliganek (209)...H-4
Kotlik (577)....F-2
Kotzebue (3,201)..C-3
Koyuk (338)....E-3
Koyukuk (96)....E-4
Kwethluk (721)....G-3
Kwigillingok (321)..H-2
Larsen Bay (87)...I-5
Lime Village (29)..G-4
Lower Kalskag
(282)....G-2
Manley Hot Springs
(89)....E-6
Manokotak (442)..H-3

Marshall (414)....F-3
McCarthy (28)....G-8
McGrath (346)....F-5
Medfra....E-6
Mekoryuk (191)...G-1
Metlakatla
(1,405)....J-13
Minto (210)....D-6
Moose Pass
(219)....H-6
Mountain Village
(813)....F-2
Mount Baker (35)..J-12
Napakiak (354)....G-2
Napaskiak (405)...G-2
Nenana (378)....E-6
New Stuyahok
(510)....H-4
Newhalen (190)...H-5
Newtok (354)....G-2
Nikolai (94)....F-5
Nikolski (18)....L-4
Ninilchik (883)...H-6
Noatak (468)....C-4
Nome (3,598)....E-2
Nondalton (164)...H-5
Noorvik (668)....C-3
Nulato (264)....E-4
Old Harbor (218)..J-5

Ophir....F-4
Ouzinkie (161)....J-5
Palmer (5,937)...G-6
Paxson (40)....F-7
Pelican (88)....I-11
Petersburg
(2,948)....I-12
Petersville (4)....F-6
Pilot Point (68)....J-4
Pilot Station (568)..F-2
Platinum (61)....H-2
Point Baker (35)..J-12
Point Hope (674)..B-2
Point Lay (189)....A-4
Poorman....E-5
Port Alexander
(52)....J-12
Port Alsworth
(159)....H-5
Port Heiden (102)..J-3
Port Lions (194)...J-5
Portage....H-6
Prudhoe Bay
(2,174)....A-6
Quinhagak (669)..H-2
Ruby (166)....E-5
Russian Mission
(312)....G-3
Sagwon....B-6
Sand Point (976)..L-6

Scammon Bay
(474)....F-2
Selawik (829)....C-4
Seldovia (255)....H-6
Seward (2,693)...H-6
Shageluk (83)....F-3
Shaktoolik (251)..E-3
Shishmaref (563)..C-2
Shungnak (262)...C-4
Sitka (8,881)....I-11
Skagway (920)..H-11
Skwentna (37)....G-6
Slana (147)....F-8
Sleetmute (86)....G-4
Soldotna (4,163)..H-6
St. Michael (401)..E-3
Stebbins (556)....E-3
Sterling (5,617)...H-6
Stony River (54)...G-4
Sutton....G-6
Takotna (52)....F-4
Talkeetna (876)...F-6
Tanacross (136)...F-8
Tanana (246)....E-6
Tatitlek (88)....G-7
Teller (229)....D-2
Tenakee Springs
(131)....I-11

Tetlin (127)....F-8
Thorne Bay
(471)....J-12
Togiak (817)....H-3
Tok (1,258)....F-8
Toksook Bay
(590)....G-2
Trapper Creek
(481)....G-6
Tuluksak (373)...G-3
Tununak (327)....G-1
Twin Hills (69)....H-3
Unalakleet (688)..E-3
Unalaska (4,376)..L-5
Valdez (3,976)....G-7
Venetie (166)....D-7
Wainwright (556)..A-4
Wales (145)....D-1
Wasilla (7,831)....G-6
White Mountain
(190)....E-3
Whittier (220)....G-7
Willow (2,102)....G-6
Wiseman (14)....D-6
Wrangell (2,369)..I-12
Yakutat (662)....H-9

NORTHWEST TERRITORIES

Aklavik (633)....B-10
Deline (472)....C-13

Detah (210)....C-16
Edzo....D-16
Enterprise (87)....E-16
Fort Good Hope
(515)....C-12
Fort Liard (536)...F-14
Fort McPherson
(792)....C-10
Fort Providence
(734)....D-17
Fort Resolution
(474)....D-17
Fort Simpson
(1,238)....E-14
Fort Smith
(2,093)....D-18
Hay River
(3,606)....E-16
Inuvik (3,463)....B-10
Jean Marie River
(59)....E-15
Nahanni Butte
(102)....F-14
Norman Wells
(727)....C-12
Trout Lake (92)...F-15
Tsiigehtchic
(143)....C-10
Tuktoyaktuk
(854)....A-10

Tulita (478)....D-13
Wha Ti (500)....D-15
Wrigley (133)....D-14
Yellowknife
(19,234)..C-16, I-18

YUKON

Aishihik....G-10
Beaver Creek
(103)....F-9
Burwash Landing
(95)....G-9
Carcross (289)..G-11
Carmacks (503)..F-10
Champagne....G-10
Dawson City
(1,319)....D-9
Destruction Bay
(35)....G-9
Eagle Plains....D-10
Elsa....D-9
Faro (344)....F-11
Flat Creek....E-9
Haines Junction
(593)....G-10
Herschel....A-9

Keno....E-10
Kluane....G-9
Koidern....F-9
Mayo (226)....E-10
Minto....F-10
Old Crow (245)..C-9
Pelly Crossing
(336)....E-10
Rancheria....G-12
Ross River (352)..F-11
Shingle Point....B-9
Sixtymile....F-9
Snag....F-9
Stewart Crossing
(25)....E-10
Stewart River....D-9
Sulphur....F-9
Swift River....G-12
Tagish (391)....G-11
Teslin (122)....G-12
Watson Lake
(802)....G-13
Whitehorse
(23,276)..G-11, K-8
Yukon Crossing..F-10

NA008-15

IN WINTER ICE BRIDGES REPLACE FERRIES IN YUKON & NW TERRITORIES

KILOMETERS IN CANADA
KILOMETERS x 0.62 = MILES

INQUIRE LOCALLY FOR CURRENT CONDITIONS BEFORE DRIVING ON UNIMPROVED ROADS SHOWN ON THIS MAP

FAIRBANKS, AK 1:114,048

YELLOWKNIFE NT 1:95,040

ANCHORAGE, AK 1:142,560

JUNEAU, AK 1:3E016

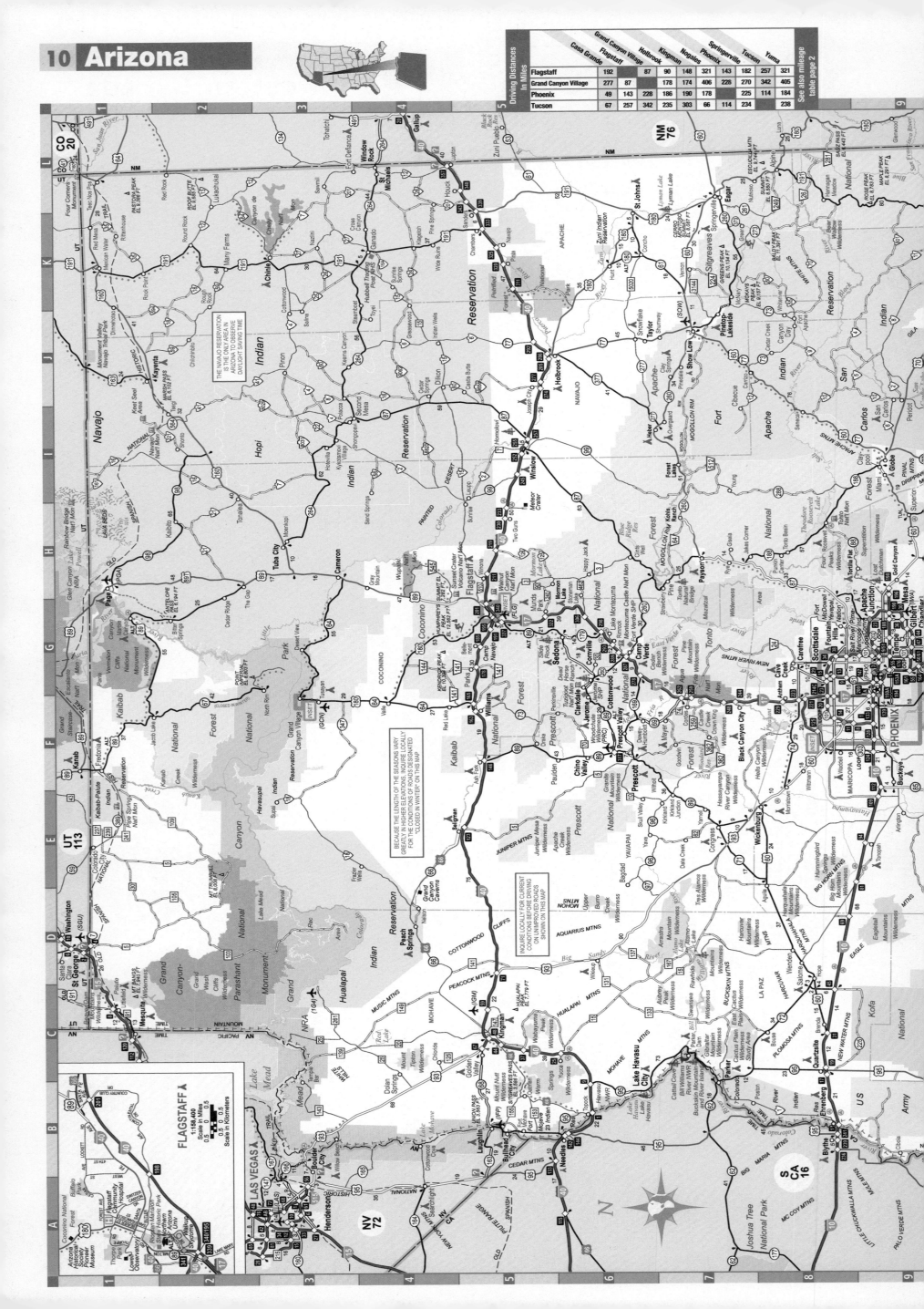

Driving Distances In Miles	Casa Grande	Grand Canyon Village	Flagstaff	Holbrook	Kingman	Nogales	Phoenix	Springerville	Tucson	Yuma
Flagstaff	192		87	90	148	321	143	182	257	321
Grand Canyon Village	277	87		178	174	406	228	270	342	405
Phoenix	49	143	228	186	190	178		225	114	184
Tucson	67	257	342	235	303	66	114	234		238

See also mileage table on page 2

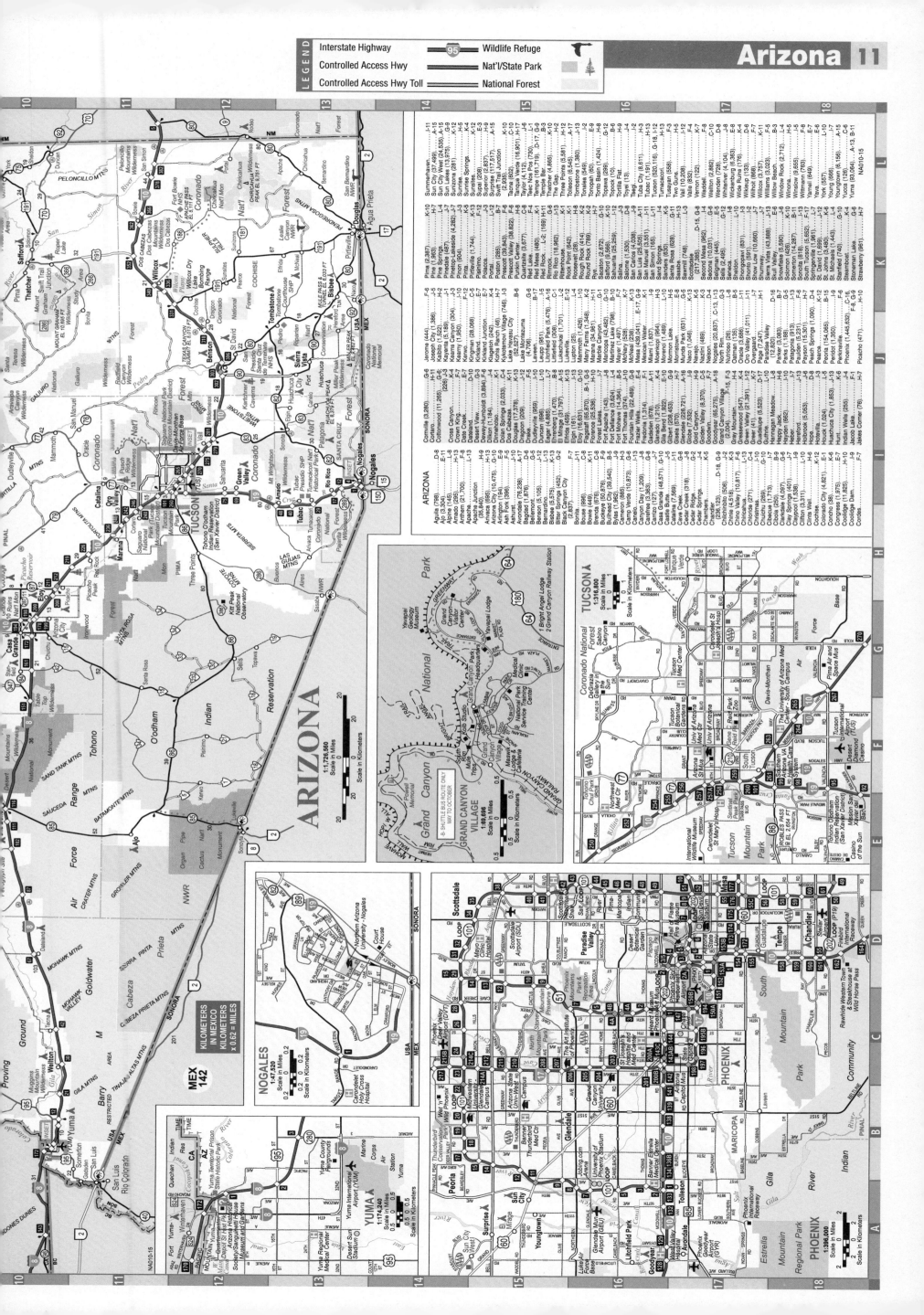

See also mileage table on page 2

Driving Distances In Miles	Branson, MO	El Dorado	Fayetteville	Fort Smith	Hot Springs	Jonesboro	Little Rock	Memphis, TN	Pine Bluff	Texarkana
Fort Smith	158	259	58		131	257	158	287	200	181
Little Rock	170	117	188	158		56	130	134	44	143
Memphis, TN	273	251	318	287	191	70	134		177	276
Texarkana	305	87	237	181	114	271	143	276	153	

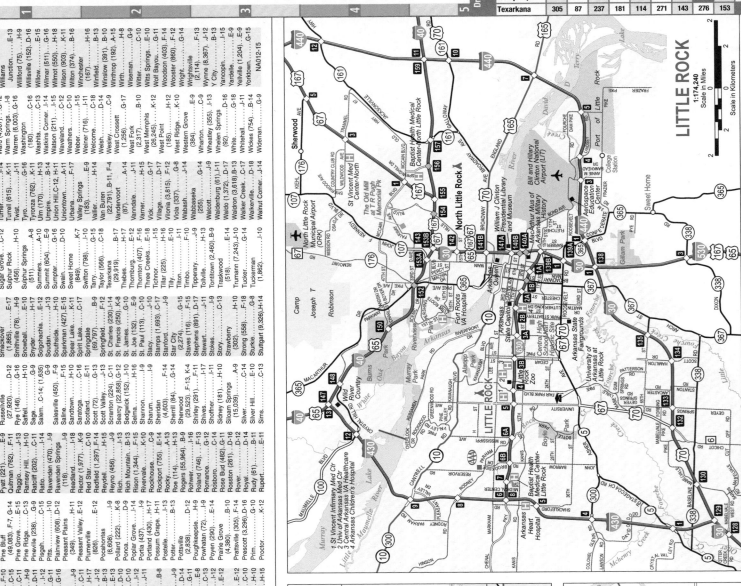

LITTLE ROCK
1:174,240
Scale in Miles
Scale in Kilometers

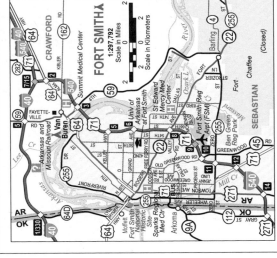

FORT SMITH
1:297,792
Scale in Miles
Scale in Kilometers

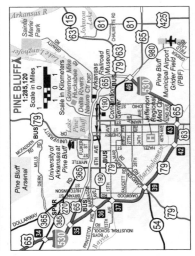

PINE BLUFF
1:285,120
Scale in Miles
Scale in Kilometers

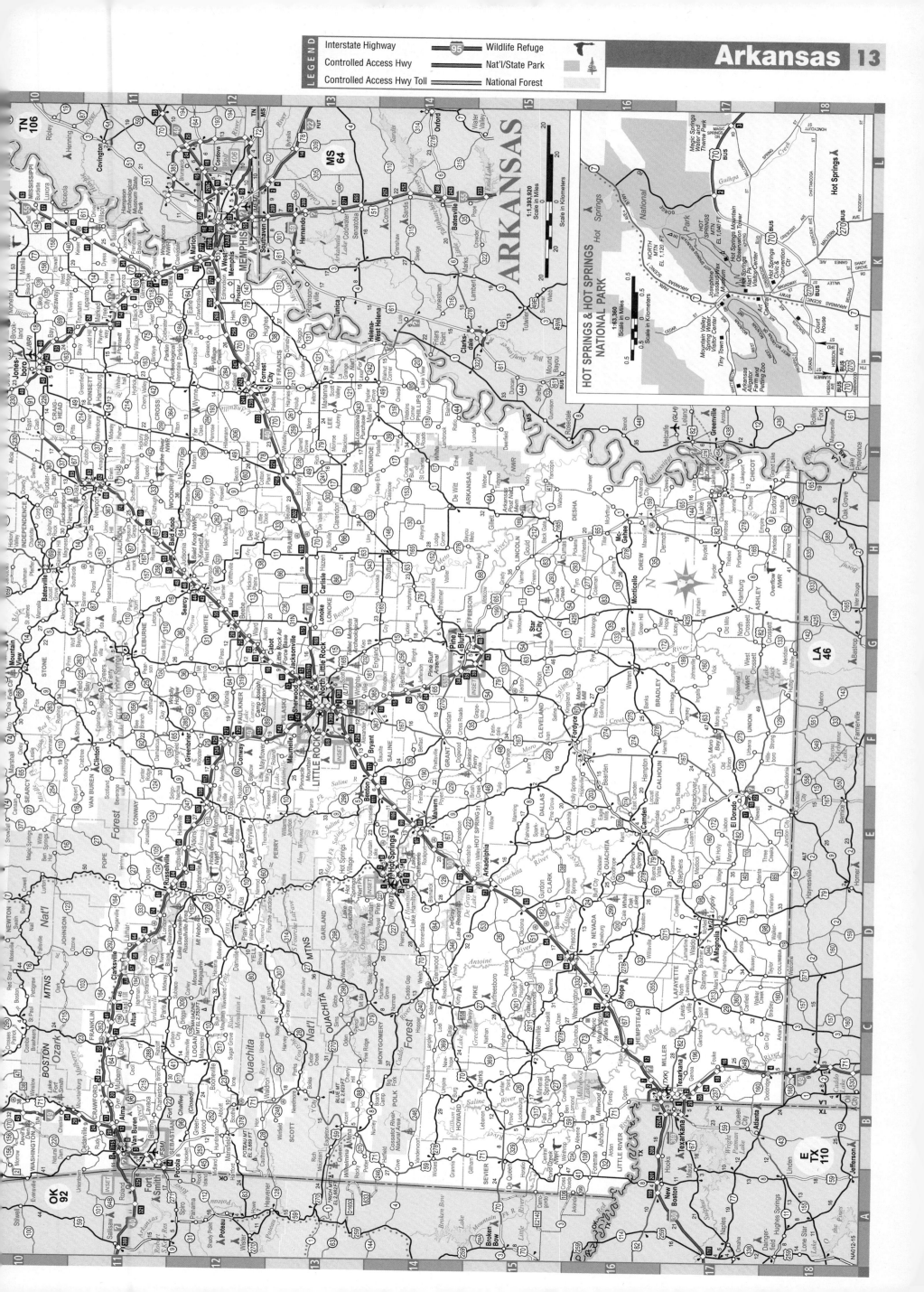

LEGEND

Interstate Highway	Wildlife Refuge
Controlled Access Hwy	Nat'l/State Park
Controlled Access Hwy Toll	National Forest

HOT SPRINGS & HOT SPRINGS NATIONAL PARK

1:63,360
Scale in Miles
Scale in Kilometers

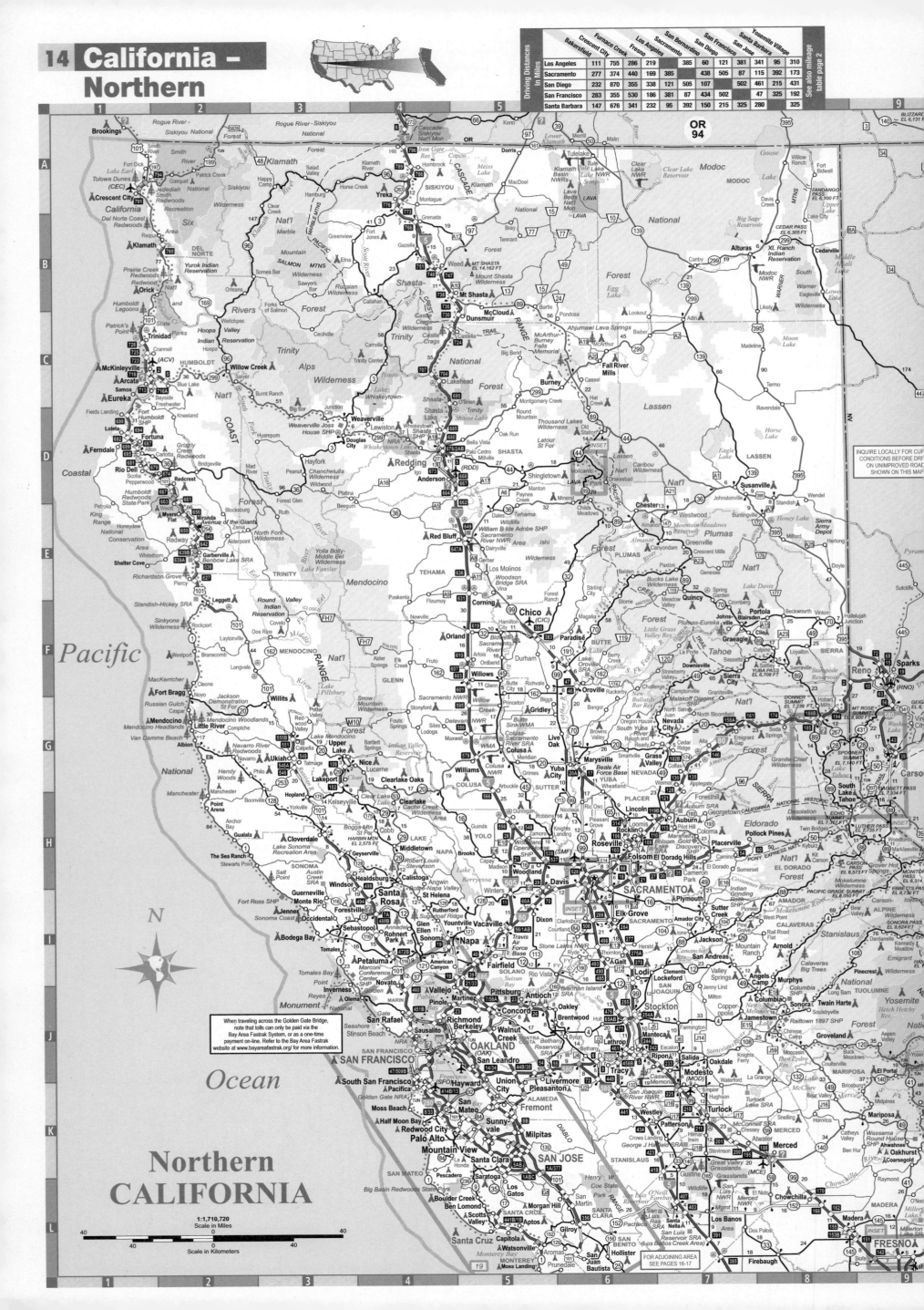

Driving Distances In Miles

	Bakersfield	Crescent City	Furnace Creek	Fresno	Los Angeles	Sacramento	San Bernardino	San Diego	San Francisco	San Jose	Santa Barbara	Yosemite Village
Los Angeles	111	755	286	219		385	60	121	381	341	95	310
Sacramento	277	374	440	169	385		438	505	87	115	392	173
San Diego	232	870	355	338	121	505	107		502	461	215	431
San Francisco	283	355	530	186	381	87	434	502		47	235	192
Santa Barbara	147	676	341	232	95	392	150	215	325	280		325

See also page 2 mileage table

Northern CALIFORNIA

1:1,710,720
Scale in Miles
Scale in Kilometers

When traveling across the Golden Gate Bridge, note that tolls can only be paid via the Bay Area Fastrak System, or as a one-time payment on-line. Refer to the Bay Area Fastrak website at www.bayareafastrak.org/ for more information.

INQUIRE LOCALLY FOR CURRENT CONDITIONS BEFORE DRIVING ON UNIMPROVED ROADS SHOWN ON THIS MAP.

FOR ADJOINING AREA SEE PAGES 16-17

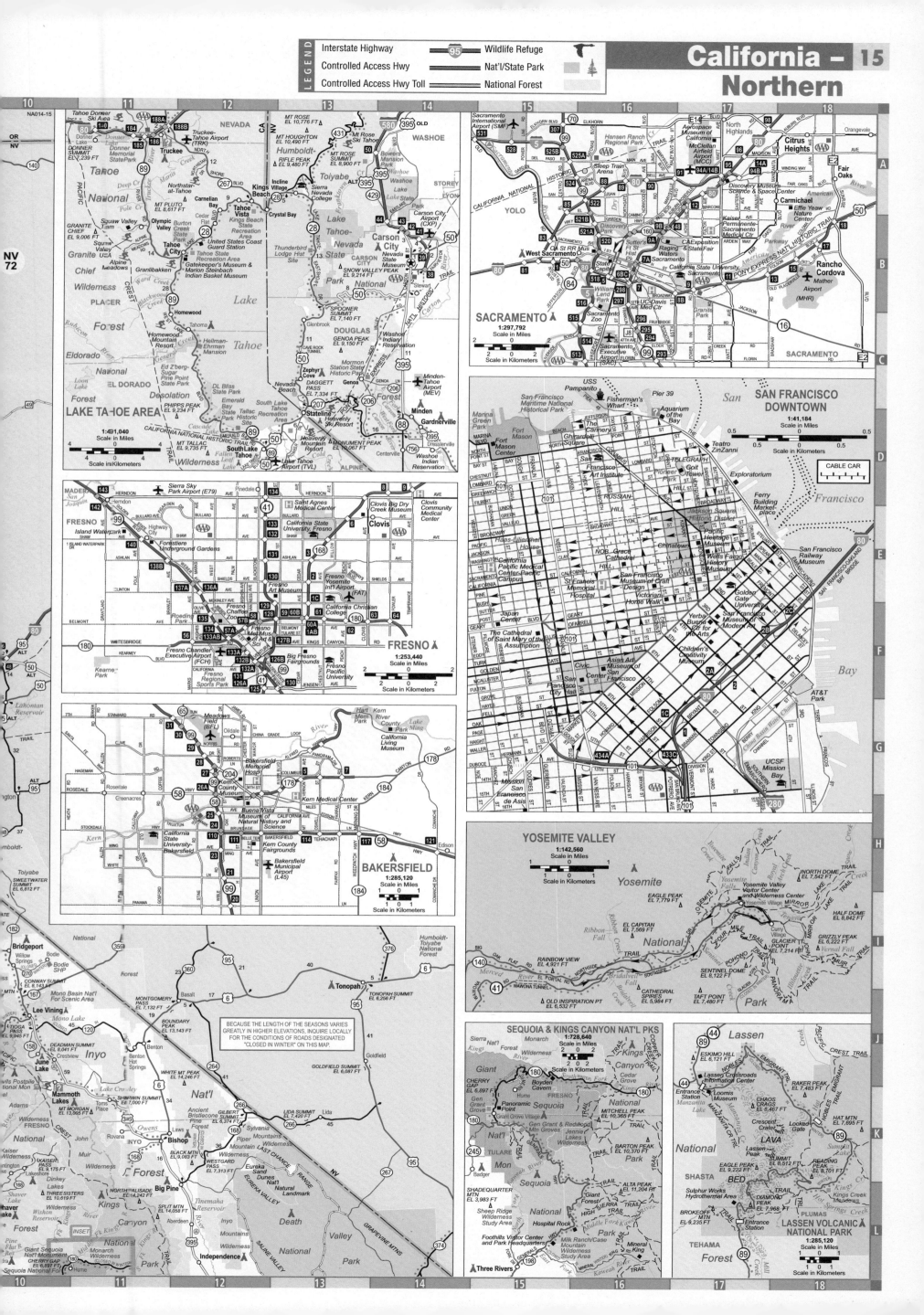

LEGEND
- Interstate Highway
- Controlled Access Hwy
- Controlled Access Hwy Toll
- Wildlife Refuge
- Nat'l/State Park
- National Forest

LAKE TAHOE AREA

SACRAMENTO
1:297,792

SAN FRANCISCO DOWNTOWN
1:41,184

FRESNO
1:253,440

BAKERSFIELD
1:285,120

YOSEMITE VALLEY
1:142,560

SEQUOIA & KINGS CANYON NAT'L PKS
1:728,640

LASSEN VOLCANIC NATIONAL PARK
1:285,120

BECAUSE THE LENGTH OF THE SEASONS VARIES GREATLY IN HIGHER ELEVATIONS, INQUIRE LOCALLY FOR THE CONDITIONS OF ROADS DESIGNATED "CLOSED IN WINTER" ON THIS MAP.

See also mileage table on page 2

Driving Distances In Miles	Bakersfield	Crescent City	Furnace Creek	Fresno	Los Angeles	Sacramento	San Bernardino	San Diego	San Francisco	San Jose	Santa Barbara	Yosemite Village
Los Angeles	111	755	286	219		385	60	121	381	341	95	310
Sacramento	277	374	440	169	385		438	505	87	115	392	173
San Diego	232	870	355	338	121	505	107		502	461	215	431
San Francisco	283	341	230	186	381	87	434	502		47	325	192
Santa Barbara	147	676	341	236	95	392	150	215	325	280		325

CALIFORNIA

Towns with asterisk (*) are keyed to the maps on pages 14-15.

Towns with double asterisks (**) are keyed to the maps on pages 18-19.

MONTEREY PENINSULA

1:152,064

Scale in Miles

Scale in Kilometers

NA016-15

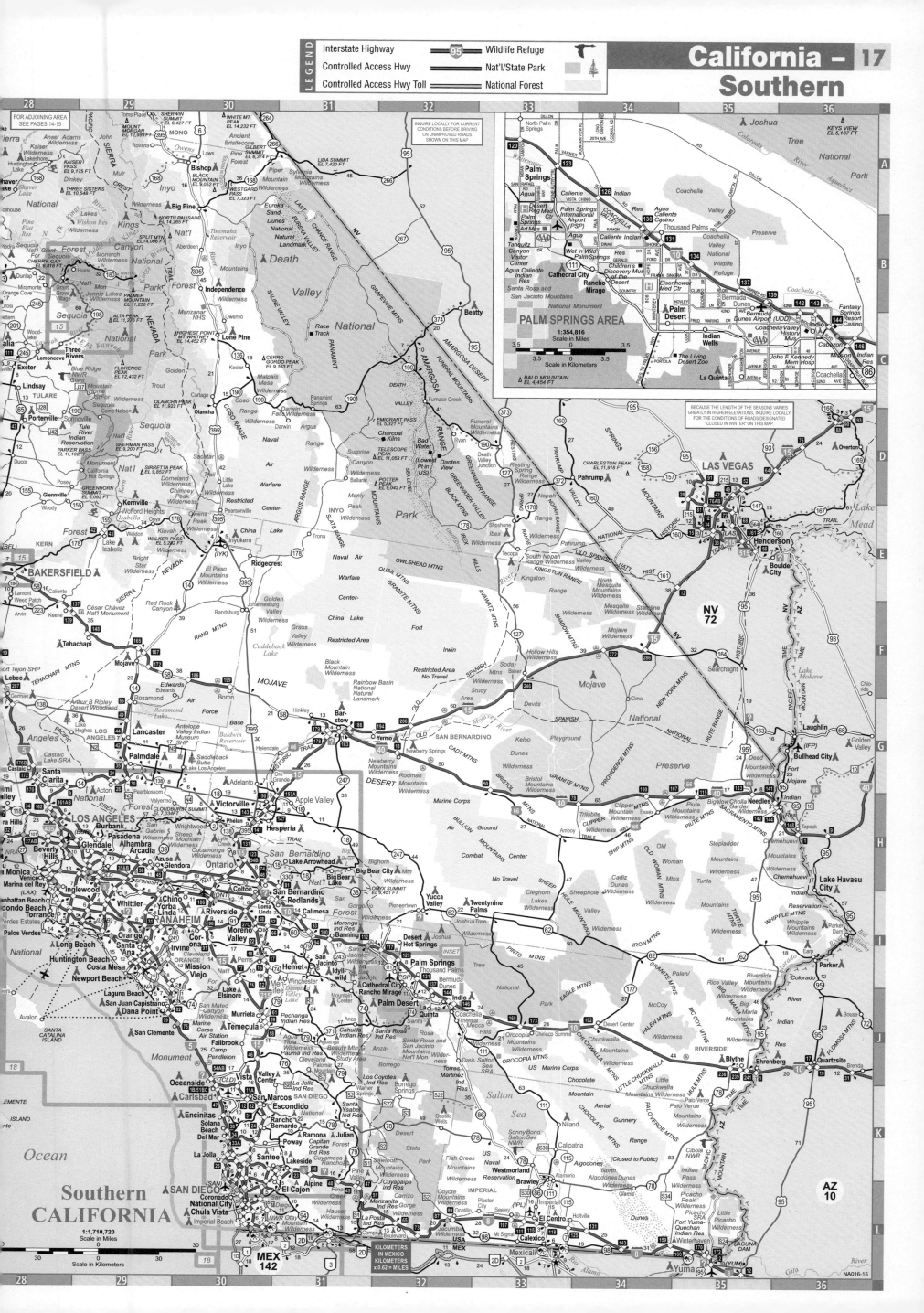

Southwestern CALIFORNIA

1:633,600
Scale in Miles
10 10
Scale in Kilometers
10 10

NA018-15

SANTA BARBARA, CA
1:174,240
Scale in Miles
0.5 0.5
Scale in Kilometers
0.5 0.5

VENTURA / OXNARD CA
1:253,440
Scale in Miles
1 0 1
Scale in Kilometers
1 0 1

DOWNTOWN LOS ANGELES, CA
1:79,200
Scale in Miles
0.5 0.5
Scale in Kilometers
0.5 0.5

DOWNTOWN SAN DIEGO, CA
1:38,016
Scale in Miles
0.2 0.2
Scale in Kilometers
0.2 0.2

TIJUANA / ENSENADA MEXICO
1:1,203,840
Scale in Kilometers
Scale in Miles

KILOMETERS IN MEXICO
KILOMETERS x 0.62 = MILES

Pacific Ocean

California Coastal National Monument

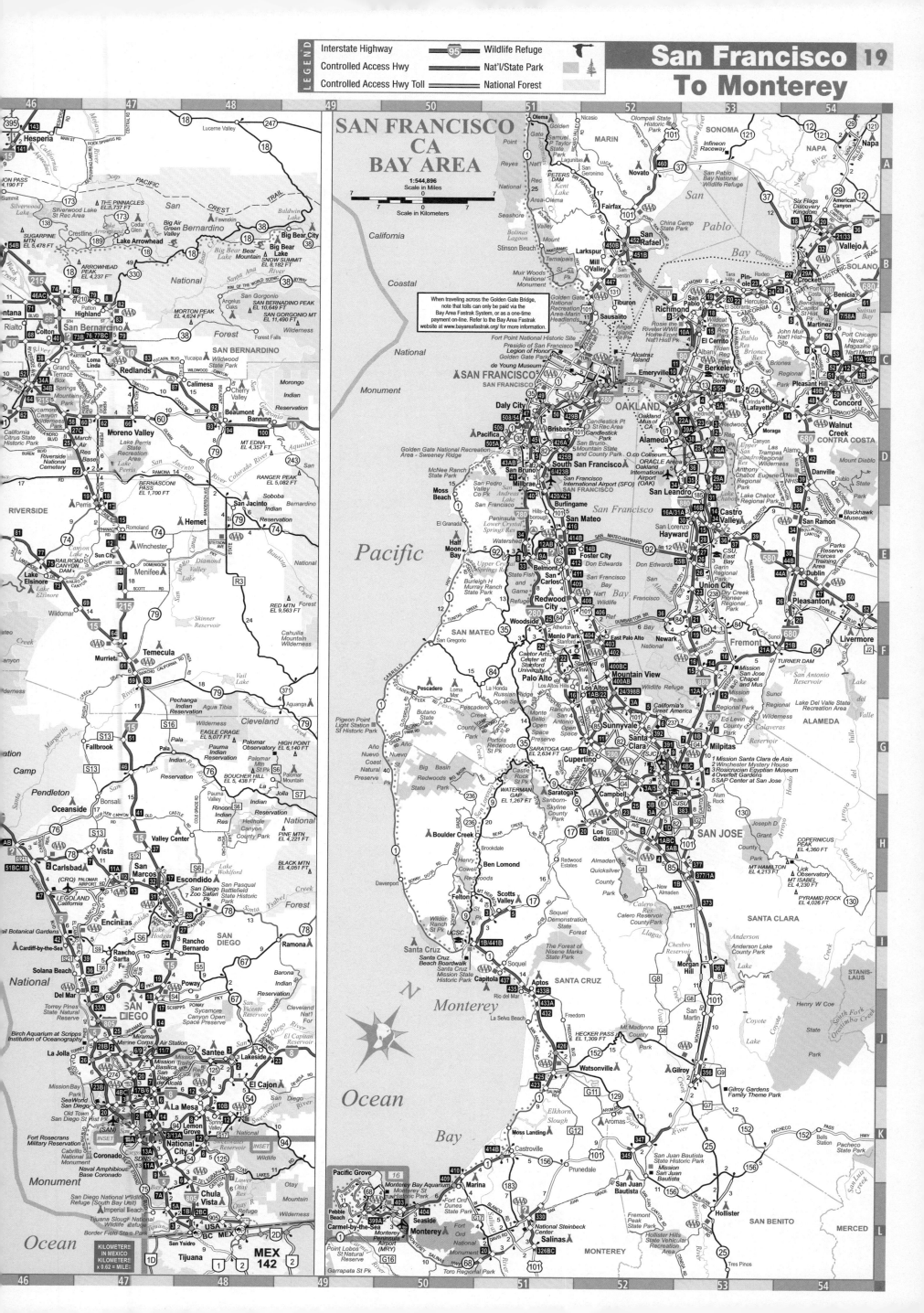

LEGEND
Interstate Highway — 95
Controlled Access Hwy
Controlled Access Hwy Toll
Wildlife Refuge
Nat'l/State Park
National Forest

SAN FRANCISCO CA BAY AREA
1:544,896
Scale in Miles
Scale in Kilometers

When traveling across the Golden Gate Bridge, note that tolls can only be paid via the Bay Area Fastrak System, or as a one-time payment on-line. Refer to the Bay Area Fastrak website at www.bayareafastrak.org/ for more information.

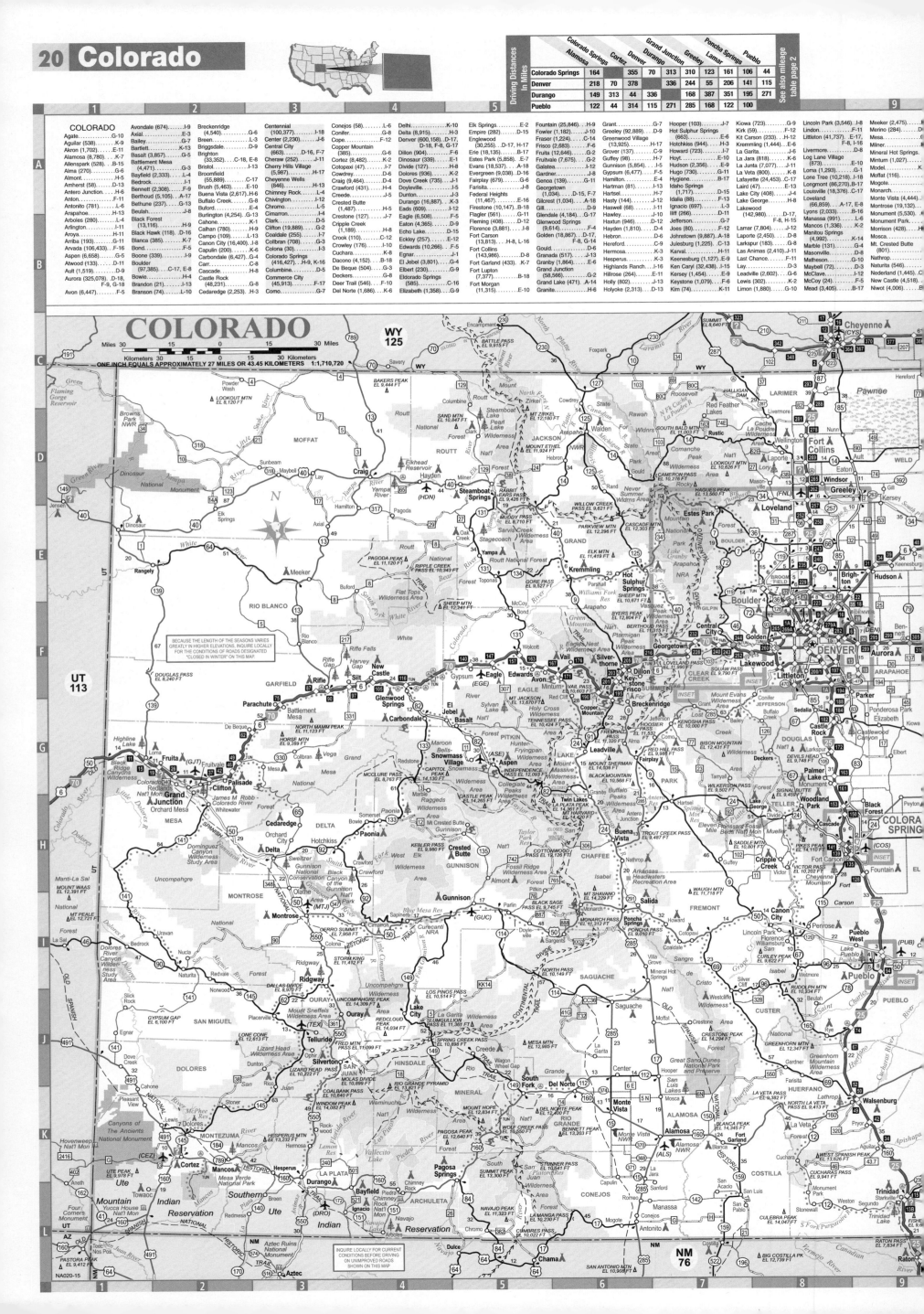

Driving Distances In Miles	Alamosa	Colorado Springs	Cortez	Denver	Durango	Grand Junction	Greeley	Lamar	Poncha Springs	Pueblo
Colorado Springs	164		355	70	313	310	123	161	106	44
Denver	218	70	378		336	244	55	206	141	115
Durango	149	313	44	336		168	387	351	195	271
Pueblo	122	44	314	115	271	285	168	122	100	

See also mileage table page 2

COLORADO

Agate...G-10
Aguilar (538)...K-9
Akron (1,702)...E-11
Alamosa (8,780)...K-7
Allenspark (528)...B-15
Alma (270)...G-6
Almont...H-5
Amherst (58)...D-13
Antero Junction...H-6
Anton...H-11
Antonito (781)...L-6
Arapahoe...H-13
Arboles (280)...L-4
Arlington...I-11
Aroya...G-11
Arriba (193)...G-11
Arvada (106,433)...F-16
Aspen (6,658)...G-5
Atwood (133)...D-11
Ault (1,519)...D-9
Aurora (325,078)...D-18, F-9, G-18
Avon (6,447)...F-5

Avondale (674)...I-9
Axial...E-3
Bailey...G-7
Basalt (3,857)...G-5
Bartlett...K-13
Battlement Mesa (4,471)...G-4
Bayfield (2,333)...L-4
Bedrock...H-1
Bennett (2,308)...F-9
Berthoud (5,105)...D-8
Bethune (237)...G-13
Beulah...I-8
Black Forest...H-8
Black Hawk (118)...D-16
Blanca (385)...K-7
Bond...F-5
Boone (339)...I-9
Boulder (97,385)...C-17, E-8
Bowie...H-4
Brandon (21)...I-13
Branson (74)...L-10

Breckenridge (4,540)...I-18
Breen...L-3
Briggsdale...D-9
Brighton (33,352)...C-18, E-8
Bristol...I-13
Broomfield (55,889)...C-17
Brush (5,463)...E-10
Buena Vista (2,617)...H-6
Buffalo Creek...G-7
Buford...E-4
Burlington (4,254)...G-13
Cahone...K-1
Calhan (780)...H-9
Campo (109)...L-13
Canon City (16,400)...I-8
Capulin (200)...K-6
Carbondale (6,427)...G-4
Carr...E-8
Cascade...H-8
Castle Rock (48,231)...G-8
Cedaredge (2,253)...H-3

Centennial (100,377)...I-18
Center (2,230)...J-6
Central City (663)...D-16, F-7
Cheraw (252)...J-11
Cherry Hills Village (5,987)...I-18
Cheyenne Wells (846)...H-13
Chimney Rock...L-4
Chivington...I-12
Chromo...L-5
Clark...E-4
Clifton (19,889)...G-2
Coaldale (255)...I-7
Collbran (708)...G-3
Colona...G-2
Colorado Springs (416,427)...H-9, K-16
Columbine...C-17
Commerce City (45,913)...F-17
Como...G-7

Conejos (58)...L-6
Conifer...F-7
Cope...F-12
Copper Mountain (385)...F-6
Cortez (8,482)...K-2
Cotopaxi (47)...I-7
Cowdrey...D-6
Craig (9,464)...D-4
Crawford (431)...H-4
Creede...J-5
Crested Butte (1,487)...H-5
Crestone (127)...J-7
Cripple Creek (1,189)...H-8
Crook (110)...C-12
Crowley (176)...I-10
Cuchara...K-8
Dacono (4,152)...E-8
De Beque (504)...G-3
Deckers...G-7
Deer Trail (546)...F-10
Como...G-7

Delhi...K-10
Delta (8,915)...H-3
Denver (600,158)...D-17, F-8, G-17
Dillon (904)...F-6
Dinosaur (319)...E-1
Divide (127)...H-8
Dolores (936)...K-2
Dove Creek (735)...J-1
Doyleville...I-5
Dunton...J-2
Durango (16,887)...K-3
Eads (609)...I-12
Eagle (6,508)...F-5
Eaton (4,365)...D-9
Eckley (257)...E-12
Edwards (10,266)...F-5
Egnar...J-1
El Jebel (3,801)...G-4
Elbert (230)...G-9
Eldorado Springs (585)...C-16
Elizabeth (1,358)...G-9

Elk Springs...E-2
Empire (282)...D-15
Englewood (30,255)...D-17, H-17
Erie (18,135)...D-18, E-8
Estes Park (5,858)...E-7
Evans (18,537)...A-18
Evergreen (9,038)...D-16
Fairplay (679)...G-6
Farisita...J-8
Federal Heights (11,467)...C-18
Firestone (10,147)...B-18
Flagler (561)...G-12
Fleming (408)...D-12
Florence (3,881)...I-8
Fort Carson (13,813)...H-8, L-16
Fort Collins (143,986)...D-8
Fort Garland (433)...K-7
Fort Lupton (7,377)...B-18
Fort Morgan (11,315)...E-10

Fountain (25,846)...H-9
Fowler (1,182)...J-10
Fraser (1,224)...C-14
Frisco (2,683)...F-6
Fruita (12,646)...G-2
Fruitvale (7,675)...G-2
Galatea...I-12
Gardner...J-8
Genoa (189)...G-11
Georgetown (1,034)...D-15, F-7
Gilcrest (1,034)...A-18
Gill...A-18
Glendale (4,184)...G-17
Glenwood Springs (9,614)...F-4
Golden (18,867)...D-17, F-8, G-14
Gould...D-6
Granada (517)...J-13
Granby (1,864)...C-14
Grand Junction (58,566)...G-2
Grand Lake (471)...A-14
Granite...H-6

Grant...G-7
Greeley (92,889)...D-9
Greenwood Village (13,925)...H-17
Grover (137)...C-9
Guffey (98)...H-7
Gunnison (5,854)...I-5
Gypsum (6,477)...F-5
Hamilton...E-4
Hartman (81)...I-13
Hasty (144)...J-12
Haswell (88)...I-11
Hawley...J-10
Haxtun (946)...D-12
Hebron...D-6
Hereford...C-9
Hermosa...K-3
Hesperus...K-3
Highlands Ranch (96,154)...I-16
Hillrose (264)...E-11
Holly (802)...J-13
Holyoke (2,313)...D-13

Hooper (103)...J-7
Hot Sulphur Springs (663)...E-6
Hotchkiss (944)...H-3
Hovenweep...K-1
Howard (723)...I-7
Hoyt...E-10
Hudson (2,356)...E-8
Hugo (730)...G-11
Hygiene...B-17
Idaho Springs (1,717)...D-15
Iliff (266)...D-11
Ignacio (697)...L-3
Idalia (88)...F-13
Jefferson...G-7
Joes (80)...F-12
Johnstown (9,887)...A-18
Julesburg (1,225)...C-13
Karval...H-11
Keenesburg (1,127)...E-8
Ken Caryl (32,438)...I-15
Keota...C-9
Keystone (1,079)...F-6
Kim (74)...K-11

Kiowa (723)...G-9
Kirk (59)...F-12
Kit Carson (233)...H-12
La Garita...K-6
La Jara (818)...K-6
La Junta (7,077)...J-11
La Veta (800)...K-8
Lafayette (24,453)...C-17
Laird (47)...E-13
Lake City (408)...J-4
Lake George...H-8
Lakewood (142,980)...F-8, H-15
Lamar (7,804)...J-12
Laporte (2,450)...D-8
Larkspur (183)...G-8
Las Animas (2,410)...J-11
Last Chance...F-11
Leadville (2,602)...G-6
Lewis (302)...K-2
Limon (1,880)...G-10

Lincoln Park (3,546)...I-8
Lindon...F-11
Littleton (41,737)...F-17, F-8, I-16
Livermore...C-8
Log Lane Village (873)...E-10
Loma (1,293)...G-1
Lone Tree (10,218)...I-18
Longmont (86,270)...B-17
Louisville (18,376)...C-17
Loveland (66,859)...A-17, E-8
Lyons (2,033)...B-16
Manassa (991)...L-6
Mancos (1,336)...K-2
Manitou Springs (4,992)...K-14
Marble (131)...G-4
Masonville...D-8
Matheson...G-10
Maybell (72)...D-3
McClave...J-12
McCoy (24)...F-5
Mead (3,405)...B-17

Meeker (2,475)...E-3
Merino (284)...D-11
Mesa...G-3
Milner...D-4
Mineral Hot Springs...J-7
Model...L-10
Moffat (117)...J-6
Mogote...L-6
Monarch...H-6
Monte Vista (19,132)...K-6
Montrose...H-2
Monument (5,530)...H-8
Monument Park...K-14
Morrison (428)...F-7
Mt. Crested Butte (801)...H-5
Naturita (546)...I-1
Nathrop...H-6
Nederland (1,445)...F-7
New Castle (4,518)...F-4
Niwot (4,006)...B-17

BECAUSE THE LENGTH OF THE SEASONS VARIES GREATLY IN HIGHER ELEVATIONS, INQUIRE LOCALLY FOR THE CONDITIONS OF ROADS DESIGNATED "CLOSED IN WINTER" ON THIS MAP.

INQUIRE LOCALLY FOR CURRENT CONDITIONS BEFORE DRIVING ON UNIMPROVED ROADS SHOWN ON THIS MAP.

Miles 30 15 0 15 30 Miles
Kilometers 30 15 0 15 30 Kilometers
ONE INCH EQUALS APPROXIMATELY 27 MILES OR 43.45 KILOMETERS 1:1,710,720

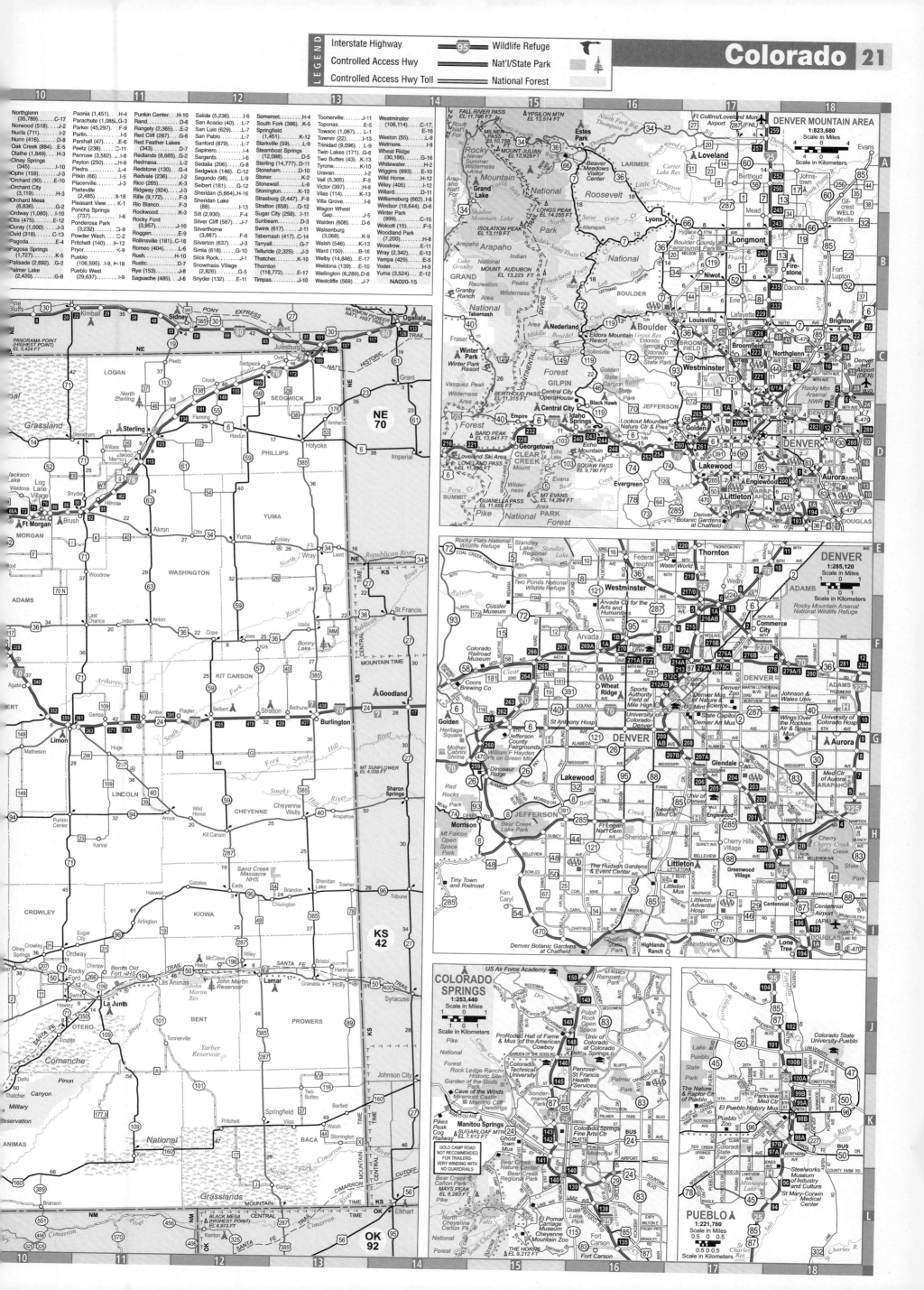

LEGEND

Interstate Highway
Controlled Access Hwy
Controlled Access Hwy Toll
Wildlife Refuge
Nat'l/State Park
National Forest

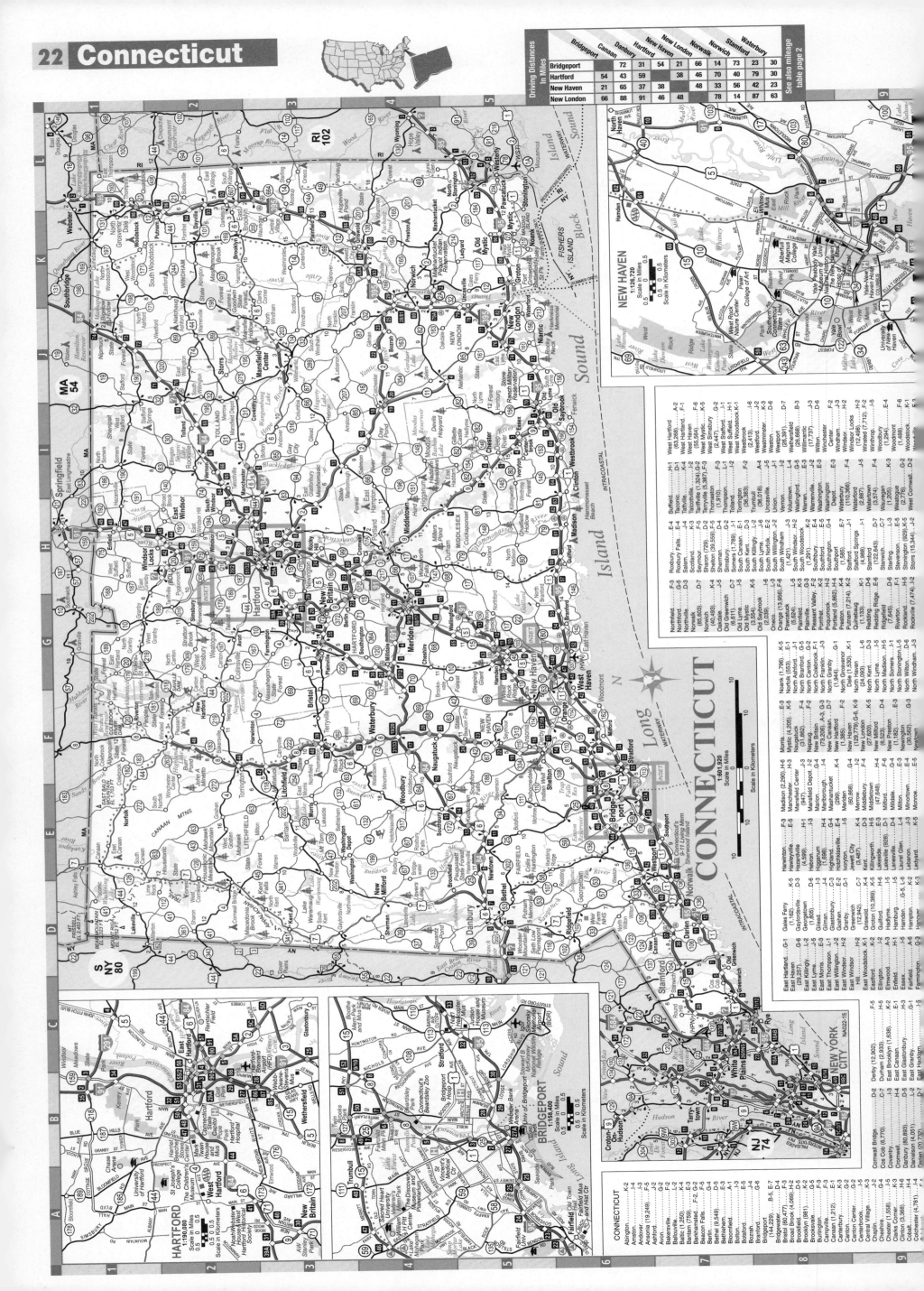

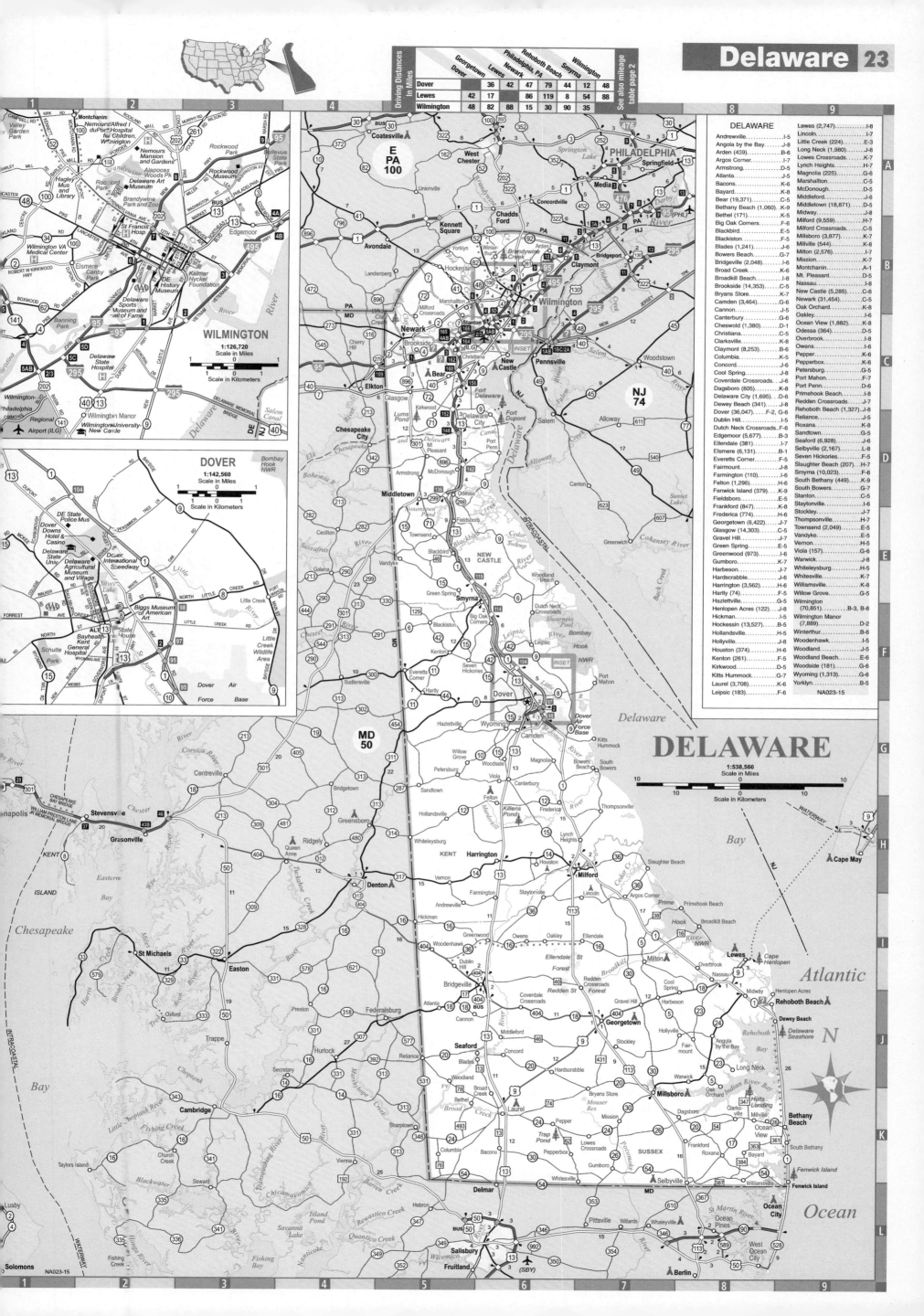

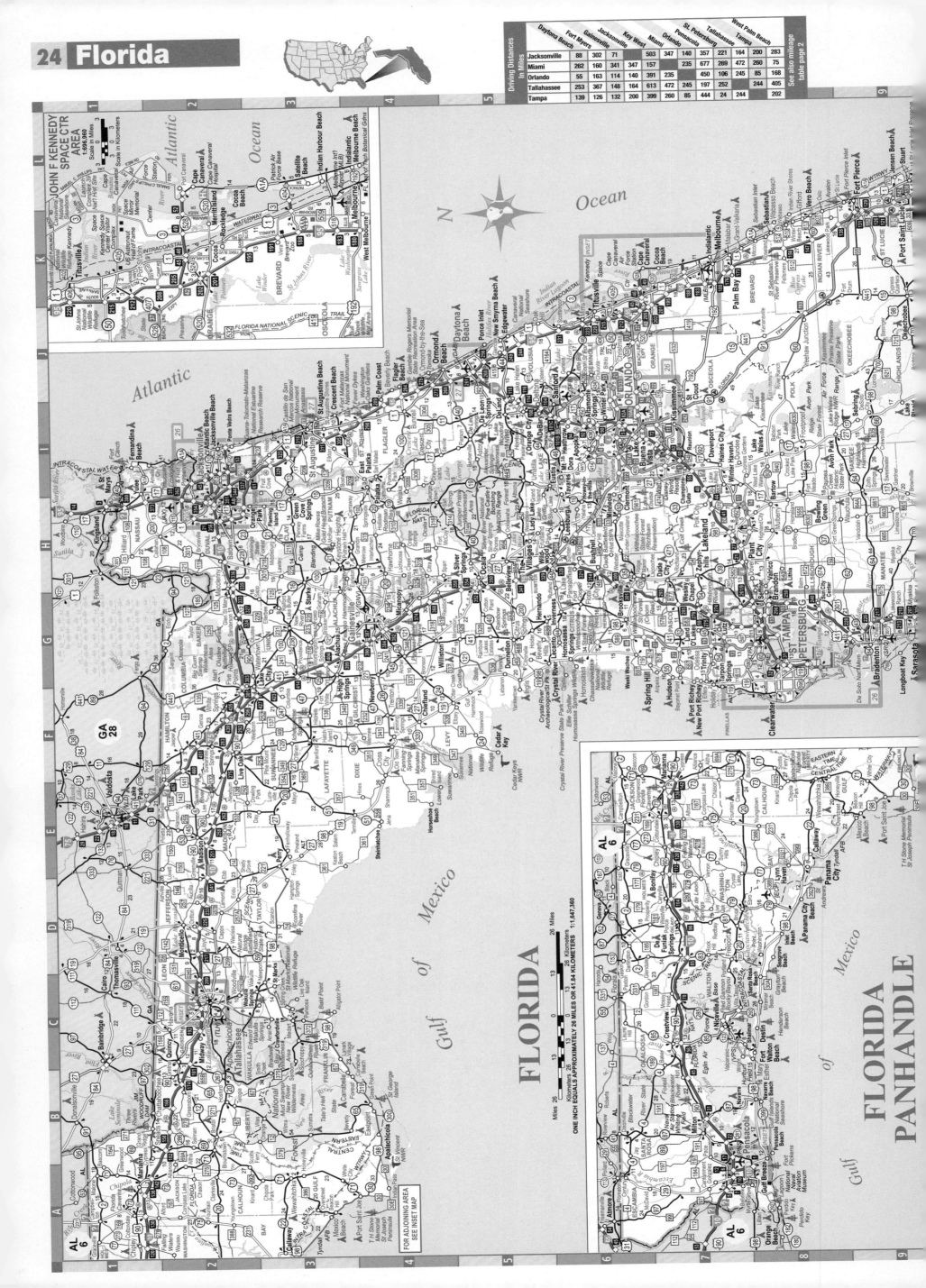

Driving Distances in Miles — See also page 2 mileage table

	Daytona Beach	Fort Myers	Gainesville	Jacksonville	Key West	Miami	Orlando	Pensacola	St. Petersburg	Tallahassee	Tampa	West Palm Beach
Jacksonville	88	302	71		503	347	140	357	221	164	200	275
Miami	262	160	341	347	157		235	677	269	472	260	75
Orlando	55	163	114	140	391	235		450	106	245	85	168
Tallahassee	253	367	148	164	613	472	245	197	252		244	405
Tampa	139	126	132	200	399	260	85	444	24	244		202

FLORIDA

FLORIDA PANHANDLE

LEGEND

Interstate Highway 95	Wildlife Refuge
Controlled Access Hwy	Nat'l/State Park
Controlled Access Hwy Toll	National Forest

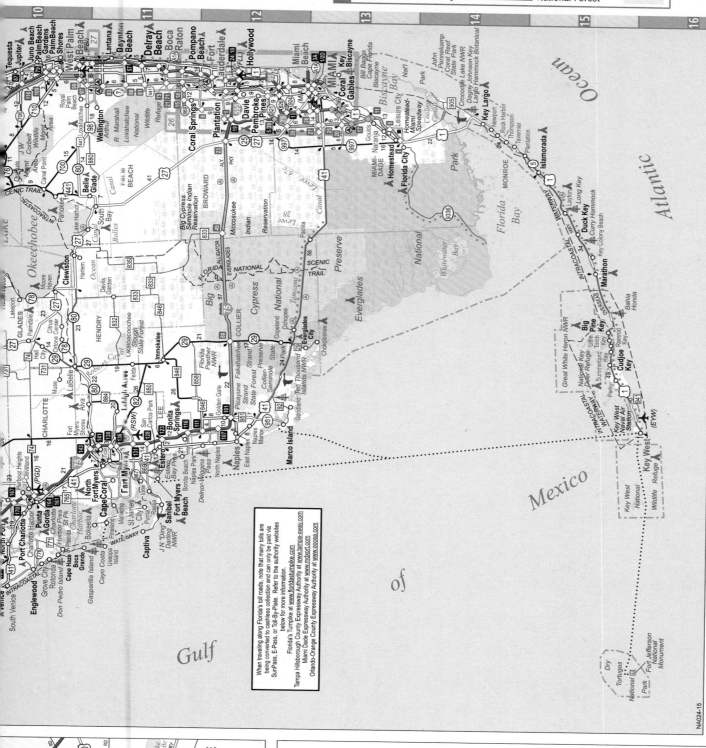

When traveling along Florida's toll roads, note that many tolls are being converted to cashless collection and can only be paid via SunPass, E-Pass, or Toll-By-Plate. Refer to the authority websites below for more information.

Tampa Hillsborough County Expressway Authority at www.tampa-xway.com
Florida's Turnpike at www.floridasturnpike.com
Miami Dade Expressway Authority at www.mdxdot.com
Orlando-Orange County Expressway Authority at www.oocea.com

ORLANDO, FL
1:364,320
Scale in Miles
Scale in Kilometers

JACKSONVILLE FL
1:380,160
Scale in Miles
Scale in Kilometers

TAMPA / ST PETERSBURG FL AREA
1:411,840
Scale in Miles
Scale in Kilometers

MIAMI / FT LAUDERDALE, FL AREA
1:316,800
Scale in Miles
Scale in Kilometers

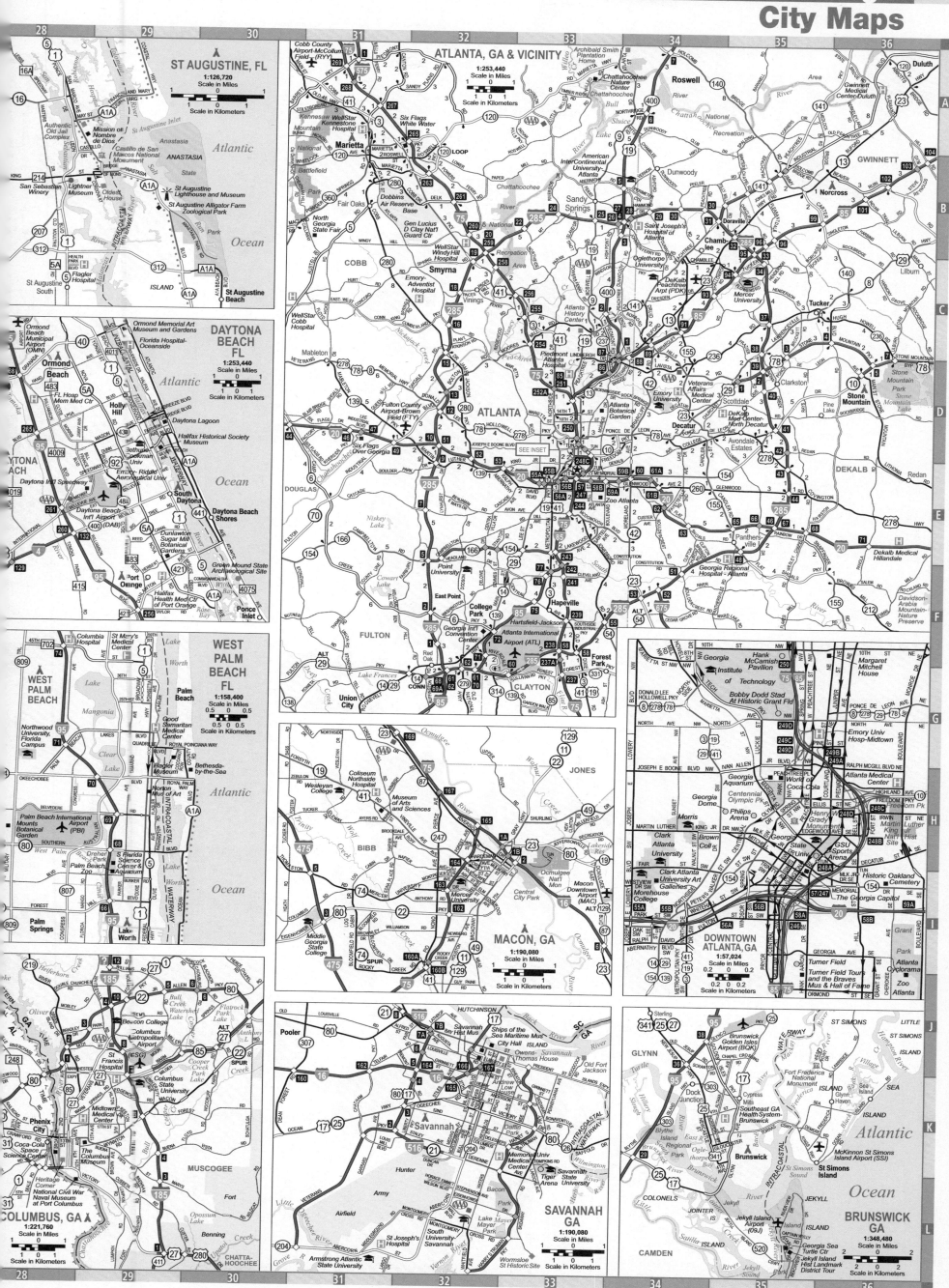

Driving Distances In Miles	Albany	Athens	Atlanta	Augusta	Brunswick	Columbus	Macon	Rome	Savannah	Statesboro	Tifton	Valdosta
Albany		198	182	229	174	86	105	232	251	212	42	80
Atlanta	182	71		148	273	107	84	69	248	209	181	228
Augusta	229	97	148		200	249	124	217	126	80	228	238
Columbus	86	180	107	249	258		99	142	250	210	126	174
Macon	105	93	84	124	191	99		152	166	127	104	151

See also mileage table page 2

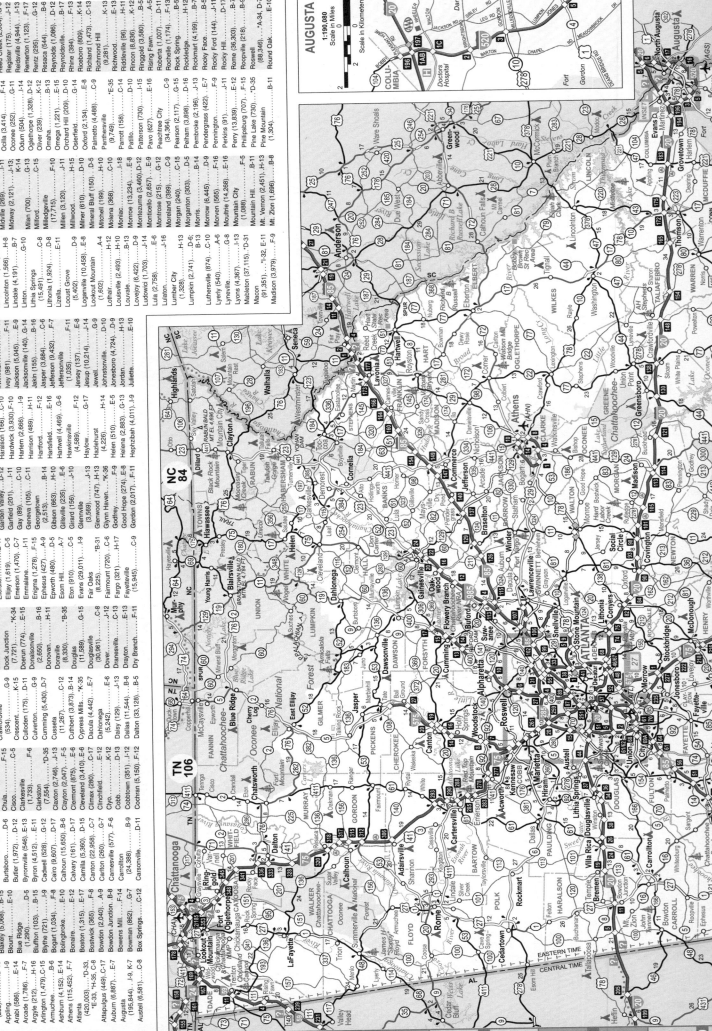

GEORGIA

AUGUSTA

1:1,298,880 Scale in Miles
1:1,190,080 Scale in Kilometers

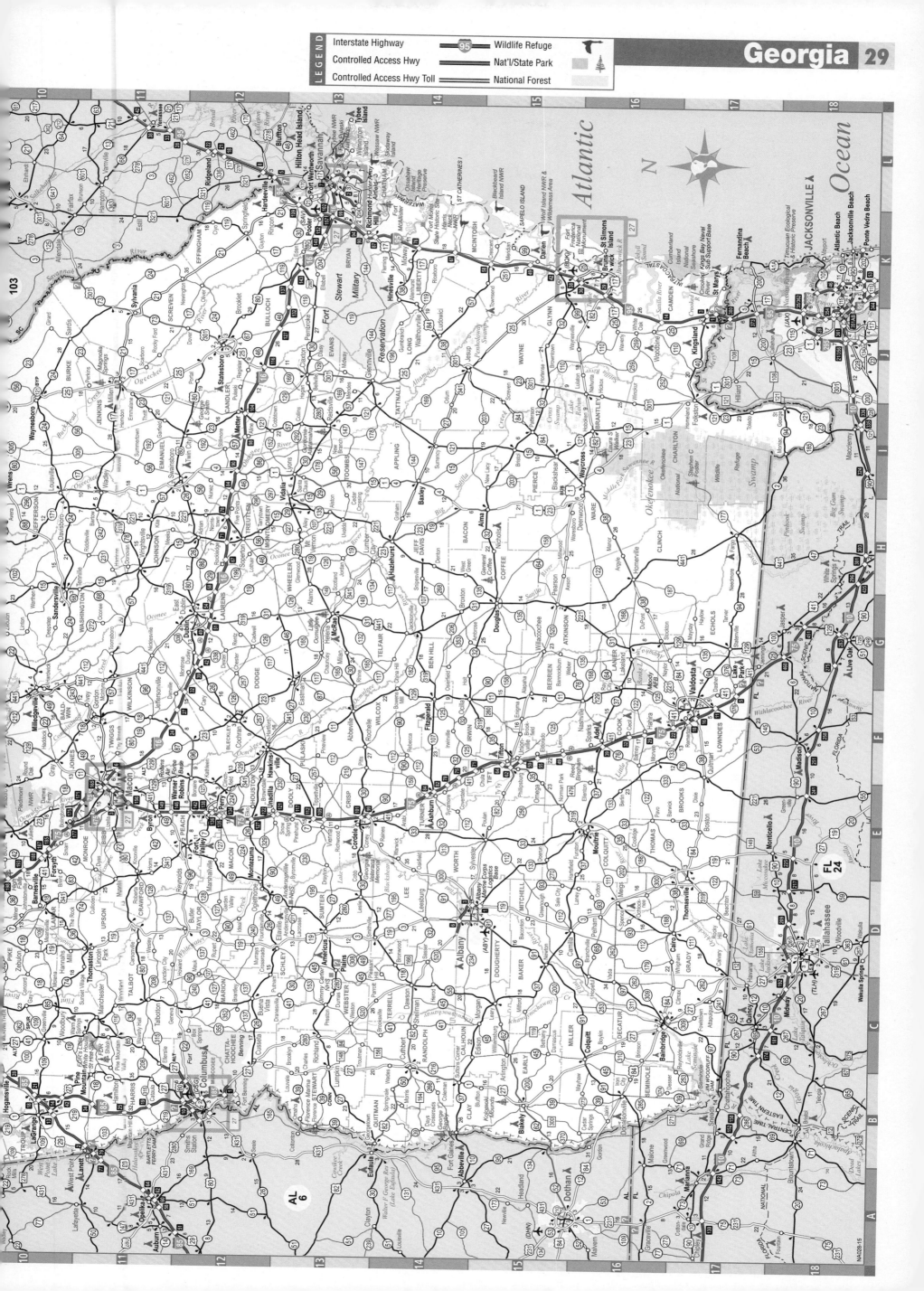

LEGEND
Interstate Highway
Controlled Access Hwy
Controlled Access Hwy Toll
Wildlife Refuge
Nat'l/State Park
National Forest

HAWAI'I

Amauulu Camp......J-17
Captain Cook (3,429)..........G-13
Hakalau..............J-11
Halaula (469)........K-12
Hanaipoe.............I-11
Hawi (1,081)........G-10
Hilea................I-15
Hilo (43,263). .J-12, K-17
Hoea................G-10
Holualoa (8,538)....G-13
Honalo (2,423)......G-13
Honaunau (2,567)...G-13
Honohina............J-11
Honokaa (2,258).....I-11
Honokohau.........G-12
Honomu (509).......J-11
Honuapo............I-15
Hookena............G-14
Huehue Ranch......G-12
Kaalualu...........H-15
Kahaluu (3,549).....G-13
Kahuku.............J-11
Kahuku Ranch......H-15
Kailua-Kona.........G-12
Kaimu..............K-14
Kainaliu............G-13
Kalaoa (9,644)......G-12
Kamaili.............K-13
Kaniahiku Village....K-13
Kapaau (1,734).....G-10
Kapalaoa...........G-11
Kapehu.............J-11
Kapoho.............K-13
Kapulena............I-10
Kaueleau...........K-13
Kaumana............J-12
Kaupulehu..........G-12
Kawaihae...........G-11
Keaau (2,253).......K-13
Kealakekua (2,019)..G-13
Kealia..............G-14
Keamuku...........H-12
Keauhou (3,549)....G-13
Keaukaha...........L-16
Keawaiki............G-11
Keei................G-13
Kehena.............K-14
Keokea.............G-13
Kiholo..............G-12
Koae...............K-13
Kuhio Village........H-11
Kukaiau.............I-11
Kukui...............J-13
Kukuihaele (336)....H-10
Kurtistown (1,298)...J-13
Laupahoehoe (581). .J-11
Mahaiula...........G-12
Mahukona..........G-10
Makahalau..........I-11
Makapala...........H-10
Meyer Camp.........I-14
Milolii..............G-14
Mountain View (3,924)...........J-13
Naalehu (866).......H-15
Napoopoo (2,567)...G-13
Ninole..............J-11
Onomea............J-12
Ookala.............J-11
Opihikao............K-13
Paauhau............I-11
Paauilo (595).........I-11
Pahala (1,356).......I-14
Pahoa (945).........K-13
Papa...............G-14
Papaikou (1,314)....J-12
Paukaa (425). .J-12, J-15
Pepeekeo (1,789). . .J-12
Pepeekeo Mill.......J-12
Piihonua.......H-17, J-12
Pohoiki.............K-13
Pua Akala............I-12
Puako (772).........G-11
Punaluu.............I-15
Puu Hue Ranch.....G-10
Puu Waawaa Ranch............G-12
Puuanahulu.........G-12
Puueo..............J-17
Volcano (2,575)......J-13
Waiaka.............H-11
Waiakea............K-17
Waikapuna..........H-15
Waikii..............H-12
Waikoloa Village (6,362)............H-11
Wailea..............J-11
Waimea (9,212).....H-11
Wainaku (1,224).....J-16
Waiohinu...........H-15
Weloka.............J-11

KAUA'I

Anahola (2,223)......E-7
Eleele (2,390)........B-9
Haena (431)..........C-6
Hanalei (450).........C-6
Hanamaulu (3,835)...D-8
Kaawanui............B-9
Kalaheo (4,595)......C-9
Kalihiwai (428).......D-6
Kapaa (10,699).......D-7
Kapaia...............D-8
Kaumakani (749).....B-9
Kealia...............E-7
Kekaha (3,537).......A-8
Kilauea (2,803).......D-6
Kipu.................D-9
Kokee...............B-7
Koloa (2,144)........C-9
Kukuiula.............C-9
Lawai (2,363)........C-9
Lihue (6,455).........D-8
Mana................A-8
Niumalu.............D-9
Numila...............C-9
Omao (1,301)........C-9
Pakala Village (294)..B-9
Poipu (979)..........D-9
Princeville (2,158)....C-6
Puhi (2,906)..........D-8
Wailua (2,254).......E-8
Waimea (1,855)......B-8
Wainiha (318)........C-6
Waipouli.............E-8

LĀNA'I

Kaumalapau........G-18
Lāna'i City (3,102). .H-17

MAUI

Haiku...............C-15
Haliimaile (964).....C-15
Hamoa.............F-16
Hana (1,235)........F-16
Haou...............F-16
Honolua............A-14
Kaanapali (1,045)...A-15
Kaeleku............F-16
Kahana.............A-14
Kahului (20,146)....B-15
Kailua..............D-15
Kanahena..........C-17
Kapalua (353)......A-14
Kaupakulua.........D-15
Kaupo..............E-17
Keanae.............E-15
Keawakapu.........C-16
Kelawea............A-15
Keokea (1,612).....C-16
Keoneoio...........C-17
Kihei (16,749)......C-16
Kipahulu............E-17
Kokomo............D-15
Kuau...............C-15
Kula (6,452)........C-16
Lahaina (9,118).....A-15
Maalaea (352)......B-16
Makawao (7,184)...C-15
Makena (99)........C-17
Mala...............A-15
Mokulau............E-17
Muolea.............F-16
Nahiku.............E-15
Napili..............A-14
Olinda (1,084)......D-15
Olowalu (80)........A-15
Paia (2,668)........C-15
Pauwela............D-15
Pukalani (7,574)....C-15
Spreckelsville.......C-15
Ulupalakua Ranch. .C-17
Waiakoa............C-16
Waihee-Waiehu (8,841)...........B-15
Waikapu (2,965)....B-15
Wailea (5,938)......C-16
Wailua.............E-15
Wailuku (15,313)....B-15
Wailuku Heights....B-15

MOLOKA'I

Halawa.............F-11
Halena.............A-12
Hoolehua...........C-11
Kalae...............C-11
Kalanianaole Colony...........C-12
Kalaupapa..........D-11
Kalawao............D-11
Kaluaaha...........E-12
Kamalo.............E-12
Kamiloloa...........C-12
Kaunakakai (3,425)..C-12
Kawela.............D-12
Kualapuu (2,027). . .C-11
Maunaloa (376).....B-11
Moomomi...........B-11
Pauwalu............F-12
Pukoo..............E-12
Ualapue (425)......E-12
Waialua............F-12

O'AHU

Aiea (9,338)..........F-1
Ewa.................H-8
Ewa Beach (14,955)..H-9
Foster Village........F-1
Halawa (14,014).....F-1
Haleiwa (3,970)......G-5
Honolulu (371,657)...I-2, J-9, K-9
Kaaawa (1,379)......J-6
Kahaluu (4,738)......J-7
Kahuku (2,614).......I-4
Kailua (38,635).......K-8
Kaneohe (34,597)....K-7
Kapolei (15,186).....G-8
Laie (6,138)...........I-5
Lualualei.............G-8
Makakilo City (18,248)...........G-8
Mililani Town (27,629)...........H-7
Mokuleia (1,811).....G-5
Nanakuli (12,666)....G-8
Olomana............K-8
Opaeula Camp......G-5
Paumalu............H-4
Pearl City (47,698)....I-7
Wahiawa (17,821). . .H-6
Waianae (13,177)....F-7
Waimanalo (5,451). . .L-8
Waimanalo Beach (4,481)............L-8
Waimea.............H-5
Waipahu (38,216)....H-8
Waipio (11,674)......H-7

NA030-15

HONOLULU, O'AHU
1:110,880
Scale in Miles
Scale in Kilometers
Pacific Ocean

STATE OF HAWAI'I
1:6,336,000
Scale in Miles
Scale in Kilometers
Pacific Ocean

O'AHU
1:316,800
Scale in Miles
Scale in Kilometers
Pacific Ocean

KAUA'I
1:411,840
Scale in Miles
Pacific Ocean

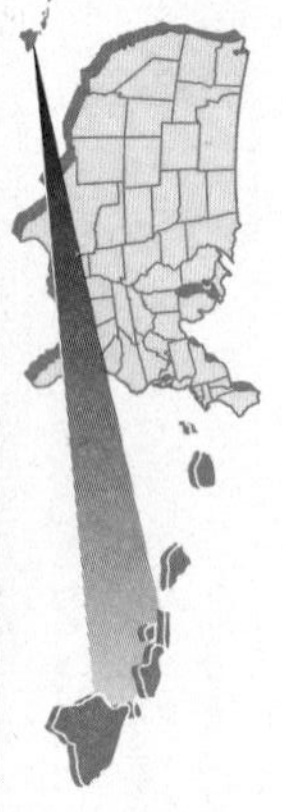

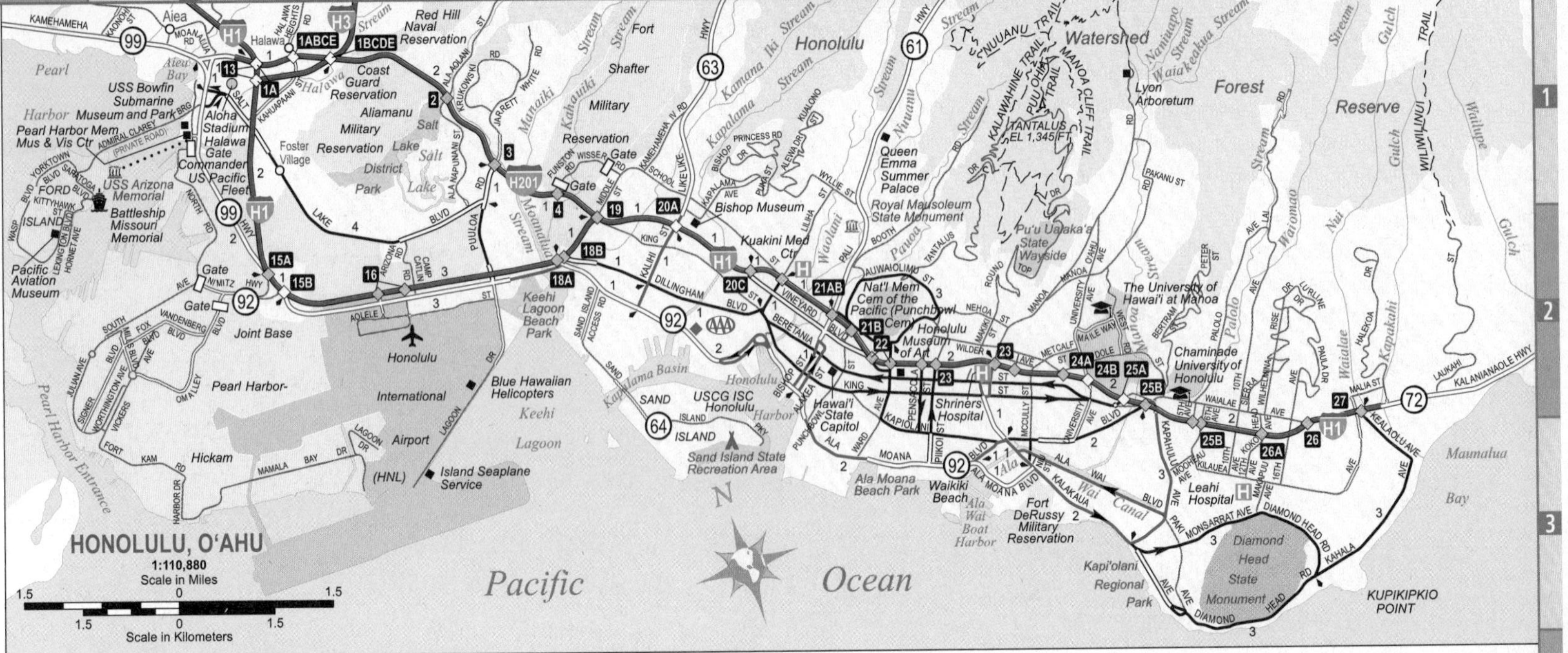

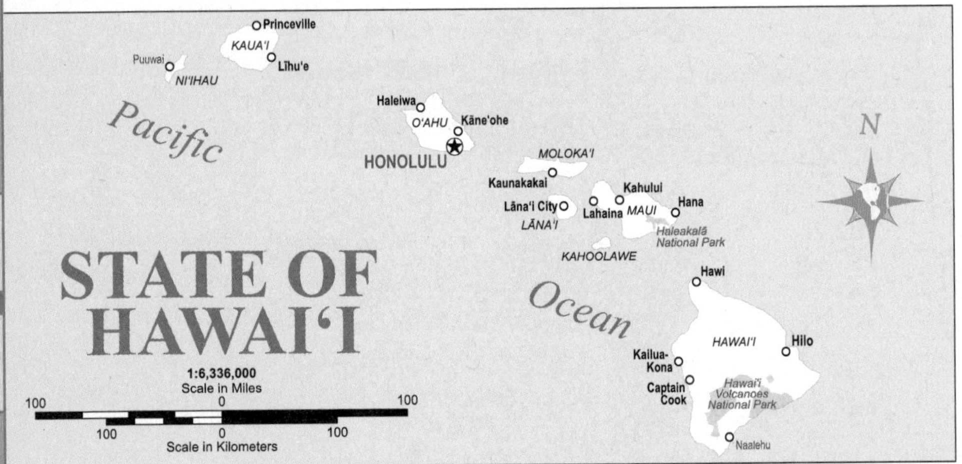

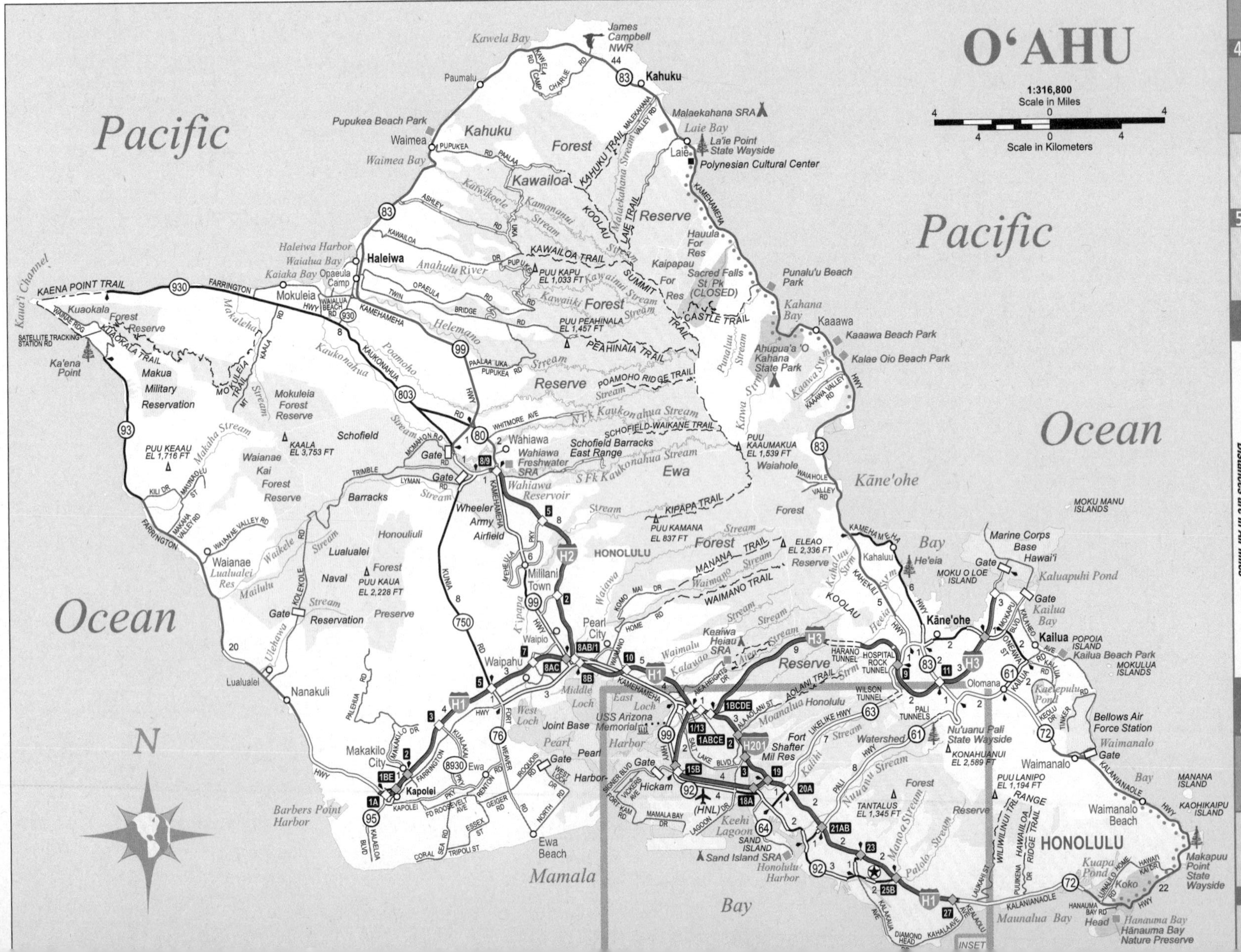

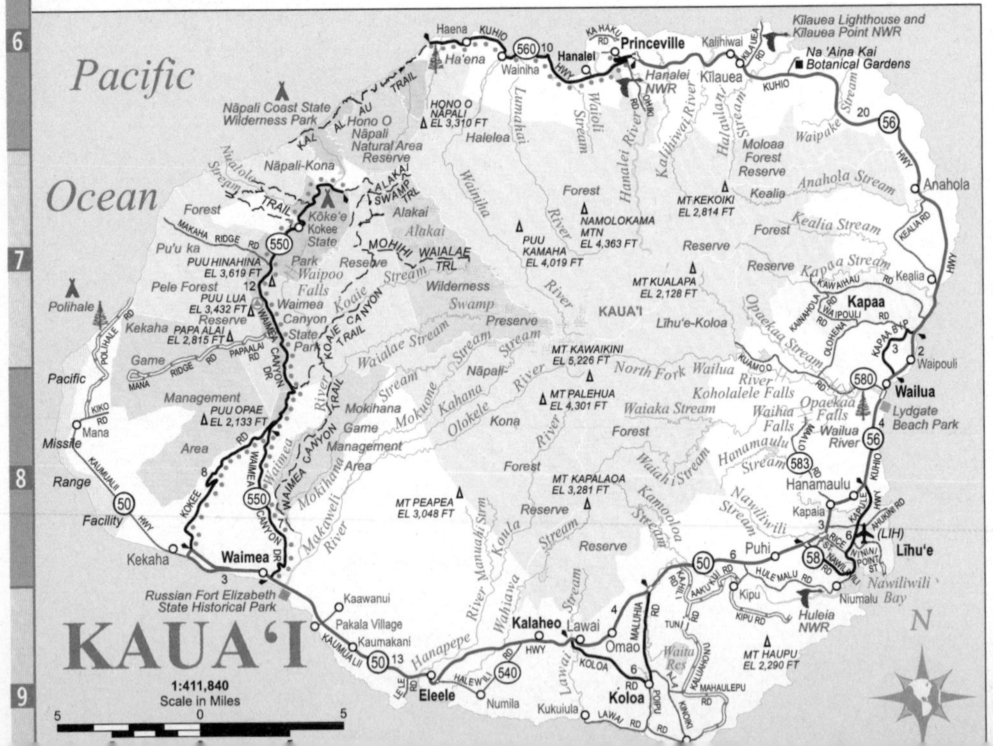

Driving Distances In Miles

	Hilo	Honolulu	Hoolehua	Kahului	Kailua-Kona	Lāna'i City	Līhu'e	Waimea
Hilo		216	162	121	62	141	317	45
Honolulu	216		55	94	169	74	102	172
Līhu'e	317	102	158	201	263	177		284

Distances are in Air Miles

See also mileage table page 2

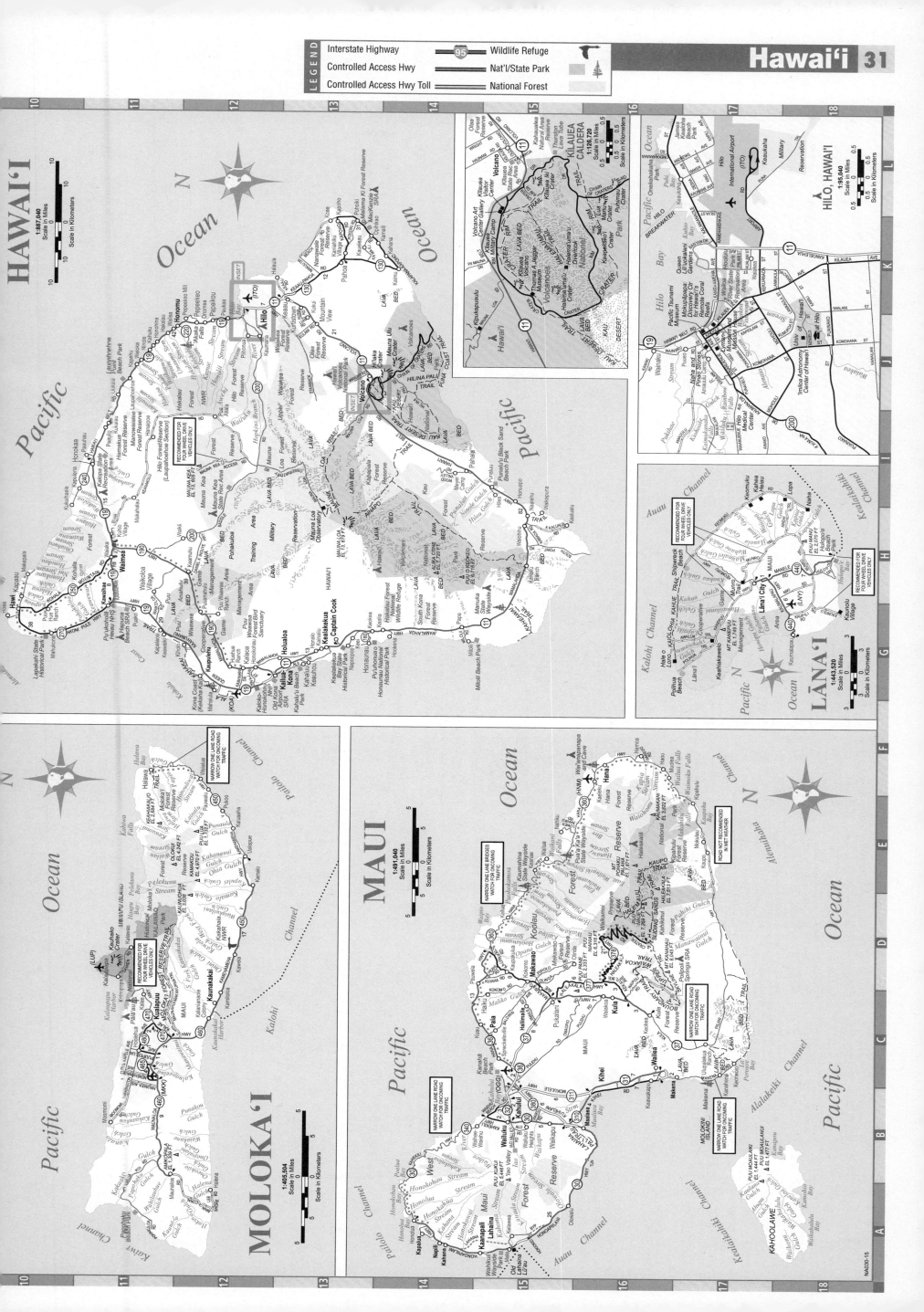

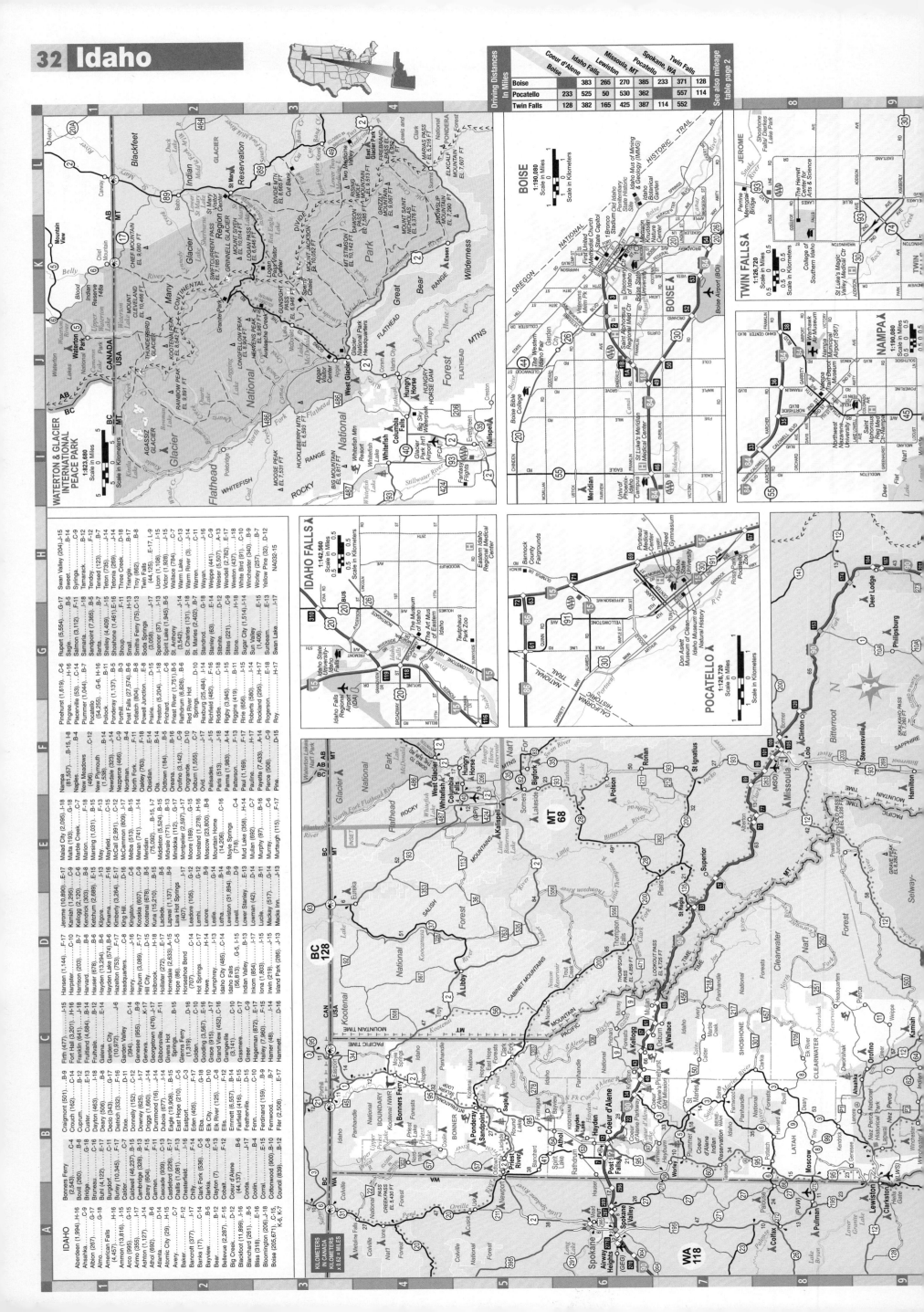

See also mileage table page 2

Driving Distances in Miles

	Boise	Coeur d'Alene	Idaho Falls	Lewiston	Missoula, MT	Pocatello	Spokane, WA	Twin Falls
Boise		383	265	270	385	233	371	128
Pocatello	233	525	50	530	362		557	114
Twin Falls	128	382	165	425	387	114		552

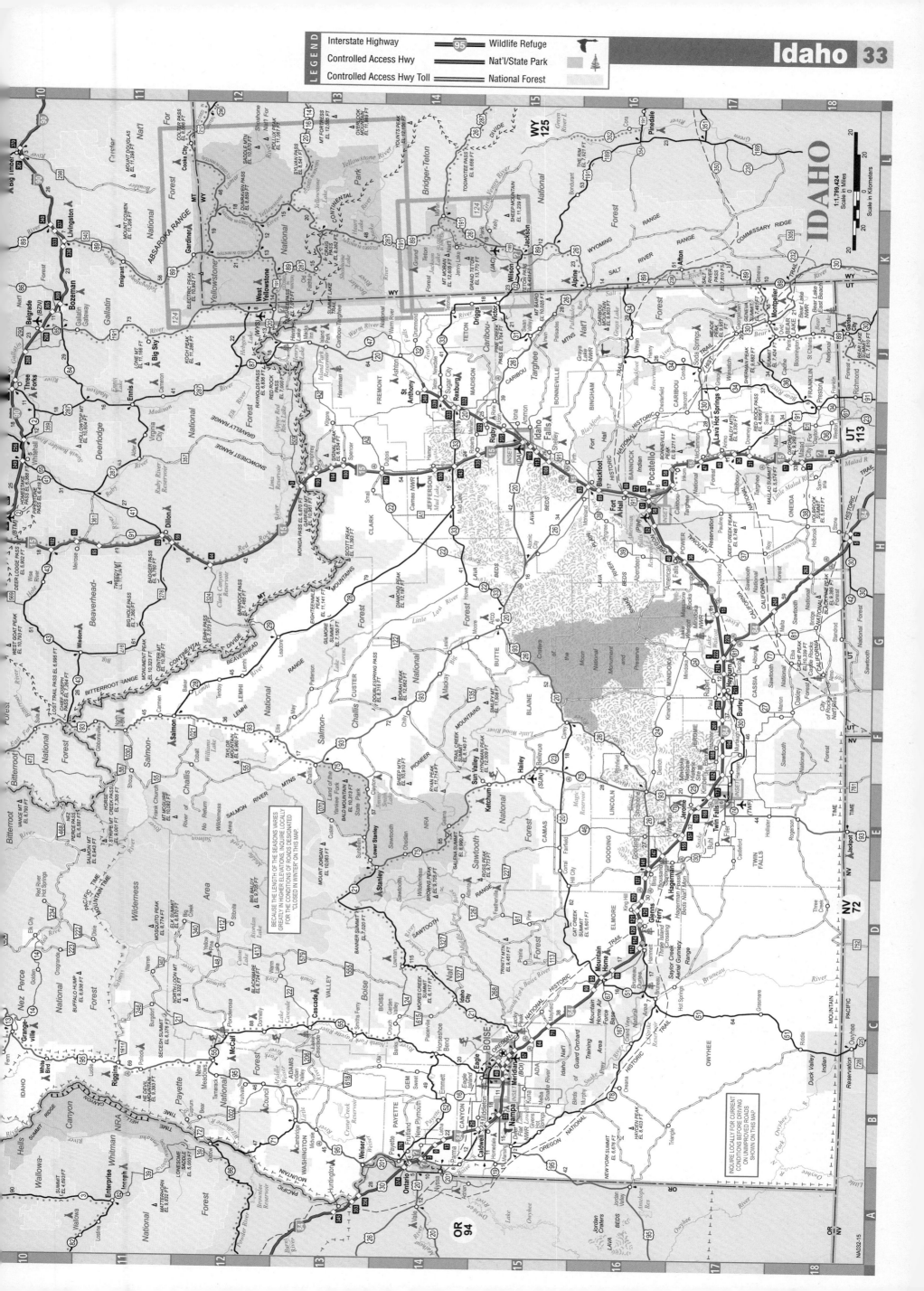

LEGEND

Interstate Highway · 95 · Wildlife Refuge
Controlled Access Hwy · Nat'l/State Park
Controlled Access Hwy Toll · National Forest

IDAHO

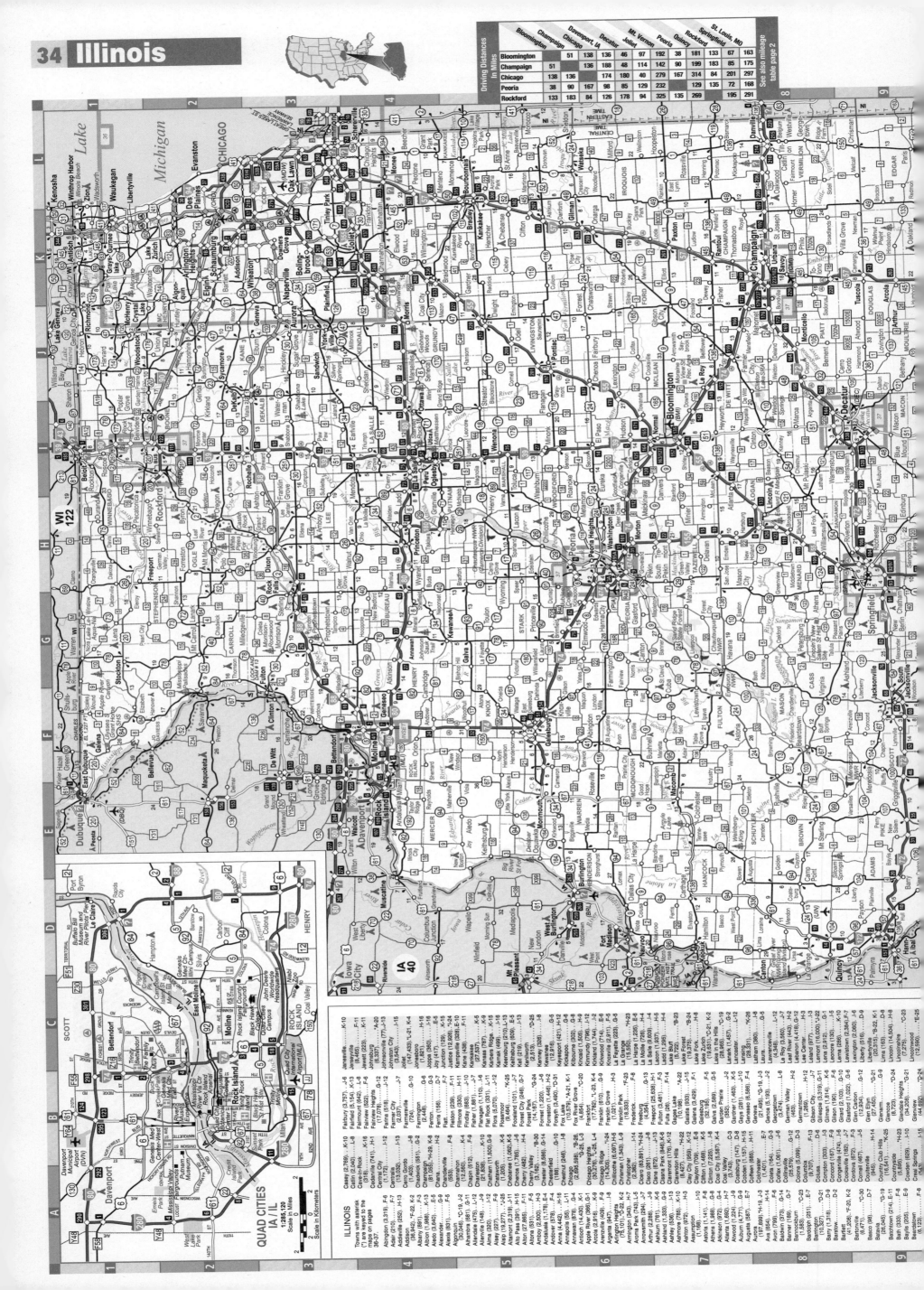

LEGEND
Interstate Highway (95)
Controlled Access Hwy
Controlled Access Hwy Toll
Wildlife Refuge
Nat'l/State Park
National Forest

ILLINOIS
1:1,298,880
Scale in Miles
20 0 20
20 0 20
Scale in Kilometers
NA034-15

NA034-15

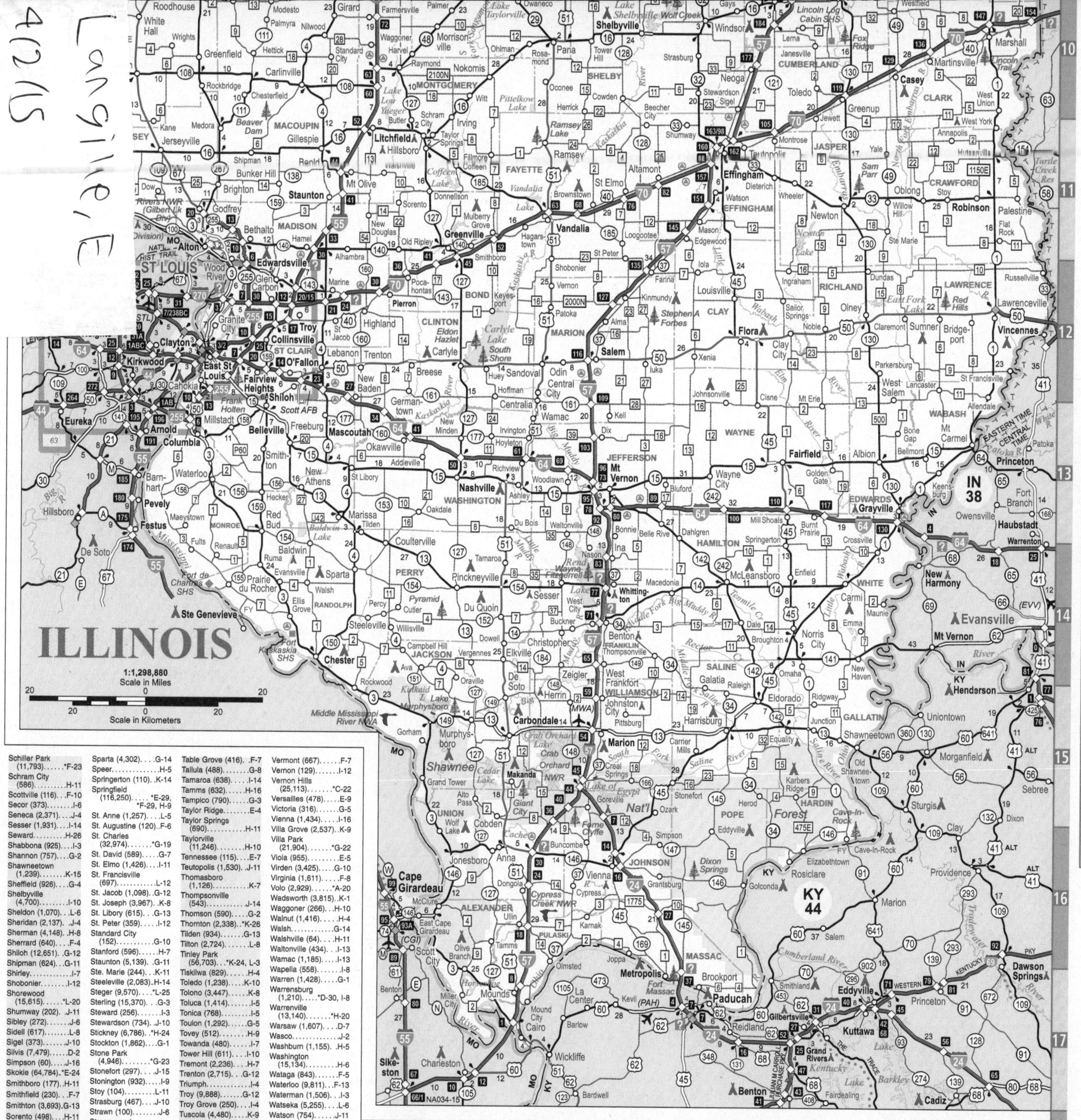

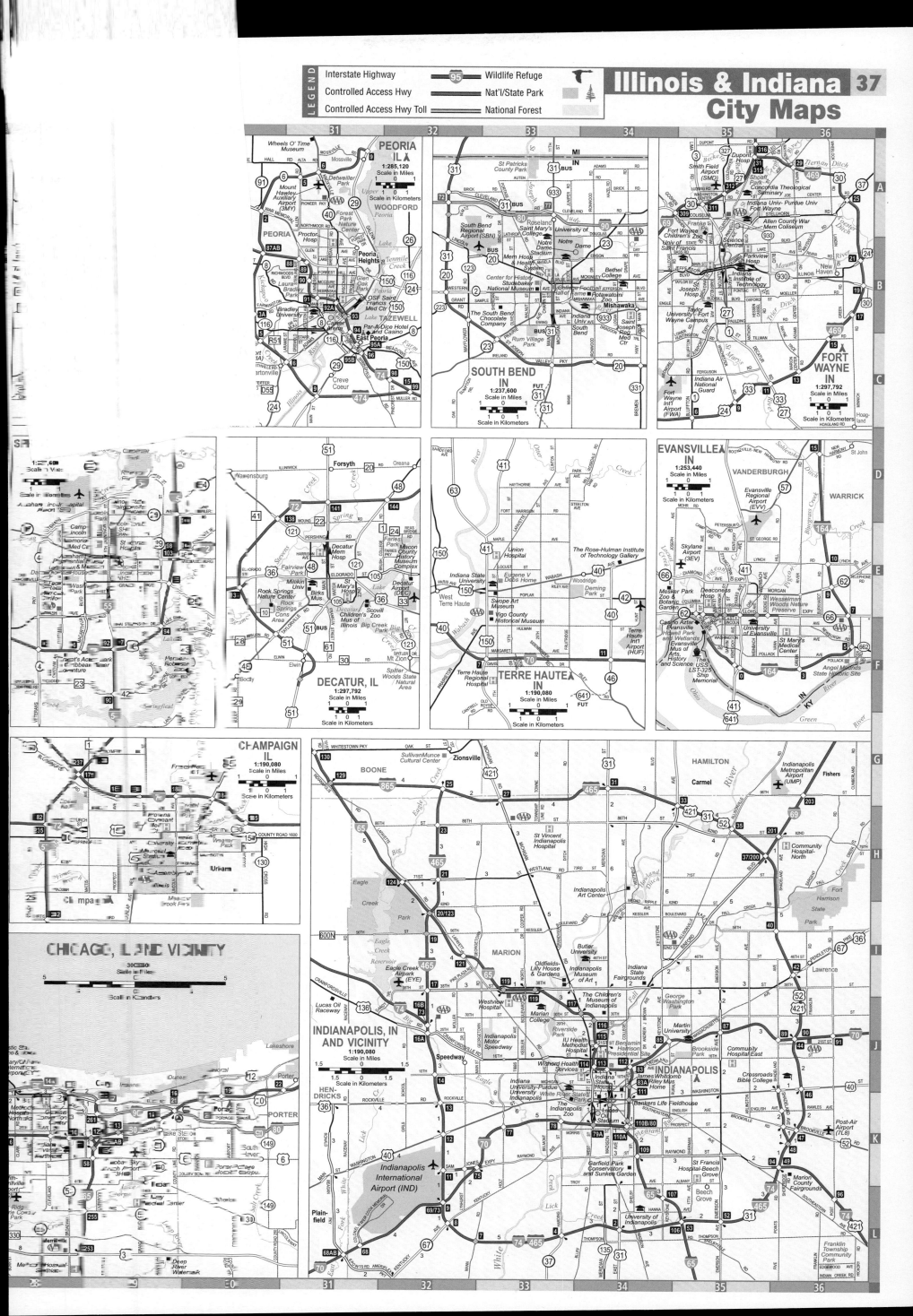

LEGEND

Interstate Highway — 95 — Wildlife Refuge
Controlled Access Hwy — Nat'l/State Park
Controlled Access Hwy Toll — National Forest

PEORIA IL
1:285,120
Scale in Miles
Scale in Kilometers

SOUTH BEND IN
1:237,600
Scale in Miles
Scale in Kilometers

FORT WAYNE IN
1:297,792
Scale in Miles
Scale in Kilometers

DECATUR, IL
1:297,792
Scale in Miles
Scale in Kilometers

TERRE HAUTE IN
1:190,080
Scale in Miles
Scale in Kilometers

EVANSVILLE IN
1:253,440
Scale in Miles
Scale in Kilometers

CHAMPAIGN IL
1:190,080
Scale in Miles
Scale in Kilometers

CHICAGO, IL AND VICINITY
Scale in Miles
Scale in Kilometers

INDIANAPOLIS, IN AND VICINITY
1:190,080
Scale in Miles
Scale in Kilometers

Driving Distances In Miles

	Bloomington	Chicago, IL	Columbus	Evansville	Fort Wayne	Indianapolis	Lafayette	Louisville	Michigan City	South Bend	Terre Haute
Fort Wayne	176	166	168	311		122	115	118	36	93	20
Indianapolis	60	186	46	182	122		63	15	72	138	7
Michigan City	200	58	197	304	118	152	92				19
Richmond	122	256	89	254	96	72	134		205	1	
Terre Haute	59	177	103	110	206	77	87	19	15	216	

See also mileage

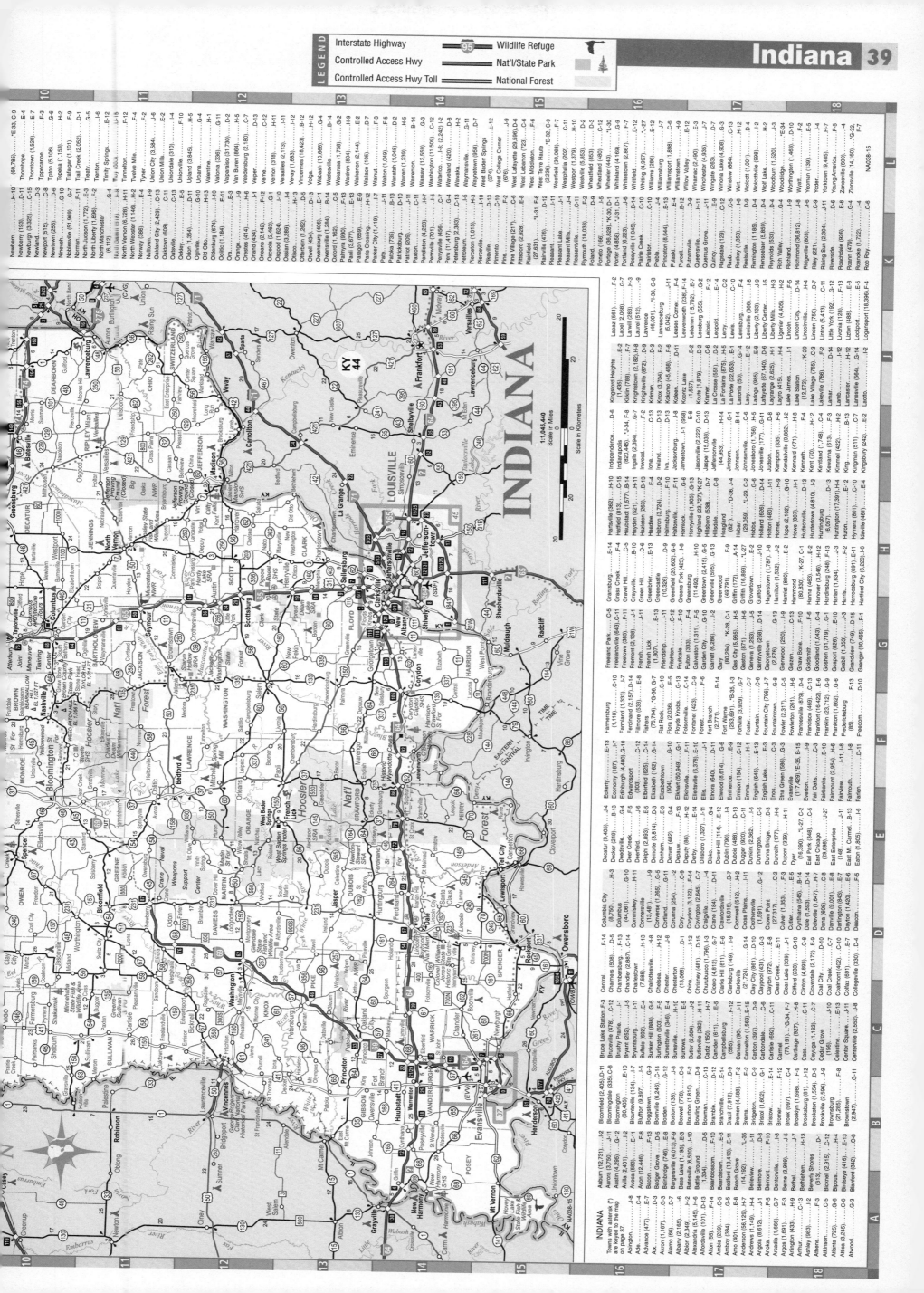

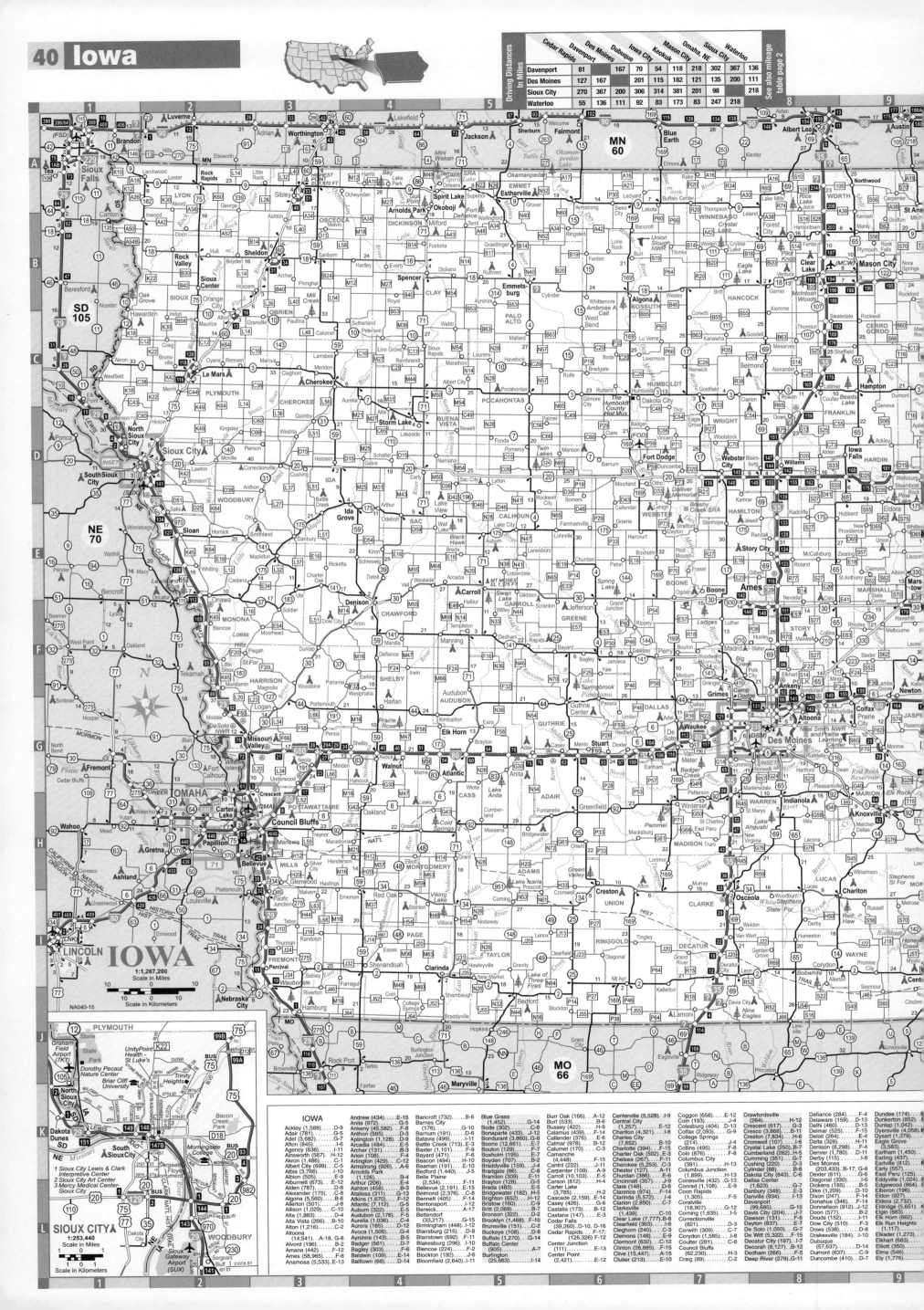

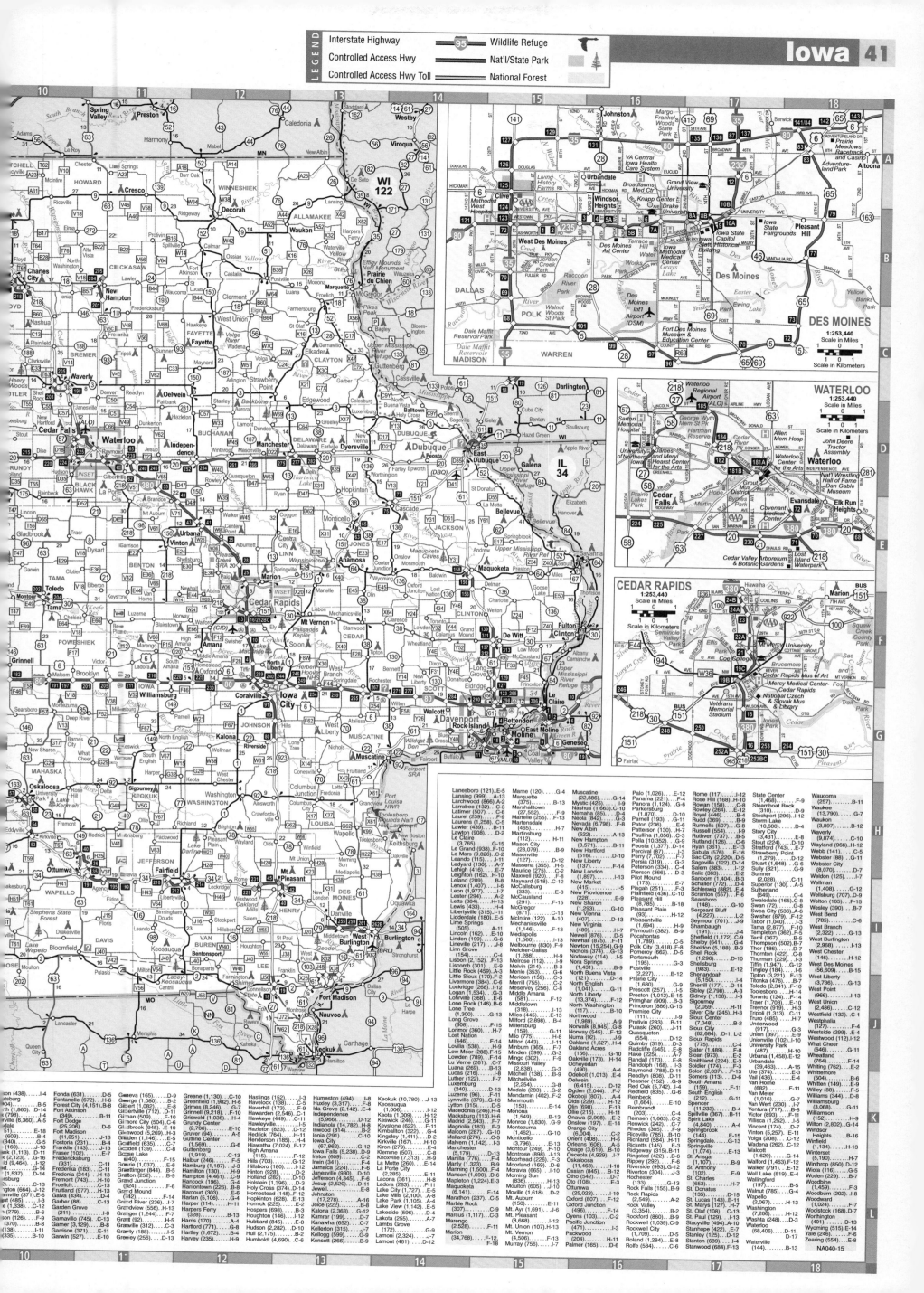

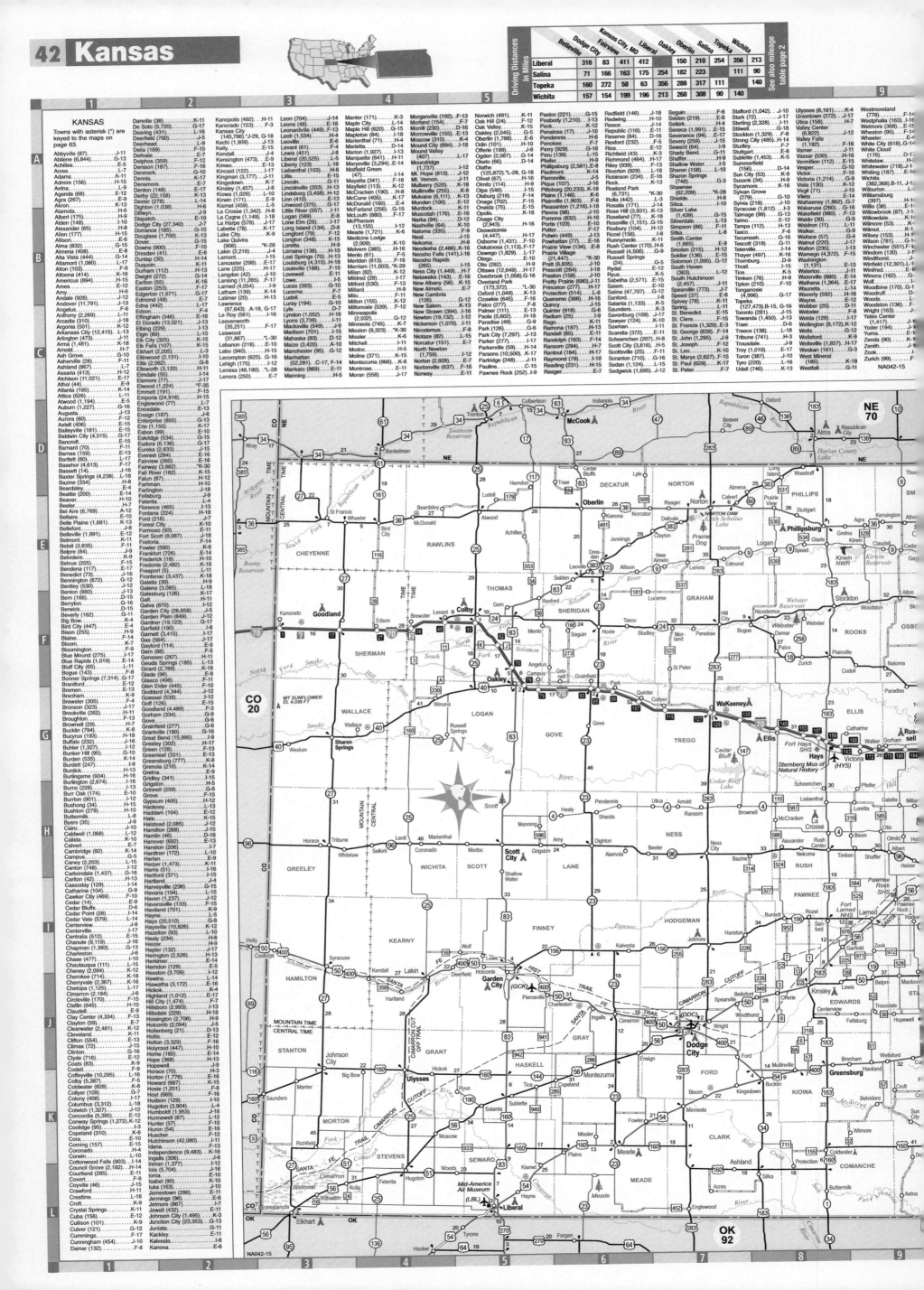

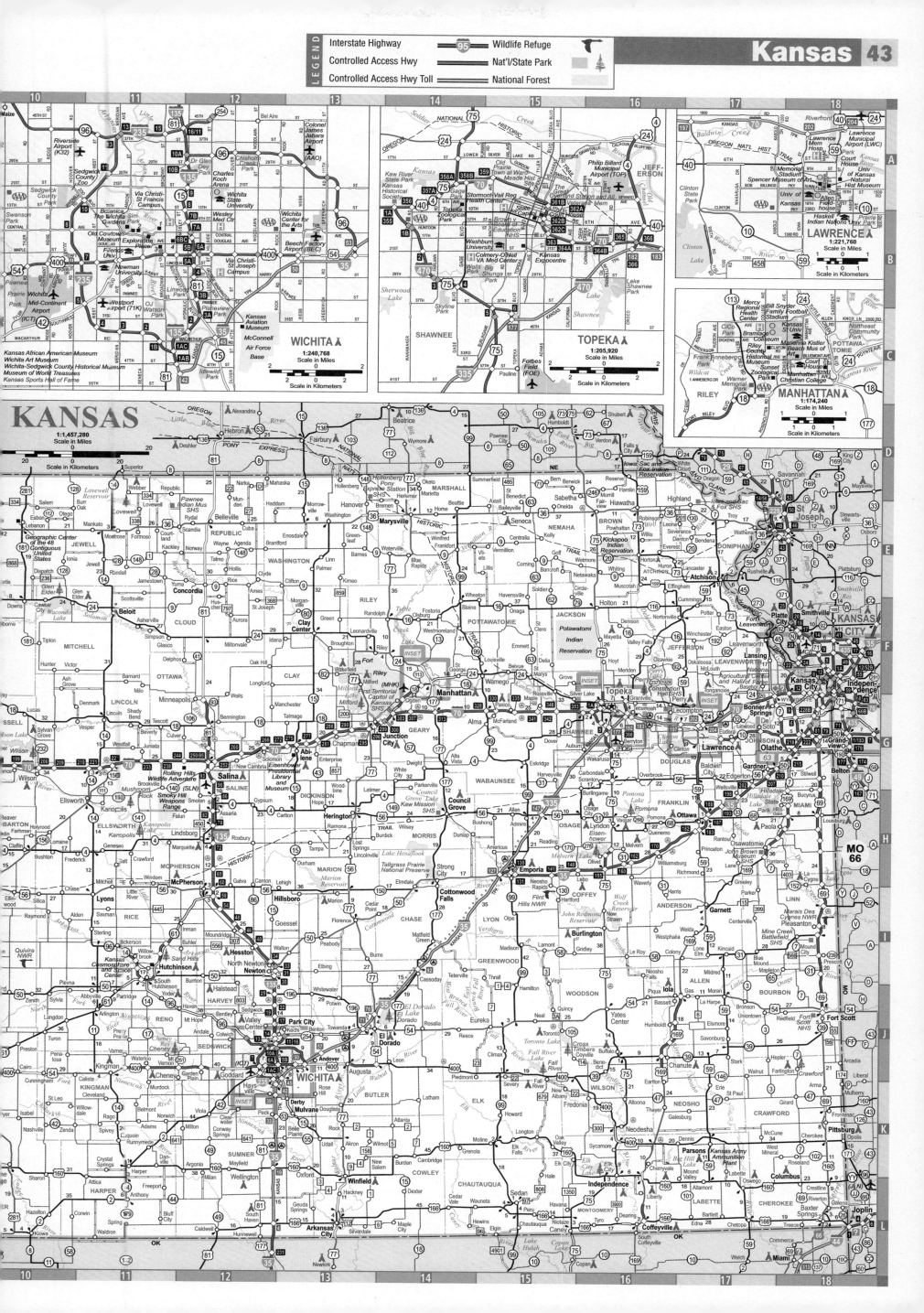

LEGEND

Interstate Highway — 95 — Wildlife Refuge
Controlled Access Hwy — Nat'l/State Park
Controlled Access Hwy Toll — National Forest

WICHITA
1:240,768
Scale in Miles

TOPEKA
1:205,920
Scale in Miles

LAWRENCE
1:221,760
Scale in Kilometers

MANHATTAN
1:174,240
Scale in Miles

KANSAS
1:1,457,280
Scale in Miles
Scale in Kilometers

MO

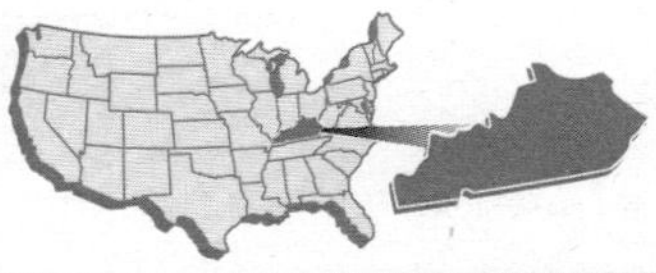

Driving Distances In Miles	Ashland	Bowling Green	Cincinnati, OH	Corbin	Evansville, IN	Frankfort	Lexington	Louisville	Madisonville	Middlesboro	Owensboro	Paducah
Cincinnati, OH	135	211		169	220	80	83	100	251	211	213	314
Evansville, IN	304	111	220	269		174	189	114	48	316	41	109
Frankfort	141	146	80	114	174		28	53	187	156	158	250
Lexington	118	152	83	87	189	28		74	192	129	178	255
Louisville	190	151	100	163	114	53	74		154	205	106	217

See also mileage table page 2

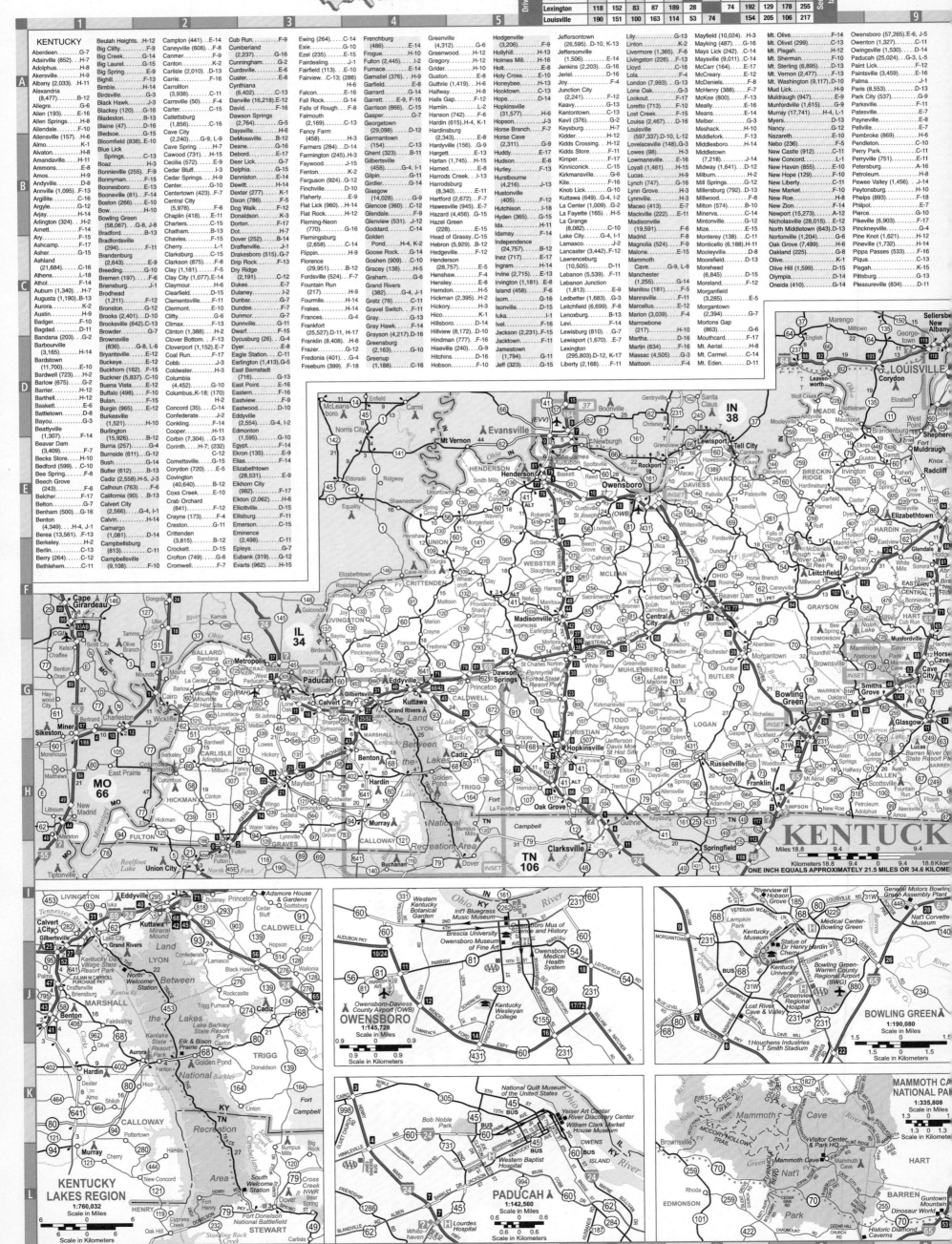

KENTUCKY

Aberdeen. G-7
Adairville (852). . .H-7
Adolphus. H-8
Akersville. H-9
Albany (2,033). .H-11
Alexandria (8,477). B-12
Allegre. G-6
Allen (193). E-16
Allen Springs. H-8
Allendale. F-10
Allensville (157). .H-6
Almo. K-1
Alvaton. H-8
Amandaville. H-11
Ammons. E-8
Amos. H-9
Andyville. D-8
Annville (1,095). .F-13
Argillite. C-16
Argyle. G-12
Arjay. H-14
Arlington (324). . .H-2
Arnett. F-14
Ary. F-15
Ashcamp. F-17
Asher. G-15
Ashland (21,684). C-16
Athens. L-18
Athol. F-14
Auburn (1,340). . .H-7
Augusta (1,190)..B-13
Aurora. K-2
Austin. H-9
Badger. F-10
Bagdad. D-11
Bandana (203). . .G-2
Barbourville (3,165). H-14
Bardstown (11,700). E-10
Bardwell (723). . . .H-2
Barlow (675). G-2
Barrier. H-12
Barthell. H-12
Baskett. E-6
Battletown. D-8
Bayou. G-3
Beattyville (1,307). F-14
Beaver Dam (3,409). F-7
Becks Store. H-10
Bedford (599). . .C-10
Bee Spring. F-8
Beech Grove (243). F-6
Belcher. F-17
Belton. G-7
Benham (500). . .G-16
Benton (4,349). . . .H-4, J-1
Berea (13,561). .F-13
Berkeley. H-2
Berlin. C-13
Berry (264). C-12
Bethlehem. C-11
Beulah Heights. .H-12
Big Clifty. F-9
Big Creek. G-14
Big Laurel. G-15
Big Spring. E-9
Bighill. F-13
Bimble. H-14
Birdsville. G-3
Black Hawk. J-3
Blackey (120). . . .G-16
Bladeston. B-13
Blaine (47). D-16
Bledsoe. G-15
Bloomfield (838)..E-10
Blue Lick Springs. C-13
Boaz. H-3
Bonnieville (255). .F-9
Bonnyman. F-15
Boonesboro. E-13
Booneville (81). . .F-14
Boston (266). E-10
Bow. H-10
Bowling Green (58,067). . .G-8, J-8
Bradford. B-13
Bradfordsville (294). F-11
Brandenburg (2,643). E-9
Breeding. G-10
Bremen (197). F-6
Briensburg. J-1
Brodhead (1,211). F-12
Bronston. G-12
Brooks (2,401). . .D-10
Brooksville (642).C-13
Browder. G-7
Brownsville (836). G-8, L-6
Bryantsville. E-12
Buckeye. E-12
Buckhorn (162). .F-15
Buckner (5,837)..C-10
Buena Vista. E-12
Buffalo (498). F-10
Bulan. F-15
Burgin (965). E-12
Burkesville (1,521). H-10
Burlington (15,926). B-12
Burna (257). G-4
Burnside (611). . .G-12
Bush. G-14
Butler (612). B-13
Cadiz (2,558).H-5, J-3
Calhoun (763). F-6
California (90). . .B-13
Calvert City (2,566). G-4, I-1
Calvin. H-14
Camargo (1,081). D-14
Campbellsburg (813). C-11
Campbellsville (9,108). F-10
Campton (441). . .E-14
Caneyville (608). . .F-8
Canmer. F-9
Canton. K-2
Carlisle (2,010). .D-13
Carrie. F-16
Carrollton (3,938). C-11
Carrsville (50). F-4
Carter. C-15
Catlettsburg (1,856). C-16
Cave City (2,240). G-9, L-9
Cave Spring. H-7
Cawood (731). . .H-15
Cecilia (572). E-9
Cedar Bluff. I-3
Cedar Springs. . . .H-9
Center. G-10
Centertown (423). .F-7
Central City (5,978). F-6
Chaplin (418). . . .E-11
Charters. C-15
Chatham. B-13
Chavies. F-15
Cherry. L-1
Clarksburg. C-15
Clarkson (875). . . .F-8
Clay (1,181). F-5
Clay City (1,077).E-14
Claymour. H-6
Clearfield. D-15
Clementsville. F-11
Clermont. E-10
Clifty. G-6
Climax. F-13
Clinton (1,388). . . .H-2
Clover Bottom. . .F-13
Cloverport (1,152).E-7
Coal Run. F-17
Cobb. J-3
Coldwater. H-3
Columbia (4,452). G-10
Columbus..K-18; (170) H-2
Concord (35). . . .C-14
Confederate. J-2
Conkling. F-14
Cooper. H-11
Corbin (7,304). . .G-13
Corinth. H-7; (232) C-12
Cornettsville. G-15
Corydon (720). . . .E-5
Covington (40,640). B-12
Coxs Creek. E-10
Crab Orchard (841). F-12
Crayne (173). F-4
Creston. G-11
Crittenden (3,815). B-12
Crockett. D-15
Crofton (749). G-6
Cromwell. F-7
Cub Run. F-9
Cumberland (2,237). G-16
Cunningham. G-2
Curdsville. E-6
Custer. E-8
Cynthiana (6,402). C-13
Danville (16,218).E-12
David. F-16
Dawson Springs (2,764). G-5
Daysville. H-6
DeMossville. B-12
Deane. G-16
Debord. E-17
Deer Lick. G-7
Delphia. G-15
Denniston. E-14
Dewitt. H-14
Dexter (277). K-1
Dixon (786). F-5
Dog Walk. F-12
Donaldson. K-3
Dorton. F-17
Dot. H-7
Dover (252). B-14
Draffenville. J-1
Drakesboro (515)..G-7
Drip Rock. F-13
Dry Ridge (2,191). C-12
Dukes. E-7
Dulaney. I-2
Dunbar. G-7
Dundee. F-7
Dunmor. G-7
Dunnville. G-11
Dwarf. F-15
Dycusburg (26). . .G-4
Dyer. E-8
Eagle Station. . . .C-11
Earlington (1,413).G-5
East Bernstadt (716). G-13
East Point. E-16
Eastern. F-16
Eastview. F-9
Eastwood. D-10
Eddyville (2,554). G-4, I-2
Edmonton (1,595). G-10
Egypt. F-14
Ekron (135). E-9
Elias. F-14
Elizabethtown (28,531). E-9
Elkhorn City (982). F-17
Elkton (2,062). H-6
Elliottville. D-15
Ellisburg. F-11
Emerson. C-15
Eminence (2,498). C-11
Epleys. G-7
Eubank (319). . . .G-12
Evarts (962). H-15
Ewing (264). C-14
Exie. G-10
Ezel (235). E-15
Fairdealing. J-1
Fairfield (113). . .E-10
Fairview. .C-13; (286) H-6
Falcon. E-16
Fall Rock. G-14
Falls of Rough. . . .F-8
Falmouth (2,169). C-13
Fancy Farm (458). H-3
Farmers (284). . .D-14
Farmington (245)..H-3
Faywood. J-15
Fenton. K-2
Ferguson (924). .G-12
Finchville. D-10
Flaherty. E-9
Flat Lick (960). . .H-14
Flat Rock. H-12
Fleming-Neon (770). G-16
Flemingsburg (2,658). C-14
Flippin. H-9
Florence (29,951). B-12
Fordsville (524). . .F-7
Fountain Run (217). H-9
Fourmile. H-14
Frakes. H-14
Frances. G-4
Frankfort (25,527).D-11, H-17
Franklin (8,408). .H-8
Frazer. G-12
Fredonia (401). . .G-4
Freeburn (399). .F-18
Frenchburg (486). E-14
Frogue. H-10
Fulton (2,445). I-2
Furnace. E-14
Gamaliel (376). . .H-9
Garfield. E-8
Garrard. G-14
Garrett. E-9, F-16
Garrison (866). .C-15
Gasper. G-7
Georgetown (29,098). D-12
Germantown (154). C-13
Ghent (323). B-11
Gilbertsville (458). G-4, I-1
Gilpin. G-11
Girdler. G-14
Glasgow (14,028). G-9
Glencoe (360). . .C-12
Glendale. F-9
Glenview (531). .J-12
Goddard. C-14
Golden Pond. H-4, K-2
Goose Rock. . . .G-14
Goshen (909). . .C-10
Gracey (138). H-5
Graham. G-6
Grand Rivers (382). G-4, J-1
Gratz (78). C-11
Gravel Switch. . .F-11
Gray. G-13
Gray Hawk. F-14
Grayson (4,217).D-16
Greensburg (2,163). G-10
Greenup (1,188). C-16
Greenville (4,312). G-6
Greenwood. H-12
Gregory. H-12
Grider. H-10
Guston. E-8
Guthrie (1,419). . .H-6
Halfway. H-8
Halls Gap. F-12
Hamlin. L-2
Hanson (742). F-6
Hardin (615).H-4, K-1
Hardinsburg (2,343). E-8
Hardyville (156). .G-9
Hargett. E-13
Harlan (1,745). . .H-15
Harned. E-8
Harrods Creek. . .I-13
Harrodsburg (8,340). E-11
Hartford (2,672). . .F-7
Hawesville (945). .E-7
Hazard (4,456). .G-15
Hazel Green (228). E-15
Head of Grassy..C-15
Hebron (5,929). .B-12
Hedgeville. F-12
Henderson (28,757). E-5
Henshaw. F-4
Hensley. E-8
Herndon. H-5
Hickman (2,395). .H-2
Hickory. H-3
Hico. K-1
Hillsboro. D-14
Hillview (8,172). .D-10
Hindman (777). .F-16
Hiseville (240). . . .G-9
Hitchins. D-16
Hobson. F-10
Hodgenville (3,206). F-9
Hollyhill. H-13
Holmes Mill. H-16
Holt. E-8
Holy Cross. E-10
Honeybee. H-13
Hooktown. C-13
Hope. D-14
Hopkinsville (31,577). H-6
Hopson. J-3
Horse Branch. F-7
Horse Cave (2,311). G-9
Huddy. E-17
Hudson. E-8
Hurley. F-13
Hurstbourne (4,216). J-13
Hustonville (405). F-12
Hutchison. I-18
Hyden (365). . . .G-15
Ida. H-11
Idamay. F-14
Independence (24,757). B-12
Inez (717). E-17
Ingram. H-14
Irvine (2,715). . . .E-13
Irvington (1,181). .E-8
Island (458). F-6
Isom. G-16
Isonville. D-15
Iuka. I-1
Ivel. F-16
Jackson (2,231)..F-15
Jacktown. F-11
Jamestown (1,794). G-11
Jeff (323). G-15
Jeffersontown (26,595). .D-10, K-13
Jeffersonville (1,506). E-14
Jenkins (2,203). . .G-16
Jeriel. D-16
Joy. F-4
Junction City (2,241). F-12
Keavy. G-13
Kentontown. C-13
Kevil (376). G-2
Keysburg. H-7
Kidder. H-12
Kidds Crossing. . .H-12
Kidds Store. F-11
Kimper. F-17
Kinniconick. C-15
Kirkmansville. G-6
Kite. F-16
Knob Lick. G-10
Kuttawa (649). .G-4, I-2
La Center (1,009). .G-2
La Fayette (165). . .H-5
La Grange (8,082). C-10
Lake City. G-4, I-1
Lamasco. J-2
Lancaster (3,442)..F-12
Lawrenceburg (10,505). D-11
Lebanon (5,539). .F-11
Lebanon Junction (1,813). E-9
Ledbetter (1,683). .G-3
Leitchfield (6,699). .F-8
Lenoxburg. B-13
Levi. F-14
Lewisburg (810). . .G-7
Lewisport (1,670). .E-7
Lexington (295,803).D-12, K-17
Liberty (2,168). . . .F-11
Lily. G-13
Linton. K-2
Livermore (1,365). .F-6
Livingston (226). . .F-13
Lloyd. C-16
Lola. F-4
London (7,993). . .G-13
Lone Oak. G-3
Lookout. F-17
Loretto (713). F-10
Lost Creek. F-15
Louisa (2,467). . . .D-16
Louisville (597,337).D-10, L-12
Lovelaceville (148).G-3
Lowes (98). H-3
Lowmansville. E-16
Loyall (1,461). H-15
Lucas. H-9
Lynch (747). G-16
Lynn Grove. H-3
Lynnville. H-3
Maceo (413). E-7
Mackville (222). . . .E-11
Madisonville (19,591). F-6
Madrid. F-8
Magnolia (524). F-9
Malone. E-15
Mammoth Cave. G-9, L-8
Manchester (1,255). G-14
Manitou (181). F-5
Mannsville. F-11
Marcellus. E-12
Marion (3,039). F-4
Marrowbone (217). H-10
Martha. D-16
Martin (634). F-16
Massac (4,505). . . .G-3
Mattoon. F-4
Mayfield (10,024). .H-3
Mayking (487). . . .G-16
Mays Lick (242). .C-14
Maysville (9,011). .C-14
McCarr (164). E-17
McCreary. E-12
McDaniels. F-8
McHenry (388). F-7
McKee (800). F-13
Meally. E-16
Means. E-14
Melber. G-3
Meshack. H-10
Middlefork. F-13
Middlesboro. H-14
Middletown (7,218). J-14
Midway (1,641). . .D-12
Milburn. H-2
Mill Springs. G-12
Millersburg (792). .D-13
Millwood. F-8
Milton (574). B-10
Minerva. C-14
Mintonville. G-12
Mize. E-15
Monterey (138). . .C-11
Monticello (6,188).H-11
Mooleyville. D-8
Moorefield. D-13
Morehead (6,845). D-15
Moreland. F-12
Morganfield (3,285). E-5
Morgantown (2,394). G-7
Mortons Gap (863). G-6
Mouthcard. F-17
Mt. Aerial. H-8
Mt. Carmel. C-14
Mt. Eden. D-11
Mt. Olive. F-14
Mt. Olivet (299). C-13
Mt. Pisgah. H-12
Mt. Sherman. F-10
Mt. Sterling (6,895). D-13
Mt. Vernon (2,477). F-13
Mt. Washington (9,117)..D-10
Mud Lick. H-9
Muldraugh (947). E-9
Munfordville (1,615). G-9
Murray (17,741). H-4, L-1
Myers. D-13
Nancy. G-12
Nazareth. E-10
Nebo (236). F-5
New Castle (912). C-11
New Concord. L-1
New Haven (855). E-10
New Hope (129). F-10
New Liberty. C-11
New Market. F-10
New Roe. H-8
New Zion. F-14
Newport (15,273). A-12
Nicholasville (28,015). . .E-12
North Middletown (643).D-13
Nortonville (1,204). G-6
Oak Grove (7,489). H-6
Oakland (225). G-8
Olive. K-1
Olive Hill (1,599). D-15
Olympia. D-14
Oneida (410). G-14
Owensboro (57,265).E-6, J-5
Owenton (1,327). C-11
Owingsville (1,530). D-14
Paducah (25,024). . .G-3, L-5
Paint Lick. F-12
Paintsville (3,459). E-16
Palma. J-1
Paris (8,553). D-13
Park City (537). G-9
Parksville. F-11
Patesville. E-7
Payneville. E-8
Pellville. E-7
Pembroke (869). H-6
Pendleton. C-10
Perry Park. C-11
Perryville (751). E-11
Petersburg. A-16
Petroleum. H-8
Pewee Valley (1,456). . .J-14
Peytonsburg. H-10
Phelps (893). F-18
Philpot. E-7
Pierce. G-10
Pikeville (6,903). F-17
Pinckneyville. G-4
Pine Knot (1,621). H-12
Pineville (1,732). H-14
Pippa Passes (533). F-16
Piqua. C-13
Pisgah. K-15
Pittsburg. G-13
Pleasureville (834). D-11

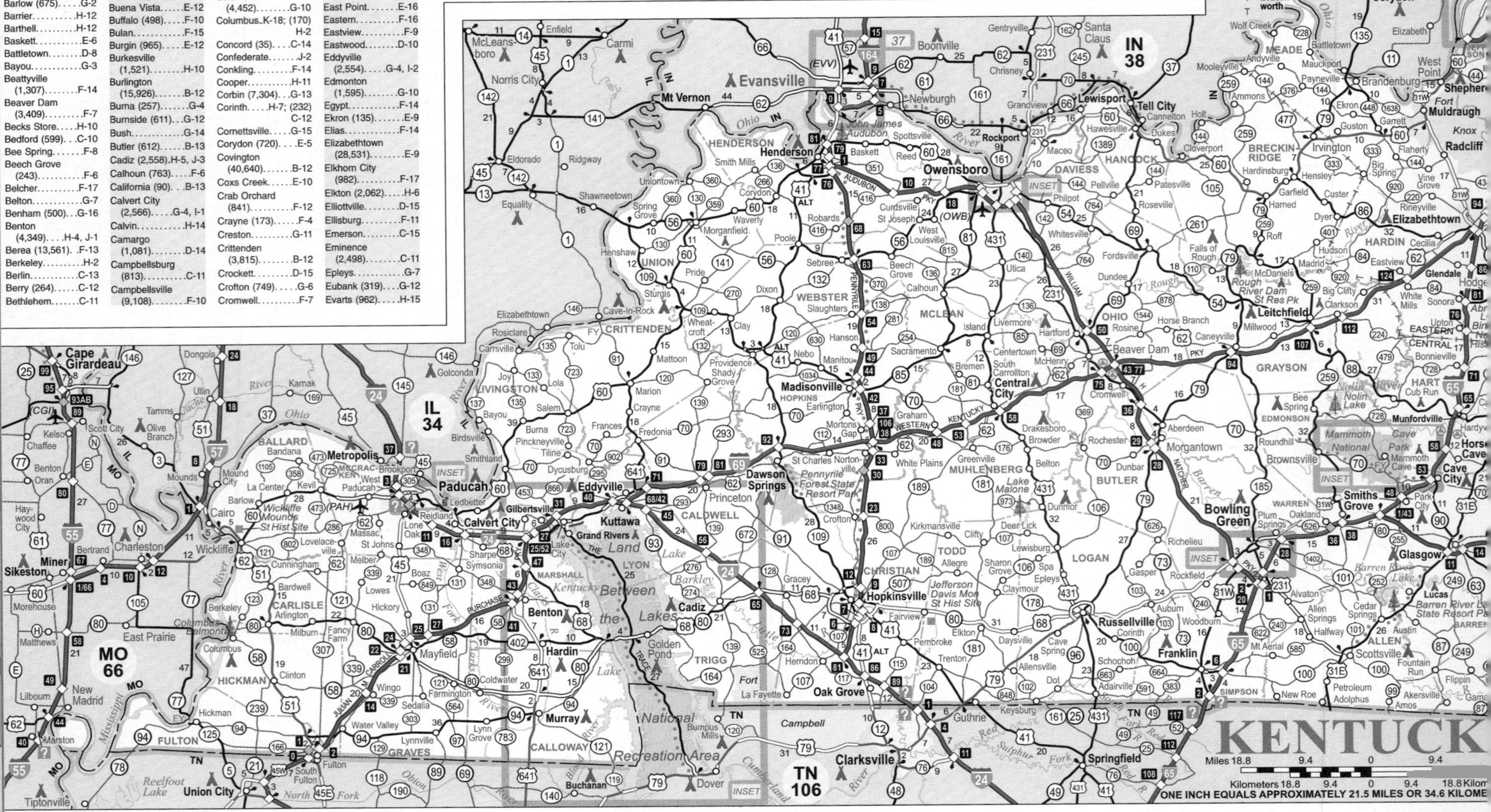
KENTUCK
Miles 18.8 9.4 0 9.4
Kilometers 18.8 9.4 0 9.4 18.8
ONE INCH EQUALS APPROXIMATELY 21.5 MILES OR 34.6 KILOME

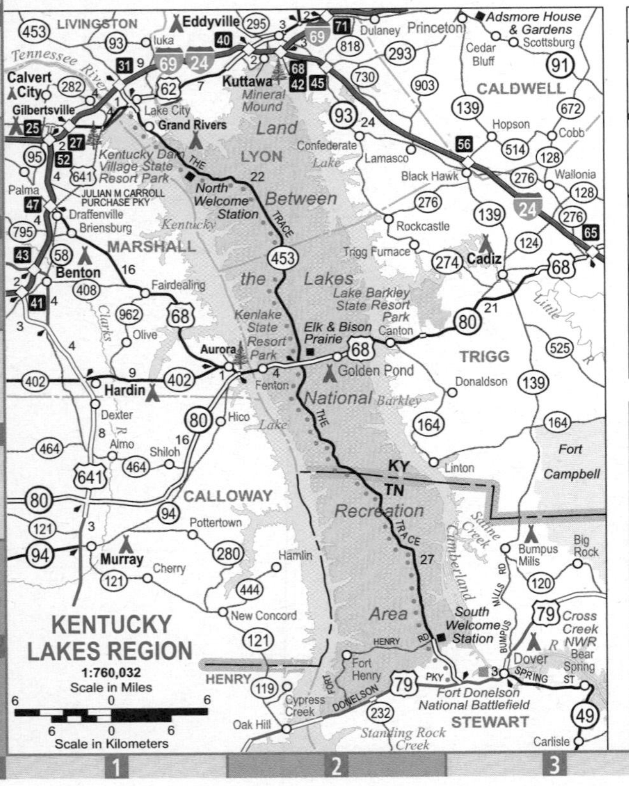
KENTUCKY LAKES REGION
1:760,032
Scale in Miles
6 0 6
6 0 6
Scale in Kilometers

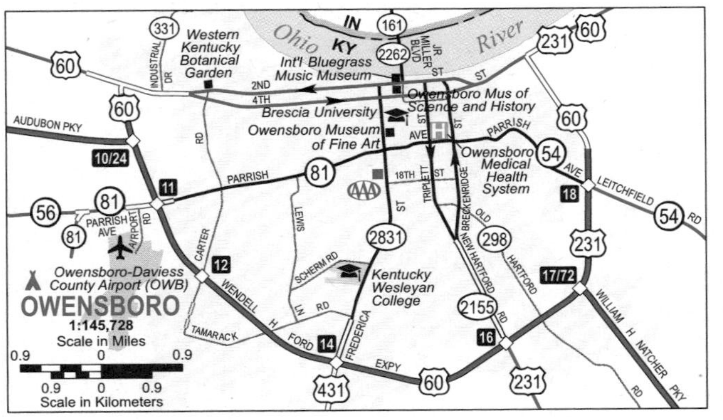
OWENSBORO
1:145,728
Scale in Miles
0.9 0 0.9
0.9 0 0.9
Scale in Kilometers

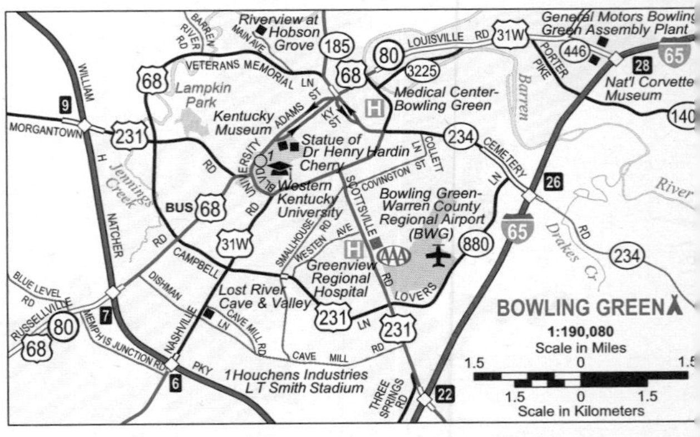
BOWLING GREEN
1:190,080
Scale in Miles
1.5 0 1.5
1.5 0 1.5
Scale in Kilometers

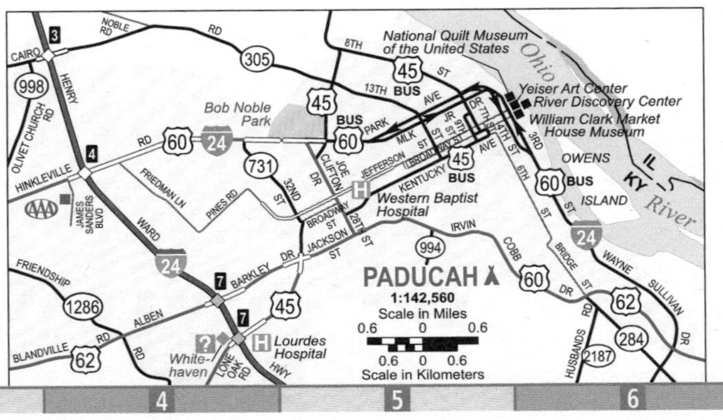
PADUCAH
1:142,560
Scale in Miles
0.6 0 0.6
0.6 0 0.6
Scale in Kilometers

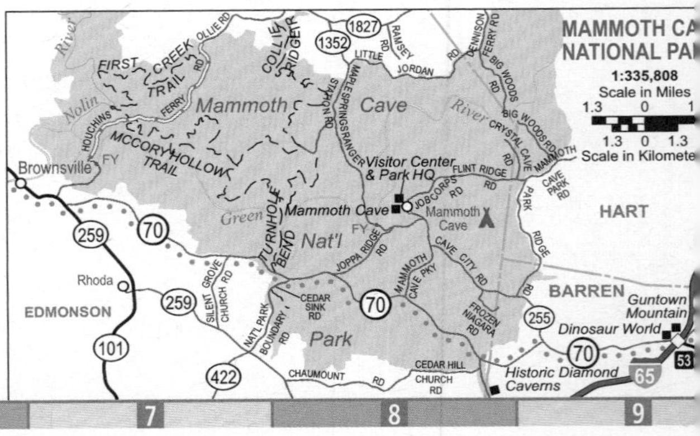
1:335,808

LEGEND

Interstate Highway	95 Wildlife Refuge
Controlled Access Hwy	Nat'l/State Park
Controlled Access Hwy Toll	National Forest

Plum Springs (453)....G-8
Plummers Landing....D-14
Poole....E-5
Pottertown....K-1
Powersville....C-13
Preachersville....F-12
Prestonsburg (3,255)..E-16
Pricetown....F-5
Pride....F-5
Princeton (6,329)...G-5, I-3
Prospect (4,698)....I-13
Providence....L-16, (3,193) F-5
Pryse....E-14
Quincy....H-15
Quincy....C-15
Radcliff (21,688)....E-9

Ravenna (605)....E-13
Raywick (134)....F-10
Redfox....G-16
Reidland (4,491)....G-3
Reed....L-7
Renfro Valley....F-13
Rhoda....L-7
Richelieu....G-7
Richmond (31,364)....E-13
Ribolt....C-14
Rineyville....E-9

Roark....G-14
Robards (515)....E-5
Robinson Creek....F-17
Rochester (152)....G-7
Rockbridge....H-10
Rockcastle....J-2
Rockfield....F-4
Rockholds (390)....H-13
Roff....E-9
Rogers....E-14
Roseville....E-7
Rosine (113)....F-7
Roundhill....F-7
Rowland....F-12
Roxana....G-16
Royalton....E-16
Rush....E-16
Russell (3,380)....C-16
Russell Springs (2,441)....G-11
Russellville (6,960)..H-7

Sacramento (468)....F-6
Sadieville (303)....C-12
Salem (752)....F-4
Salt Lick (303)....D-14
Salvisa (420)....E-11
Salyersville (1,883)..E-15
Sanders (238)....C-11
Sandgap....E-13
Sandy Hook (675)....D-15
Sardis (103)....C-14
Sassafras....G-16
Science Hill (693)..G-12
Scottsburg....I-3
Scottsville (4,226)..H-8
Sebree (1,603)....F-5
Sedalia (295)....H-3

Shady Grove....F-5
Sharkey....D-14
Sharon Grove....H-6
Sharpsburg (323)...D-14
Shelbiana....F-17
Shelbyville (14,045)..D-11
Shepherdsville (11,222)....E-10
Sherburne....D-14
Sherman....B-12
Shiloh....K-1
Shipley....H-11
Shively (15,264)....K-11
Sidney....E-17
Siler....H-14

Simpsonville (2,484)....D-10
Slade....E-14
Slaughters (216)....F-6
Smilax....G-16
Smith Mills....E-5
Smithfield (106)....C-11
Smithland (301)....F-4
Smiths Grove (714)..G-8
Soldier....D-15
Sonora (513)....F-9
South Carrollton (184)....F-6
South Shore....B-16
Spa....G-7

Sparta (231)....C-11
Spottsville (325)....E-6
Spring Grove....F-14
Springfield (2,519)..E-11
St. Charles (277)....G-5
St. Johns....G-3
St. Joseph....E-6
St. Mary....F-10
St. Matthews (17,472)....J-13
St. Paul....C-15
Staffordsville....E-16
Stamping Ground (643)....D-12
Stanford (3,487)....F-12
Stanton (2,733)....E-14
Static....H-11

Stearns (1,416)....H-12
Stinnett....G-15
Stoney Fork....H-14
Sturgis (1,898)....F-4
Sulphur....C-11
Summer Shade (307)..H-10
Summersville (568)..F-10
Sunnybrook....H-11
Symsonia (615)....G-3
Tannery....C-15
Tateville....G-12
Taylorsville (763)....D-10
Tilden....D-14
Tiline....G-4
Tilton....D-14
Tollesboro....C-14
Tomahawk....E-16
Tompkinsville (2,402)..H-10
Totz....G-15
Trenton (384)....H-6
Trigg Furnace....J-2
Tyner....F-14
Ulysses....E-16
Union (5,379)....B-12
Uniontown (1,002)....E-5
Upton (683)....F-9
Utica....F-6
Vanceburg (1,518)....C-15
Vancleve....E-15
Verona (1,455)....B-12
Versailles (8,568)....D-12
Vincent....E-13
Vine Grove (4,520)....E-9
Virgie (279)....F-17
Waco....E-13
Waddy....D-11
Wagersville....F-13
Wallingford....C-14
Wallins Creek (156)..H-15
Wallonia....B-3
Walton (3,635)....B-12
Waneta....F-13

Warfield (269)....E-17
Warsaw (1,615)....B-11
Washington....C-14
Water Valley (279)...H-5
Wavely (308)....G-11
Waverly (426)....F-16
Waynesburg....F-12
Wayland....E-16
Webbville....D-16
West Liberty (3,435)..E-6
West Louisville....E-6
West Matthews....J-13
West Paducah (780)..F-6
West Point (797)....E-9
Wheatcroft (160)....F-5
Wheelwright (780)...E-16
White Mills....F-9
White Plains (884)...G-6
Whitesburg (2,139)..G-16
Whitesville (552)....E-5
Whitley City (1,170)..H-12
Wickliffe (688)....G-2
Willard....D-16
Williamsburg (5,245)..H-13
Williamstown (3,925)..C-12
Williamsport (282)...E-11
Wilmore (3,686)....E-12
Winchester (18,368)..E-13
Wingo (632)....H-3
Winston....E-13
Wittensville....E-16
Wolf Creek....H-3
Woodbine....H-13
Woodburn (355)....H-8
Woodine....F-13
Wooton....G-15
Worthville (185)....C-11

Yamacraw....H-12
Yeaddiss....G-15
Yosemite....F-12
Yuma....G-11
Zion Hill....I-15
Zoe....E-14
Zula....H-11

NA044-15

NA044-15
240

FRANKFORT
1:158,400
Scale in Miles
Scale in Kilometers

LOUISVILLE AND VICINITY
1:297,792
Scale in Miles
Scale in Kilometers

LEXINGTON AND VICINITY
1:237,600
Scale in Miles
Scale in Kilometers

Driving Distances In Miles	Alexandria	Baton Rouge	Hammond	Lafayette	Lake Charles	Monroe	New Orleans	Shreveport	Tallulah	Winnfield
Baton Rouge	115		47	56	126	185	81	233	164	171
Lake Charles	97	126	172	75		192	206	221	221	145
New Orleans	218	81	57	135	206	264		341	246	265
Shreveport	124	233	289	212	221	98	341		154	94

See also mileage table page 2

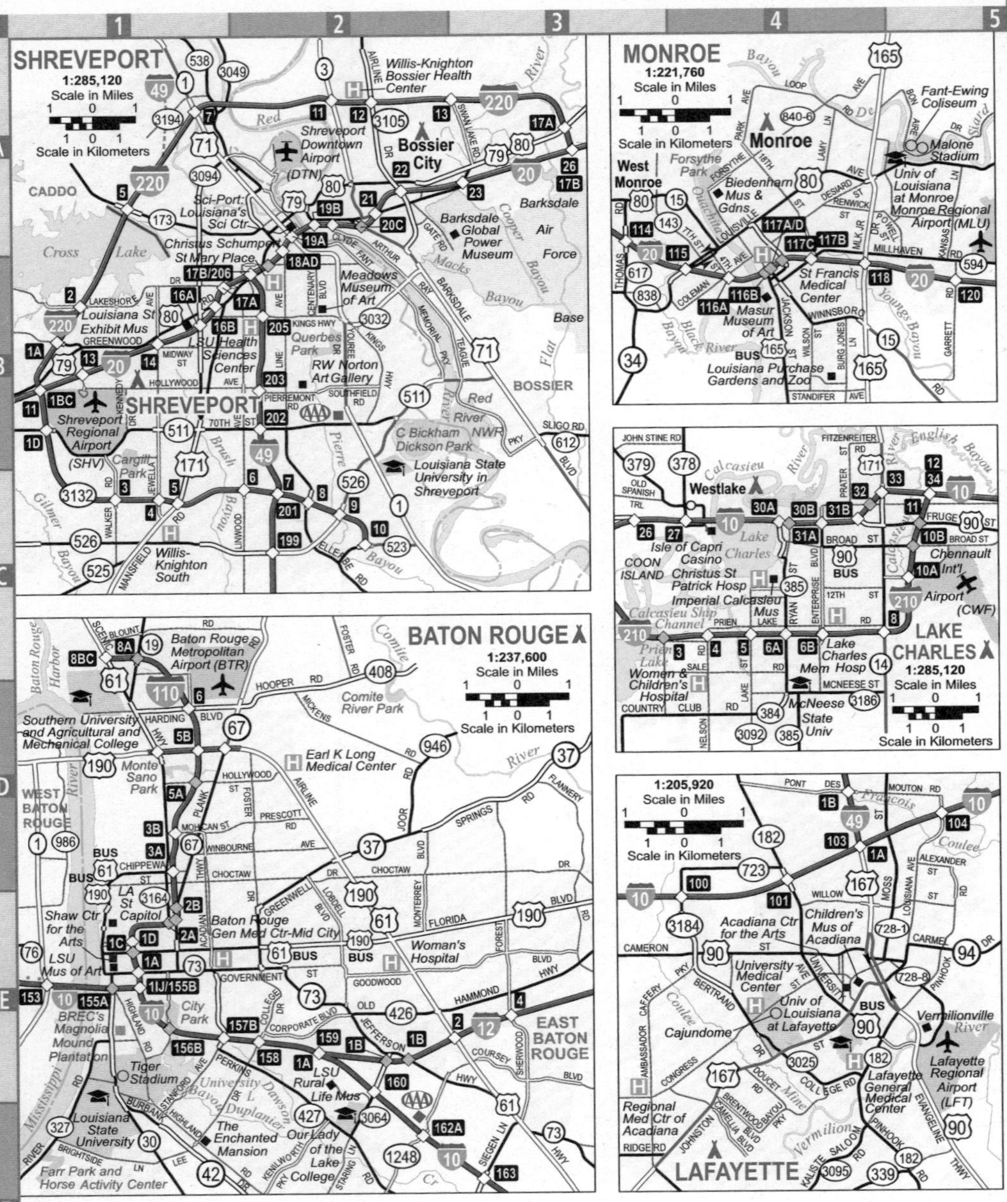

SHREVEPORT 1:285,120
Scale in Miles
Scale in Kilometers

SHREVEPORT

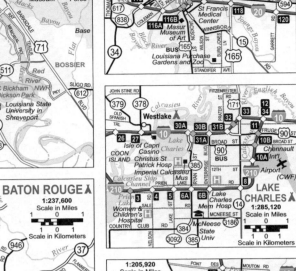

MONROE 1:221,760
Scale in Miles
Scale in Kilometers

Monroe
West Monroe

LAKE CHARLES 1:285,120
Scale in Miles
Scale in Kilometers

Westlake
LAKE CHARLES

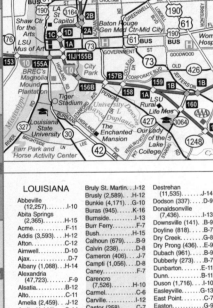

BATON ROUGE 1:237,600
Scale in Miles
Scale in Kilometers

BATON ROUGE
EAST BATON ROUGE
WEST BATON ROUGE

LAFAYETTE 1:205,920
Scale in Miles
Scale in Kilometers

LAFAYETTE

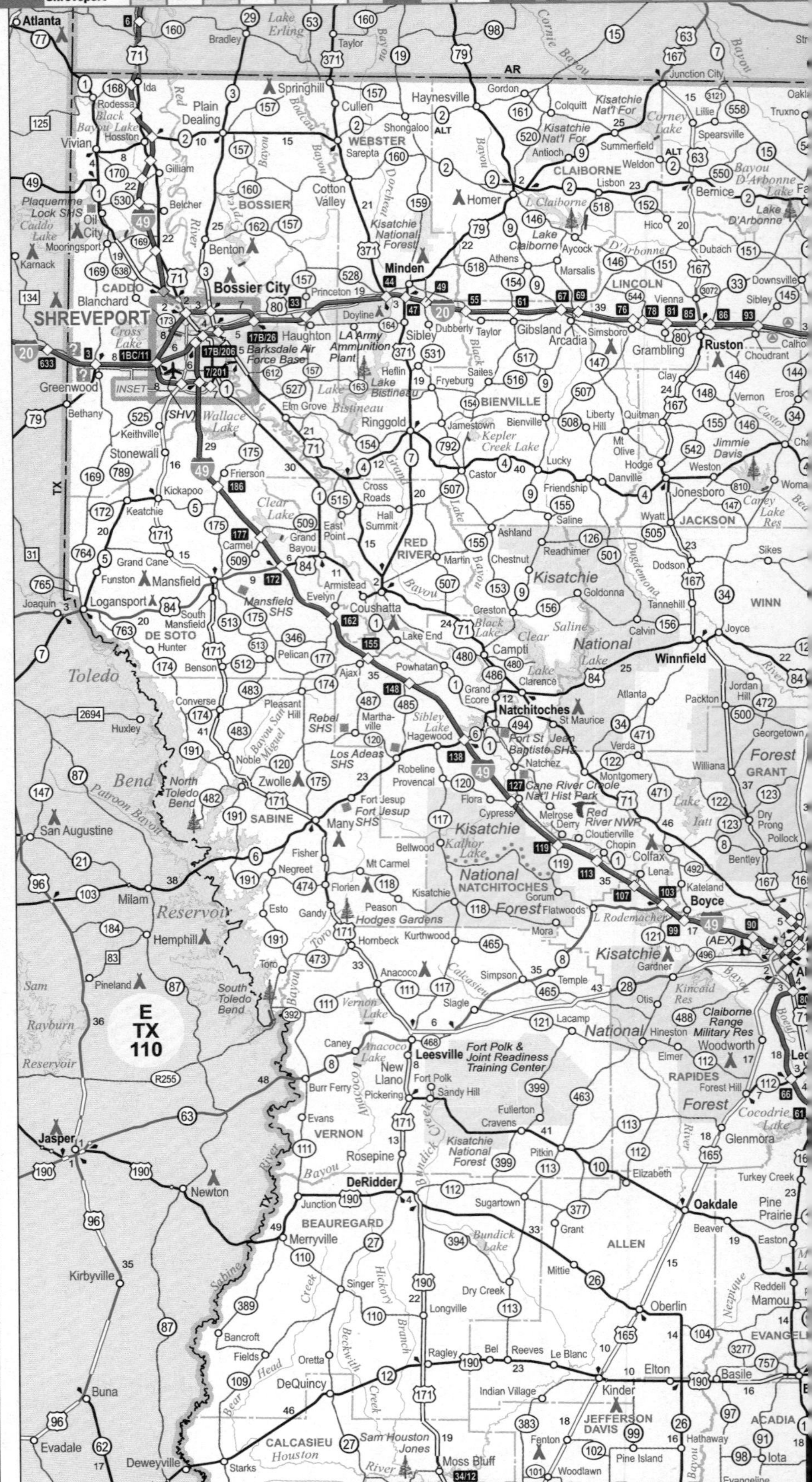

LOUISIANA

Abbeville (12,257)...I-10
Abita Springs (2,365)...H-15
Acme...F-11
Addis (3,593)...H-12
Afton...C-12
Amwell...D-10
Ajax...G-7
Albany (1,088)...H-14
Alexandria (47,723)...F-9
Alsatia...B-11
Alto...C-11
Amelia (2,459)...J-12
Amite (4,141)...G-14
Anacoco (869)...F-7
Angie (251)...G-16
Angola...G-11
Antioch...A-8
Arabi (3,635)...J-16
Arcadia (2,919)...B-8
Archibald...C-11
Argo...F-11
Armistead...D-7
Arnaudville (1,057)...H-10
Ashland (269)...C-8
Athens (249)...B-8
Atlanta (163)...D-8
Avery Island...J-10
Avondale (4,954)...C-15
Aycock...B-8
Bains...G-12
Baker (13,895)...H-12
Baldwin (2,436)...J-11
Bancroft...H-6
Baptist...H-14
Baskin (254)...C-11
Baskinton...C-11
Bastrop (11,365)...B-10
Batchelor...G-11
Baton Rouge (229,493)...F-2, H-12
Bayou Cane (19,355)...J-13
Bayou Chicot...G-9
Bayou Goula...H-12
Bayou Sorrel...H-12
Beaver...G-9
Beekman...A-11
Bel...G-8
Belcher (263)...B-6
Bell City...J-8
Bell River...J-12
Belle Rose (1,902)...J-13
Bellwood...F-8
Benson...D-6
Bentley...E-9
Benton (1,948)...B-6
Bernice (1,689)...A-9
Berwick (4,946)...J-11
Bethany...C-5
Bienville (218)...C-8
Big Bend...F-11
Blanchard (2,899)...B-6
Bogalusa (12,232)...G-15
Bonita (484)...A-11
Bordelonville (525)...F-10
Bossier City (61,315)...B-2, B-6
Boudreaux...K-13
Bougere...F-11
Bourg (2,919)...K-14
Boyce (1,004)...E-9
Braithwaite...J-15
Branch (388)...I-10
Breaux Bridge (8,139)...I-10
Brouillette...F-10
Broussard (8,197)...I-10

Bruly St. Martin...I-12
Brusly (2,589)...H-12
Buras (945)...K-16
Burnside...I-13
Burr Ferry...F-6
Bush...H-15
Calhoun (679)...B-9
Calvin (238)...D-8
Cameron (406)...J-7
Campti (1,056)...D-8
Caney...C-10
Carencro (7,526)...H-10
Carmel...I-12
Carville...I-12
Castor (258)...C-7
Center Point (492)...F-10
Centerville...J-11
Chalmette (16,751)...C-18, J-15
Charenton (1,903)...J-11
Chase...A-11
Chataignier (364)...H-9
Chatham (557)...C-9
Chauvin (2,912)...K-14
Cheneyville (625)...F-10
Chipola...G-13
Chopin...E-8
Choudrant (845)...B-9
Church Point (4,560)...H-10
Clarence (499)...D-8
Clarks (1,017)...D-10
Clay...C-9
Clayton (711)...E-11
Clifton...G-5
Clinton (1,653)...G-13
Cloutierville...E-8
Cocodrie...K-14
Colfax (1,558)...E-9
Collinston (287)...B-11
Colquitt...A-8
Columbia (390)...C-10
Concord...A-12
Convent (711)...I-13
Converse (440)...D-6
Cooper Point...C-10
Corey...C-11
Cotton Plant...C-10
Cotton Valley (1,009)...A-7
Cottonport (2,006)...F-10
Coushatta (1,964)...D-7
Covington (8,765)...H-15
Cravens...G-7
Creston...D-8
Crew Lake...B-11
Cross Roads...A-9
Crowley (13,265)...I-9
Crown Point...J-15
Crowville (499)...C-11
Cullen (1,163)...A-7
Cut Off (5,976)...K-14
Cypress...F-8
Danville...C-8
Darlington...G-13
Darnell...D-6
DeQuincy (3,235)...H-7
DeRidder (10,578)...G-7
Deer Park...G-12
Delcambre (1,866)...J-10
Delhi (2,919)...B-11
Delta (284)...C-11
Denham Springs (10,215)...H-12
Dennis Mills...G-13
Derry...E-8

Destrehan (11,535)...J-14
Dodson (337)...D-9
Donaldsonville (7,436)...I-12
Downsville (141)...B-9
Doyline (818)...B-7
Dry Creek...G-8
Dry Prong (436)...E-9
Dubach (961)...B-9
Dubberly (273)...B-7
Dunbarton...E-11
Dunn...B-11
Duson (1,716)...I-10
Easleyville...G-13
East Point...C-7
Easton...C-7
Echo...F-10
Eden...E-10
Edgard (2,441)...I-14
Effie...F-10
Elizabeth (532)...G-8
Elm Grove...C-7
Elton (1,128)...H-8
Eola...G-10
Enterprise...D-11
Epps (854)...B-12
Erath (2,114)...I-10
Erwinville...H-12
Eros (155)...C-9
Estherwood (889)...I-9
Esto...C-10
Eunice (10,398)...H-9
Evangeline...I-9
Evans...G-7
Evergreen (310)...G-10
Extension...D-11
Fairbanks...A-10
Farmerville (3,860)...B-9
Felixville...G-13
Felps...G-13
Fenton (377)...H-8
Ferriday (3,511)...E-11
Fields...G-7
Fifth Ward (800)...F-10
Fisher (230)...C-7
Fiske...A-11
Flatwoods...E-9
Fluker...G-14
Floyd...B-12
Folsom (716)...H-15
Fordoche (928)...H-11
Forest (355)...B-11
Forest Hill (818)...F-9
Forked Island...I-10
Fort Jesup (509)...E-7
Fort Necessity...B-11
Fort Polk...F-7
Foules...D-11
Franklin (7,660)...J-11
Franklinton (3,857)...G-15
French Settlement (1,116)...I-13
Frierson (487)...C-6
Frogmore...E-11
Fryeburg...D-7
Fullerton...G-8
Funston...D-6
Galion...D-11
Galliano (7,676)...K-14
Gandy...D-11
Gardner...F-9
Geismar...I-12
Georgetown (327)...D-10
Gheens (979)...J-13
Gibson (739)...J-13
Gilbert (520)...C-11

Gilliam (164)...A-6
Girard...B-11
Glencoe (211)...J-11
Glenmora (1,342)...G-9
Golden Meadow (2,101)...K-15
Goldman...D-11
Goldonna (430)...D-8
Gonzales (9,781)...I-12
Goodwill...B-11
Gordon...B-11
Gorum...E-8
Goudeau...G-10
Grambling (4,949)...B-9
Gramercy (3,613)...I-13
Grand Bayou (242)...C-7
Grand Chenier...J-8
Grand Coteau (947)...H-10
Grand Ecore...D-8
Grand Isle...K-15
Grand Lake...I-7
Grangeville...H-14
Gray (5,584)...J-13
Grayson (532)...D-10
Greensburg (718)...G-14
Greenwell Springs...H-13
Greenwood (3,219)...C-5
Gretna (17,736)...C-17, J-15
Grosse Tete (647)...H-12
Gueydan (1,261)...I-9
Hackberry (1,261)...I-7
Hagewood...E-7
Hahnville (3,344)...I-14
Haile...B-9
Hall Summit (300)...C-7
Hammond (20,019)...H-14
Harahan (9,277)...C-15
Harrisonburg (348)...D-11
Harvey...I-15
Hathaway (8,679)...H-9
Haughton (3,454)...B-7
Hayes (780)...I-8
Haynesville (2,327)...A-8
Hebert...B-10
Helm (244)...D-7
Henderson...I-11
Hermitage...H-12
Hessmer (802)...F-10
Hico...B-9
Highland...A-12
Hineston...F-8
Hodge (470)...C-9
Holden...H-13
Holly Beach...J-7
Holly Ridge...B-11
Holton...G-14
Holum...D-8
Homer (3,237)...A-8
Hornbeck (480)...F-7
Hosston (318)...A-6
Houma (33,727)...K-13
Husser...G-14
Ida (223)...A-6
Independence (1,665)...H-14
Indian Bayou...I-10
Indian Village...I-8
Innis...G-11
Intracoastal City...J-10
Iota (1,500)...I-9
Iowa (2,996)...I-8
Jackson (3,842)...G-13
Jamestown (139)...C-7
Jean Lafitte (1,903)...J-15

Jeanerette (5,530)...J-11
Jena (3,398)...E-10
Jennings (10,383)...I-9
Jigger...D-11
Johnsons Bayou...J-7
Jones...A-11
Jonesboro (4,704)...C-9
Jonesville (2,265)...E-11
Jordan Hill (211)...D-9
Joyce (384)...D-9
Junction...D-9
Junction City (321)...A-9
Kaplan (4,600)...I-10
Kateland...E-9
Keatchie...C-6
Keithville (416)...A-12
Keithville...C-6
Kelly...D-10
Kenner (66,702)...A-14, H-15
Kentwood (2,198)...G-14
Kickapoo...C-6
Kilbourne (416)...A-12
Kinder (2,477)...H-8
Kisatchie...E-8
Krotz Springs (1,198)...H-11
Kurthwood...F-7
Labadieville (1,854)...J-13
Labarre...I-12
Lacamp...F-8
Lacassine (480)...I-8
Lacombe (8,679)...H-15
Lafitte (972)...J-15
Lake Arthur (2,738)...I-9
Lake Charles (71,993)...C-4, I-7
Lake End...D-7
Lake Providence (3,991)...B-12
Lakeland...G-11
Lamourie...F-9
Laplace (29,872)...I-14
Larose (7,303)...K-14
Lawtell (1,198)...H-10
Le Blanc...H-8
Lebeau...G-10
Lecompte (1,227)...F-9
Lees Landing...I-9
Leesville (6,612)...F-7
Legonier...H-11
Lemee (244)...D-7
Lena...D-8
Leonville (1,084)...H-10
Leroy...I-10
Lewiston...G-14
Libuse...E-9
Liberty Hill...C-8
Lillie (118)...A-9
Lindsay (2,904)...F-10
Linville (185)...B-8
Lisbon (185)...A-8
Little Creek...B-11
Livingston (1,555)...I-13
Livonia (1,442)...H-11
Lockport (2,578)...K-14
Log Cabin (1,441)...H-8
Logansport (1,555)...D-5
Longleaf (635)...F-9
Longville...H-8
Loreauville (887)...J-10
Lottie...H-11
Louisa...J-11
Lucky (272)...C-8
Lydia (952)...J-10

Madisonville (748)...H-15
Mamou (3,242)...H-9
Manchac...I-14
Mandeville (11,560)...H-15
Mangham (672)...C-11
Manifest...E-10
Mansfield (5,001)...D-6
Mansura (1,419)...F-10
Many (2,853)...E-7
Marringouin (1,098)...H-11
Marion (765)...A-10
Marksville (5,702)...F-10
Marrero (33,141)...J-15
Marsalis...B-8
Marthaville (327)...D-7
Martin (594)...D-7
Mathews (964)...J-13
Maurepas (964)...I-13
Maurice (964)...I-10
McManus...G-12
McNary (341)...F-9
Melrose...E-8
Melville (1,041)...G-11
Mer Rouge (629)...B-11
Meraux (5,816)...J-15
Mermentau (661)...I-9
Merryville (1,103)...G-7
Metairie (138,481)...B-16
Metropolis...D-11
Midway (1,291)...E-10
Minden (13,082)...B-7
Mittie (248)...G-8
Moncla...F-10
Monroe (48,815)...B-10, B-4
Monterey (594)...E-11
Montgomery (730)...E-8
Monticello...B-12
Mooringsport (793)...A-6
Mora...F-10
Moreauville (793)...F-10
Morgan City (12,404)...J-12
Morganza (610)...G-11
Morrow...G-10
Morse (812)...I-9
Moss Bluff (11,557)...H-7
Mt. Airy (1,084)...E-7
Mt. Hermon...G-14
Mt. Olive...C-8
Napoleonville (984)...J-13
Natalbany...H-14
Natchez (597)...E-8
Natchitoches (18,323)...D-8
Nebo...E-10
Negreet...E-6
New Iberia (30,617)...J-11
New Llano (2,504)...F-7
New Roads (4,831)...G-12
Newellton (1,227)...C-12
Newlight...D-11
Noble (577)...E-7
Norwood (322)...G-12
Oak Grove (1,723)...B-12
Oak Ridge (144)...B-11

Opelousas (16,634)...H-10
Oretta (418)...H-7
Oscar...H-12
Otis...F-8
Packton...D-9
Paincourtville (911)...J-13
Palmetto (164)...G-10
Paradis (1,298)...J-14
Patoutville (1,298)...J-11
Patterson (6,112)...J-12
Pearl River (2,506)...H-16
Peason...E-7
Pecan Island (911)...J-9
Pelican (241)...D-6
Perry...J-10
Pickering...G-7
Pierre Part (3,169)...J-12
Pigeon...J-12
Pilottown...L-17
Pine (611)...H-8
Pine Grove...G-13
Pine Island...H-8
Pine Prairie (1,610)...G-9
Pineville (14,555)...F-9
Pioneer (156)...B-12
Pitkin (572)...G-8
Plain Dealing (1,015)...A-6
Plaquemine (7,119)...I-12
Plaucheville (248)...G-10
Pleasant Hill (723)...D-7
Point...D-11
Point Blue...H-11
Pointe a la Hache (187)...K-16
Pollock (376)...E-9
Ponchatoula (6,559)...H-14
Port Allen (5,180)...H-12
Port Barre (2,055)...H-10
Powhatan (135)...D-7
Prairieville (26,895)...I-12
Pride...G-13
Princeton...B-7
Provencal (677)...E-7
Quitman (181)...C-8
Raceland (10,193)...J-14
Ragley (1,494)...H-7
Ramah...H-11
Rayne (7,953)...I-10
Rayville (3,695)...B-11
Readhimer...E-8
Reddell (733)...G-9
Reeves (232)...H-8
Rhinehart...E-10
Richmond (577)...C-12
Ridgecrest (694)...E-11
Ringgold (1,495)...C-7
River Ridge (13,494)...C-15
Robert...H-14
Robeline (174)...E-7
Rockdale...H-11
Rodessa (270)...A-5
Rosa...H-15
Rosedale (793)...H-12
Rosefield...D-10
Roseland (1,123)...G-14
Rosepine (1,692)...G-7
Ruston (21,859)...B-9
Sailes...C-8
Saline (277)...C-8
Sandy Hill...F-7
Sarepta (891)...A-7

Shelburn...A-12
Shelton...A-11
Sheridan...B-10
Shongaloo (182)...A-7
Shreveport (199,311)...B-2, B-6
Sibley...B-9, B-7
Sicily Island (526)...D-11
Sikes (119)...C-9
Simmesport (2,161)...G-11
Simpson (841)...F-8
Simsboro (841)...B-8
Singer (287)...G-7
Slagle...F-8
Slaughter (997)...G-13
Slidell (27,068)...I-16
Somerset...B-12
Sondheimer...B-12
South Mansfield (264)...D-6

Spearsville (137)...A-9
Spencer...B-10
Spokane (442)...C-7
Springfield (487)...H-14
Springhill (5,269)...A-7
St. Benedict...H-15
St. Bernard...J-16
St. Francisville (1,765)...G-12
St. Gabriel (6,677)...I-12
St. James (826)...I-13
St. Joseph (1,176)...D-12
St. Landry...G-10
St. Martinville (6,114)...I-11
St. Maurice (323)...D-8
Sandy Hill...F-7
Standard...D-10
Starks (664)...H-7
State Line...G-15

Sterling (1,594)...B-10
Stonewall (1,814)...C-6
Sugartown (54)...G-8
Sulphur (20,410)...I-7
Summerfield (281)...A-8
Summerland...A-10
Sun (470)...H-15
Sunset (2,897)...H-10
Supreme (1,052)...J-13
Tacony...C-12
Tallulah (7,335)...C-12
Talisheek...H-15
Tangipahoa (748)...G-14
Tannehill...D-9
Taylor...B-8
Temple...F-8
Terry...F-10
Thibodaux (14,566)...J-13
Thomas...C-11
Tickfaw (694)...H-14

Tioga...E-9
Toro...F-7
Torras...G-11
Transylvania (54)...B-12
Truxno...A-8
Tullos (395)...D-10
Turkey Creek (441)...G-9
Urania (1,313)...D-10
Vacherie...I-13
Venice (202)...L-17
Ventress (890)...G-12
Verda...E-9
Vernon...D-9
Vidalia (4,299)...E-11
Ville Platte (8,534)...G-10
Vinton (3,671)...I-7
Violet...J-15
Vivian (3,671)...A-6
Vixen...C-9
Waddil (6,138)...H-13

Walker (6,138)...H-13
Wallace Ridge (710)...E-11
Walters...C-8
Warden...A-7
Wamerton...A-8
Washington (964)...H-10
Waterproof (688)...D-12
Watson (1,047)...H-13
Waverly...C-12
Weeks...J-11
Welch (3,226)...I-9
Welsh (3,226)...I-9
West Monroe (13,065)...A-14
Westlake (4,568)...C-16
Westwego (8,534)...C-16
Weyanoke...G-12
Whitecastle (1,883)...I-12
Whitehall...E-11
Wildsville...E-11

Williana...E-8
Wilmer...G-14
Wilson (595)...G-12
Winnfield (4,840)...D-9
Winnsboro (4,910)...C-11
Wisner (964)...D-11
Womack...C-11
Woodland...C-12
Woodlawn...I-7
Woodworth (1,096)...F-9
Wyatt...E-10
Youngsville (8,105)...I-10
Zachary (14,960)...H-12
Zenoria...D-10
Zwolle (1,759)...D-6

NA046-15

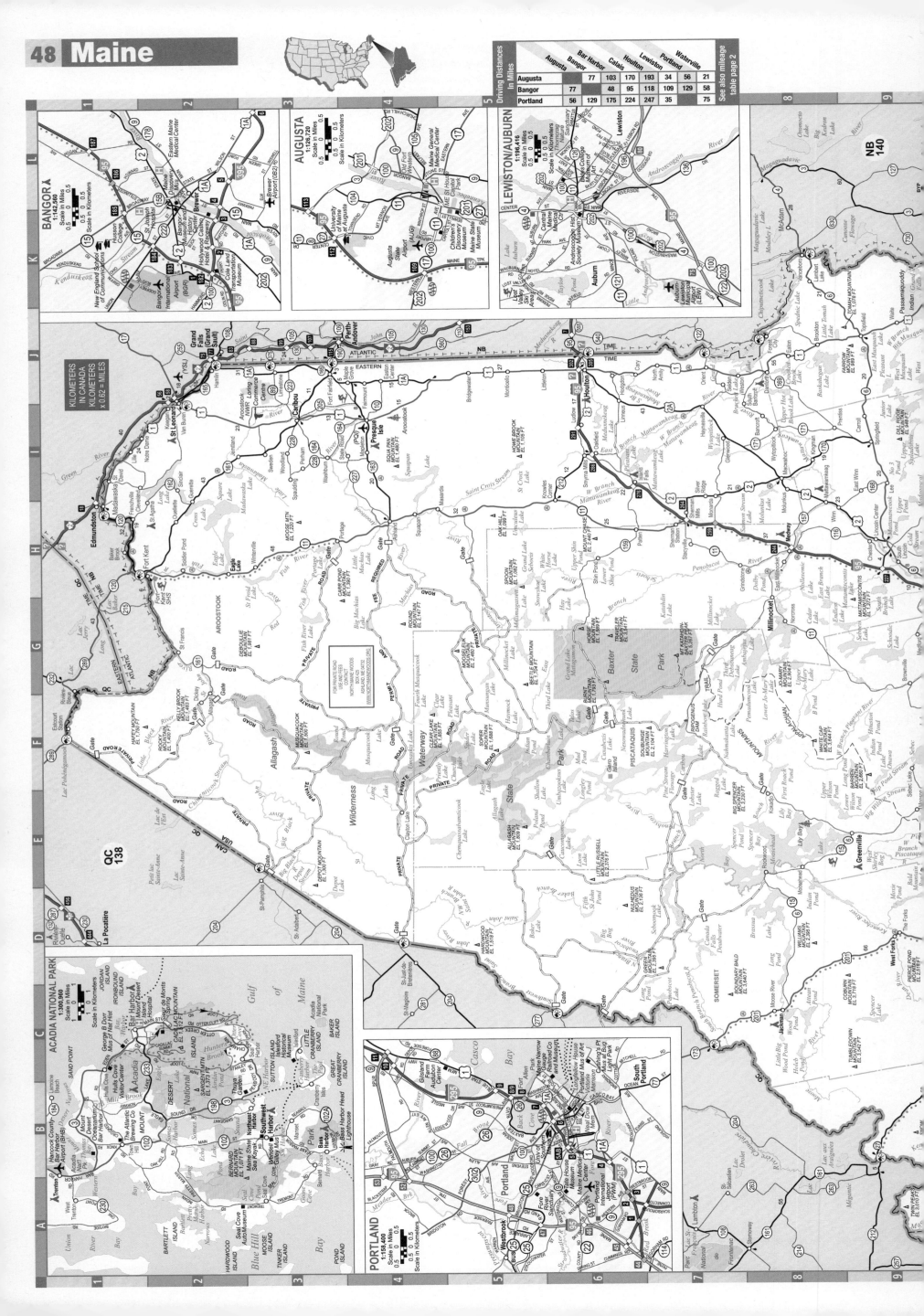

See also mileage table page 2

Driving Distances in Miles

	Augusta	Bangor	Bar Harbor	Calais	Houlton	Lewiston	Portland	Waterville
Augusta		77	103	170	193	34	56	21
Bangor	77		48	95	118	109	129	58
Portland	56	129	175	224	247	35		75

BANGOR
1:142,560

AUGUSTA
1:126,720

LEWISTON/AUBURN
1:196,416

KILOMETERS IN CANADA
KILOMETERS x 0.62 = MILES

ACADIA NATIONAL PARK
1:300,960

PORTLAND
1:158,400

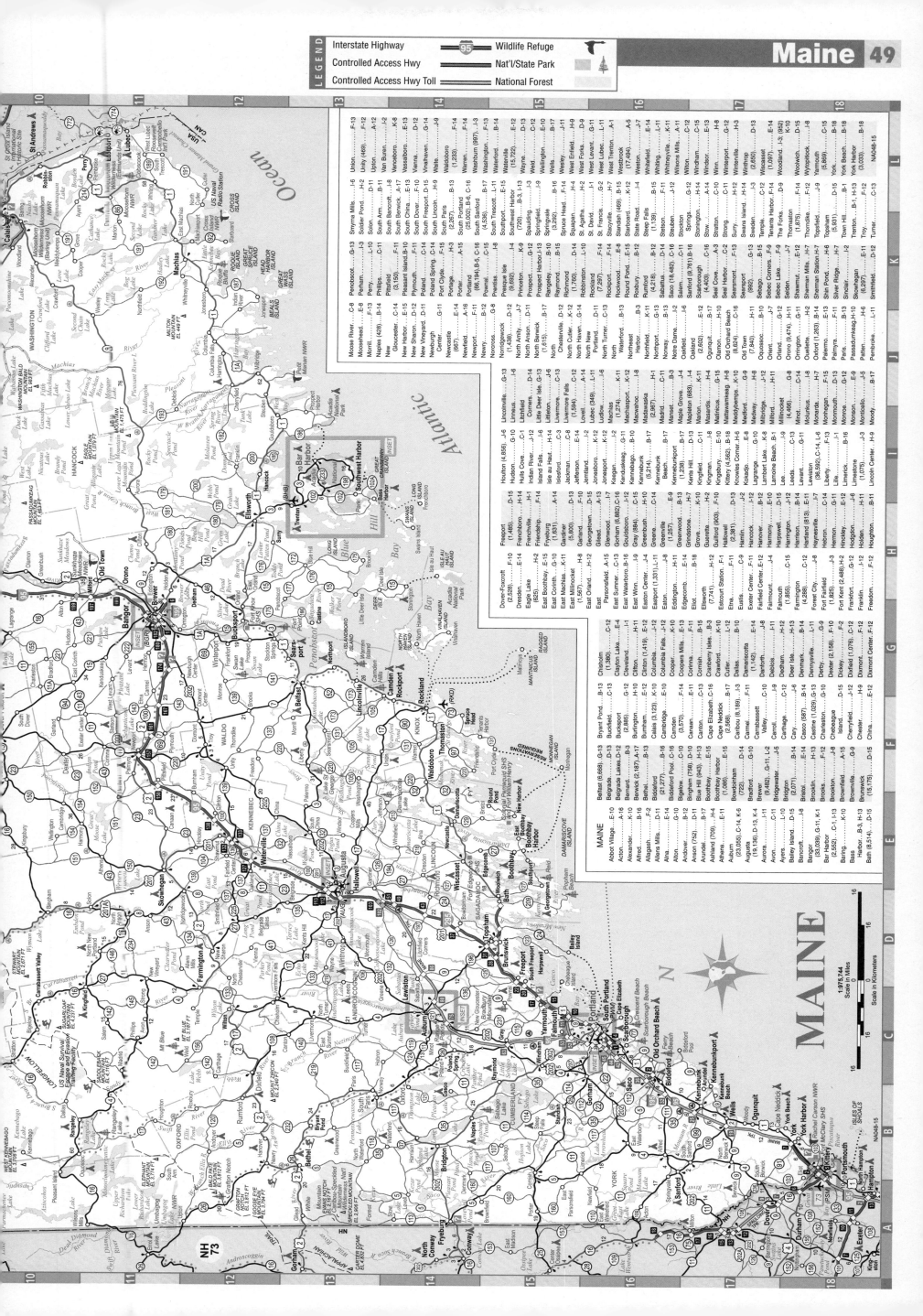

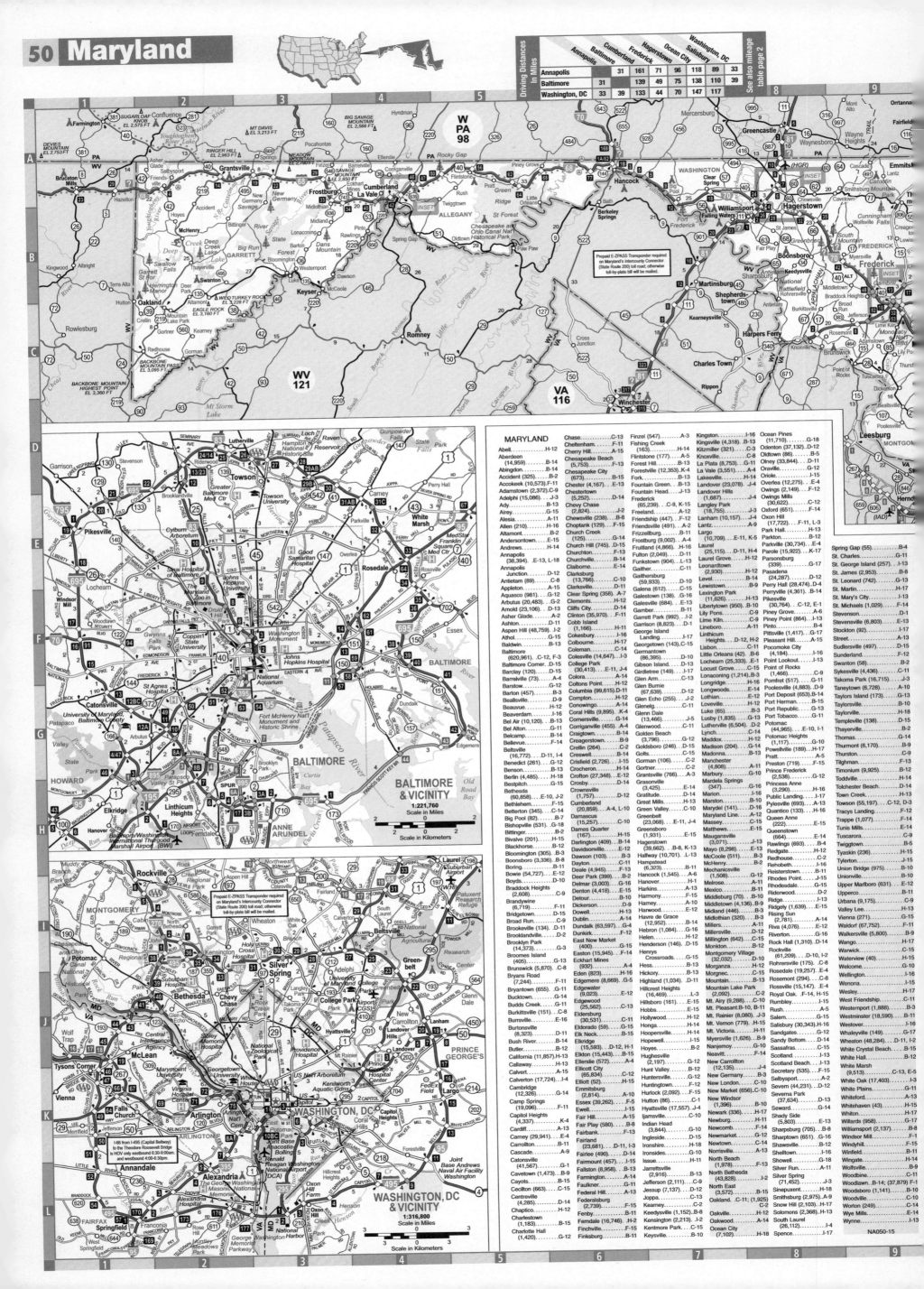

LEGEND

Interstate Highway	95	Wildlife Refuge
Controlled Access Hwy		Nat'l/State Park
Controlled Access Hwy Toll		National Forest

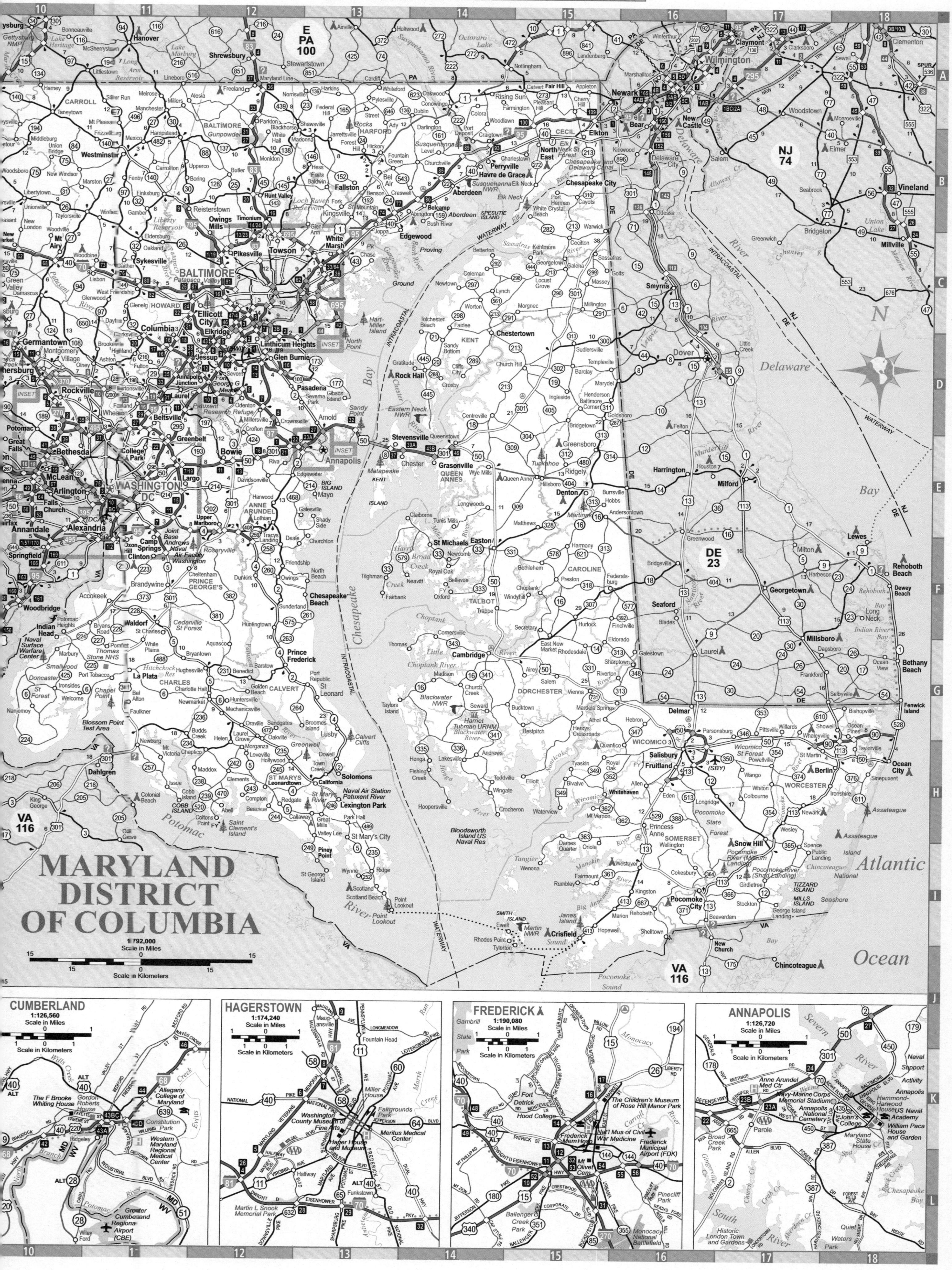

MARYLAND DISTRICT OF COLUMBIA

1:792,000
Scale in Miles
Scale in Kilometers

CUMBERLAND
1:126,560
Scale in Miles
Scale in Kilometers

HAGERSTOWN
1:174,240
Scale in Miles
Scale in Kilometers

FREDERICK
1:190,080
Scale in Miles
Scale in Kilometers

ANNAPOLIS
1:126,720
Scale in Miles
Scale in Kilometers

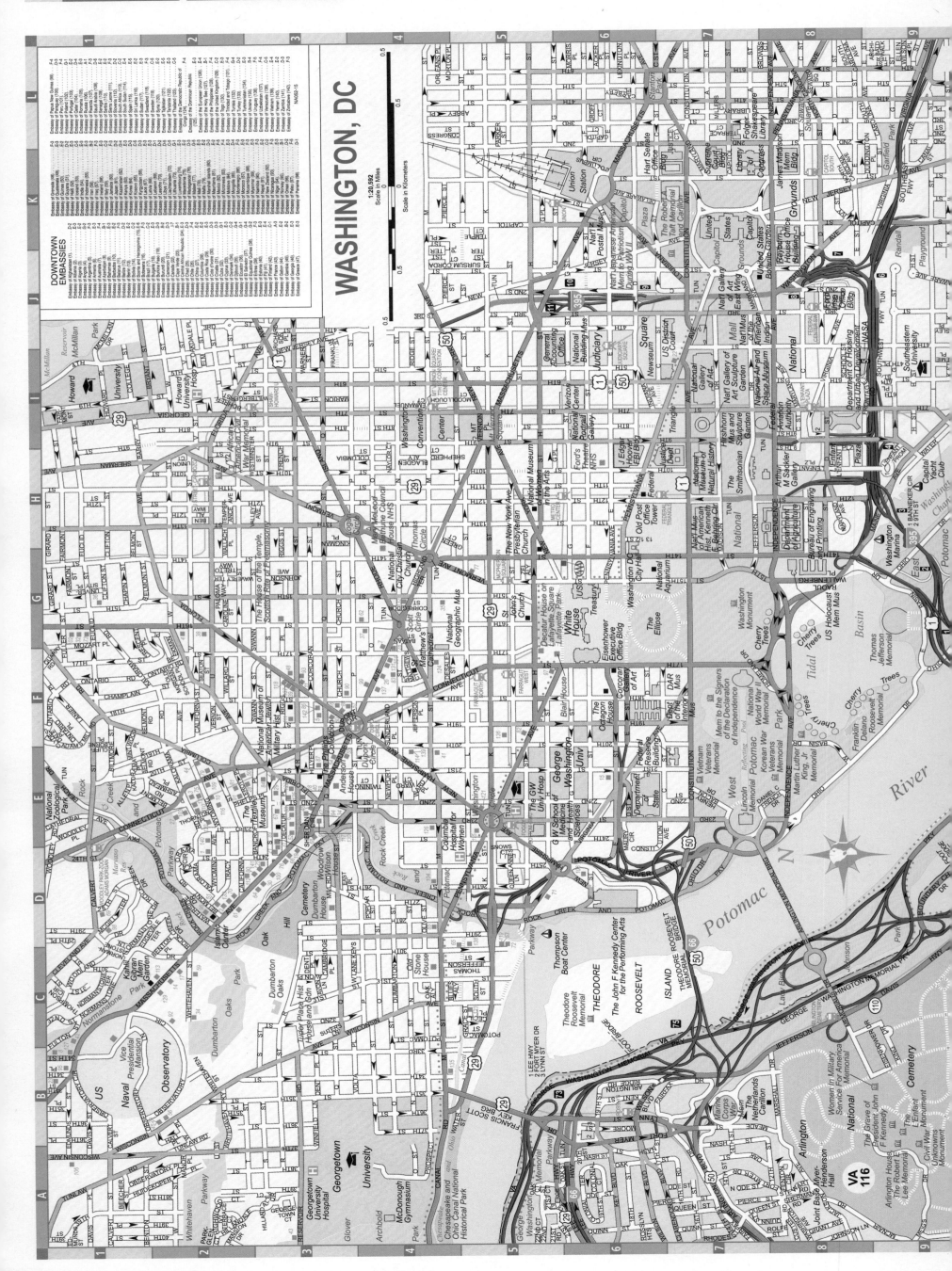

WASHINGTON, DC

1:20,592

Scale in Miles

Scale in Kilometers

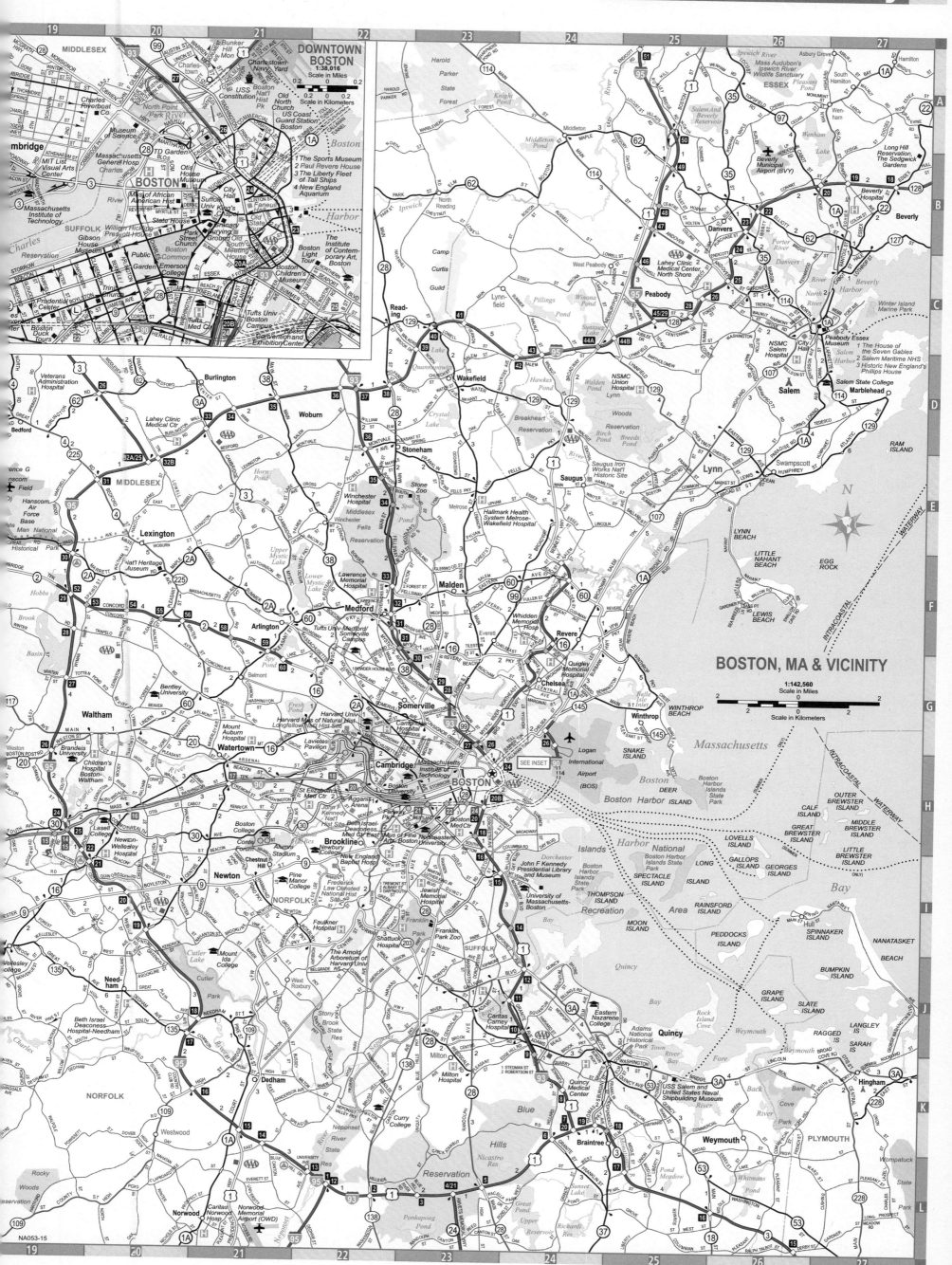

DOWNTOWN BOSTON
1:38,016
Scale in Miles
Scale in Kilometers

1 The Sports Museum
2 Paul Revere House
3 The Liberty Fleet of Tall Ships
4 New England Aquarium

BOSTON, MA & VICINITY
1:142,560
Scale in Miles
Scale in Kilometers

Peabody Essex Museum
1 The House of the Seven Gables
2 Salem Maritime NHS
3 Historic New England's Phillips House

See also mileage table page 2

Driving Distances In Miles

	Boston	Great Barrington	New Bedford	Newburyport	Plymouth	Provincetown	Sagamore	Springfield	Williamstown	Worcester
Boston		137	58	37	40	116	35	90	141	44
New Bedford	58	162		95	34	93	31	116	182	70
Springfield	90	55	116	128	124	196	134		75	52
Worcester	44	99	70	74	77	149	87	52	119	

MASSACHUSETTS

Towns with asterisk (*) are keyed to the maps on page 53.

Abington (15,985)..G-13
Acton........D-11
Adams (5,515)....C-3
Agawam (28,438)...L-1
Alford........L-14
Amesbury (16,283)...B-13
Amherst........E-6
Andover (8,762)....C-12
Aquinnah........L-14
Arlington (42,844)...*F-23
Asbury Grove....*A-27
Ashburnham........C-9
Ashby........C-9
Ashfield........D-4
Ashland........F-11
Ashley Falls....G-2
Assonet........I-13
Athol (8,265)....D-7
Attleboro (43,593)...H-12

Auburn........L-5
Avon........G-13
Ayer (2,868)....D-10
Baldwinville (2,028)...D-8
Barnstable (45,193)...J-16
Barre (1,009)....E-8
Becket........E-3
Becket Center....F-3
Belchertown (2,899)...E-6
Bellingham (4,854)....G-11
Belmont (24,729)...*G-21
Berlin........E-10
Bernardston........C-5
Beverly (39,502)...*B-27
Billerica (58,732)...*H-22
Blackstone........G-10
Blandford (393)....F-4

Bliss Corner....L-8
Bolton........E-10
Bondsville........F-6
Boston (617,594)...*B-21, *H-23, *H-24, E-13
Bourne (1,418)....I-15
Boxborough........D-10
Boxford (2,339)....C-13
Boylston........C-5
Braintree (35,744)...*F-25
Brant Rock....G-15
Brewster (2,000)....I-18
Bridgewater (7,841)...H-13
Brigsville........E-10
Brimfield........F-7
Brockton (93,810)...G-13
Brookfield (833)....F-8

Burlington (24,498)...*D-20
Buzzards Bay (3,859)....I-15
Byfield........*B-21
Cambridge (105,162)...*B-19, *G-22, E-12
Canton........D-11
Carlisle........D-11
Carver........H-14
Cataumet........G-5
Centerville........J-16
Charlemont........C-4
Charlestown........*A-21
Charlton........F-8
Charlton City....G-8
Charlton Depot....G-8
Chartley........H-12
Chatham (1,421)....J-18
Chelmsford........C-17
Chelsea (35,177)...*G-24

Chestnut Hill....*I-21
Chicopee (55,298)...J-1
Chilmark........L-14
Clarksburg........B-3
Clayton........D-6
Clinton (7,389)....E-10
Cochituate........E-11
Cohasset........F-14
Cold Spring....C-5
Colrain........C-5
Concord........E-11
Conway........D-5
Cordaville (2,650)...F-10
Cotuit........J-16
Cummington........E-4
Dalton........D-3
Danvers (26,493)...*B-26
Dedham (24,729)...*K-21, F-12
Deerfield (643)....D-5
Dell........C-4
Dennis (2,407)....I-17
Dennis Port....J-17

Dighton........I-12
Douglas........G-9
Dracut........D-18
Drury........C-3
Duxbury (1,802)....G-14
East Bridgewater....G-14
East Brookfield (6,038)....F-8
East Douglas........G-9
East Falmouth (6,569)....J-15
East Freetown........I-13
East Harwich........I-18
East Leverett....D-6
East Longmeadow....L-3
East Northfield....C-6
East Orleans........I-18
East Otis........F-3
East Templeton........D-8
East Walpole....G-12
East Wareham........I-15
East Windsor....D-3
Eastham........I-18

Easthampton........F-5
Easton........G-12
Edgartown........K-15
Elmwood........G-13
Erving........C-6
Essex (1,471)....C-14
Everett (41,667)...*F-23
Fairhaven........L-8
Fall River (88,857)...I-8, J-12
Falmouth (3,799)....J-15
Falmouth Heights....J-15
Farley........D-6
Feeding Hills....L-1
Fiskdale (2,583)....G-8
Fitchburg (40,318)...D-9
Florida........C-3
Forestdale (4,099)...I-15
Foxboro (5,625)....G-12
Framingham (68,318)...F-11
Franklin (31,635)...G-11
Gardner (20,228)...D-8
Gilbertville........E-7

Gloucester (28,789)...C-14
Goshen........E-4
Grafton........G-10
Great Barrington (2,231)...F-2
Green Harbor....G-15
Greenfield (17,456)...D-5
Griswoldville........C-5
Groton (1,124)....D-10
Hadley........E-5
Halifax........H-14
Hamilton........C-13
Hampden........G-6
Hancock........D-2
Hanover........G-14
Hanson (2,118)....G-14
Hardwick........E-7
Harvard........D-10
Harwich........I-17
Harwich Port (1,644)....J-17
Hatchville........J-15
Hatfield (1,318)....E-5

Haverhill (60,879)...C-12
Hawley........D-4
Haydenville........E-5
Heath........C-4
Hingham (5,660)...*K-27, F-14
Hinsdale........E-3
Hixville........C-14
Holbrook (10,791)...G-13
Holden........E-9
Holland (1,464)....G-7
Holliston........F-11
Holyoke (39,880)...F-5, J-1
Hoosac Tunnel....C-3
Hopedale (3,753)....G-10
Hopkinton (2,550)...F-10
Housatonic (1,109)...F-1
Hubbardston........D-8
Hudson (10,293)....*I-26
Humarock........G-15
Huntington (936)....F-4
Hyannis (14,907)...J-17

Lowell (106,519)...C-11, E-17
Konkapot........G-2
Lake Pleasant....D-6
Lancaster........E-10
Lanesborough........C-10
Lawrence (76,377)...C-12
Lee (2,051)....E-2
Leeds........E-5
Leicester........F-9
Lenox........E-2
Lenox Dale....E-2
Leominster (40,759)...D-9
Leverett........D-6
Lexington (31,394)...*F-20
Leyden........C-5
Lincoln........E-11
Lithia........E-4
Littleton........D-10
Locks Village....D-6
Longmeadow (15,784)...L-2

Lunenburg (1,760)...D-9
Lynn (90,329)...*E-26, D-13
Lynnfield (11,596)...*C-23
Lyonsville........C-5
Madaket (236)....L-17
Malden (59,450)...*F-23
Manchaug........G-9
Manchester (236)....B-13
Manomet........H-15
Mansfield........G-12
Marblehead........*D-27
Marion........I-14
Marlborough (38,499)...E-10
Marshfield........G-15
Marshfield Hills....G-15
Mattapoisett........I-14

Medfield (6,483)...F-11
Medford (56,173)...*F-22
Medway........G-11
Melrose (26,983)...*E-23
Mendon........G-10
Menemsha........L-14
Merrimac........B-13
Methuen (47,255)...C-12
Middleboro........H-13
Middlefield........E-4
Middleton........*A-24
Milford (25,555)...G-10
Millbury........G-10
Millers Falls (1,139)....D-6
Millis........F-11
Millville........G-10
Milton (27,003)...*I-23
Monponsett........G-14
Monroe Bridge....C-4
Monson (2,110)....G-7
Montague........D-5
Monterey........F-2

Montville........G-3
Monument Beach....I-15
Mt. Hermon....C-6
Mt. Washington....G-1
Nantucket (7,446)...L-17
Natick........E-11
Needham (28,886)...*I-21
New Ashford....C-3
New Bedford (95,072)...J-13, K-8
New Boston....G-3
New Braintree....E-7
New Marlborough....G-2
New Salem....D-6
Newbury........B-13
Newburyport (17,416)...B-13
Nichewaug........D-7
Norfolk........G-11
North Adams (13,708)...C-3
North Amherst....E-5

Springfield (inset)
Scale 1:190,080

Worcester (inset)
Scale 1:142,560

Fall River (inset)
Scale 1:190,080

New Bedford (inset)
Scale 1:158,400

LEGEND

Interstate Highway	Wildlife Refuge
Controlled Access Hwy	Nat'l/State Park
Controlled Access Hwy Toll	National Forest

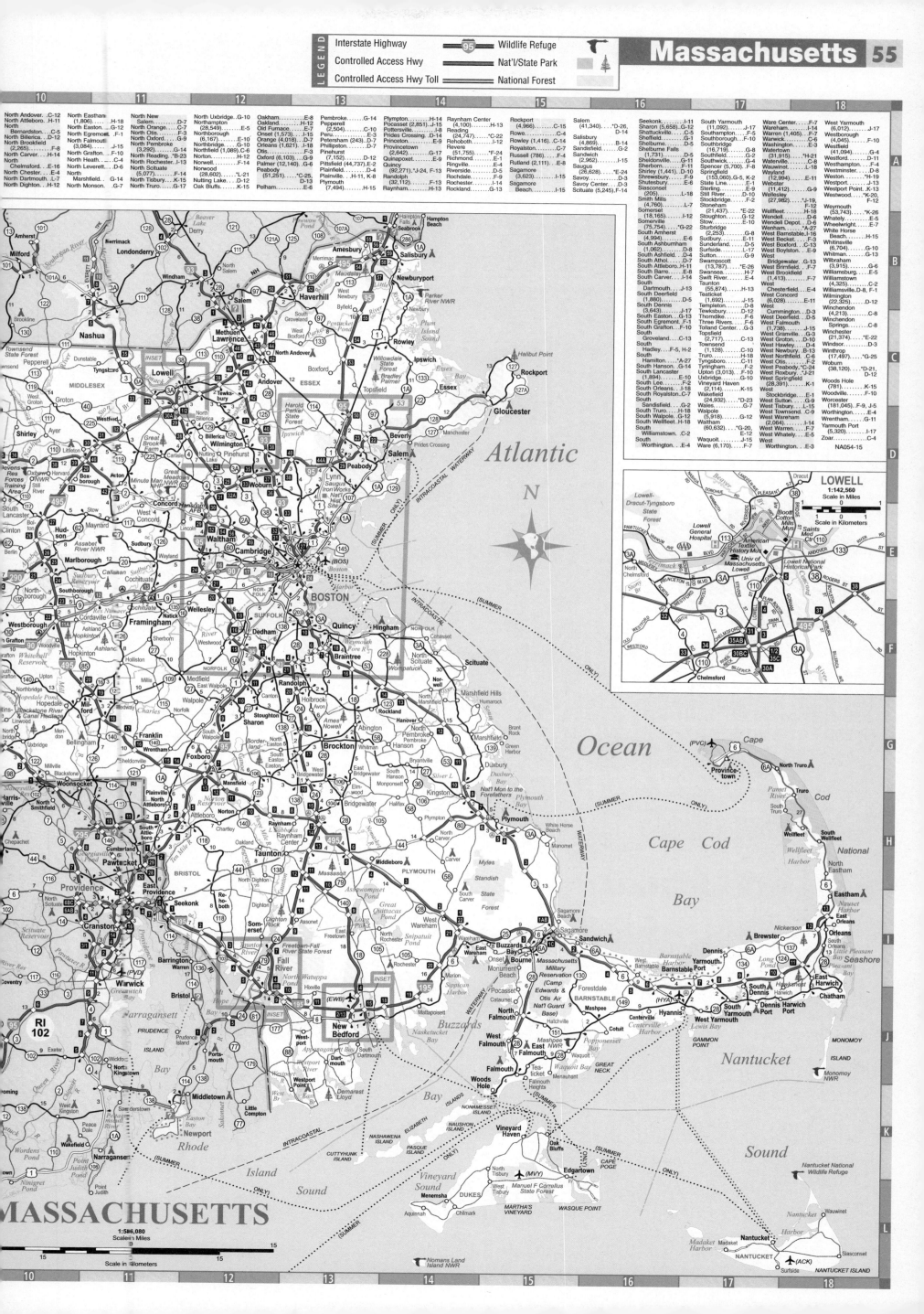

Index

North Andover...C-12
North Attleboro..H-11
North Bernardston..C-5
North Billerica...D-12
North Brookfield (2,265)...F-8
North Carver...H-14
North Chelmsford...E-16
North Chester...E-4
North Dartmouth..L-7
North Dighton..H-12

North Eastham (1,806)...H-18
North Easton...G-12
North Falmouth (3,084)...F-1
North Grafton...F-10
North Heath...C-4
North Leverett...D-6
North Marshfield...G-7
North Monson...G-7

North New Salem...D-7
North Orange...C-7
North Otis...F-3
North Oxford...G-9
North Pembroke...G-14
North Reading...*B-23
North Scituate (5,077)...F-14
North Tisbury...K-15
North Truro...G-17

North Uxbridge...G-10
Northampton (28,549)...E-5
Northborough (6,167)...E-10
Northbridge (3,292)...G-14
Northfield (1,089)...C-6
Norton...H-12
Norwell...H-13
Norwood (28,602)...*L-21
Nutting Lake...D-12

Oakham...E-8
Oakland...H-12
Old Furnace...E-8
Onset (1,573)...I-15
Orange (4,018)...D-7
Orleans (1,621)...H-18
Otis...F-3
Oxford (6,103)...G-9

Pembroke...G-14
Pepperell...C-10
Peru...E-3
Petersham (243)...D-7
Phillipston...D-7
Pinehurst...D-12
Pittsfield (44,737)...E-2
Plainfield...D-4
Plainville...H-11, K-8
Plymouth (7,494)...H-15

Plympton...H-13
Pocasset (2,851)...J-15
Pottersville...*C-22
Prides Crossing...D-14
Princeton...E-9
Provincetown (2,642)...G-17
Quincy (92,271)...J-24, F-13
Randolph (32,112)...F-13
Raynham...H-13

Raynham Center (4,100)...H-13
Rehoboth (24,747)...*C-22
Rehoboth...I-12
Revere (51,755)...*F-24
Richmond...E-4
Ringville...E-4
Riverside...E-4
Rochdale...G-9
Rochester...F-9
Rockland...G-13

Rockport (4,966)...C-15
Rowe...C-4
Rowley (1,416)...C-14
Royalston...C-7
Russell (786)...F-4
Rutland (2,111)...E-8
Sagamore...I-15
Sagamore Beach...I-15

Salem (41,340)...*D-26
Salisbury (4,869)...B-14
Sandisfield...G-2
Sandwich...I-15
Saugus (26,628)...*E-24
Savoy...D-3
Savoy Center...D-3
Scituate (5,245)...F-14

Seekonk...I-11
Sharon (5,658)...G-12
Shattuckville...C-5
Sheffield...G-1
Shelburne...C-5
Shelburne Falls...D-5
Sheldonville...G-11
Shirley (1,441)...D-10
Shrewsbury...F-9
Shutesbury...E-6
Siasconset (205)...L-18
Smith Mills (4,760)...L-7
Somerset (18,165)...I-12
Somerville...I-12
South Amherst...E-6
South Ashburnham (1,062)...D-7
South Ashfield...D-4
South Athol...C-13
South Attleboro...H-11
South Barre...E-8
South Carver...I-14
South Dartmouth (1,880)...J-13
South Deerfield (1,880)...D-5
South Dennis...I-17
South Easton...G-13
South Egremont (5,643)...G-1
South Grafton...F-10
South Groveland...C-13
South Hadley...F-5, H-2
South Hamilton...*A-27
South Hanson...G-14
South Lancaster (1,894)...E-10
South Lee...F-2
South Royalston...C-7
South Sandisfield...G-1
South Truro...H-18
South Walpole...G-12
South Wellfleet...H-18
South Williamstown...C-2
South Worthington...E-4

South Yarmouth (11,092)...J-17
Southampton...F-5
Southborough...F-10
Southbridge (16,719)...G-8
Southfield...G-1
Southwick...G-4
Spencer (5,700)...F-8
Springfield (153,060)...G-5, K-2
State Line...E-1
Sterling...E-9
Still River...D-10
Stockbridge...F-2
Stoneham (21,437)...*E-22
Stoughton (26,628)...*E-24
Stow...E-10
Sturbridge (2,253)...G-8
Sudbury...E-11
Sunderland...D-5
Surfside...L-17
Sutton...G-9
Swampscott (13,787)...*E-26
Swansea...H-7
Swift River...E-14
Taunton (55,874)...H-13
Teaticket (1,692)...J-15
Templeton...D-8
Tewksbury (24,932)...*D-23
Thorndike...F-6
Three Rivers...F-6
Tolland Center...G-3
Topsfield (2,717)...C-13
Townsend (1,128)...C-10
Truro...H-18
Tyngsboro (5,646)...C-11
Tyringham...F-2
Upton (3,013)...F-10
Uxbridge...G-10
Vineyard Haven (2,114)...K-15
Wakefield (24,804)...*D-23
Wales (1,831)...G-7
Walpole (5,918)...G-12
Waltham (60,632)...*G-20
Waquoit...J-15
Ware (6,170)...F-7

Ware Center...F-7
Wareham...I-14
Warren (1,405)...F-7
Warwick...C-6
Washington...E-3
Watertown (31,915)...*H-21
Waterville...F-4
Wauwinet...L-18
Wayland...E-11
Webster (11,412)...G-9
Wellesley (27,982)...*K-20, F-12
Wellfleet...H-18
Wendell...D-6
Wendell Depot...D-6
Wenham...*A-27
West Barnstable...I-16
West Becket...F-3
West Boxford...C-13
West Boylston...E-9
West Bridgewater...G-13
West Brimfield...F-7
West Brookfield (1,413)...F-7
West Chesterfield...E-4
West Concord (6,028)...E-11
West Cummington...D-3
West Deerfield...D-5
West Falmouth (1,738)...J-15
West Granville...G-3
West Groton...D-10
West Hawley...C-4
West Medway...F-3
West Newbury...B-13
West Newton...*L-18
West Northfield...C-6
West Otis...F-3
West Peabody...*C-24
West Roxbury...*J-21
West Springfield (28,391)...K-1
West Stockbridge...E-1
West Sutton...G-9
West Tisbury...J-15
West Townsend...C-9
West Wareham...I-14
West Warren...F-7
West Whately...E-5

West Yarmouth (6,012)...J-17
Westborough...E-10
Westfield (41,094)...G-4
Westford...D-11
Westhampton...E-4
Westminster...D-8
Weston...*H-19
Westport...J-13
Westport Point...K-13
Westwood...*K-20, F-12
Weymouth (53,743)...F-13
Whately...E-5
Wheelwright...E-7
White Horse Beach...H-15
Whitinsville (6,704)...G-10
Whitman...G-13
Wilbraham (3,915)...G-6
Williamsburg...E-5
Williamstown (4,325)...C-2
Wilmington (22,325)...D-12
Winchendon (4,213)...C-8
Winchendon Springs...C-8
Winchester (21,374)...*E-23
Windsor...D-3
Winthrop (17,497)...*G-25
Woburn (38,120)...*D-21, D-12
Woods Hole (781)...K-15
Woodville...F-10
Worcester (181,045)...F-9, J-15
Worthington...E-4
Wrentham...G-11
Yarmouth Port (5,320)...I-17
Zoar...C-4

NA054-15

LOWELL
1:142,560
Scale in Miles
Scale in Kilometers

MASSACHUSETTS
1:586,080
Scale in Miles
Scale in Kilometers

RI 102

See also page 2

Driving Distances In Miles

	Battle Creek	Bay City	Detroit	Escanaba	Flint	Grand Rapids	Ironwood	Lansing	Marquette	Muskegon	Port Huron	Sault Ste Marie
Detroit	120	115		434	68	157	599	90	455	197	63	346
Flint	110	51	68			330	534	54	391	153	67	282
Grand Rapids	65	130	157	387	113		464	68	430	41	180	299
Lansing	54	96	90	374	54	68	539		396	107	118	287
Muskegon	106	146	197	402	153	41	567	107	424		220	315

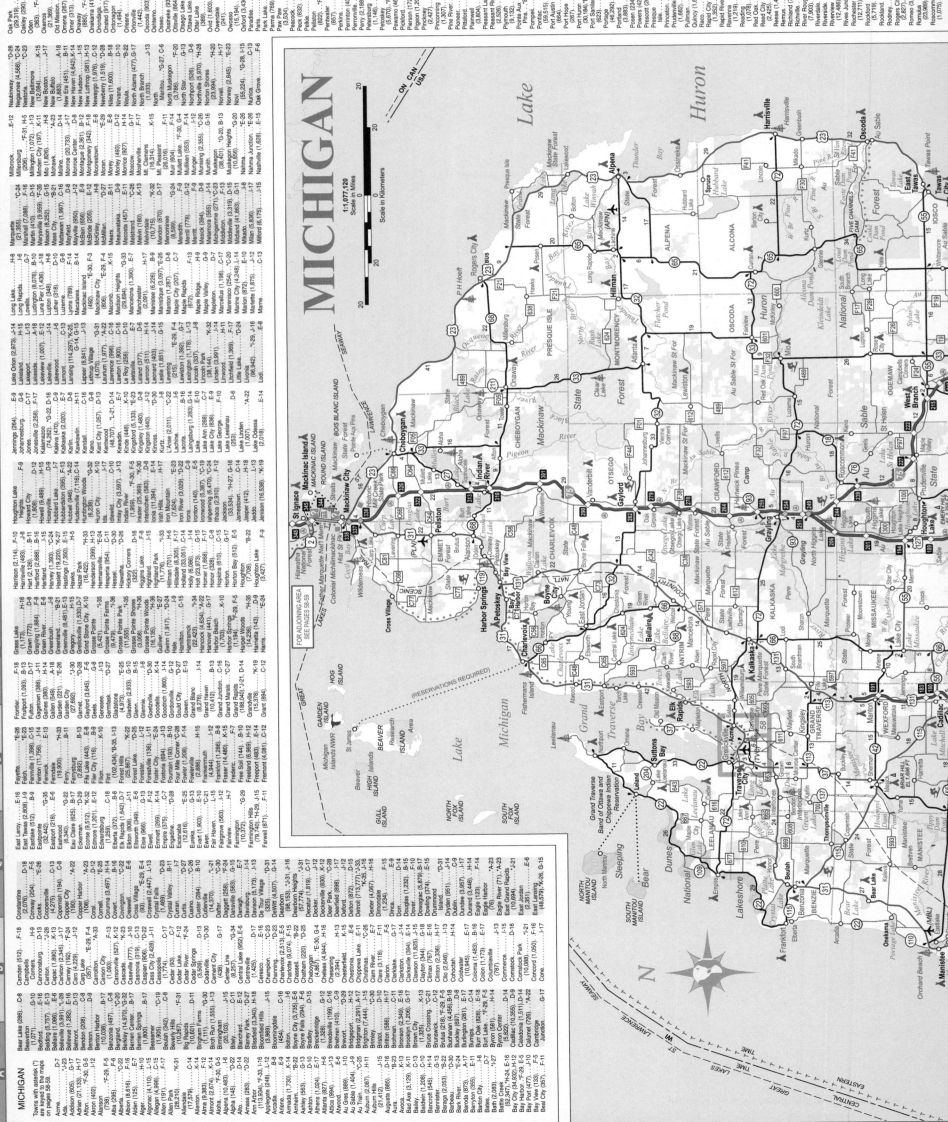

MICHIGAN

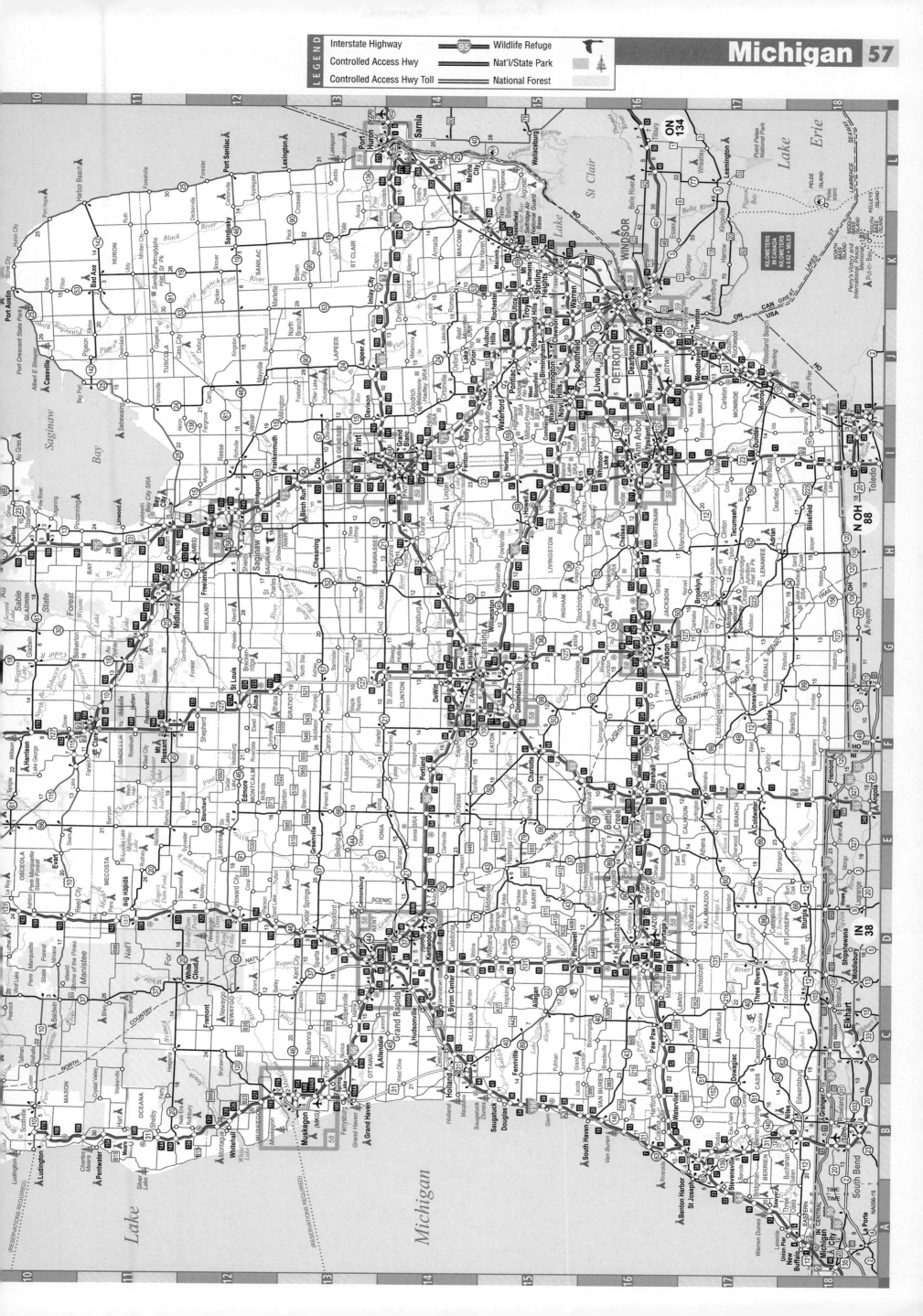

LEGEND
Interstate Highway
Controlled Access Hwy
Controlled Access Hwy Toll
Wildlife Refuge
Nat'l/State Park
National Forest

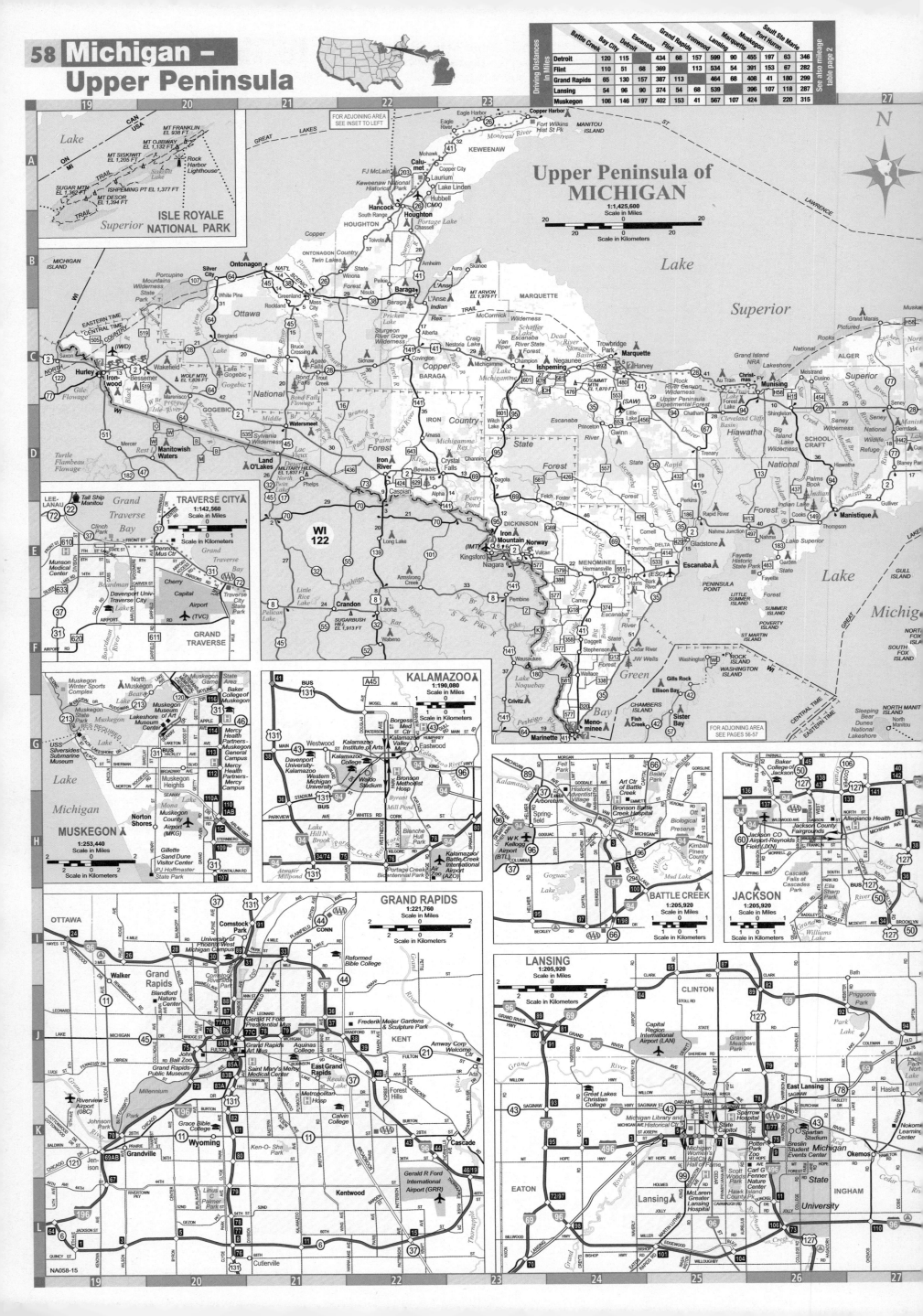

Driving Distances In Miles

	Battle Creek	Bay City	Detroit	Escanaba	Grand Rapids	Flint	Ironwood	Lansing	Marquette	Muskegon	Port Huron	Sault Ste Marie
Detroit	120	115		434	68	157	599	90	455	197	63	346
Flint	110	51	68	369	113		534	54	391	153	67	282
Grand Rapids	65	130	157	387		113	464	68	408	41	180	299
Lansing	54	96	90	374	54	68	539		396	107	118	287
Muskegon	106	146	197	402	41	153	567	107	424		220	315

See also mileage table on page 2

Upper Peninsula of MICHIGAN
1:1,425,600

NA058-15

See also mileage table page 2

Driving Distances In Miles

	Albert Lea	Bemidji	Duluth	Fargo, ND	International Falls	Minneapolis	Rochester	St. Cloud	St. Paul	Sioux Falls, SD
Duluth	249	153		253	162	155	234	147	151	391
International Falls	387	112	162	250		294	372	270	290	512
Minneapolis	97	224	155	234	294		87	70	10	237
Rochester	62	311	234	323	372	87		159	77	237

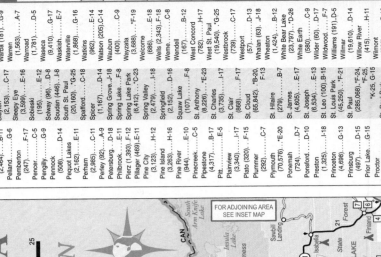

MINNESOTA

Towns with asterisk are keyed to the map on page 62.

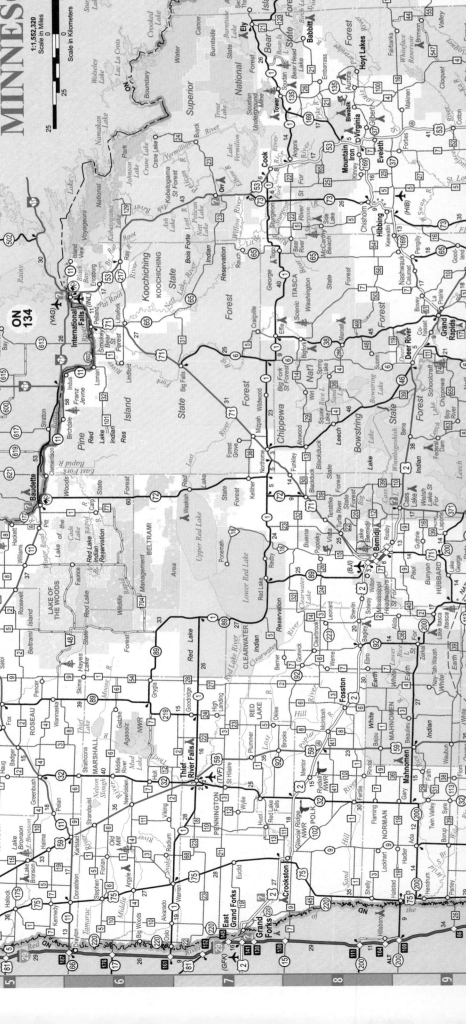

MINNESOTA

1:1,552,320

Scale in Miles

Scale in Kilometers

FOR ADJOINING AREA SEE INSET MAP

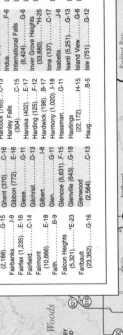

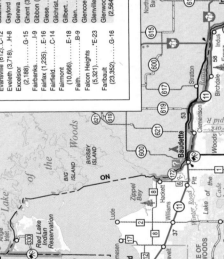

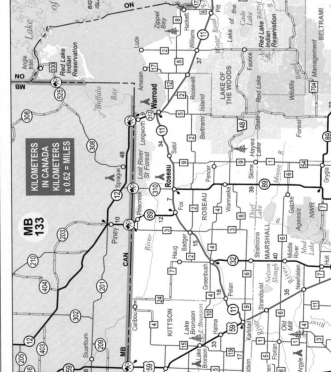

KILOMETERS IN CANADA
KILOMETERS x 0.62 = MILES

LEGEND

Interstate Highway	Wildlife Refuge
Controlled Access Hwy	Nat'l/State Park
Controlled Access Hwy Toll	National Forest

NORTHEAST MINNESOTA

SCALE SAME AS PRINCIPAL MAP

KILOMETERS IN CANADA
KILOMETERS x 0.62 = MILES

ON 134

WI 122

MI 58

IA 40

SD 105

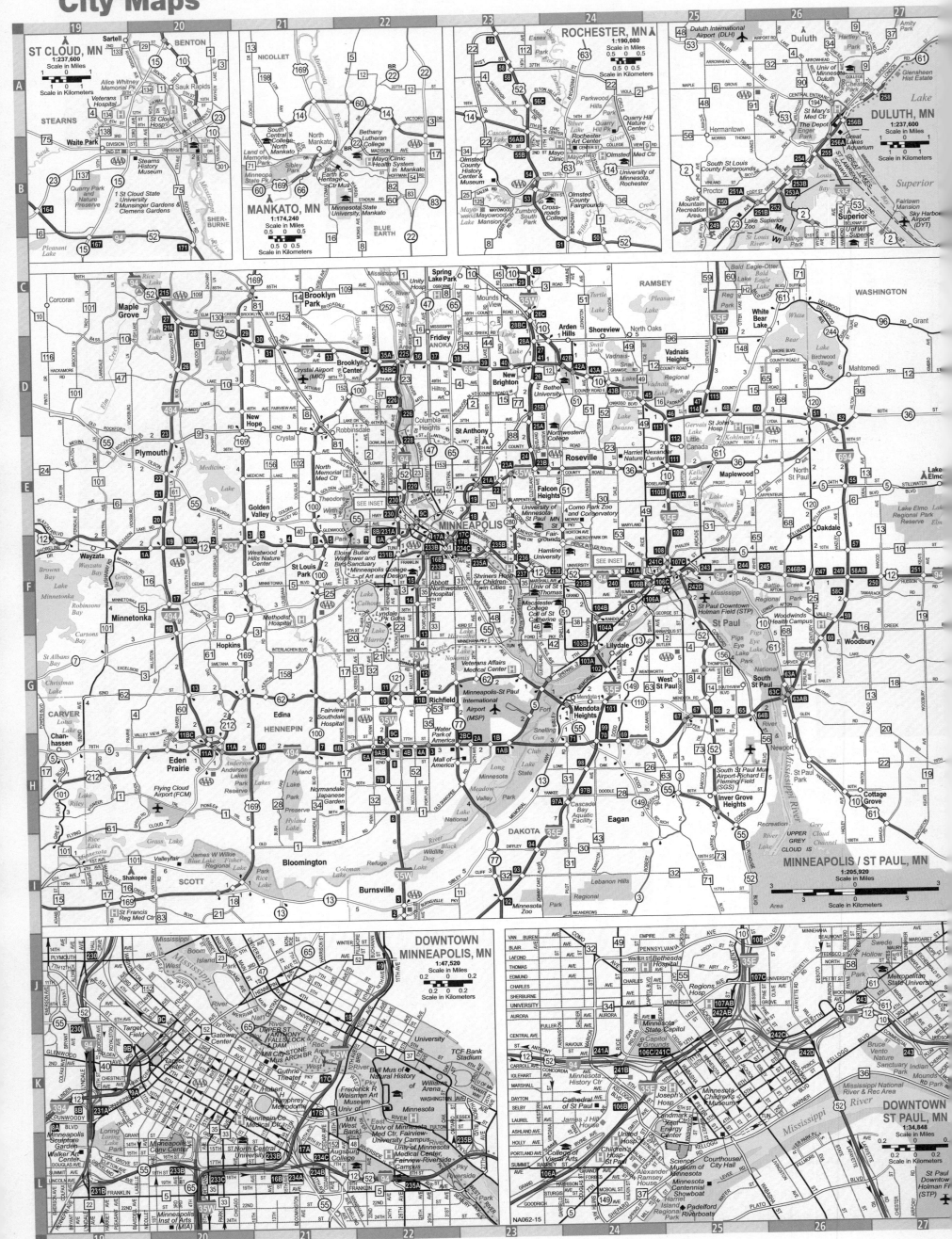

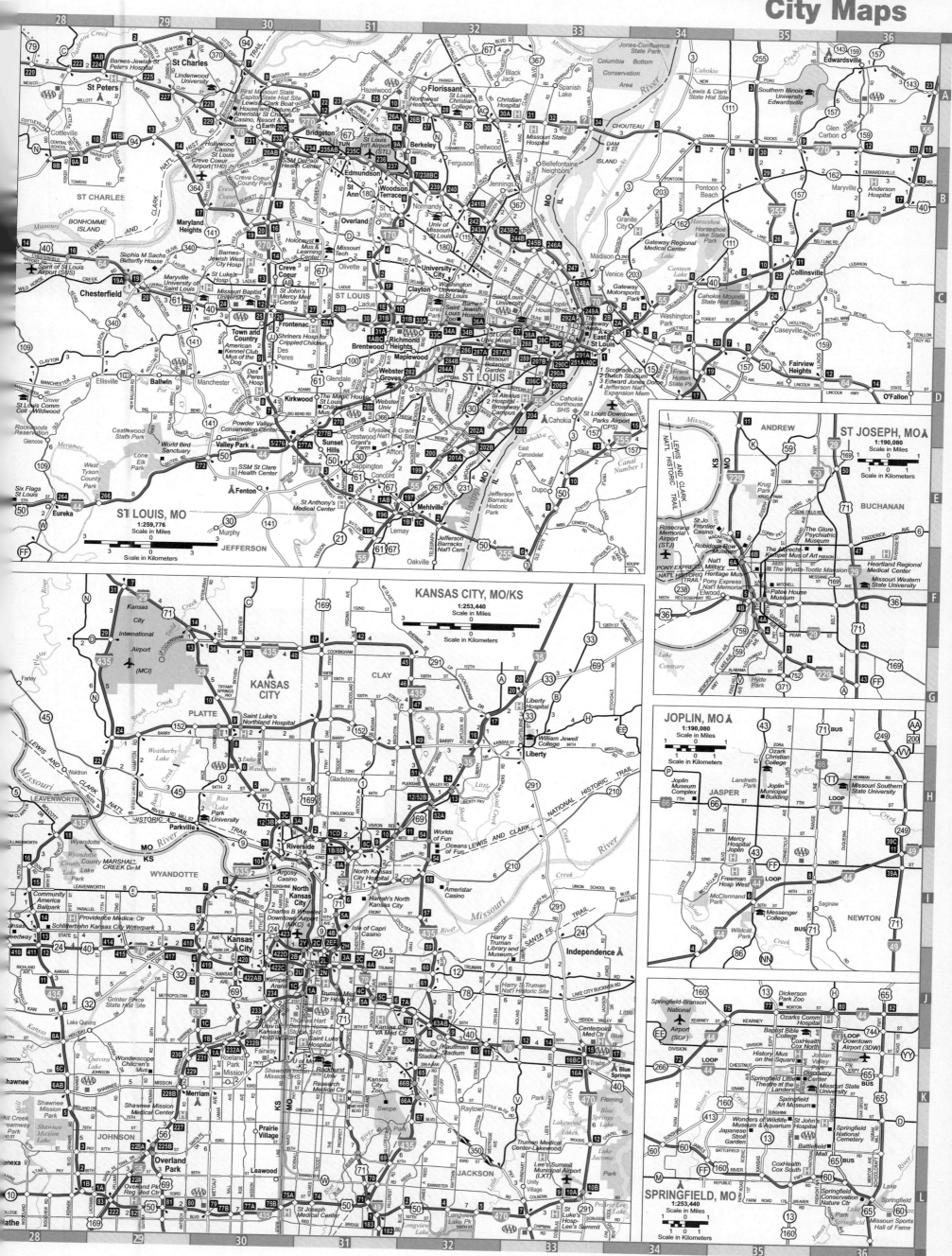

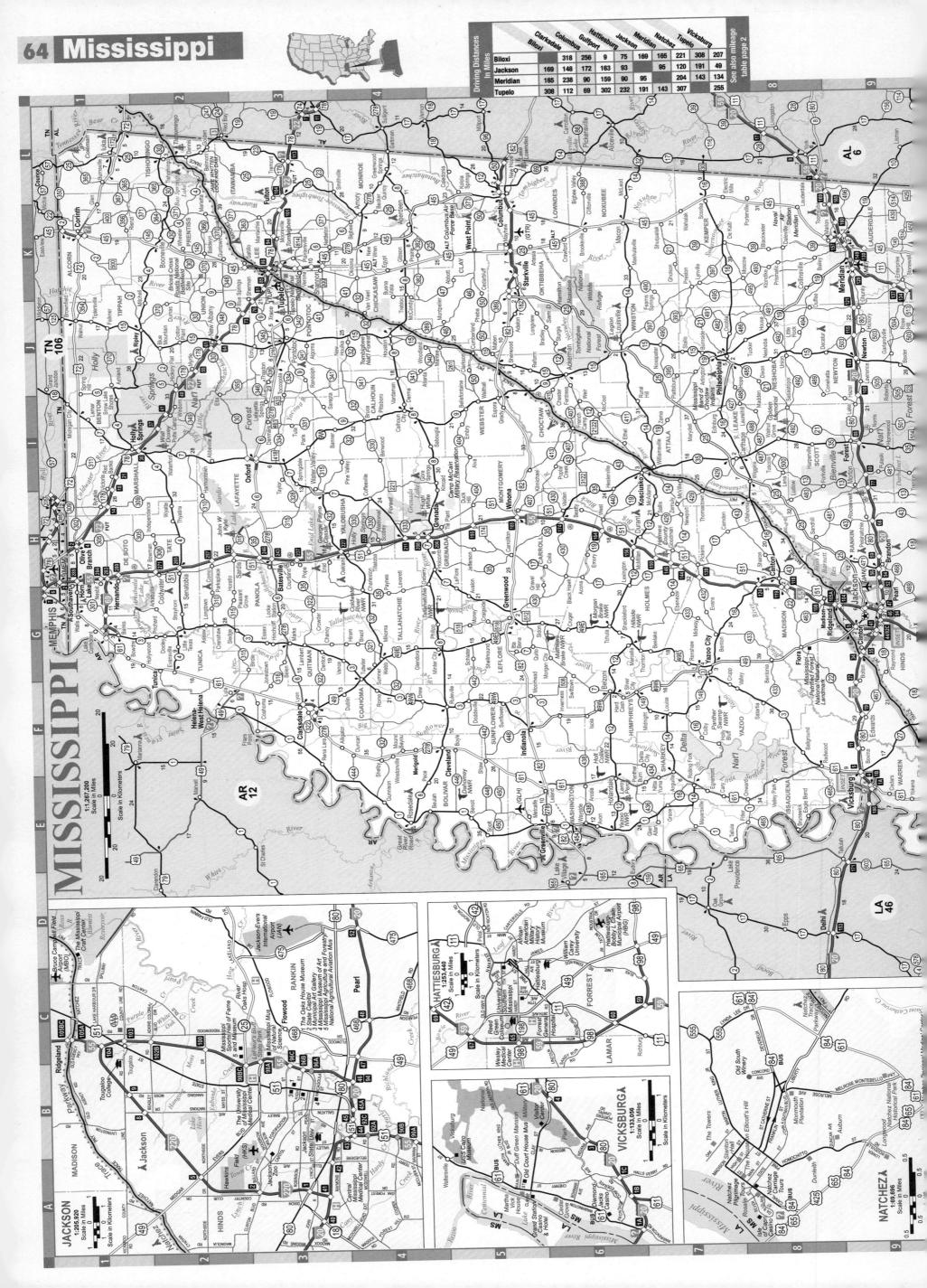

See also mileage table page 2

Driving Distances In Miles

	Biloxi	Clarksdale	Columbus	Gulfport	Hattiesburg	Jackson	Meridian	Natchez	Tupelo	Vicksburg
Biloxi		318	256	9	75	169	165	221	308	207
Jackson	169	148	172	163	93		95	120	191	49
Meridian	165	238	90	159	90	95		204	143	134
Tupelo	308	112	69	302	232	191	143	307		255

LEGEND

- Interstate Highway
- Controlled Access Hwy
- Controlled Access Hwy Toll
- Wildlife Refuge
- Nat'l/State Park
- National Forest

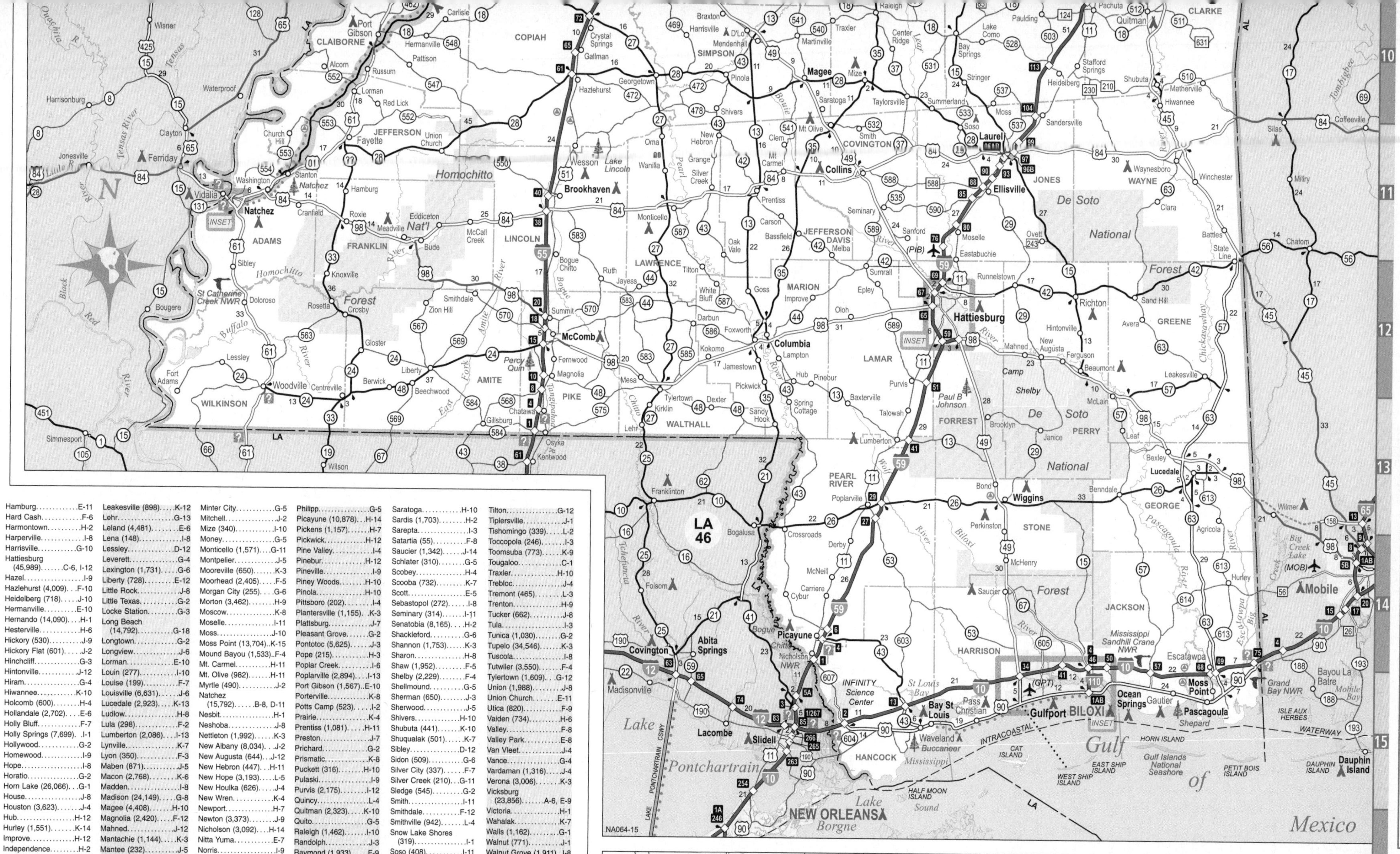
NA064-15

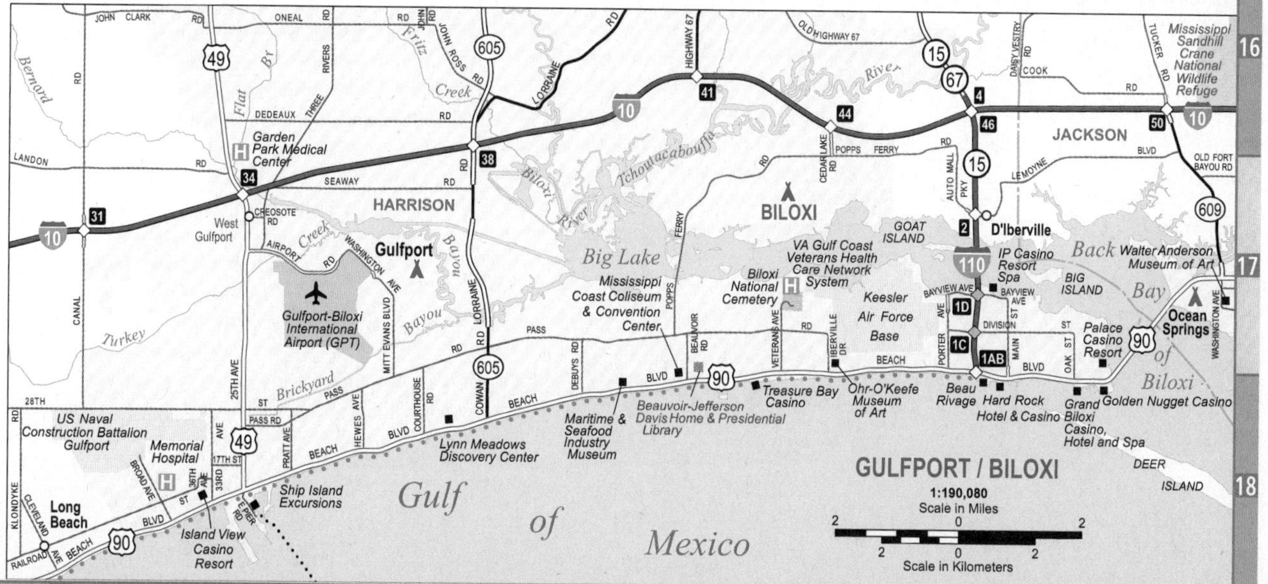
GULFPORT / BILOXI
1:190,080
Scale in Miles
Scale in Kilometers

Abbeville (419)....I-2
Abbott....K-5
Aberdeen (5,612)....K-4
Ackerman (1,510)....J-6
Acona....G-6
Adaton....J-5
Agricola....K-13
Alcorn....E-10
Algoma (590)....J-3
Alligator (208)....F-4
Alva....I-5
Amory (7,316)....K-4
Anguilla (726)....E-7
Arcola (361)....E-6
Arkabutla....G-2
Arlington....J-7
Artesia (440)....K-6
Ashland (569)....J-1
Askew....G-2
Atlanta....J-4
Avalon....G-5
Avera....K-12
Avon....E-6
Bailey....K-8
Baldwyn (3,297)....K-2
Ballground....F-8
Banks....G-1
Banner....I-4
Bassfield (254)....H-11
Batesville (7,463)....H-3
Battles....K-11
Baxter....J-9
Baxterville....I-13
Bay Springs (1,786)....I-10
Bay St Louis (9,260)....I-15
Beatty....H-6
Beaumont (951)....J-12
Becker....K-4
Beechwood....E-12
Beelake....G-7
Belen....G-3
Bellefontaine....I-5
Belmont (2,021)....L-2
Belzoni (2,235)....F-6
Benndale....K-13
Benoit (477)....E-5
Benton....G-7
Bentonia (440)....G-8
Benwood....I-4
Berwick....E-12
Beulah (348)....E-4
Bexley....K-13
Bigbee....K-4
Bigbee Valley....L-6
Biloxi (44,054)....J-15, K-17
Birdie....G-3
Black Hawk....G-6
Blackwater....K-8
Blue Mountain (920)....J-2
Blue Springs (228)....J-3
Bogue Chitto (522)....F-12
Bolton (567)....F-9
Bond....J-13
Booneville (8,743)....K-2
Bovina....F-9
Bowdre....G-1
Bowman....H-2
Boyle (650)....F-5
Bradley....J-6
Brandon (21,705)....H-9
Braxton (183)....H-10
Brazil....G-4
Brookhaven (12,513)....F-11
Brooklyn....J-13
Brooksville (1,223)....K-6
Brownfield....J-1
Bruce (1,939)....I-4
Brunswick....E-8
Bude (1,063)....E-11
Buena Vista....J-4
Burns....I-9
Burnside....J-7
Burnsville (936)....L-1
Byhalia (1,302)....H-1
Caledonia (1,041)....L-5
Calhoun City (1,774)....I-4
Camden....H-7
Canton (13,189)....G-8
Carlisle....E-10
Carriere....H-14
Carrollton (190)....H-5
Carson....H-11
Carthage (5,075)....I-8
Cary (313)....E-7
Cedarbluff....J-5
Cedars....E-9
Center Ridge....I-10
Centreville (1,684)....E-13
Chancy....G-3
Charleston (2,193)....G-4
Chatawa....F-13
Chester....I-6
Chunky (326)....J-9
Church Hill....D-11
Clara (410)....K-11
Clarksdale (17,962)....F-3
Clarkson....J-5
Clem....H-11
Cleveland (12,334)....F-5
Cliftonville....K-6
Clinton (25,216)....G-9
Coahoma (377)....F-3
Coffeeville (905)....H-4
Coila....H-6
Coldwater (1,677)....H-2
Collins (2,586)....I-11
Collinsville (1,948)....J-8
Columbia (6,582)....H-12
Columbus (23,640)....K-5
Como (1,279)....H-2
Conehatta (1,342)....I-8
Corinth (14,573)....K-1
Cotton Plant....J-2
Courtland (511)....H-3
Craigside....G-5
Cranfield....D-11
Crawford (641)....K-6
Crenshaw (885)....G-2
Crosby (318)....E-12
Crossroads....H-14
Crowder (712)....G-3
Cruger (386)....G-6
Crupp....F-7
Crystal Springs (5,044)....G-10
Cumberland....J-5
Cybur....H-14
D'Iberville (9,486)....K-17
D'Lo (452)....H-10
Daleville....K-8
Darbun....G-12
De Kalb (1,164)....K-7
Decatur (1,841)....J-8
Delta City....F-7
Denmark....I-3
Dennis....L-2
Denton....G-3
Derby....I-14
Derma (1,025)....I-4
Dexter....H-13
Dixon....I-8
Doddsville (98)....F-5
Doloroso....D-12
Dooley....G-2
Drew (1,927)....F-4
Dublin....F-4
Duck Hill (732)....H-5
Duffee....J-8
Dumas (470)....J-2
Duncan (423)....F-4
Durant (2,673)....H-7
Eagle Bend....E-8
Eastabuchie....I-12
Ebenezer....G-7
Ecru (895)....J-3
Eddiceton....E-11
Edinburg....I-7
Edwards (1,034)....F-9
Egremont....E-7
Egypt....K-4
Electric Mills....K-7
Ellisville (4,448)....J-11
Embry....I-5
Emory....H-6
Enid....H-3
Enterprise (526)....K-9
Epley....I-12
Escatawpa (3,722)....K-14
Essex....G-3
Ethel (418)....I-6
Etta....I-2
Eupora (2,197)....I-5
Evans....G-7
Evansville....G-2
Falkner (514)....J-1
Fayette (1,614)....E-11
Fearns Springs....J-7
Fentress....I-6
Ferguson....J-12
Fernwood....F-12
Fitler....E-8
Flora (1,886)....G-8
Florence (4,141)....G-9
Flowood (7,823)....C-3
Forest (5,684)....I-9
Forkville....H-8
Fort Adams....C-13
Foxworth (603)....H-12
French Camp (174)....I-6
Friars Point (1,200)....F-3
Fulton (3,961)....K-3
Gallman....G-10
Garlandville....J-9
Gattman (90)....L-4
Gautier (18,572)....K-15
Georgetown (286)....G-10
Gholson....K-7
Gibson....K-4
Gillsburg....F-13
Glen (412)....K-1
Glen Allan....E-7
Glendora (151)....G-4
Gloster (960)....E-12
Golden (191)....L-2
Goodman (1,386)....H-7
Gore Springs....H-5
Goss....H-12
Grace....E-7
Grady....I-5
Grange....H-11
Gravel Hill....G-6
Greenville (34,400)....E-6
Greenwood (15,205)....G-5
Greenwood Springs....L-4
Grenada (13,092)....H-4
Gulfport (67,793)....H-17, J-15
Gunnison (452)....E-4
Guntown (2,083)....K-2
Hamburg....E-11
Hard Cash....F-6
Harmontown....H-2
Harperville....I-8
Harrisville....G-10
Hattiesburg (45,989)....C-6, I-12
Hazel....I-9
Hazlehurst (4,009)....F-10
Heidelberg (718)....J-10
Hermanville....E-10
Hernando (14,090)....H-1
Hesterville....H-6
Hickory (530)....J-9
Hickory Flat (601)....J-2
Hinchcliff....G-3
Hintonville....J-12
Hiram....G-4
Hiwannee....K-10
Holcomb (600)....H-4
Hollandale (2,702)....E-6
Holly Bluff....F-7
Holly Springs (7,699)....I-1
Hollywood....G-2
Homewood....I-9
Hope....I-8
Horatio....G-2
Horn Lake (26,066)....G-1
House....J-8
Houston (3,623)....J-4
Hub....H-12
Hurley (1,551)....K-14
Improve....H-12
Independence....H-2
Indianola (10,683)....F-5
Inverness (1,019)....F-6
Isola (713)....F-6
Itta Bena (2,049)....G-5
Iuka (3,028)....L-1
Jackson (173,514)....B-4, G-9
Jamestown....H-12
Janice....J-13
Jayess....G-12
Jefferson....H-5
Jonestown (1,298)....F-3
Kilmichael (699)....I-5
Kincaid....H-5
Kirklin....G-13
Klondike....K-8
Knoxville....E-12
Kokomo....G-12
Kolola Springs....L-5
Kosciusko (7,402)....I-7
Lafayette Springs....I-3
Lake (324)....I-9
Lake Como....J-10
Lake Cormorant....G-1
Lamar....I-1
Lambert (1,638)....G-3
Lampton....H-12
Lauderdale (442)....K-8
Laurel (18,540)....J-11
Laurelhill....I-8
Lawrence....I-9
LeFlore....G-5
Leaf....K-13
Leakesville (898)....K-12
Lehr....G-13
Leland (4,481)....E-6
Lena (148)....I-8
Lessley....D-12
Leverett....G-4
Lexington (1,731)....G-6
Liberty (728)....E-12
Little Rock....J-8
Little Texas....G-2
Locke Station....G-3
Long Beach (14,792)....G-18
Longtown....G-2
Longview....J-6
Lorman....E-10
Louin (277)....I-10
Louise (199)....F-7
Louisville (6,631)....J-6
Lucedale (2,923)....K-13
Ludlow....H-8
Lula (298)....F-2
Lumberton (2,086)....I-13
Lynville....K-7
Lyon (350)....F-3
Maben (871)....J-5
Macon (2,768)....K-6
Madden....I-8
Madison (24,149)....G-8
Magee (4,408)....H-10
Magnolia (2,420)....F-12
Mahned....J-12
Mantachie (1,144)....K-3
Mantee (232)....J-5
Marcella....G-6
Marietta (256)....K-2
Marion (1,479)....K-9
Marks (1,735)....G-3
Martinville....H-10
Marydell....I-7
Mashulaville....K-7
Matherville....K-10
Mayersville (547)....E-7
Mayhew....K-5
McAdams....H-7
McCall Creek....F-11
McComb (12,790)....F-12
McCondy....J-4
McCool (135)....I-6
McHenry....J-14
McLain (441)....K-13
McLeod....K-7
McMillan....H-6
McNeill....H-14
McVille....H-7
Meadville (449)....E-11
Melba....H-12
Mendenhall (2,504)....H-10
Meridian (41,148)....K-9
Merigold (439)....F-4
Mesa....G-12
Metcalfe (1,067)....E-5
Michigan City....I-1
Midnight....F-7
Midway....G-7
Mikoma....G-4
Minter City....G-5
Mitchell....J-2
Mize (340)....I-10
Money....G-5
Monticello (1,571)....G-11
Montpelier....J-5
Mooreville (650)....K-3
Moorhead (2,405)....F-5
Morgan City (255)....G-6
Morton (3,462)....H-9
Moscow....K-8
Moselle....I-11
Moss....J-10
Moss Point (13,704)....K-15
Mound Bayou (1,533)....F-4
Mt. Carmel....H-11
Mt. Olive (982)....H-11
Myrtle (490)....J-2
Natchez (15,792)....B-8, D-11
Nesbit....H-1
Neshoba....J-8
Nettleton (1,992)....K-3
New Albany (8,034)....J-2
New Augusta (644)....J-12
New Hebron (447)....H-11
New Hope (3,193)....L-5
New Houlka (626)....J-4
New Wren....K-4
Newport....H-7
Newton (3,373)....J-9
Nicholson (3,092)....H-14
Nitta Yuma....E-7
Norris....I-9
Noxapater (472)....J-7
Oak Vale....H-12
Oakland (527)....H-4
Ocean Springs (17,442)....K-15, L-17
Ocobla....J-8
Ofahoma....H-8
Okolona (2,692)....K-4
Olive Branch (33,484)....H-1
Oloh....I-12
Oma....G-11
Onward....E-8
Osyka (440)....F-13
Ovett....J-11
Oxberry....G-4
Oxford (18,916)....I-3
Pace (274)....E-4
Pachuta (261)....J-10
Panther Burn....E-7
Paris....I-3
Parksplace....G-2
Pascagoula (22,392)....K-15
Pass Christian (4,613)....J-15
Pattison....E-10
Paulding....J-10
Paynes....G-4
Pearl (25,092)....C-4, G-9
Pelahatchie (1,334)....H-9
Perkinston....J-14
Petal (10,454)....D-5
Pheba....J-5
Philadelphia (7,477)....J-7
Philipp....G-5
Picayune (10,878)....H-14
Pickens (1,157)....H-7
Pickwick....H-12
Pine Valley....I-4
Pinebur....H-12
Pineville....I-9
Piney Woods....H-10
Pinola....H-10
Pittsboro (202)....I-4
Plantersville (1,155)....K-3
Plattsburg....J-7
Pleasant Grove....G-2
Pontotoc (5,625)....J-3
Pope (215)....H-3
Poplar Creek....I-6
Poplarville (2,894)....I-13
Port Gibson (1,567)....E-10
Porterville....K-8
Potts Camp (523)....I-2
Prairie....K-4
Prentiss (1,081)....H-11
Preston....J-7
Prichard....G-2
Prismatic....K-8
Puckett (316)....H-10
Pulaski....I-9
Purvis (2,175)....I-12
Quincy....L-4
Quitman (2,323)....K-10
Quito....G-5
Raleigh (1,462)....I-10
Randolph....J-3
Raymond (1,933)....F-9
Red Banks....I-1
Red Lick....E-10
Redwood....E-8
Reform....J-5
Rena Lara....F-3
Renshaw....G-7
Richburg....C-7
Richton (1,068)....J-12
Ridgeland (24,047)....C-1, G-9
Rienzi (317)....K-1
Ripley (5,395)....J-2
Roberts....I-9
Rolling Fork (2,143)....E-7
Rome....F-4
Rose Hill....J-9
Rosedale (1,873)....E-4
Rosetta....E-12
Roxie (497)....E-11
Ruleville (3,007)....F-5
Runnelstown....J-12
Rural Hill....I-7
Russum....E-10
Ruth....G-12
Sabougla....I-4
Sallis (134)....H-7
Saltillo (4,752)....K-3
Sand Hill....K-12
Sandersville (731)....J-10
Sandhill....H-8
Sandy Hook....H-13
Sanford....I-11
Saratoga....H-10
Sardis (1,703)....H-2
Sarepta....I-3
Satartia (55)....F-8
Saucier (1,342)....J-14
Schlater (310)....G-5
Scobey....H-4
Scooba (732)....K-7
Scott....E-5
Sebastopol (272)....I-8
Seminary (314)....I-11
Senatobia (8,165)....H-2
Shackleford....G-6
Shannon (1,753)....K-3
Sharon....H-8
Shaw (1,952)....F-5
Shelby (2,229)....F-4
Shellmound....G-5
Sherman (650)....J-3
Sherwood....J-5
Shivers....H-10
Shubuta (441)....K-10
Shuqualak (501)....K-7
Sibley....D-12
Sidon (509)....G-6
Silver City (337)....F-7
Silver Creek (210)....G-11
Sledge (545)....G-2
Smith....I-11
Smithdale....F-12
Smithville (942)....L-4
Snow Lake Shores (319)....I-1
Soso (408)....I-11
Southaven (48,982)....G-1
Spring Cottage....H-13
Spring Hill....I-1
Springdale....I-3
Stafford Springs....J-10
Stallo....J-7
Stanton....D-11
Star....G-10
Starkville (23,888)....K-5
State Line (565)....K-12
Stonewall (1,088)....K-9
Strayhorn....G-2
Stringer....I-10
Sturgis (254)....J-6
Summerland....I-10
Summit (1,705)....F-12
Sumner (316)....G-4
Sumrall (1,421)....I-12
Sunflower (1,159)....F-5
Swiftown....F-6
Tallula....E-7
Talowah....I-13
Taylor (322)....I-3
Taylorsville (1,353)....I-10
Tchula (2,096)....G-6
Terry (1,063)....G-10
Thaxton (643)....J-3
Thomastown....H-7
Thornton....G-7
Thyatira....H-2
Tie Plant....H-5
Tillatoba (91)....H-4
Tilton....G-12
Tiplersville....J-1
Tishomingo (339)....L-2
Toccopola (246)....I-3
Toomsuba (773)....K-9
Tougaloo....C-1
Traxler....H-10
Trebloc....J-4
Tremont (465)....L-3
Trenton....H-9
Tucker (662)....J-8
Tula....I-3
Tunica (1,030)....G-2
Tupelo (34,546)....K-3
Tuscola....I-8
Tutwiler (3,550)....F-4
Tylertown (1,609)....G-12
Union (1,988)....J-8
Union Church....E-11
Utica (820)....F-9
Vaiden (734)....H-6
Valley....F-8
Valley Park....E-8
Van Vleet....J-4
Vance....G-4
Vardaman (1,316)....J-4
Verona (3,006)....K-3
Vicksburg (23,856)....A-6, E-9
Victoria....H-1
Wahalak....K-7
Walls (1,162)....G-1
Walnut (771)....J-1
Walnut Grove (1,911)....I-8
Waltersville....A-4
Walthall (144)....I-5
Wanilla....G-11
Washington....D-11
Water Valley (3,392)....H-3
Waterford....I-2
Waveland (6,435)....I-15
Waynesboro (5,043)....K-11
Wayside....E-6
Webb (565)....G-4
Weir (459)....I-6
Wesson (1,925)....F-11
West (185)....H-6
West Gulfport....H-17
West Point (11,307)....K-5
Wheeler....K-2
White Bluff....H-12
Wiggins....H-8; (4,390) J-13
Williamsville....I-7
Winborn....I-2
Winchester....K-11
Winona (5,043)....H-5
Winstonville (191)....F-4
Woodland (125)....J-4
Woodville (1,096)....D-12
Wyatte....H-2
Yazoo City (11,403)....F-7
Yokena....E-9
Zama....I-7
Zemuly....H-7
Zion Hill....E-12

NA064-15

	Branson	Columbia	Jefferson City	Joplin	Kansas City	Poplar Bluff	Sikeston	Springfield	St. Joseph	St. Louis
Kansas City	210	126	150	157		357	381	166	53	250
Sikeston	262	257	252	303	381	48		236	435	147
Springfield	44	167	133	71	166	190	236		223	215
St. Louis	252	126	134	284	250	153	147	215	302	

Driving Distances In Miles

See also mileage table page 2

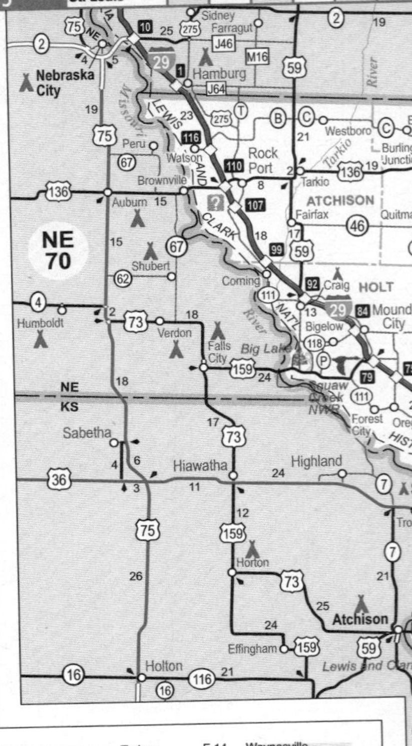
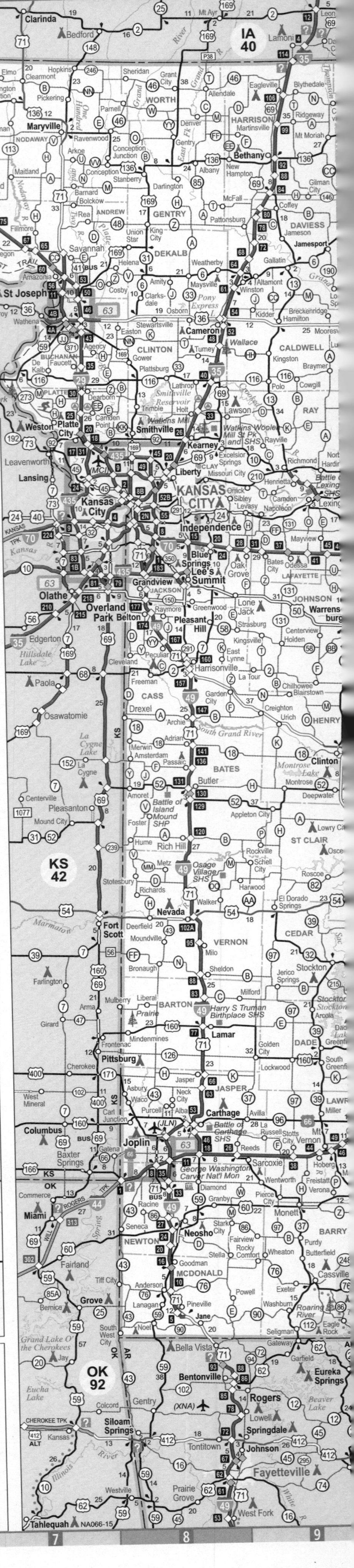
Nebraska City
Hamburg
Clarinda
Bedford
IA 40
NE 70
St Joseph
Atchison
Maryville
Savannah
Bethany
Cameron
Kansas City
Independence
Lee's Summit
Liberty
Olathe
Overland Park
Belton
Harrisonville
Clinton
Nevada
Fort Scott
Pittsburg
Lamar
Carthage
Joplin
Neosho
Miami
Columbus
KS 42
OK 92
Grove
Bentonville
Rogers
Springdale
Fayetteville
Siloam Springs
Tahlequah
Eureka Springs

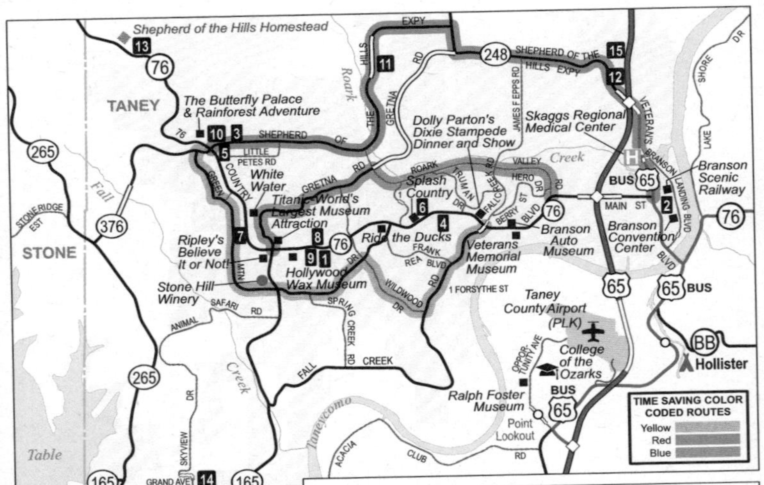
Shepherd of the Hills Homestead
TANEY
The Butterfly Palace & Rainforest Adventure
Dolly Parton's Dixie Stampede Dinner and Show
Skaggs Regional Medical Center
Branson Scenic Railway
White Water
Titanic World's Largest Museum Attraction
Ripley's Believe It or Not!
Ride the Ducks
Branson Auto Museum
Branson Convention Center
Veterans Memorial Museum
Hollywood Wax Museum
Stone Hill Winery
STONE
Taney County Airport (PLK)
College of the Ozarks
Hollister
Ralph Foster Museum
Point Lookout
TIME SAVING COLOR CODED ROUTES
Yellow
Red
Blue
Shepherd of the Hills Fish Hatchery
Kayak Branson
Showboat Branson Belle
BRANSON
1:110,880
Scale in Miles
Scale in Kilometers

THEATERS

1. Baldknobbers Country Music Theatre ... J-5
2. Branson Hot Hits Theatre ... J-6
3. Branson's IMAX Entertainment Complex ... I-4
4. God and Country Theatre ... J-5
5. Golden Corral Showroom ... I-4
6. Grand Country Music Hall ... J-5
7. Jim Stafford Theatre ... J-4
8. New Americana Theatre ... J-5
9. Presleys' Country Jubilee ... J-5
10. RFD-TV The Theatre ... I-4
11. Sight & Sound Theatres ... I-5
12. The Oak Ridge Boys Theatre ... I-6
13. The Shepherd of the Hills Outdoor Theatre ... I-4
14. Welk Resort Theatre ... K-4
15. Yakov Smirnoff Theatre ... I-6

NA066-15

MISSOURI

Towns with asterisk (*) are keyed to the map on page 63.

Adrian (1,677)...F-8
Advance (1,347)...J-17
Affton (20,307)...*E-31
Agency (684)...C-7
Alba (555)...I-8
Albany (1,730)...B-8
Aldrich (80)...H-10
Alexandria (159)...B-14
Allendale (53)...A-8
Alma (402)...E-10
Altamont (204)...C-9
Altenburg (352)...H-17
Alton (871)...K-14
Amazonia (312)...C-7
Amity (54)...C-8
Amoret (190)...G-8
Amsterdam (242)...F-8
Anderson (1,961)...K-8
Annada (29)...D-15
Annapolis (345)...I-15
Anniston (232)...J-18
Appleton City (1,127)...G-9
Arbela (41)...A-13
Arbyrd (509)...L-16
Arcadia (608)...H-15
Archie (1,170)...F-8
Arcola (55)...H-9
Argyle (162)...G-13
Arkoe (68)...B-7
Armstrong (284)...D-11
Arnold (20,808)...F-16
Arrow Rock (56)...E-11
Asbury (207)...I-8
Ash Grove (1,472)...I-10
Ashburn (52)...D-14
Ashland (3,707)...E-12
Atlanta (385)...C-12
Augusta (253)...F-15
Aurora (7,508)...J-9
Auxvasse (983)...E-13
Ava (2,993)...J-11
Avilla (125)...I-9
Baker (3)...J-17
Bakersfield (246)...K-12
Ballwin (30,404)...*D-29
Baring (132)...B-12
Barnard (221)...B-7
Barnett (203)...F-11
Bates City (219)...E-9
Beaufort...F-14
Belgrade...H-15
Bell City (448)...J-17
Belle (1,545)...G-13
Bellefontaine Neighbors (10,860)...*B-33
Belleview...H-15
Bellflower (393)...E-14
Belton (23,116)...E-8
Benton (863)...I-18
Benton City (104)...E-13
Berger (221)...F-14
Berkeley (8,978)...*B-31
Bernie (1,958)...K-17
Bethany (3,292)...B-9
Bethel (122)...C-13
Bevier (718)...C-12
Biehle (48)...H-17
Bigelow (27)...B-6
Billings (1,035)...J-10
Birch Tree (679)...J-14
Bismarck (1,546)...H-15
Bixby...H-14
Black...H-15
Black Jack (6,929)...*A-32
Blackburn (249)...E-10
Blackwater (162)...E-11
Blairstown (97)...F-9
Bland (539)...G-13
Blodgett (213)...J-18
Bloomfield (1,933)...J-17
Bloomsdale (521)...G-16
Blue Eye (167)...K-10
Blue Springs (52,575)...*K-34, E-8
Blythedale (193)...A-9
Bogard (164)...D-10
Bois D'Arc...I-10
Bolckow (187)...B-7
Bolivar (10,325)...H-10
Bonne Terre (6,864)...H-16
Bonnots Mill...F-13
Boonville (8,319)...E-11
Boss...H-14
Bosworth (305)...D-10
Bourbon (1,632)...G-14
Bowling Green (5,334)...D-14
Bradleyville...J-11
Bragg City (149)...L-17
Braggadocio...L-17
Brandsville (161)...K-13
Branson (10,520)...J-5; (6,050) K-10
Branson West (478)...K-10
Brashear (273)...B-12
Braymer (878)...C-9
Breckenridge (383)...C-9
Brentwood (8,055)...*D-31
Bridgeton (11,550)...*B-31
Brighton...I-10
Brimson (63)...B-9
Brinktown...G-13
Brixey...J-12
Bronaugh (249)...H-8
Brookfield (4,542)...C-11
Broseley...K-16
Browning (265)...B-11
Brownington (107)...G-9
Brumley (91)...G-12
Bruner...J-11
Brunswick (858)...D-11
Bucklin (467)...C-11
Bucyrus...I-13
Buffalo (3,084)...H-11
Bunceton (354)...E-11
Bunker (407)...I-14
Burfordville...I-17
Burlington Junction (537)...A-7
Butler (4,219)...G-8
Butterfield (470)...J-9
Cabool (2,146)...I-13
Cainsville (290)...A-9
Cairo (292)...D-12
Caledonia (130)...H-15
Calhoun (469)...F-10
California (4,278)...F-12
Callao (292)...C-12
Camden (191)...D-9
Camden Point (474)...D-7
Camdenton (3,718)...G-11
Cameron (9,933)...C-8
Campbell (1,992)...K-17
Canton (2,377)...B-14
Cape Fair...J-10
Cape Girardeau (37,941)...I-18
Cardwell (713)...L-16
Carl Junction (7,445)...I-8
Carrollton (3,784)...D-10
Carthage (14,378)...I-8
Caruthersville (6,168)...L-17
Cascade...I-16
Cassville (3,266)...K-9
Catron (67)...K-17
Caulfield...K-13
Cedarcreek...K-11
Center (508)...D-14
Centertown (278)...F-12
Centerview (267)...F-9
Centerville (191)...I-15
Centralia (4,027)...D-12
Chadwick...J-11
Chaffee (2,955)...I-17
Chamois (396)...F-13
Charleston (5,947)...J-18
Cherryville...H-14
Chesterfield (47,484)...*C-29
Chestnutridge...J-10
Chilhowee (325)...F-9
Chillicothe (9,515)...C-10
Chula (210)...C-10
Clarence (813)...C-12
Clark (298)...D-12
Clarksburg (334)...F-11
Clarksdale (271)...C-8
Clarksville (442)...D-15
Clarkton (1,288)...K-17
Clayton (15,939)...*C-31, F-16
Clearmont (170)...A-7
Cleveland (661)...F-8
Clever (2,139)...J-10
Clifton Hill (114)...D-11
Climax Springs (124)...G-11
Clinton (9,008)...F-9
Coatsville...A-12
Cobalt City (226)...H-16
Coffey (166)...B-9
Cole Camp (1,121)...F-10
Collins (159)...H-10
Columbia (108,500)...B-17; (84,531) E-12
Commerce (67)...I-18
Conception (210)...B-8
Conception Junction (198)...B-8
Concord (16,421)...*E-31
Concordia (2,450)...E-10
Conway (788)...I-11
Cooter (469)...L-17
Corder (404)...E-10
Corning (15)...B-6
Cosby (124)...C-8
Cottleville (3,075)...*B-28
Couch...K-14
Cowgill (188)...D-9
Craig (248)...B-6
Crane (1,462)...J-10
Creighton (349)...F-9
Crestwood (11,912)...*D-31
Creve Coeur (17,833)...*C-30
Crocker (1,110)...G-12
Cross Timbers (216)...G-10
Cuba (3,356)...G-14
Curryville (225)...D-14
Dadeville (234)...I-9
Dalton (17)...D-11
Danville (34)...E-14
Darlington (121)...B-8
Davisville...H-14
Dawn (128)...C-10
De Kalb (220)...C-7
De Soto (6,400)...G-16
De Witt...D-10
Dearborn (496)...D-7
Deepwater (433)...G-9
Deerfield (81)...H-8
Defiance (155)...F-15
Dellwood (5,025)...*B-32
Delta (438)...I-17
Denver (39)...A-8
Des Arc (177)...I-15
Des Peres (8,373)...*D-30
Desloge (5,054)...H-16
Devils Elbow...H-13
Dexter (7,864)...J-17
Diamond (902)...J-8
Diehlstadt (161)...J-18
Diggins (299)...I-11
Dittmer...G-15
Dixon (1,549)...G-13
Doe Run (915)...H-16
Doniphan (1,997)...K-15
Doolittle (630)...H-13
Dora...J-12
Dover (103)...D-9
Downing (335)...A-12
Drexel (965)...F-8
Duke...H-13
Dunnegan...H-10
Durham...C-13
Eagle Rock (199)...K-9
Eagleville (316)...A-9
Earth City...*A-30
East Lynne (303)...F-8
East Prairie (3,176)...J-18
Easton (234)...C-8
Edgar Springs (208)...H-13
Edina (1,176)...B-12
Edmundson (834)...*B-31
Edwards...G-10
El Dorado Springs (3,593)...H-9
Eldon (4,567)...G-12
Eldridge...H-11
Elk Creek...I-13
Elkland...I-11
Ellington (987)...I-15
Ellisville (9,133)...*D-28
Ellsinore (446)...J-15
Elmer (80)...C-11
Elmo (168)...A-7
Elsberry (1,934)...D-15
Emden...C-13
Eminence (600)...I-14
Emma (233)...E-10
Eolia (522)...D-15
Essex (472)...J-17
Ethel (62)...C-11
Eugene...F-12
Eunice...I-13
Eureka (10,189)...*E-28
Everton (319)...I-9
Ewing (456)...B-13
Excello (49)...C-12
Excelsior Springs (11,084)...D-8
Exeter (772)...K-9
Fair Grove (1,393)...I-10
Fair Play (475)...H-10
Fairdealing (676)...K-15
Fairfax (638)...B-6
Fairview (383)...J-9
Falcon...H-12
Farber (322)...D-14
Farley (269)...*G-28
Farmington (16,240)...H-16
Farrar...H-17
Faucett...C-7
Fayette (2,688)...E-11
Fenton (4,022)...*E-30
Ferguson (21,203)...*B-32
Festus (11,602)...G-16
Fillmore (184)...B-7
Fisk (342)...J-16
Flemington (148)...H-10
Fletcher...G-15
Flint Hill (525)...E-15
Florence...F-11
Florida...D-13
Florissant (52,158)...*A-32
Foley (161)...E-15
Fordland (800)...I-11
Forest City (268)...B-7
Foristell (505)...E-15
Forsyth (2,255)...K-11
Fortuna...F-11
Foster (117)...G-8
Frankford (323)...D-14
Franklin (95)...E-11
Fredericktown (3,985)...H-16
Freeburg (437)...G-13
Freeman (482)...F-8
Freistatt (163)...J-9
Fremont (129)...J-14
French Village...G-16
Frohna (254)...H-17
Frontenac (3,482)...*C-30
Fulton (12,790)...E-13
Gainesville (773)...K-12
Galena (440)...J-10
Gallatin (1,786)...C-9
Galt (253)...B-10
Garden City (1,642)...F-8
Gasconade (223)...F-14
Gatewood...K-15
Gentry (72)...B-8
Gerald (1,345)...F-14
Gerster (25)...G-10
Gibbs (107)...B-12
Gideon (1,093)...K-17
Gilliam (197)...D-11
Gilman City (383)...B-9
Gladstone (25,410)...*H-31
Glasgow (1,103)...D-11
Glenallen (85)...I-17
Glencoe...*E-28
Glendale (5,925)...*D-31
Glenwood (196)...A-12
Gobler...L-17
Golden (280)...K-9
Golden City (765)...I-9
Goodman (1,248)...J-8
Gordonville (391)...I-17
Gorin...B-13
Gower (1,526)...C-8
Graff...I-12
Granby (2,134)...J-8
Grand Pass (66)...D-10
Grandin (243)...J-15
Grandview (24,475)...E-8
Granger (34)...A-13
Grant City (859)...A-8
Gravois Mills (144)...G-11
Gray Summit (2,701)...F-15
Green City (657)...B-11
Green Ridge (476)...F-10
Greencastle (275)...B-11
Greenfield (1,371)...I-9
Greentop (442)...B-12
Greenville (511)...I-16
Greenwood (5,221)...E-8
Grover...*D-28
Grovespring...I-12
Grubville...G-15
Hale (419)...C-10
Halfway (173)...H-10
Hallsville (1,491)...E-12
Halltown (173)...I-9
Hamilton (1,809)...C-9
Hannibal (17,916)...C-14
Hardenville...K-12
Hardin (569)...D-9
Harris (61)...B-10
Harrisburg (266)...E-12
Harrisonville (10,019)...F-8
Hartford...A-11
Hartsburg (103)...F-12
Hartshorn...I-13
Hartville (613)...I-12
Harviell (106)...K-16
Harwood (47)...G-9
Hawk Point (669)...E-14
Hayti (2,939)...L-17
Hayward (131)...K-17
Haywood City (206)...J-17
Hazelwood (25,703)...*A-31
Helena...C-8
Hematite...G-16
Henley...G-12
Henrietta (369)...D-9
Herculaneum (3,468)...G-16
Hermann (2,431)...F-14
Hermitage (467)...H-10
Higbee (568)...D-12
Higginsville (4,797)...E-9
High Hill (195)...E-14
Highlandville (911)...J-10
Hillsboro (2,821)...G-16
Hoberg (56)...J-9
Hogan...I-15
Holcomb (635)...K-17
Holden (2,252)...F-9
Holland (229)...L-17
Holliday (137)...D-12
Hollister (4,426)...J-6
Holt (447)...D-8
Holts Summit (3,247)...F-12
Homestown (151)...K-17
Hopkins (532)...A-7
Hornersville (663)...L-17
Houston (2,081)...I-13
Houstonia (220)...E-10
Howardville (383)...K-18
Huggins...I-12
Hughesville (183)...E-10
Humansville (1,048)...H-10
Hume (336)...G-8
Humphreys (118)...B-10
Hunnewell (184)...C-13
Huntsville (1,564)...D-12
Hurdland (163)...B-12
Hurley (178)...J-10
Iberia (736)...G-12
Independence (113,288)...E-8; (116,830) *J-33
Ionia (88)...F-10
Irondale (445)...H-15
Ironton (1,460)...H-15
Isabella...K-12
Jackson (13,758)...I-17
Jacksonville (151)...C-12
Jadwin...I-14
Jameson (133)...B-9
Jamesport (524)...B-9
Jamestown (386)...E-12
Jane...K-8
Jasper (931)...I-8
Jefferson City (39,636)...F-12; (43,079) D-17, F-12
Jennings (14,712)...*B-32
Jerico Springs (228)...H-9
Jerome...H-13
Jonesburg (768)...E-14
Joplin (45,504)...J-8; (50,150) *I-35
Kahoka (2,078)...A-13
Kaiser...G-12
Kansas City (441,545)...E-8; (459,787) *K-31
Kearney (8,381)...D-8
Kelso (586)...I-18
Kennett (10,932)...L-17
Kewanee...K-18
Keytesville (471)...D-11
Kidder (323)...C-9
Kimberling City (2,400)...K-10
Kimmswick (157)...F-16
King City (1,013)...B-8
Kingdom City (128)...E-13
Kingston (348)...C-9
Kingsville (269)...F-9
Kirbyville (207)...K-10
Kirksville (17,505)...B-12
Kirkwood (27,540)...*D-31
Kissee Mills (1,109)...K-11
Knob Lick...H-16
Knob Noster (2,709)...E-10
Knox City (216)...B-13
Koeltztown...G-13
Koshkonong (212)...K-13
La Belle (660)...B-13
La Grange (931)...B-14
La Monte (1,140)...E-10
La Plata (1,366)...B-12
La Russell (114)...I-9
La Tour (62)...F-9
Laclede (345)...C-10
Laddonia (513)...D-13
Ladue (8,521)...*C-31
Lake Ozark (1,586)...G-12
Lake Spring...H-13
Lamar (4,532)...I-8
Lampe...K-10
Lanagan (419)...K-8
Lancaster (728)...A-12
Laquey...H-12
Laredo (198)...B-10
Latham...F-11
Lathrop (2,086)...D-8
Laurie (945)...G-11
Lawson (2,473)...D-8
Leadwood (1,282)...H-15
Leasburg (338)...G-14
Lebanon (14,474)...H-11
Lee's Summit (91,364)...E-8
Leeton (566)...F-9
Lemay (16,645)...*E-31
Lentner...C-12
Leonard (61)...C-12
Leslie (171)...F-14
Lesterville...I-15
Levasy (83)...E-9
Lewistown (534)...B-13
Lexington (4,726)...D-9
Liberal (759)...H-8
Liberty (29,149)...*H-33, D-8
Licking (3,124)...I-13
Lilbourn (1,190)...K-17
Lincoln (1,190)...F-10
Linn (1,459)...F-13
Linn Creek (244)...G-11
Linneus (278)...C-10
Livonia (74)...A-11
Lock Springs (57)...C-9
Lockwood (936)...I-9
Lodi...I-16
Lohman (163)...F-12
Lone Jack (1,050)...E-9
Lonedell...G-15
Long Lane...H-11
Longtown (102)...H-17
Loose Creek...F-13
Louisburg (122)...H-10
Louisiana (3,364)...D-15
Lowndes...I-16
Lowry City (640)...G-9
Lucerne (85)...A-10
Ludlow (137)...C-9
Lupus (33)...E-12
Luray (99)...A-13
Macks Creek (244)...G-11
Macomb...J-12
Macon (5,471)...C-12
Madison (554)...D-12
Maitland (343)...B-7
Malden (4,275)...K-17
Malta Bend (250)...D-10
Manchester (18,094)...*D-29
Mansfield (1,296)...J-12
Maplewood (8,046)...*D-31
Marble Hill (1,477)...I-17
Marceline (2,233)...C-11
Marionville (2,225)...J-9
Marquand (203)...I-16
Marshall (13,065)...E-10
Marshfield (6,633)...I-11
Marston (503)...K-17
Marthasville (1,136)...F-15
Martinsburg (304)...E-13
Martinsville...B-9
Maryland Heights (27,472)...*B-30
Maryville (11,972)...B-7
Matthews (628)...J-18
Maysville (1,114)...C-8
Mayview (212)...E-9
Maywood...C-13
McFall (93)...B-8
McGee...J-16
McGirk...F-12
McKittrick (61)...F-14
Meadville (462)...C-10
Mehlville (28,380)...*E-31
Memphis (1,822)...A-12
Mendon (171)...C-11
Mercer (318)...A-10
Merwin (58)...F-8
Meta (229)...G-12
Metz (49)...G-8
Mexico (11,543)...D-13
Miami (175)...D-10
Middlebrook...H-15
Middletown (167)...E-14
Milan (1,960)...B-11
Milford (26)...H-8
Mill Spring (189)...J-15
Millard (89)...B-12
Miller (699)...I-9
Millersville...I-17
Milo (90)...H-8
Mindenmines (365)...I-8
Miner (984)...J-18
Mineral Point (351)...G-15
Missouri City (267)...D-8
Moberly (13,974)...D-12
Mokane (185)...F-13
Monett (8,873)...J-9
Monroe City (2,531)...C-13
Montgomery City (2,834)...E-14
Monticello (98)...B-13
Montier (98)...J-14
Montreal...G-12
Montrose (384)...G-9
Moody...K-13
Mooresville (91)...C-9
Mora...F-10
Morehouse (973)...J-17
Morrison (139)...F-13
Morrisville (388)...I-10
Moscow Mills (2,509)...E-15
Mound City (1,159)...B-7
Moundville (124)...H-8
Mountain Grove (4,789)...J-12
Mountain View (2,719)...J-13
Mt. Leonard (87)...E-10
Mt. Moriah (87)...B-9
Mt. Vernon (4,575)...J-9
Murphy (8,690)...*E-30
Myrtle...K-14
Napoleon (222)...E-9
Naylor (632)...K-16
Neck City (186)...I-8
Neelyville (483)...K-16
Nelson (192)...E-11
Neosho (11,835)...J-8
Nevada (8,386)...H-8
New Bloomfield (669)...F-13
New Boston...C-11
New Cambria (195)...C-11
New Florence (769)...E-14
New Franklin (1,089)...E-11
New Hampton (291)...B-9
New Haven (2,089)...F-14
New London (974)...C-14
New Madrid (3,116)...K-18
New Melle (475)...F-15
Newark (94)...B-13
Newburg (470)...H-13
Newtown (183)...B-10
Niangua (405)...I-11
Nixa (19,022)...J-10
Noel (1,832)...K-8
Norborne (708)...D-9
Normandy (5,008)...*B-32
North Kansas City (4,208)...*I-31
Norwood...J-12
Novelty (139)...B-12
Novinger (456)...B-11
O'Fallon (79,329)...E-15
Oak Grove (7,795)...E-9
Oak Ridge (243)...I-17
Oakville (36,143)...*F-32
Odessa (5,300)...E-9
Old Appleton (85)...H-17
Old Monroe (265)...E-15
Oldfield...J-11
Olean (128)...F-12
Olivette (7,737)...*C-31
Olney...E-14
Oran (1,294)...J-17
Oregon (857)...B-7
Orrick (837)...D-9
Osage Beach (4,351)...G-11
Osborn (423)...C-8
Osceola (947)...G-9
Osgood (48)...B-10
Otterville (454)...F-11
Overland (16,062)...*B-31
Owensville (2,676)...G-14
Oxly (200)...K-15
Ozark (17,820)...J-10
Pacific (7,002)...F-15
Palmyra (3,595)...C-14
Paris (1,220)...D-13
Park Hills (8,759)...H-16
Parkville (5,554)...*H-29
Parma (713)...K-17
Parnell (191)...A-8
Pascola (108)...L-17
Passaic (34)...G-8
Patterson...I-16
Patton...I-17
Pattonsburg (348)...B-9
Paynesville (77)...D-15
Peace Valley...J-13
Peculiar (4,608)...F-8
Perkins...J-17
Perry (693)...D-13
Perryville (8,225)...H-17
Pevely (5,484)...G-16
Philadelphia...C-13
Phillipsburg (202)...H-11
Pickering (160)...A-7
Piedmont (1,977)...I-15
Pierce City (1,292)...J-9
Pilot Grove (768)...E-11
Pineville (791)...K-8
Pittsburg...H-10
Plato (109)...I-12
Platte City (4,691)...D-7
Plattsburg (2,319)...C-8
Pleasant Hill (8,113)...E-8
Pleasant Hope (614)...I-10
Plevna (21)...C-13
Pocahontas (114)...I-17
Point Lookout...K-6
Pollock (89)...B-11
Polo (575)...D-9
Pomona (511)...J-13
Ponce de Leon...J-10
Pontiac (175)...K-12
Poplar Bluff (17,023)...J-16
Portage Des Sioux (328)...E-16
Portageville (3,228)...K-17
Portland...F-13
Potosi (2,660)...G-15
Pottersville...K-13
Powell...K-8
Powersite...K-11
Powersville (60)...A-10
Prairie Home (280)...E-12
Preston (223)...H-10
Princeton (1,166)...A-10
Protem...K-11
Purcell (408)...I-8
Purdin (190)...C-10
Purdy (1,098)...J-9
Puxico (881)...J-16
Queen City (598)...A-12
Quincy...G-10
Quitman (45)...A-7
Qulin (458)...K-16
Racine...J-8
Ravenwood (440)...B-8
Raymondville (363)...I-13
Raymore (19,206)...E-8
Raytown (29,526)...*K-32
Rayville (223)...D-9
Rea (50)...B-7
Redford...I-15
Reeds (95)...J-8
Reeds Spring (913)...J-10
Renick (172)...D-12
Rensselaer (228)...C-14
Republic (14,751)...J-10
Revere (79)...A-13
Reynolds...I-15
Rhineland (142)...F-14
Rich Hill (1,396)...G-8
Richards (96)...H-8
Richland (1,863)...H-12
Richmond (5,797)...D-9
Richmond Heights (8,603)...*C-32
Richwoods...G-15
Ridgedale...K-10
Ridgeway (464)...A-9
Risco (346)...K-17
Riverside (2,937)...*I-30
Rives (63)...L-17
Roach...G-11
Robertsville...F-15
Roby...I-12
Rocheport (239)...E-12
Rock Port (1,318)...A-6
Rockbridge...J-12
Rockville (166)...G-9
Rocky Comfort...J-9
Rogersville (3,073)...J-11
Rolla (19,559)...H-13
Rombauer...J-16
Roscoe (124)...G-9
Rosebud (409)...F-14
Rothville (99)...C-11
Rueter...K-11
Rush Hill (151)...D-13
Russellville (807)...F-12
Rutledge (109)...B-13
Saginaw (297)...*I-35
Salem (4,950)...H-14
Salisbury (1,618)...D-11
Santa Fe...D-13
Sappington (7,580)...*E-31
Sarcoxie (1,330)...J-9
Savannah (5,057)...C-7
Saverton...C-14
Schell City (249)...G-9
Scott City (4,565)...I-18
Sedalia (21,387)...F-10
Sedgewickville (173)...H-17
Seligman (851)...K-9
Senath (1,767)...L-16
Seneca (2,336)...J-8
Seymour (1,921)...I-11
Shelbina (1,704)...C-13
Shelbyville (552)...C-13
Sheldon (543)...H-8
Shell Knob (1,379)...K-9
Sheridan (195)...A-8
Shrewsbury (6,254)...*D-31
Sibley (357)...D-8
Sikeston (16,318)...J-18
Silex (187)...E-15
Silva...I-16
Slater (1,856)...D-11
Smithton (570)...F-11
Smithville (8,425)...D-8
Solo...I-13
South Gifford (50)...B-11
South Greenfield (90)...I-9
South West City (970)...K-8
Spanish Lake (19,650)...*A-33
Sparta (1,756)...J-11
Spickard (254)...B-10
Spokane (177)...J-10
Springfield (151,580)...I-10; (159,498) *K-35
Squires...J-12
St. Albans...F-15
St. Ann (13,020)...*B-31
St. Charles (60,321)...E-16; (65,794) *B-29
St. Clair (4,724)...G-15
St. Elizabeth (336)...G-12
St. James (4,216)...G-13
St. John (6,517)...*B-31
St. Joseph (73,990)...C-7; (76,780) *F-35
St. Louis (319,294)...*C-32; (348,189) F-16
St. Martins (1,140)...F-12
St. Marys (360)...H-17
St. Patrick...B-13
St. Peters (52,575)...*A-28
St. Robert (4,340)...H-12
St. Thomas (263)...F-12
Stanberry (1,185)...B-8
Stanton...G-15
Stark City (139)...J-8
Ste. Genevieve (4,410)...G-17
Steedman...F-13
Steele (2,172)...L-17
Steelville (1,642)...G-14
Stella (158)...J-8
Stewartsville (750)...C-8
Stockton (1,819)...H-9
Stotesbury (18)...G-8
Stotts City (220)...J-9
Stoutland (192)...H-12
Stoutsville (36)...D-13
Stover (1,094)...F-11
Strafford (2,358)...I-10
Strasburg (141)...E-9
Sturdivant...J-17
Sturgeon (872)...D-12
Success...I-13
Sullivan (7,081)...G-14
Summersville (502)...I-13
Sumner (102)...C-10
Sunrise Beach (431)...G-11
Sunset Hills (8,496)...*E-31
Swedeborg...H-12
Sweet Springs (1,484)...E-10
Syracuse (172)...F-11
Tallapoosa (168)...K-17
Taneyville (396)...J-11
Taos (878)...F-13
Tarkio (1,583)...A-6
Taylor...C-14
Tebbetts...F-13
Tecumseh...K-12
Thayer (2,243)...K-14
Theodosia (243)...K-11
Thompson...D-13
Thornfield...K-11
Tiff...G-15
Tiff City...K-8
Tightwad (69)...G-10
Tina (157)...D-10
Tindall (77)...B-10
Tipton (3,262)...F-11
Town and Country (10,815)...*C-30
Treloar...F-14
Trenton (6,001)...B-10
Trimble (646)...D-8
Triplett (41)...D-10
Troy (10,540)...E-15
Truxton (91)...E-14
Tunas...H-11
Turners...I-10
Turney (148)...C-8
Tuscumbia (203)...G-12
Ulman...G-12
Union (10,204)...F-15
Union Star (437)...B-8
Unionville (1,865)...A-11
Unity Village (99)...*L-33
University City (35,371)...*C-32
Urbana (417)...H-10
Urich (505)...F-9
Utica (269)...C-10
Valles Mines...G-16
Valley Park (6,942)...*E-30
Van Buren (819)...J-15
Vandalia (3,899)...D-14
Vandiver (71)...E-13
Vanzant...J-12
Verona (619)...J-9
Versailles (2,482)...F-11
Viburnum (693)...H-14
Vichy...G-13
Vienna (610)...G-13
Viola...K-10
Vista (54)...G-9
Vulcan...I-15
Waco (87)...I-8
Waldron...*H-28
Walker (270)...H-8
Walnut Grove (665)...I-10
Walnut Shade...J-10
Wappapello...J-16
Wardell (427)...K-17
Wardsville (1,506)...F-12
Warrensburg (18,838)...E-9
Warrenton (7,880)...E-14
Warsaw (2,127)...G-10
Washburn (435)...K-9
Washington (13,982)...F-15
Wasola (113)...J-12
Watson (100)...A-6
Waverly (849)...D-10
Wayland (533)...A-14
Waynesville (4,830)...H-12
Weatherby (107)...C-8
Weaubleau (418)...H-10
Webster Groves (22,995)...*D-31
Wellsville (1,217)...E-14
Wentworth (147)...J-9
Wentzville (29,070)...E-15
Wesco...H-14
West Plains (11,986)...J-13
Westboro (141)...A-6
Weston (1,641)...D-7
Westphalia (389)...F-13
Wheatland (371)...G-10
Wheaton (696)...J-9
Wheeling (271)...C-10
Whiteoak...K-17
Whiteside (75)...D-15
Whitewater (125)...I-17
Wildwood (35,517)...F-15
Willard (5,288)...I-10
Williamsburg...E-13
Williamstown...B-13
Williamsville (342)...J-16
Willow Springs (2,184)...J-13
Wilson City (115)...J-18
Windsor (2,901)...F-10
Winfield (1,404)...E-15
Winigan (44)...B-11
Winona (1,335)...J-14
Winston (259)...C-9
Wolf Island...J-18
Woodson Terrace (4,063)...*B-31
Wooldridge (61)...E-12
Worthington (81)...A-11
Wright City (3,119)...E-15
Wyaconda (227)...A-13
Wyatt (319)...J-18
Zalma (122)...I-17
Zanoni...K-12

NA066-15

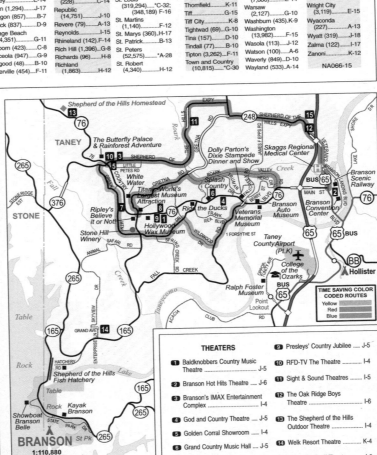

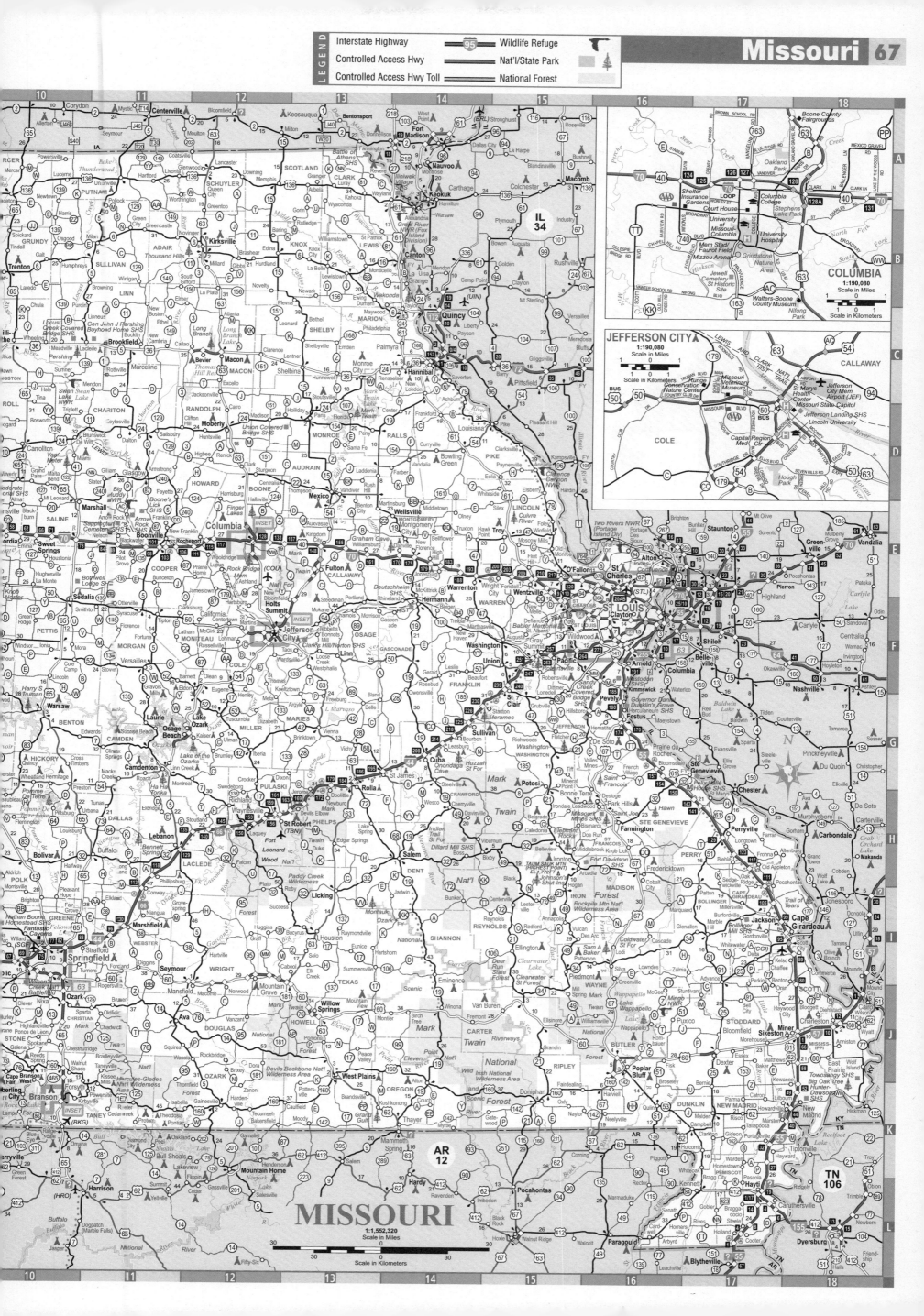

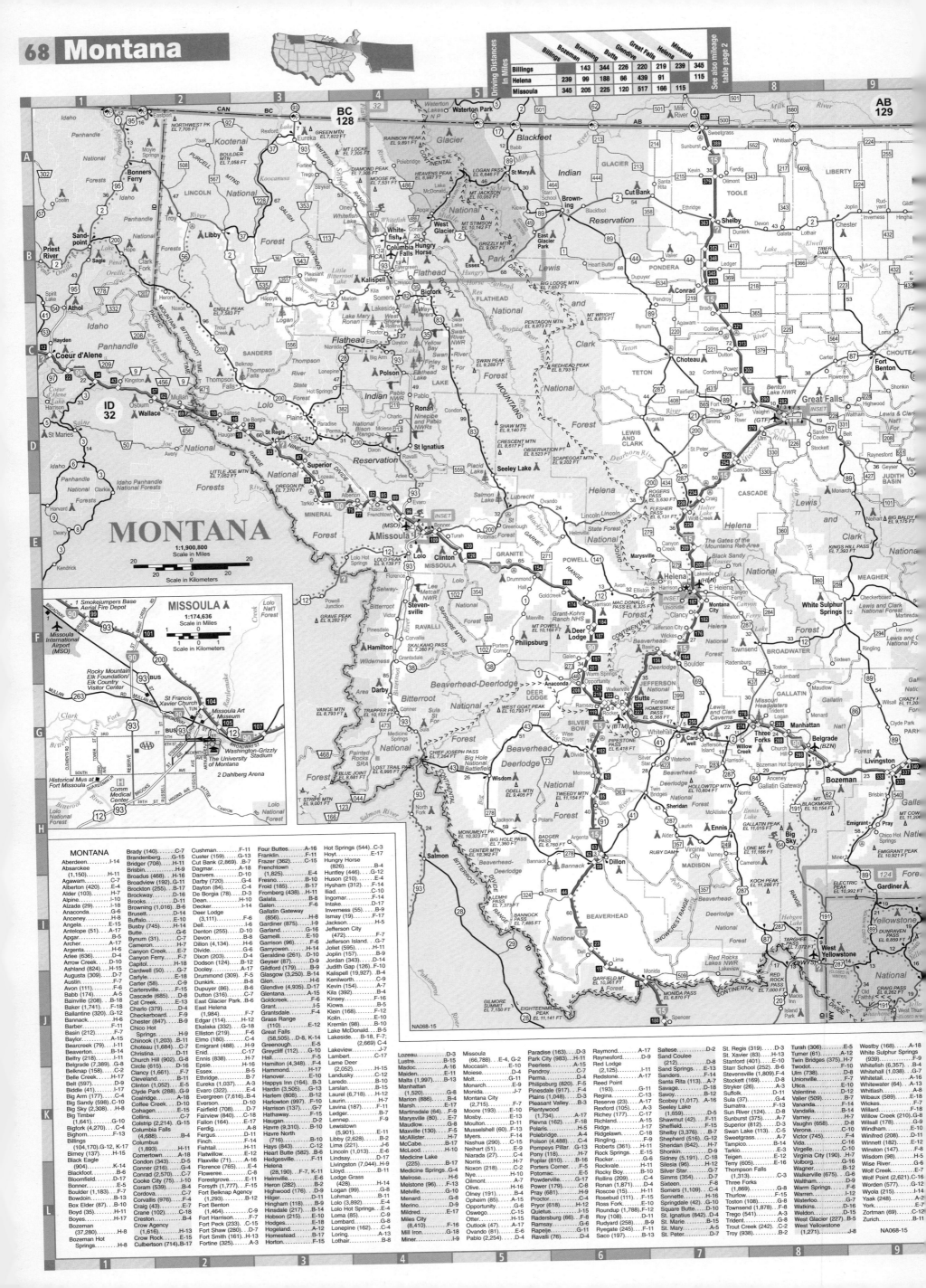

LEGEND

Interstate Highway	Wildlife Refuge
Controlled Access Hwy	Nat'l/State Park
Controlled Access Hwy Toll	National Forest

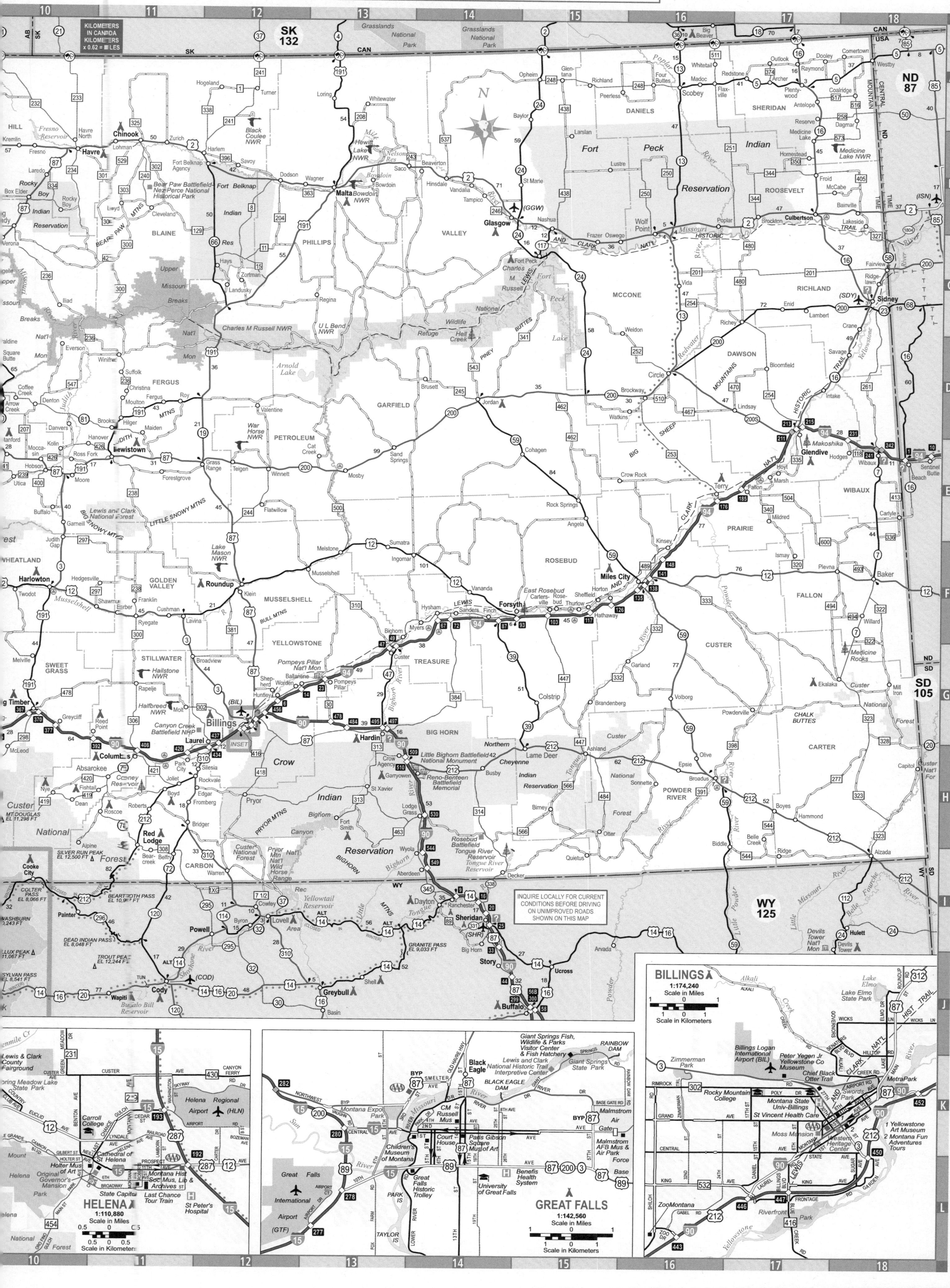

KILOMETERS IN CANADA
KILOMETERS x 0.62 = MILES

HELENA
1:110,880
Scale in Miles
Scale in Kilometers

GREAT FALLS
1:142,560
Scale in Miles
Scale in Kilometers

BILLINGS
1:174,240
Scale in Miles
Scale in Kilometers

INQUIRE LOCALLY FOR CURRENT
CONDITIONS BEFORE DRIVING
ON UNIMPROVED ROADS
SHOWN ON THIS MAP

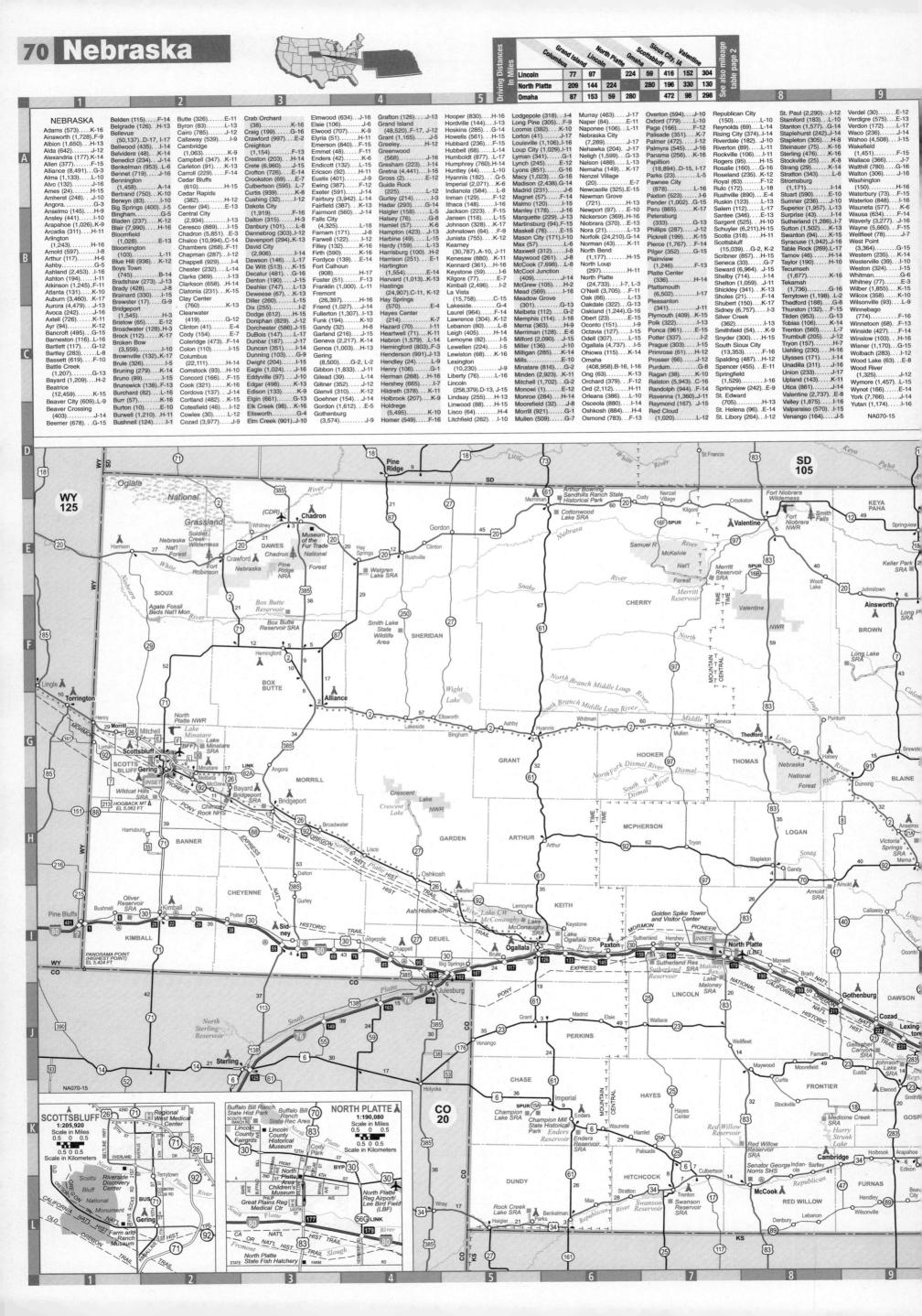

Driving Distances In Miles	Columbus	Grand Island	Lincoln	North Platte	Omaha	Scottsbluff	Sioux City IA	Valentine
Lincoln	77	97		224	59	416	152	304
North Platte	209	144	224		280	196	330	130
Omaha	87	153	59	280		472	98	298

See also mileage table on page 2

NEBRASKA

Adams (573)....K-16
Ainsworth (1,728)..F-9
Albion (1,650)...H-13
Alda (642).......J-12
Alexandria (177)..K-14
Allen (377).......F-15
Alliance (8,491)...G-3
Alma (1,133)....L-10
Alvo (132).......J-16
Ames (24).......H-15
Amherst (248)...J-10
Angora (145)....H-9
Anselmo (145)...H-9
Ansley (441)....I-10
Arapahoe (1,026)..K-9
Arcadia (311)...I-11
Arlington (1,243)..H-16
Arnold (597)....I-8
Arthur (117).....H-6
Ashby...........G-5
Ashland (2,453)..I-16
Ashton (194)....I-11
Atkinson (1,245)..F-11
Atlanta (131)...K-10
Auburn (3,460)...K-17
Aurora (4,479)..I-13
Avoca (242).....J-16
Axtell (726)....K-11
Ayr (94).......K-12
Bancroft (495)..G-15
Barneston (116)..L-16
Bartlett (117)...G-12
Bartley (283)...L-8
Bassett (619)...F-10
Battle Creek (1,207)..G-14
Bayard (1,209)...H-2
Beatrice (12,459)..K-15
Beaver City (609)..L-9
Beaver Crossing (403)..J-14
Beemer (678)...G-15

Belden (115)....F-14
Belgrade (126)...H-13
Bellevue (50,137)..D-17, I-17
Belvidere (48)..K-14
Benedict (234)..I-14
Benkelman (953)..L-6
Bennet (719)....J-16
Bennington (1,458)..A-14
Bertrand (750)...K-10
Berwyn (83)....I-10
Big Springs (400)..I-5
Bingham........G-5
Bladen (237)...K-12
Blair (7,990)...H-16
Bloomfield (1,028)..E-13
Bloomington (103)..L-11
Blue Hill (936)..K-12
Boys Town........
Bradshaw (273)..I-13
Brady (428).....J-8
Brainard (351)..I-15
Brewster (17)...G-9
Bridgeport (1,545)..H-3
Bristow (65)....E-12
Brock (112)....K-17
Broken Bow (3,559)..I-10
Brownlee........G-8
Brownville (132)..K-17
Brule (326).....I-5
Bruning (279)..K-14
Bruno (99).....I-15
Brunswick (128)..H-3
Burchard (82)..L-16
Burr (57).......K-16
Burton (10).....E-10
Burwell (1,210)..H-11
Bushnell (124)..I-1

Butte (326).....E-11
Byron (83)......L-13
Cairo (785)....J-12
Callaway (539)..I-9
Cambridge (1,063)..K-9
Carleton (91)..K-13
Carroll (229)...F-14
Cedar Bluffs (610)..H-15
Cedar Rapids (382)..H-12
Center (94)....E-13
Central City (2,934)..I-13
Ceresco (889)..I-15
Chadron (5,851)..E-3
Chalco (10,994)..C-14
Chambers (268)..F-11
Chapman (287)..I-12
Chappell (929)..I-4
Chester (232)..L-14
Clarks (369)...I-13
Clarkson (658)..H-14
Clatonia (231)..K-15
Clay Center (760)..K-13
Clearwater (419)..G-12
Clinton (41)....E-4
Cody (154)....E-7
Coleridge (473)..F-14
Colon (110)...I-15
Columbus (22,111)..H-14
Comstock (93)..H-10
Concord (166)..F-15
Cook (321)....K-16
Cordova (137)..J-14
Cortland (482)..K-15
Cotesfield (46)..I-12
Cowles (33)....L-12
Cozad (3,977)..J-9

Crab Orchard (38)..K-16
Craig (199)....G-16
Crawford (997)..E-2
Creighton (1,154)..F-13
Cresson (203)..H-14
Crete (6,960)..J-15
Crofton (726)..E-14
Crookston (92)..E-7
Culbertson (595)..L-7
Curtis (939)...K-8
Cushing (32)...I-12
Dakota City (1,919)..F-16
Dalton (315)..H-3
Danbury (101)..L-8
Dannebrog (303)..I-12
Davenport (294)..K-13
David City (2,906)..I-14
Dawson (164)..L-17
De Witt (513)..K-15
Decatur (481)..G-16
Denton (190)..J-15
Deshler (747)..L-13
Deweese (67)..K-13
Diller (260)...L-15
Dix (255).....I-2
Dodge (612)...H-15
Doniphan (829)..J-12
Dorchester (586)..J-15
DuBois (147)..L-17
Dunbar (187)..J-17
Duncan (351)..I-14
Dunning (103)..G-9
Dwight (204)..I-15

Elmwood (634)..J-16
Elsie (106)....J-6
Elwood (707)..K-9
Elyria (51)....H-11
Emerson (840)..F-15
Emmet (48)....F-11
Enders (42)....K-6
Endicott (132)..L-15
Ericson (92)...H-11
Eustis (401)...J-9
Ewing (392)...G-12
Exeter (591)...J-14
Fairbury (3,942)..L-14
Fairfield (387)..K-13
Fairmont (560)..J-14
Falls City (4,325)..L-18
Farnam (171)..J-8
Farwell (122)..I-12
Filley (132)...K-16
Firth (590)...K-16
Fordyce (130)..E-14
Fort Calhoun (908)..H-17
Foster (51)....F-13
Franklin (1,000)..L-11
Fremont (26,397)..H-16
Friend (1,027)..J-14
Fullerton (1,307)..I-13
Funk (194)....K-10
Gandy (30)....H-8
Garland (216)..J-15
Geneva (2,217)..K-14
Genoa (1,003)..H-13
Gering (8,500)..G-2, L-2
Gibbon (1,833)..J-11
Gilead (39)...L-14
Giltner (352)..J-12
Glenvil (310)..K-12
Goehner (154)..J-14
Gordon (1,612)..E-5
Gothenburg (3,574)..J-9

Grafton (126)..J-13
Grand Island (48,520)..F-17, J-12
Grant (1,165)..J-5
Greeley (466)..H-12
Greenwood (568)..J-16
Gresham (223)..I-14
Gretna (4,441)..I-16
Gross (2)......E-12
Guide Rock (225)..L-12
Gurley (199)..I-3
Hadar (293)..F-14
Haigler (158)..L-5
Halsey (76)...G-9
Hamlet (57)..K-6
Hampton (423)..J-13
Harbine (49)..L-15
Hardy (159)..L-13
Harrisburg (100)..H-1
Harrison (251)..E-1
Hartington (1,554)..E-14
Harvard (1,013)..K-13
Hastings (24,907)..C-11, K-12
Hay Springs (570)..E-4
Hayes Center (214)..K-7
Hazard (71)...I-11
Heartwell (71)..K-11
Hebron (1,579)..L-14
Hemingford (803)..F-3
Henderson (991)..J-13
Hendley (24)..L-9
Henry (106)..G-1
Herman (268)..G-16
Hershey (665)..I-7
Hildreth (378)..K-11
Holbrook (207)..K-9
Holdrege (5,495)..K-10
Homer (549)..F-16

Hooper (830)..H-16
Hordville (144)..I-13
Hoskins (285)..G-14
Howard City..H-13
Howells (561)..H-15
Hubbard (236)..F-15
Hubbell (58)..L-14
Humboldt (877)..L-17
Humphrey (760)..H-14
Huntley (44)..L-10
Hyannis (182)..G-5
Imperial (2,071)..K-6
Indianola (584)..L-8
Inman (129)..F-12
Ithaca (148)..I-16
Jackson (223)..F-16
Jansen (118)..L-15
Johnson (326)..K-17
Johnstown (86)..F-9
Juniata (755)..K-12
Kearney (30,787)..A-10, J-11
Kenesaw (880)..K-11
Kennard (361)..H-16
Keystone (59)..I-6
Kilgore (77)..E-7
Kimball (2,496)..I-2
La Vista (15,758)..C-15
Lakeside.....G-4
Laurel (964)..F-14
Lawrence (304)..K-12
Lebanon (80)..L-8
Leigh (405)..H-14
Lewellen (224)..I-5
Lewiston (68)..K-16
Lexington (10,230)..J-9
Liberty (76)..L-16
Lincoln (258,379)..D-13, J-15
Lindsay (265)..H-13
Linwood (88)..I-15
Lisco (64)....H-4
Litchfield (262)..I-10

Lodgepole (318)..I-4
Long Pine (305)..F-9
Loomis (382)..K-10
Lorton (41)...K-17
Louisville (1,106)..I-16
Loup City (1,029)..I-11
Lyman (341)..G-1
Lynch (245)..E-12
Lyons (851)..G-15
Macy (1,023)..F-16
Madison (2,438)..G-14
Madrid (231)..J-6
Magnet (57)..F-14
Malcolm (421)..G-?
Malmo (120)..I-15
Manley (178)..J-16
Marquette (229)..I-13
Martinsburg (94)..F-15
Maskell (54)..E-15
Mason City (171)..I-10
Maxwell (313)..I-8
Maywood (267)..J-8
McCook (7,698)..L-8
McCool Junction (409)..J-14
McGrew (105)..H-2
Mead (569)..I-16
Meadow Grove (298)..G-13
Melbeta (107)..G-2
Memphis (114)..I-16
Merna (363)..H-9
Merriman (118)..E-6
Milford (2,090)..J-15
Miller (136)..J-10
Milligan (285)..K-14
Minatare (816)..G-2, K-2
Minden (2,923)..K-11
Mitchell (1,702)..G-2
Monowi (1).....E-12
Monroe (284)..H-14
Moorefield (32)..J-8
Morrill (921)..G-1

Murray (463)..J-17
Naper (84)...E-11
Naponee (106)..L-11
Nebraska City (7,289)..J-17
Nehawka (204)..J-17
Neligh (1,599)..G-13
Nelson (488)..L-13
Nemaha (149)..K-17
Nenzel (20)...E-7
Newcastle (325)..E-15
Newman Grove (721)..G-13
Nickerson (369)..H-16
Niobrara (370)..E-13
Nora (21)....L-13
Norfolk (24,210)..G-14
Norman (43)..K-11
North Bend (1,177)..H-15
North Loup (297)..H-11
North Platte (24,733)..I-7, L-3
Oak (66)....L-13
Oakdale (322)..G-13
Oakland (1,244)..G-16
Obert (23)....E-15
Oconto (161)..I-9
Octavia (127)..I-15
Odell (307)..L-15
Ogallala (4,737)..I-5
Ohiowa (115)..K-14
Omaha (408,958)..B-16, I-16
Ong (63)....K-13
Ord (2,112)..H-11
Orchard (379)..F-12
Orleans (386)..L-10
Osceola (880)..I-14
Oshkosh (884)..H-4
Osmond (783)..F-13

Overton (594)..J-10
Oxford (779)..L-10
Page (166)...F-12
Palisade (354)..K-7
Palmer (472)..I-12
Palmyra (545)..J-16
Panama (256)..K-16
Papillion (18,894)..D-15, I-17
Parks (23)...L-6
Pawnee City (878)..L-16
Paxton (523)..I-6
Pender (1,002)..G-15
Peru (865)...K-17
Petersburg (333)..G-13
Phillips (287)..J-12
Pickrell (199)..K-15
Pierce (1,767)..F-14
Pilger (352)..G-15
Plainview (1,246)..F-13
Platte Center (336)..H-14
Plattsmouth (6,502)..I-17
Pleasanton (341)..J-11
Plymouth (409)..K-15
Polk (322)...I-13
Ponca (961)..E-15
Potter (337)..I-3
Prague (303)..I-15
Primrose (61)..H-12
Prosser (66)..J-12
Purdum (8)...G-8
Ragan (58)..K-11
Ralston (5,943)..C-16
Randolph (944)..F-14
Ravenna (1,360)..J-11
Raymond (162)..J-15
Red Cloud (1,020)..L-12

Republican City (150)..L-10
Reynolds (69)..L-14
Rising City (374)..I-14
Riverdale (182)..J-10
Riverton (89)..L-11
Rockville (106)..I-11
Rogers (95)..H-15
Rosalie (160)..G-16
Roseland (235)..K-12
Royal (63)...F-12
Rulo (172)...L-18
Rushville (886)..E-4
Ruskin (123)..L-13
Salem (112)..L-17
Sargent (525)..H-10
Schuyler (6,211)..H-15
Scotia (318)..H-11
Scottsbluff (15,039)..G-2, K-2
Scribner (857)..H-15
Seneca (33)..G-7
Seward (6,964)..J-15
Shelby (714)..I-14
Shelton (1,059)..J-11
Shickley (341)..K-13
Sholes (21)..F-14
Shubert (150)..K-17
Sidney (6,757)..I-3
Silver Creek (362)..I-13
Smithfield (54)..K-9
Snyder (300)..H-15
South Sioux City (13,353)..F-16
Spalding (487)..H-12
Spencer (455)..E-11
Springfield (1,529)..I-16
Springview (242)..E-9
St. Edward (781)..H-13

St. Paul (2,290)..I-12
Stamford (183)..L-10
Stanton (1,577)..G-14
Staplehurst (242)..J-14
Stapleton (305)..H-8
Steinauer (75)..K-16
Sterling (476)..K-16
Stockville (25)..K-8
Stratton (343)..L-6
Stromsburg (1,171)..I-14
Stuart (593)..F-10
Sumner (236)..J-10
Superior (1,957)..L-13
Sutherland (1,286)..I-7
Sutton (1,502)..K-13
Swanton (94)..K-15
Syracuse (1,942)..J-16
Table Rock (269)..L-17
Talmage (46)..J-17
Taylor (190)..H-10
Tecumseh (1,677)..K-16
Tekamah (1,736)..G-16
Terrytown (1,198)..L-2
Thedford (188)..G-8
Thurston (132)..F-15
Tilden (953)..G-13
Tobias (106)..K-14
Trenton (560)..L-7
Trumbull (205)..J-12
Tryon (157)...H-7
Uehling (230)..H-16
Ulysses (171)..I-14
Unadilla (311)..J-16
Union (225)..J-17
Upland (143)..K-11
Utica (861)...J-14
Valentine (2,737)..E-8
Valley (1,875)..I-16
Valparaiso (570)..I-15
Venango (164)..J-5

Verdel (30)..E-12
Verdigre (575)..E-13
Verdon (172)..L-17
Wahoo (4,508)..I-15
Wakefield (1,451)..F-15
Wallace (366)..J-7
Walthill (780)..G-15
Walton (306)..J-16
Washington (150)..H-16
Waterbury (73)..F-15
Waterloo (848)..I-16
Wauneta (577)..K-6
Wausa (634)..F-14
Waverly (3,277)..J-16
Wayne (5,660)..F-14
Wellfleet (78)..J-7
West Point (3,364)..G-15
Western (235)..K-14
Westerville (46)..I-11
Weston (324)..I-15
Whitman (77)..G-7
Wilber (1,855)..K-15
Wilcox (356)..K-11
Wilsonville (93)..L-9
Winnebago (774)..F-16
Winnetoon (68)..F-13
Winside (427)..F-14
Winslow (103)..H-16
Wisner (1,170)..G-15
Wolbach (283)..I-12
Wood Lake (63)..E-8
Wood River (1,325)..J-12
Wymore (1,457)..L-15
Wynot (166)..E-14
York (7,766)..J-14
Yutan (1,174)..I-16

NA070-15

WY 125

SD 105

CO 20

LEGEND

Interstate Highway	Wildlife Refuge
Controlled Access Hwy	Nat'l/State Park
Controlled Access Hwy Toll	National Forest

KEARNEY
1:253,440
Scale in Miles
0.5 0 0.5
Scale in Kilometers
0.5 0 0.5

KidZone-Kearney Area Children's Museum
Kearney Regional Airport (EAR)
Univ of NE at Kearney
Buffalo County Fairgrounds
Good Samaritan Hospital
Museum of Nebraska Art (MONA)
Great Platte River Road Archway Monument
BUFFALO
Trails and Rails Mus
Fort Kearny State Hist Park
KEARNEY

HASTINGS
1:158,400
Scale in Miles
0.5 0 0.5
Scale in Kilometers
0.5 0 0.5

Hastings Municipal Airport (HSI)
Mary Lanning Memorial Hospital
Children's Museum of Central Nebraska
Hastings Museum of Natural and Cultural History
Hastings College
Aquacourt Waterpark
Hastings Family Waterpark
Adams County Fairgrounds

LINCOLN
1:253,440
Scale in Miles
1 0 1
Scale in Kilometers
1 0 1

Lincoln Airport (LNK)
Lux Center for the Arts
Int'l Quilt Study Center & Mus
Univ of Nebraska-East Campus
Elder Art Gallery
Univ of Nebraska-Lincoln
Nebraska State Capitol
Sunken Gardens
Antelope
Saint Elizabeth Regional Medical Center
BryanLGH Medical Center East
Nat'l Mus of Roller Skating
Pioneers Park
Pioneers Park Nature Center
Union College
Holmes Lake
Holmes Park
Yankee Hill State Wildlife Mgmt Area
Yankee Hill Lake

OMAHA / COUNCIL BLUFFS
1:253,440
Scale in Miles
1 0 1
Scale in Kilometers
1 0 1

North Omaha Airport (3NO)
The Mormon Trail Center at Historic Winter Quarters and Pioneer Cemetery
Eppley Airfield (OMA)
Alegent Health Immanuel Medical Ctr
The General Crook House Mus
DOUGLAS
OMAHA
Creighton Univ
Century Link Center Omaha
The Durham Mus
Alegent Health Mercy Hospital
University of Nebraska at Omaha
College of Saint Mary
Douglas County Hospital
Lauritzen Gdns, Omaha's Botanical Center
Omaha's Henry Doorly Zoo and Aquarium
Boys Town
Methodist Hospital
One Pacific Place Park
Kaneville Tabernacle
Fun Plex Amusement Park
COUNCIL BLUFFS
Ralston Arena
Seymour L Smith Park
Lake Manawa St Pk
Millard Airport (MLE)
La Vista
Chalco
CORNHUSKER
SARPY
Papillion
Bellevue
Halleck Park
Fontenelle Forest Nature Center
Bellevue University
Bellevue Med Ctr
Alegent Health Midlands Hospital
Offutt Air Force Base
Haworth Park
Sarpy County Historical Museum

GRAND ISLAND
1:190,080
Scale in Miles
1 0 1
Scale in Kilometers
1 0 1

Central Nebraska Regional Airport (GRI)
VA Medical Center
St Francis Medical Center
Nebraska State Fairgrds at Fonner Pk
Stuhr Museum of the Prairie Pioneer
George Clayton Hall County Park

NEBRASKA
1:1,488,960
Scale in Miles
20 0 20
Scale in Kilometers

SD
IA
KS 42
MO 66
IA 40

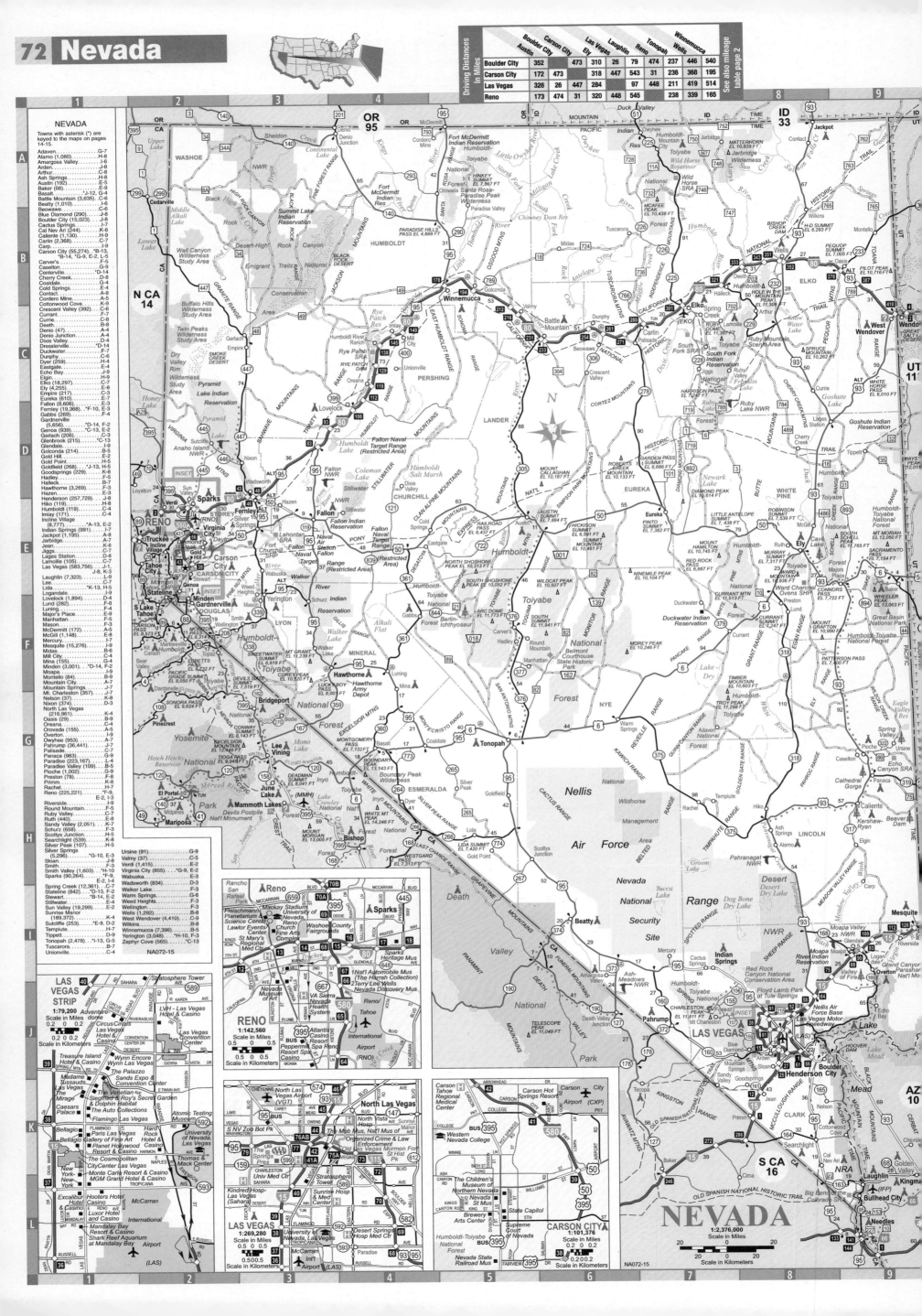

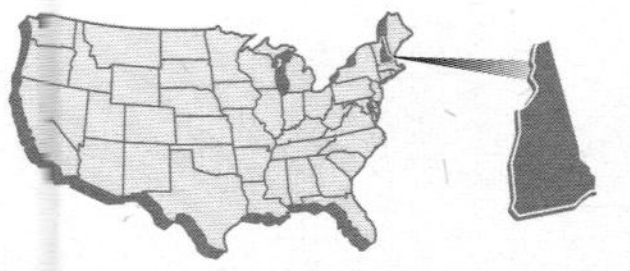

NA073-15

Driving Distances in Miles

	Colebrook	Concord	Gorham	Keene	Lebanon	Manchester	Nashua	Portsmouth	Plymouth	Twin Mountain
Concord	137		113	55	60	17	35	58	43	85
Manchester	157	17	130	66	71		19	44	60	102
Nashua	175	35	148	49	89	19		55	78	120
Portsmouth	168	58	111	107	112	44	55		101	117

See also mileage table page 2

CONCORD
1:126,720

MANCHESTER
1:205,920

1 Univ of NH at Manchester
2 Manchester Hist Assoc
3 The Currier Museum of Art
  Millyard Museum & SEE Science Center
4 Verizon Wireless Arena

PORTSMOUTH
1:126,720

NASHUA
1:142,560

NEW HAMPSHIRE
1:855,360

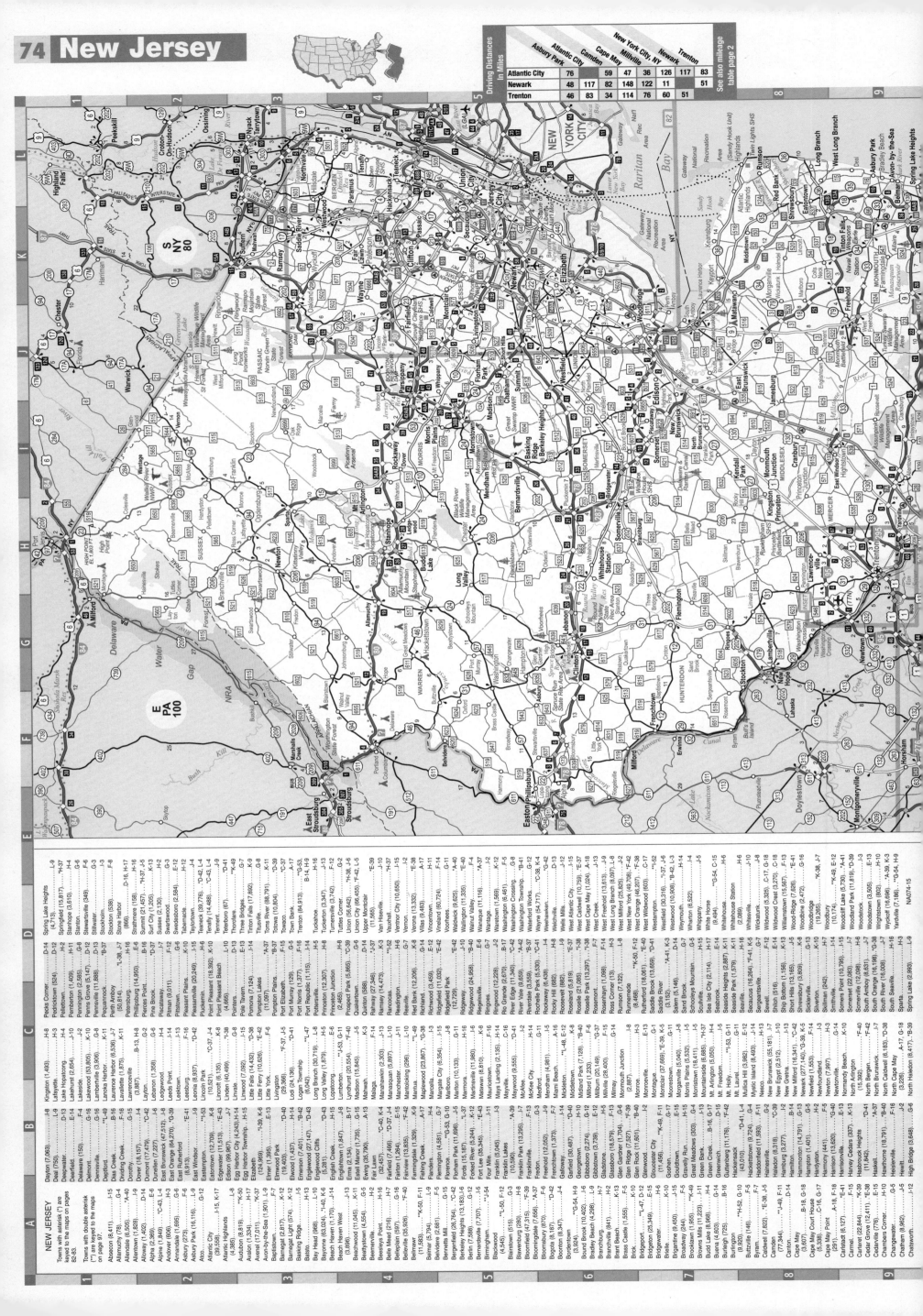

Driving Distances In Miles (See also mileage table page 2)

	Asbury Park	Atlantic City	Camden	Cape May	Millville	New York City, NY	Newark	Trenton
Atlantic City	76		59	47	36	126	117	83
Newark	48	117	82	148	122	11		51
Trenton	46	83	34	114	76	60	51	

LEGEND

Symbol	Meaning	Symbol	Meaning
95	Interstate Highway		Wildlife Refuge
	Controlled Access Hwy		Nat'l/State Park
	Controlled Access Hwy Toll		National Forest

NEW JERSEY

1:1,538,560

Scale in Miles
Scale in Kilometers

ATLANTIC CITY

1:47,520

Scale in Miles
Scale in Kilometers

CASINOS

#	Casino	Ref
1	Atlantic City Club Casino Resort	J-18
2	Bally's Atlantic City	K-18
3	Bally's Wild West Casino	K-18
4	Borgata Hotel Casino & Spa	J-16
5	Caesars Atlantic City	K-18
6	Clarige Casino Hotel	K-18
7	Golden Nugget	L-16
8	Harrah's Resort	J-16
9	Resorts	K-18
10	Showboat - The Mardis Gras Casino	K-18
11	Tropicana Casino and Resort	L-18
12	Trump Plaza Hotel & Casino	L-18
13	Trump Taj Mahal Casino Hotel	L-16

CAPE MAY

1:205,920

Scale in Miles
Scale in Kilometers

TRENTON

1:205,920

Scale in Miles
Scale in Kilometers

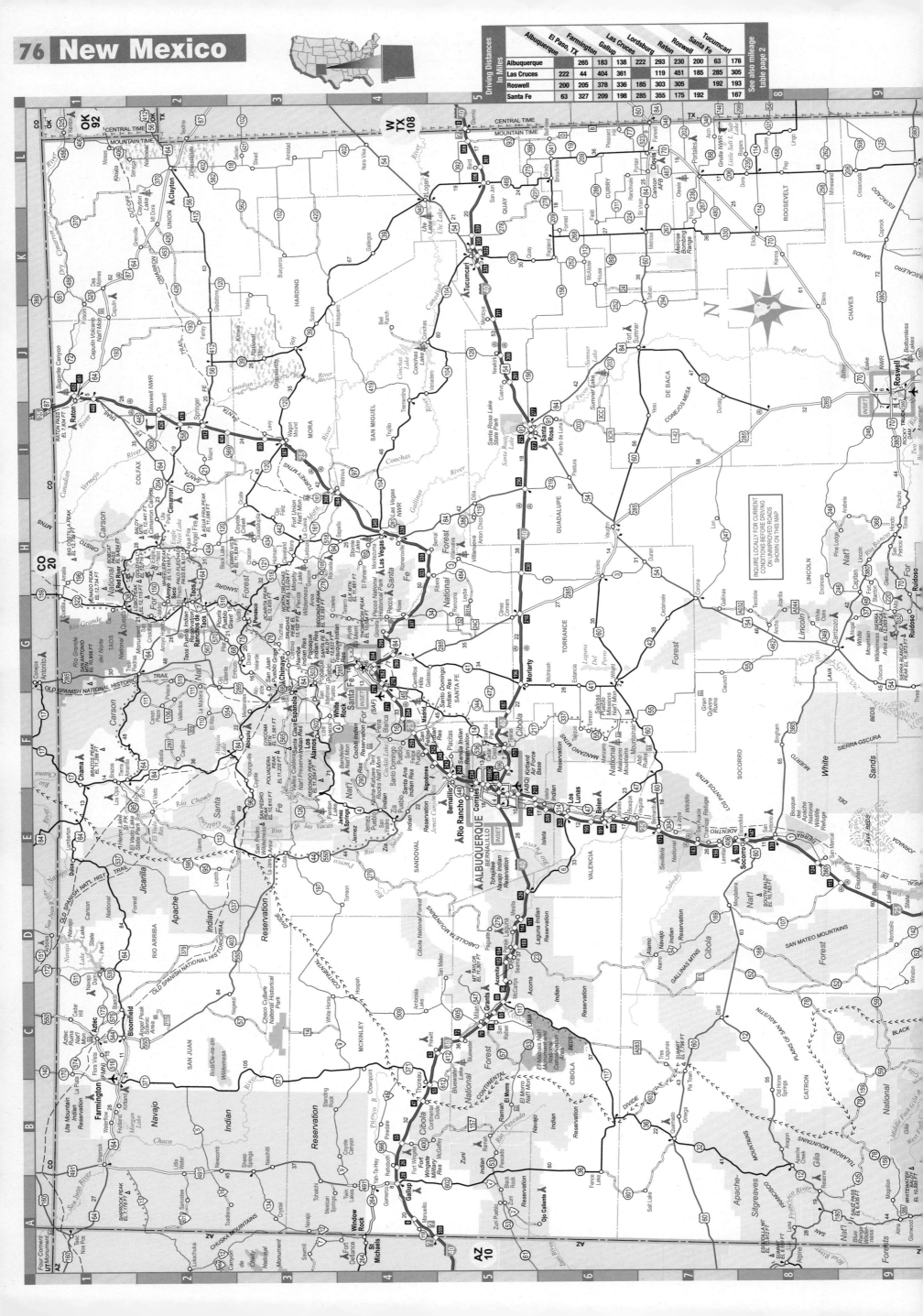

See also mileage table page 2

Driving Distances In Miles	Albuquerque	El Paso, TX	Farmington	Gallup	Las Cruces	Lordsburg	Raton	Roswell	Santa Fe	Tucumcari
Albuquerque		265	183	138	222	293	230	200	63	176
Las Cruces	222	44	404	361		119	451	185	285	305
Roswell	200	205	378	336	185	303	305		192	193
Santa Fe	63	327	209	198	285	355	175	192		167

INQUIRE LOCALLY FOR CURRENT CONDITIONS BEFORE DRIVING ON UNIMPROVED ROADS SHOWN ON THIS MAP

LEGEND

Interstate Highway	95	Wildlife Refuge	
Controlled Access Hwy		Nat'l/State Park	
Controlled Access Hwy Toll		National Forest	

NEW MEXICO

1:1,647,360

Scale in Miles
Scale in Kilometers

Abiquiu (231) D-11
Acomita H-3
Agua Fria L-2
Akela H-9
Alamo (10) H-9
Alameda G-10
Alamogordo (35,582) G-10
Albuquerque (545,852) E-5, F-15
Alcalde (285) J-10
Algodones (814) F-4
Alto I-9
Amalia J-11
Ambrosia Lake H-3
Anapra F-4
Ancho I-9
Angel Fire (1,216) H-1
Animas (237) B-14
Antelope Wells A-3
Anthony (9,360) H-5
Anton Chico (188) H-1
Apache Creek (67) B-8
Arabela J-8
Arrey (232) J-12
Arroyo Hondo H-1
Arroyo Seco J-10
Artesia (11,301) J-10
Aztec (6,763) K-1
Bard J-3
Bard (2,328) H-4
Bayard (2,328) H-4
Bell Ranch J-4
Belen (19) H-10
Bellview L-6
Bent (119) I-9
Bernalillo (8,320) H-4
Bernardo H-4
Bingham H-9
Black River Village J-12
Black Rock (1,323) A-6
Blanco (389) I-1
Bluewater (65) B-9
Boles Acres I-9
Bosque (1,638) ....
Bosque Farms (3,904) G-10
Brazos I-1
Broadview J-4
Buckhorn (200) A-10
Bueyeros J-3
Canjilon (121) D-10
Canon Plaza ....
Capitan (1,489) I-9
Caprock K-9
Carlsbad (26,138) J-11
Carrizozo (996) I-8
Causey (52) L-7
Cebolla (104) ....
Cedar Crest (956) F-6
Cedar Hill (847) I-1
Cedarvale H-7
Cerro ....
Chama (1,022) I-1
Chamberino (919) H-5
Chamical (101) H-5
Chaparral (14,631) H-5
Chilili G-3
Chimayo (3,177) J-10
Cimarron (1,021) J-2
Church L-5
Clayton (2,980) L-2
Cleveland H-1
Cliff (293) A-10
Cloudcroft (674) I-9
Clovis (37,775) L-5
Columbus (1,664) C-13
Cordova (414) ....
Corrales (8,329) F-4
Coyote (172) D-10
Coyote Canyon ....
Crownpoint (2,278) C-14
Crystal (311) A-8
Cuba (731) H-2
Cuchillo ....
Datil (54) ....
Derry ....
Des Moines (143) K-1
Dexter (1,266) J-10
Dixon (926) H-11
Dora (133) L-6
Dulce (2,743) I-1
Dunlap J-9
Duran (35) H-8
El Morro B-6
El Porvenir I-2
El Prado H-11
El Rito (808) D-11
El Valle ....
Elephant Butte (1,431) ....
Elida (197) K-8
Elkins J-9
Embudo (62) H-11
Encino (82) H-8
Escabosa ....
Espanola (10,224) H-1
Estancia (1,655) G-6
Eunice (2,922) L-11
Fairacres H-5
Farmington (45,877) ....
Faywood (33) ....
Fence Lake (42) B-7
Flora Vista (2,191) I-1
Floyd (133) L-6
Folsom (56) J-1
Forrest J-5
Fort Stanton I-9
Fort Sumner (1,031) J-7
Fort Wingate B-4
Fruitland (958) I-1
Gage F-12
Galisteo (253) ....
Gallina (158) H-2
Gallinas ....
Gallup (21,678) A-4
Gamerco (502) ....

Garfield (137) D-11
Gila (289) A-10
Gila Hot Springs. B-7
Gladstone J-2
Glencoe I-9
Glenrio (5) L-5
Glenwood (143) A-9
Glorieta (430) H-2
Grady (110) K-5
Grants (9,182) C-5
Grenville (37) K-2
Guadalupita H-1
Hachita (49) B-13
Hagerman (1,257) J-10
Hanover (167) ....
Hatch (1,648) D-12
Hernandez ....
High Rolls (834) I-9
Hillsboro (124) C-12
Hobbs (34,122) L-11
Holman H-1
Hondo (105) I-9
Hope (68) J-10
Hospah ....
Hurley (1,297) ....
Isleta ....
Jal (2,047) L-12
Jamestown ....
Jarales (2,475) ....
Jemez Pueblo ....
Jemez Springs (250) E-4
Kenna K-8
Kirtland (7,875) I-1
Kingston (32) B-12
Kirtland (7,875) I-1
La Cienega ....
La Cueva ....
La Joya (82) H-7
La Luz (1,697) I-9
La Madera (154) I-2
La Mesa (728) H-5
La Union H-5
Laguna (1,241) D-10
Lake Arthur (436) J-10
Las Cruces (97,618) E-12, E-18
Las Vegas (13,753) I-2
Lemitar (330) H-6
Levy J-3
Lindrith (128) K-10
Little Water ....
Llaves ....
Logan (1,042) J-4
Lordsburg (2,797) ....
Los Alamos (11,909) I-10
Los Lunas (14,835) E-8
Los Ojos (125) J-1
Los Padillas F-4
Loving (1,392) J-12
Lovington (11,009) L-10
Lumberton (73) I-1
Luna (158) A-8
Magdalena (938) D-7

Malaga (147) D-11
Maljamar K-10
Manuelito (29) ....
Maxwell (254) J-2
Mayhill (75) I-9
McAlister K-6
McCartys ....
McDonald L-6
McGaffey B-5
McIntosh (1,484) G-6
Medanales ....
Melrose (736) K-5
Mentmore ....
Mescalero (1,338) G-10
Mesilla (2,196) E-18
Mesita (604) ....
Mexican Springs ....
Mills ....
Milnesand (25) ....
Mimbres (667) B-11
Mogollon (15) ....
Montezuma I-2
Monticello (58) ....
Monument (206) L-11
Mora (656) I-2
Moriarty (1,910) G-5
Mosquero (93) J-3
Mountainair (928) G-7
Mt. Dora (36) ....
Nadine (200) L-11
Nageezi (287) C-10
Nara Visa (85) J-4
Naschitti (301) B-3
Navajo (2,842) A-3
Navajo Dam (281) D-5
Newcomb (339) B-2
Newkirk (7) J-5
Nogal (96) I-9
Ocate (52) I-2
Ojo Caliente (435) H-1
Ojo Feliz H-2
Old Horse Springs. B-8
Orogrande (52) H-10
Organ (323) E-12
Oscura H-9
Pastura (23) I-5
Pecos (1,392) H-2
Pena Blanca (709) F-4
Penasco (777) H-11
Peralta (3,660) F-4
Pescado ....
Petaca ....
Picacho J-9
Pie Town (186) C-7
Pilar H-11
Pinon (73) J-10
Pinos Altos (4,977) ....
Placitas (4,977) F-4
Pleasanton (151) A-9
Pojoaque Pueblo I-10
Ponderosa E-4
Portales (12,280) L-7
Prewitt D-7

St. Vrain K-7
Standing Rock. A-3
Stead L-3
Sunland Park (14,106) F-5
Sunspot ....
Taiban (130) ....
Taos (5,716) J-10
Tajique (190) G-7
Tatum (798) L-9
Tecolote I-2
Teec Nos Pos (477) ....
Tererro ....
Texico (1,130) L-5
Thoreau (1,865) B-4
Tierra Amarilla (382) I-1
Tijeras (541) F-5
Timberon ....
Tinnie ....
Tohatchi (808) A-3
Torreon (237) ....
Tres Lagunas ....
Tres Piedras H-10
Tres Ritos ....
Trujillo (73) ....
Truth or Consequences (6,475) C-11
Tucumcari (5,363) K-5
Tularosa (2,842) G-10
Twin Lakes (1,052) A-4
Tyrone (2,842) B-11
Ute Park (71) I-2
Vadito (270) H-11
Vado (541) H-5
Valdez ....
Vallecitos D-10
Varadero ....
Vaughn (446) I-7
Velarde (229) H-11
Villanueva (229) H-2
Virden (152) A-11
Wagon Mound (314) I-2
Waterflow (1,670) B-1
Weed (63) I-9
White Horse C-3
White Oaks I-9
White Rock (5,725) F-3
White Signal ....
Willard (253) G-7
Williamsburg ....
Winston (61) C-9
Yah-Ta-Hey (590) A-4
Yates ....
Youngsville (55) H-2
Zia Pueblo (737) E-4
Zuni (6,302) A-5
Zuni Pueblo (11,047) A-5

NEW MEXICO

W TX 108

E TX 86

KILOMETERS IN MEXICO
KILOMETERS x 0.62 = MILES

MEX 142

ALBUQUERQUE

1:211,760

Scale in Miles
Scale in Kilometers

ROSWELL

1:253,440

Scale in Miles
Scale in Kilometers

LAS CRUCES

1:190,080

Scale in Miles
Scale in Kilometers

SANTA FE

1:88,704

Scale in Miles
Scale in Kilometers

CARLSBAD CAVERNS NATIONAL PARK

1:190,080

Scale in Miles
Scale in Kilometers

NA076-15

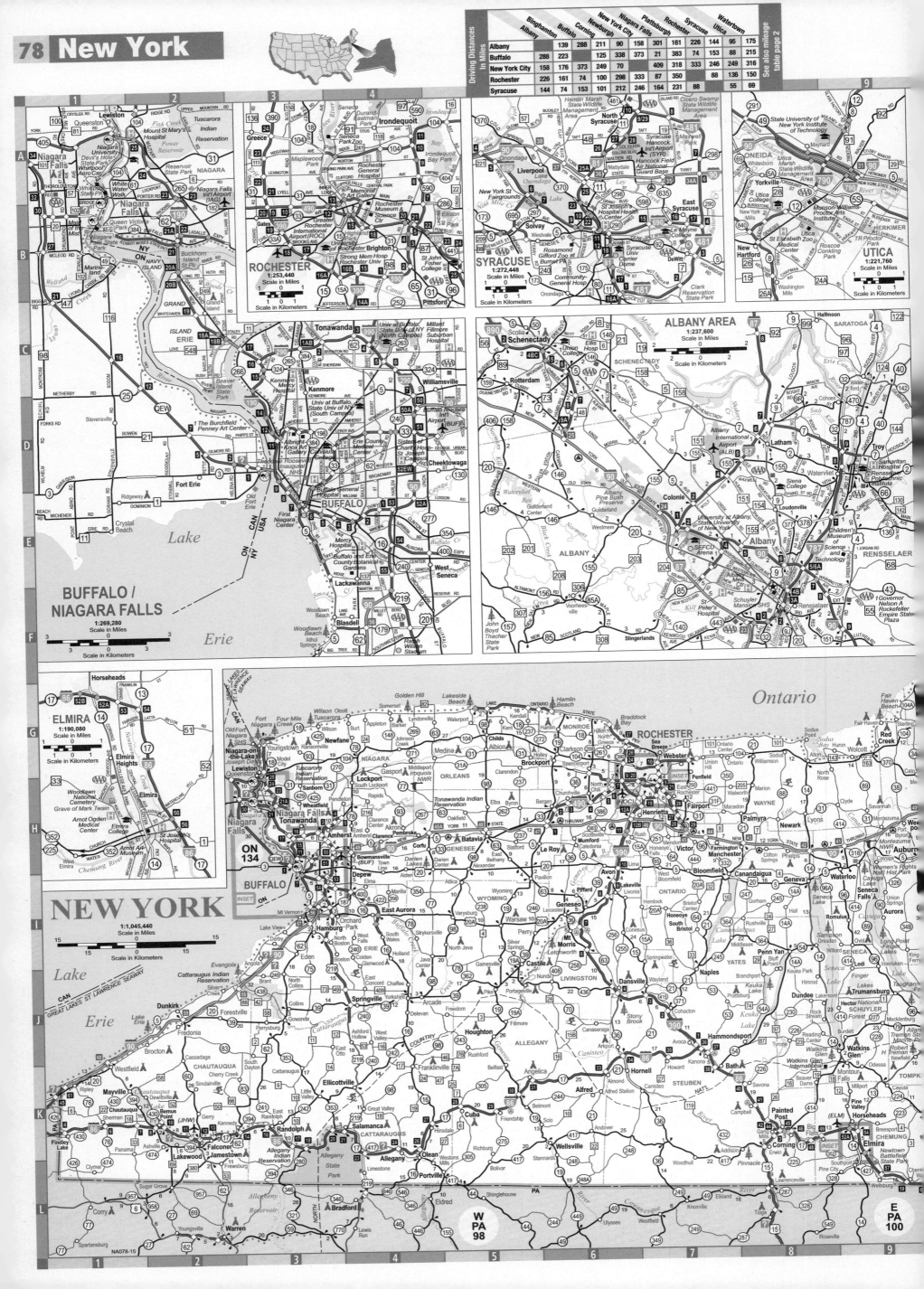

Driving Distances In Miles	Albany	Binghamton	Buffalo	Corning	Newburgh	New York City	Niagara Falls	Plattsburgh	Rochester	Syracuse	Utica	Watertown
Albany		139	288	211	90	158	301	161	226	144	95	175
Buffalo	288	223		125	338	373	21	383	74	153	88	215
New York City	158	176	373	249	70		409	318	333	246	249	316
Rochester	226	161	74	100	298	333	87	350		88	136	150
Syracuse	144	74	153	101	212	246	164	231	88		55	69

See also mileage table page 2

LEGEND

Interstate Highway
Controlled Access Hwy
Controlled Access Hwy Toll
Wildlife Refuge
Nat'l/State Park
National Forest

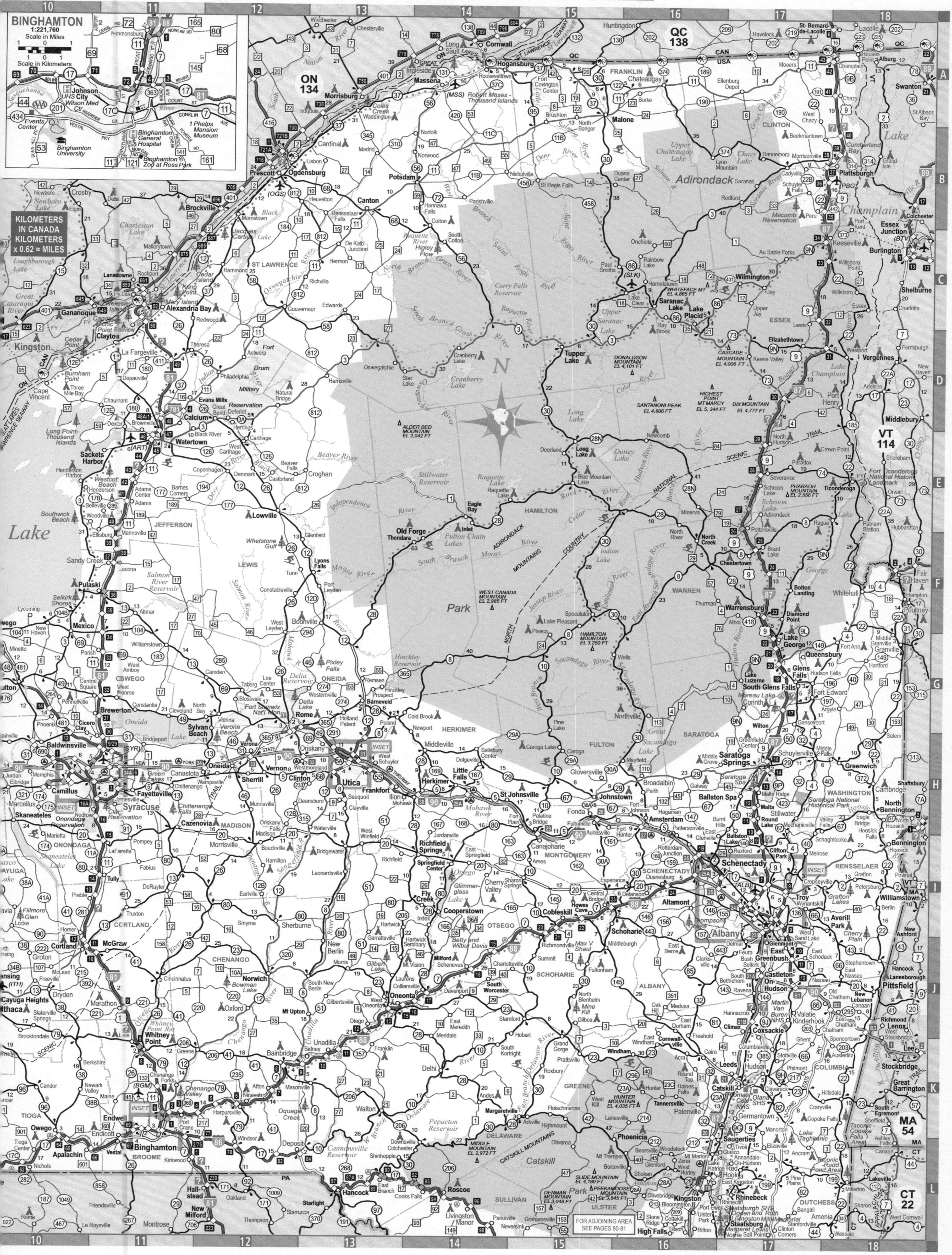

BINGHAMTON 1:221,760
Scale in Miles
Scale in Kilometers

KILOMETERS IN CANADA
KILOMETERS x 0.62 = MILES

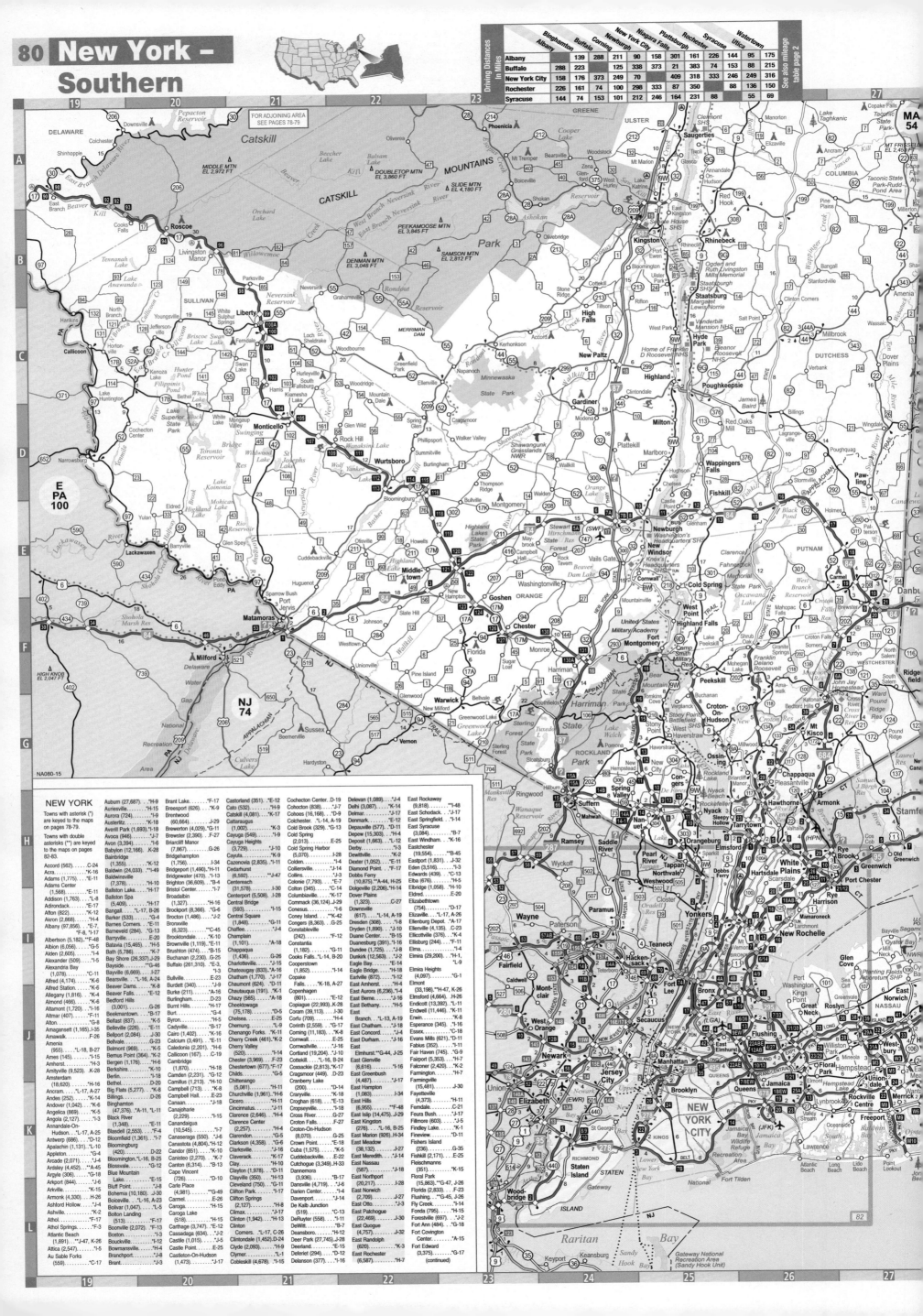

Driving Distances in Miles	Albany	Binghamton	Buffalo	Corning	Newburgh	New York City	Niagara Falls	Plattsburgh	Rochester	Syracuse	Utica	Watertown
Albany		139	288	211	90	158	301	161	226	144	95	175
Buffalo	288	223		125	338	373	21	383	74	153	88	215
New York City	158	176	373	249	70		409	318	333	246	249	316
Rochester	226	161	74	100	298	333	87	350		88	136	150
Syracuse	144	74	153	101	212	246	164	231	88		55	69

See also mileage table page 2

LEGEND

Interstate Highway	95 Wildlife Refuge
Controlled Access Hwy	Nat'l/State Park
Controlled Access Hwy Toll	National Forest

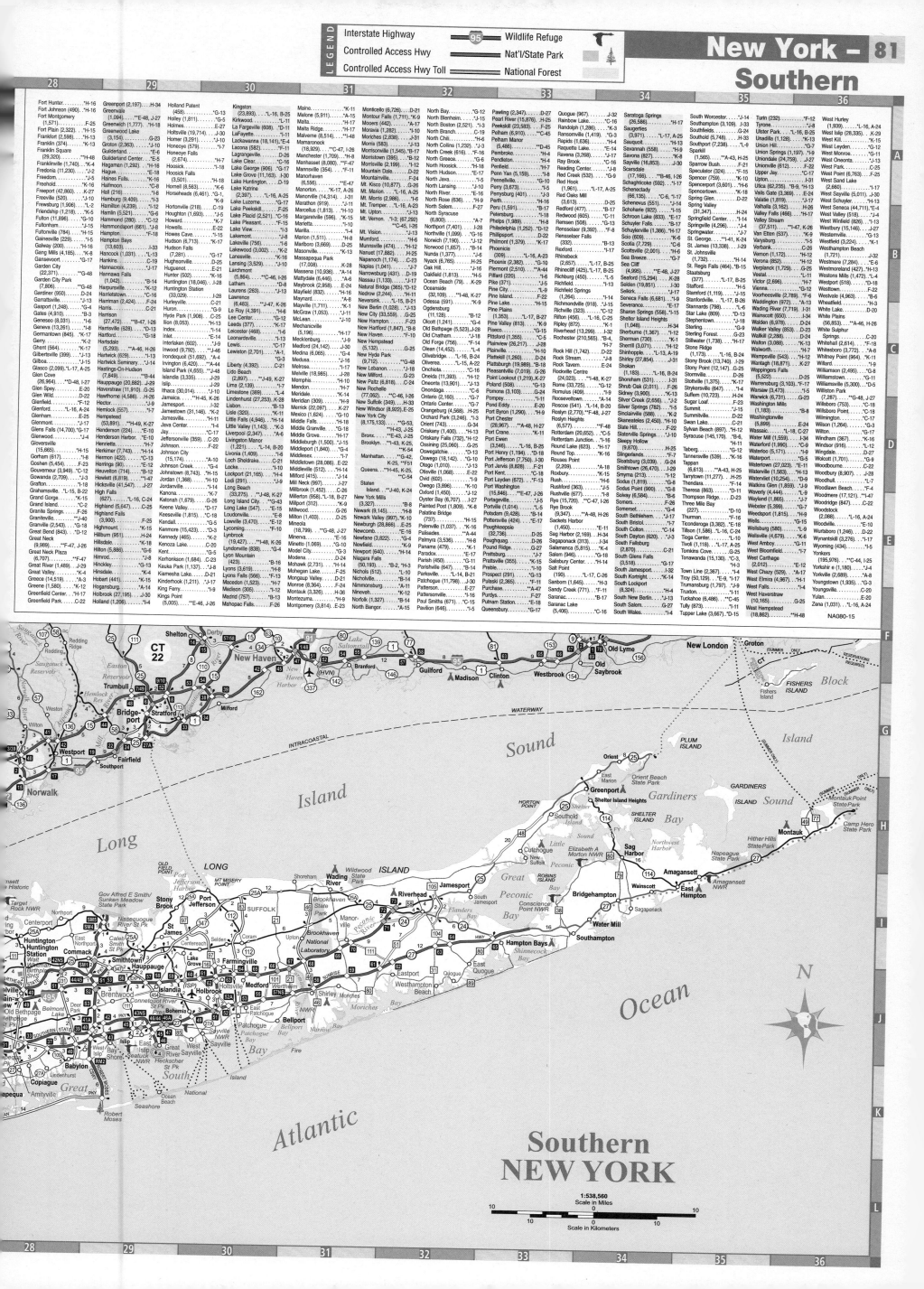

Southern
NEW YORK

1:538,560
Scale in Miles
Scale in Kilometers

NA080-15

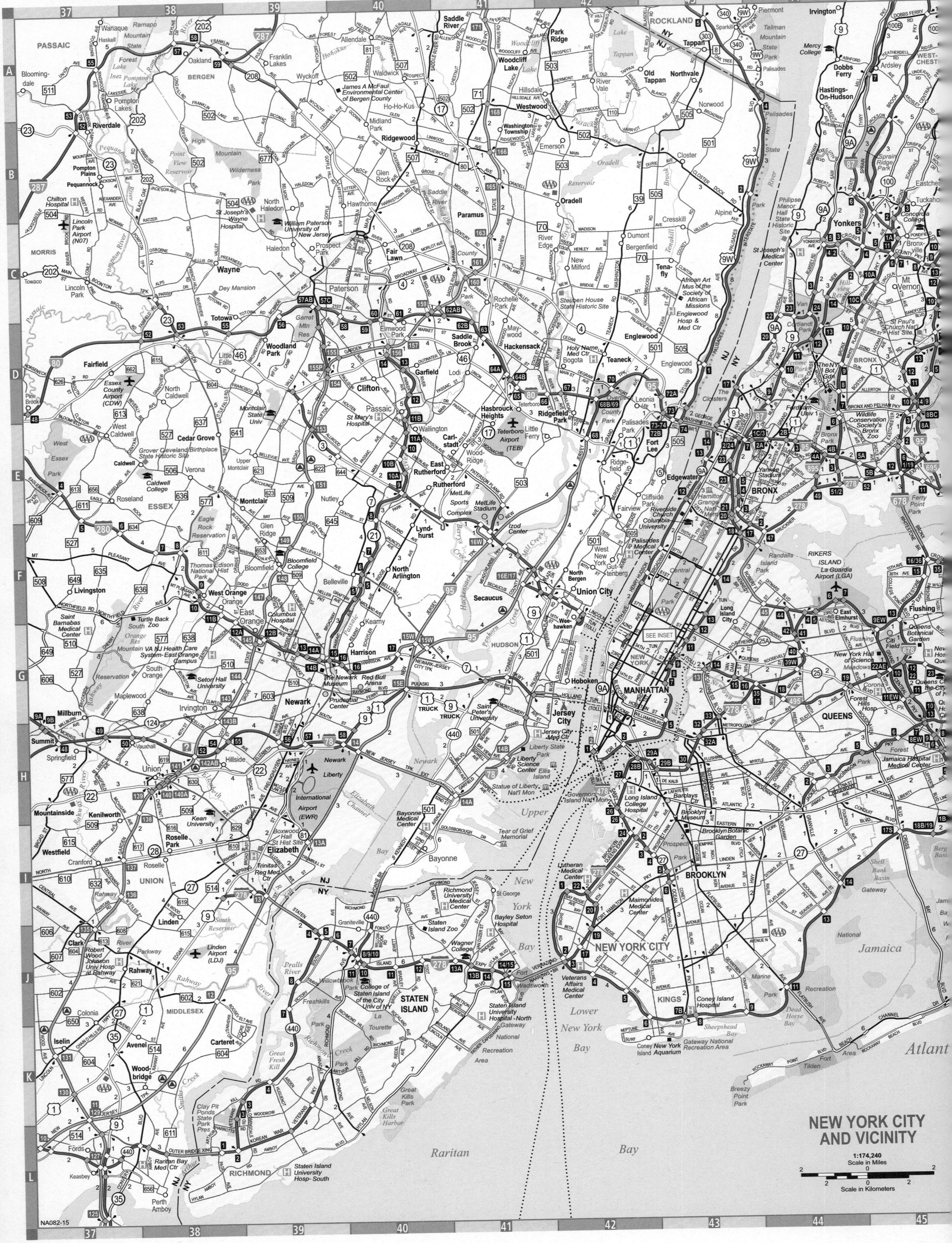
NEW YORK CITY
AND VICINITY
1:174,240
Scale in Miles
Scale in Kilometers
NA082-15
PASSAIC
BERGEN
MORRIS
ESSEX
UNION
MIDDLESEX
HUDSON
ROCKLAND
RICHMOND
QUEENS
BRONX
BROOKLYN
MANHATTAN
NEW YORK CITY
STATEN ISLAND
KINGS
NEW YORK
Paterson
Clifton
Passaic
Hackensack
Teaneck
Englewood
Fort Lee
Union City
Hoboken
Jersey City
Newark
Elizabeth
Bayonne
Linden
Rahway
Yonkers
Mt Vernon
Wayne
Paramus
Ridgewood
Montclair
West Orange
East Orange
Irvington
Secaucus
Kearny
Harrison
Rutherford
Lyndhurst
Nutley
Belleville
Bloomfield
Livingston
Millburn
Summit
Union
Cranford
Westfield
Woodbridge
Carteret
Perth Amboy
Palisades Interstate Park
Newark Liberty International Airport (EWR)
La Guardia Airport (LGA)
Teterboro Airport (TEB)
Linden Airport (LDJ)
Essex County Airport (CDW)
Lincoln Park Airport (N07)
MetLife Stadium
Statue of Liberty Nat'l Mon
Ellis Island
Governors Island Nat'l Mon
Upper Bay
Lower New York Bay
Raritan Bay
Jamaica Bay
Newark Bay
Atlant
Hudson River
Rikers Island
Fort Tilden
Breezy Point Park
Coney Island
Sheepshead Bay
Gateway National Recreation Area
Great Kills Park
Freshkills Park
Clay Pit Ponds State Park Pres
Tallman Mountain State Park
Bronx Park
Van Cortlandt Park
Forest Park
Marine Park
SEE INSET
NJ
NY

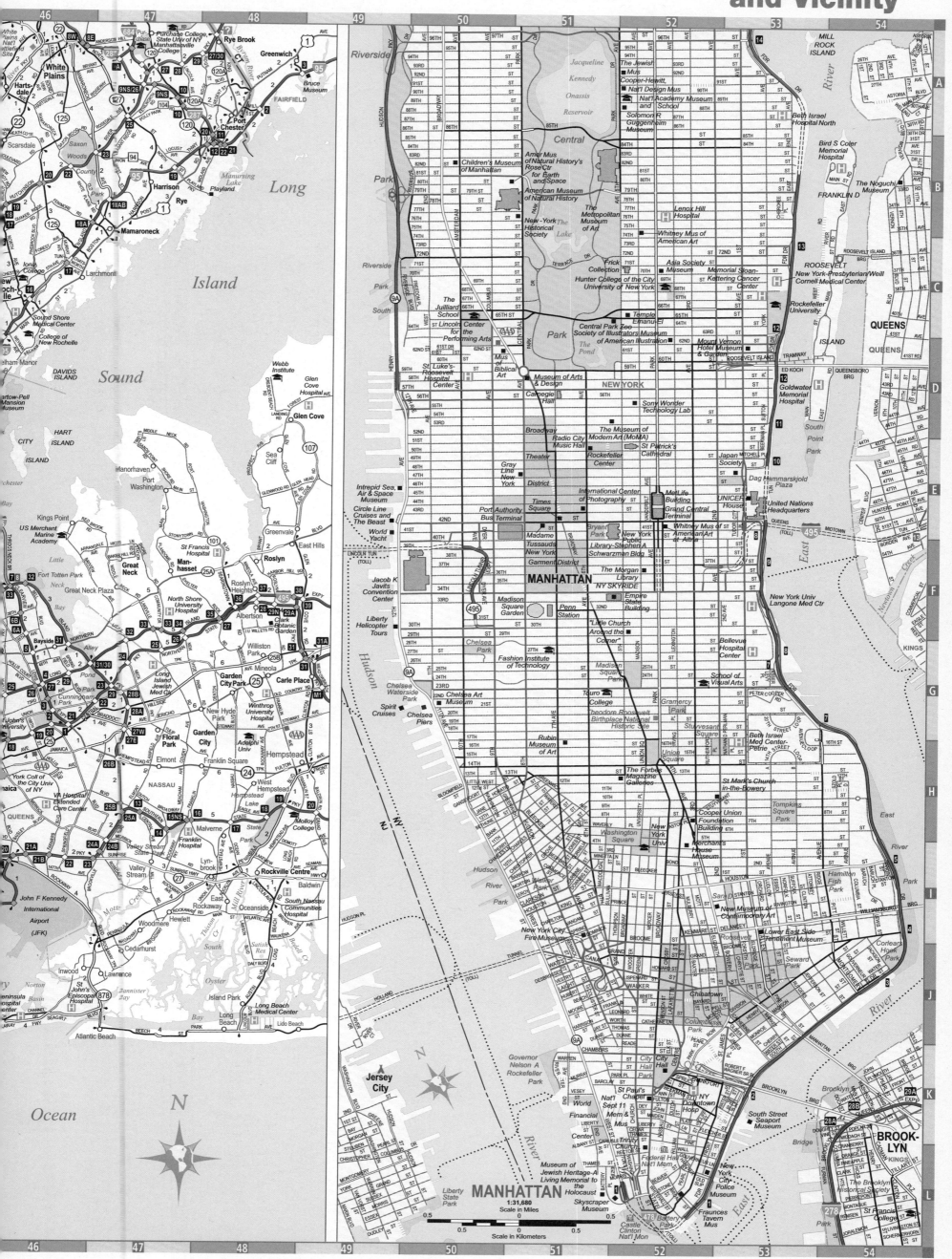

MANHATTAN
1:31,680
Scale in Miles
0.5   0.5
Scale in Kilometers
0.5   0.5

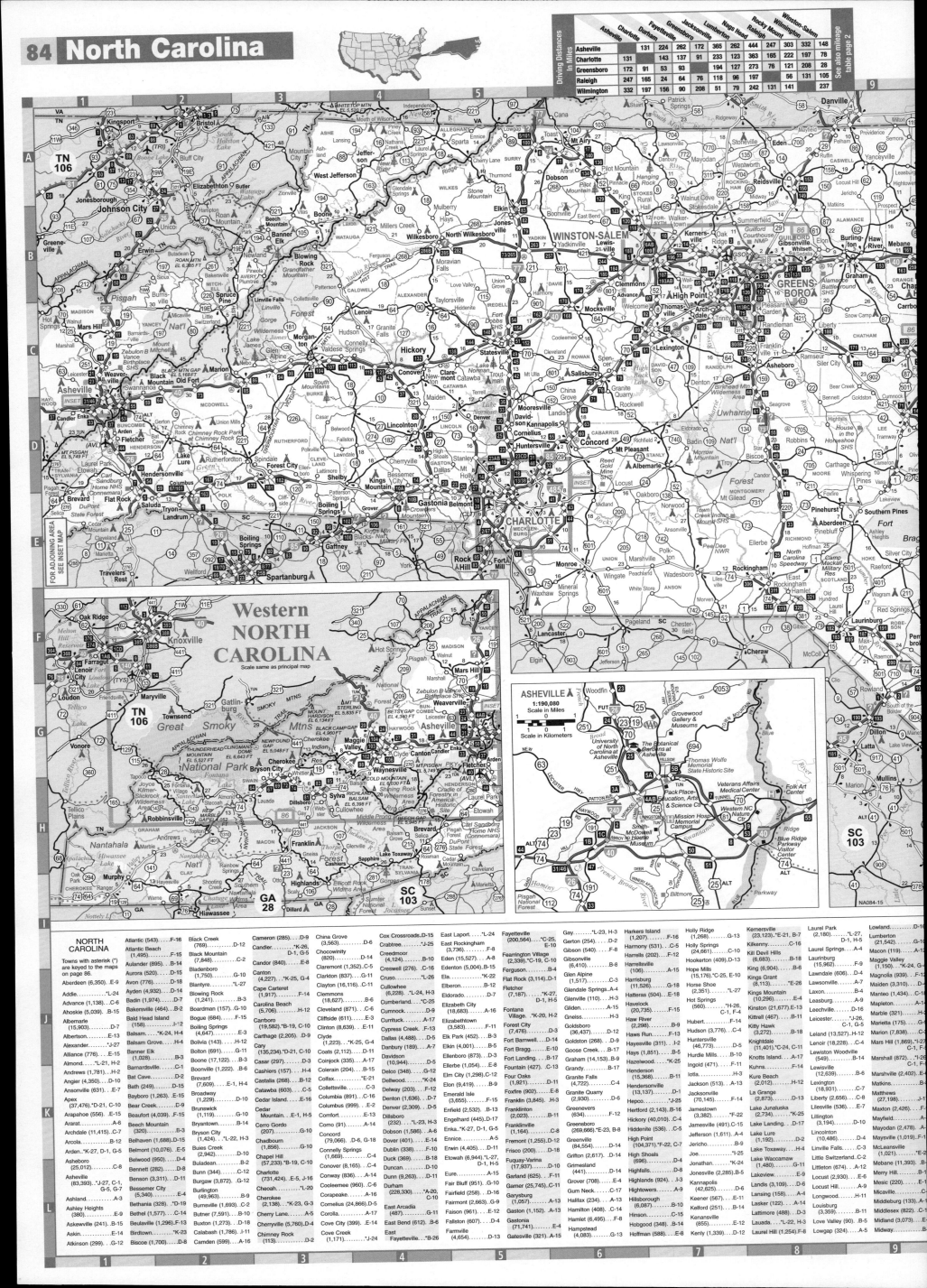

RALEIGH / DURHAM / CHAPEL HILL AREA
1:348,480
Scale in Miles
Scale in Kilometers

FAYETTEVILLE
1:253,440
Scale in Miles
Scale in Kilometers

TRIAD AREA
1:380,160
Scale in Miles
Scale in Kilometers

WILMINGTON
1:237,600
Scale in Miles
Scale in Kilometers

GREAT SMOKY MOUNTAINS NATIONAL PARK
1:570,240
Scale in Miles
Scale in Kilometers

Driving Distances In Miles	Bismarck	Churchs Ferry	Dickinson	Fargo	Grand Forks	Jamestown	Minot	Williston
Bismarck		211	99	197	272	102	110	228
Fargo	197	184	293		81	97	269	393
Grand Forks	272	108	369	81		166	212	336

See also mileage table on page 2

See also mileage table page 2

Driving Distances In Miles

	Akron	Cambridge	Canton	Cincinnati	Cleveland	Columbus	Dayton	Lima	Mansfield	Portsmouth	Toledo	Youngstown
Cincinnati	232	184	236		248	106	54	126	172	108	203	279
Cleveland	34	119	60	248		143	213	174	81	232	115	74
Columbus	126	79	128	106	143		75	103	66	90	143	173
Toledo	139	193	159	203	115	143	149	78	118	234		172
Youngstown	49	121	58	279	74	173	243	204	112	263	172	

See also mileage table page 2

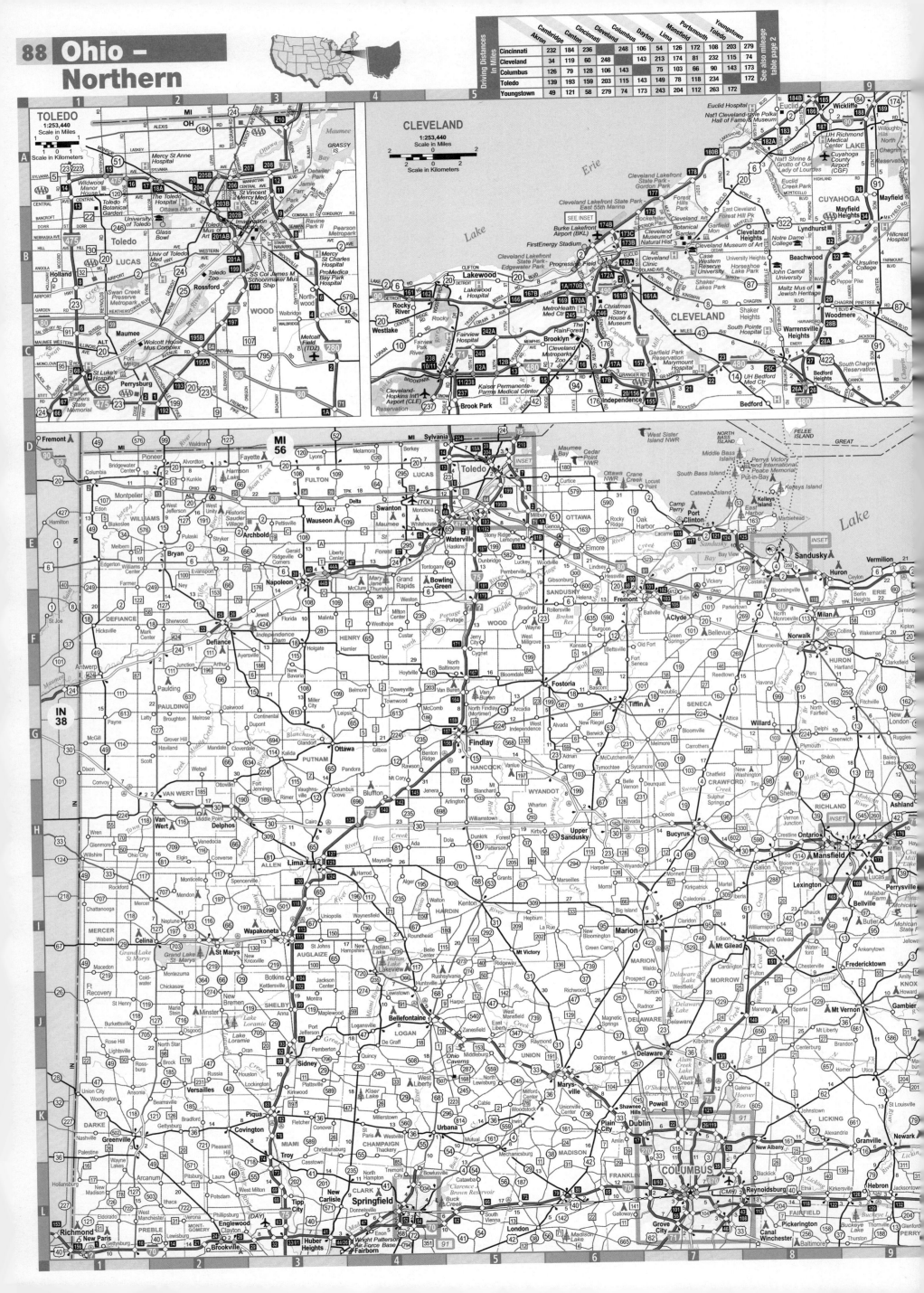

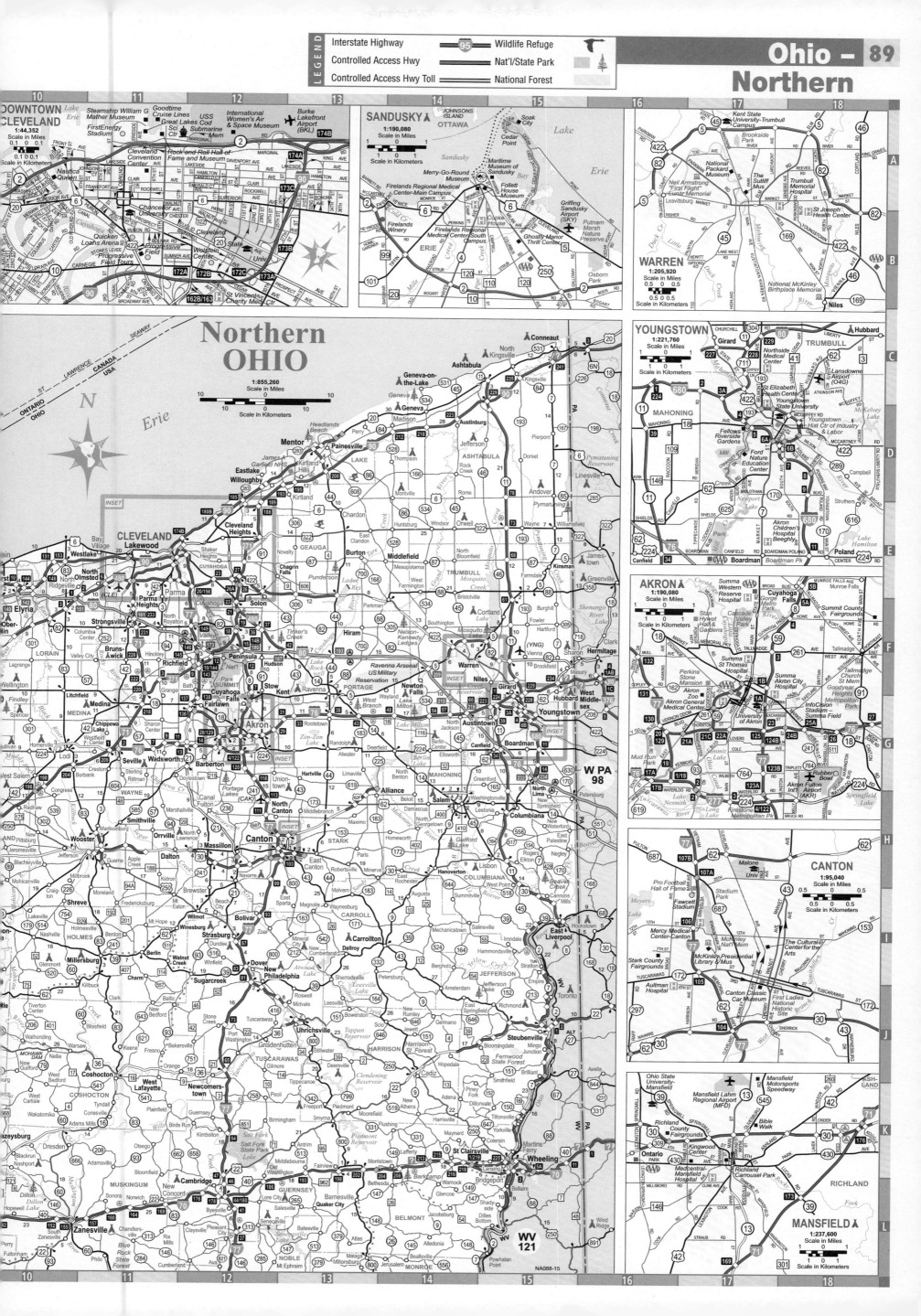

LEGEND

Interstate Highway		Wildlife Refuge	
Controlled Access Hwy		Nat'l/State Park	
Controlled Access Hwy Toll		National Forest	

DOWNTOWN CLEVELAND
1:44,352
Scale in Miles

SANDUSKY
1:190,080
Scale in Miles

Northern OHIO
1:855,260
Scale in Miles

WARREN
1:205,920
Scale in Miles

YOUNGSTOWN
1:221,760
Scale in Miles

AKRON
1:190,080
Scale in Kilometers

CANTON
1:95,040
Scale in Miles

MANSFIELD
1:237,600
Scale in Miles

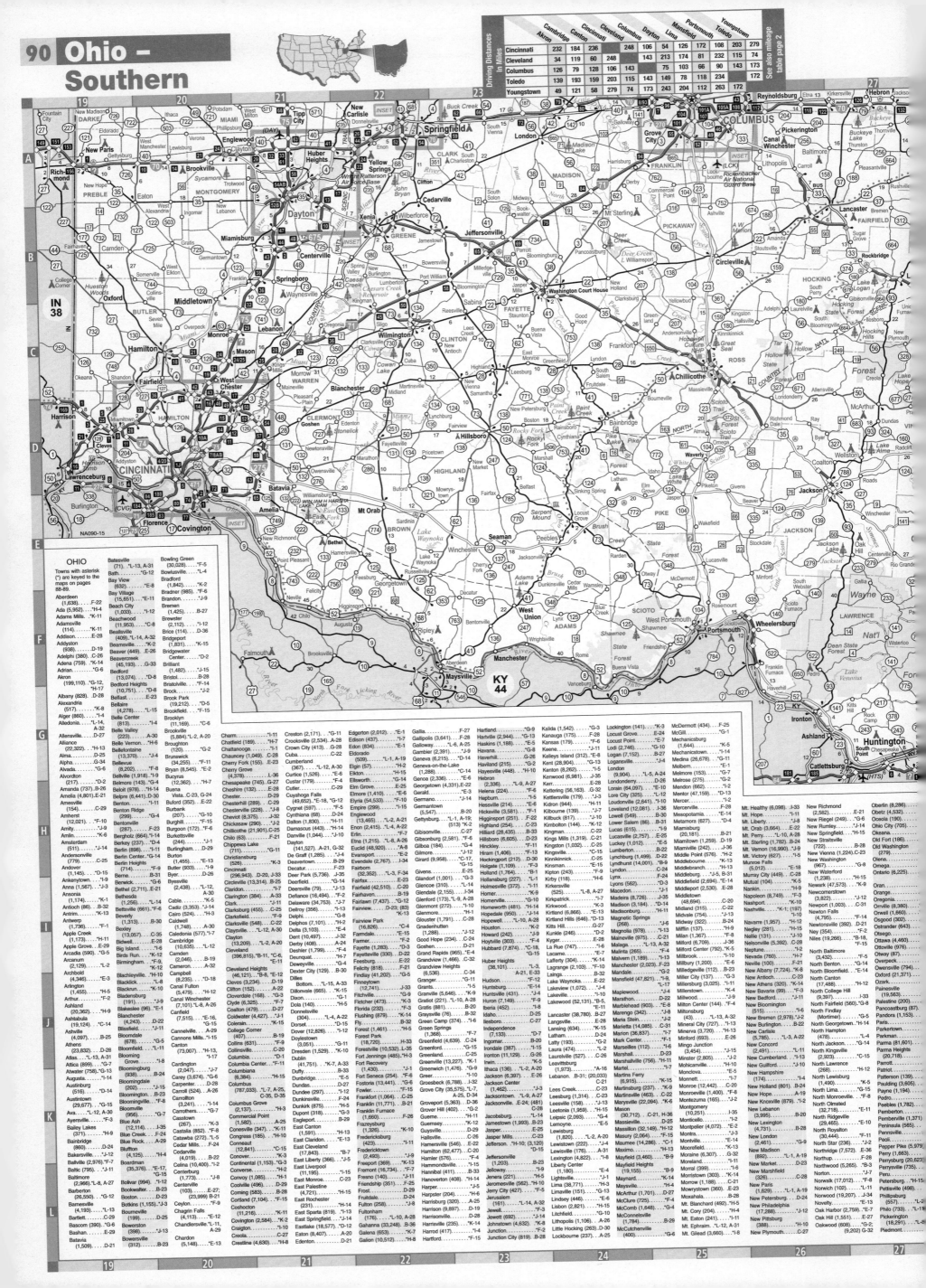

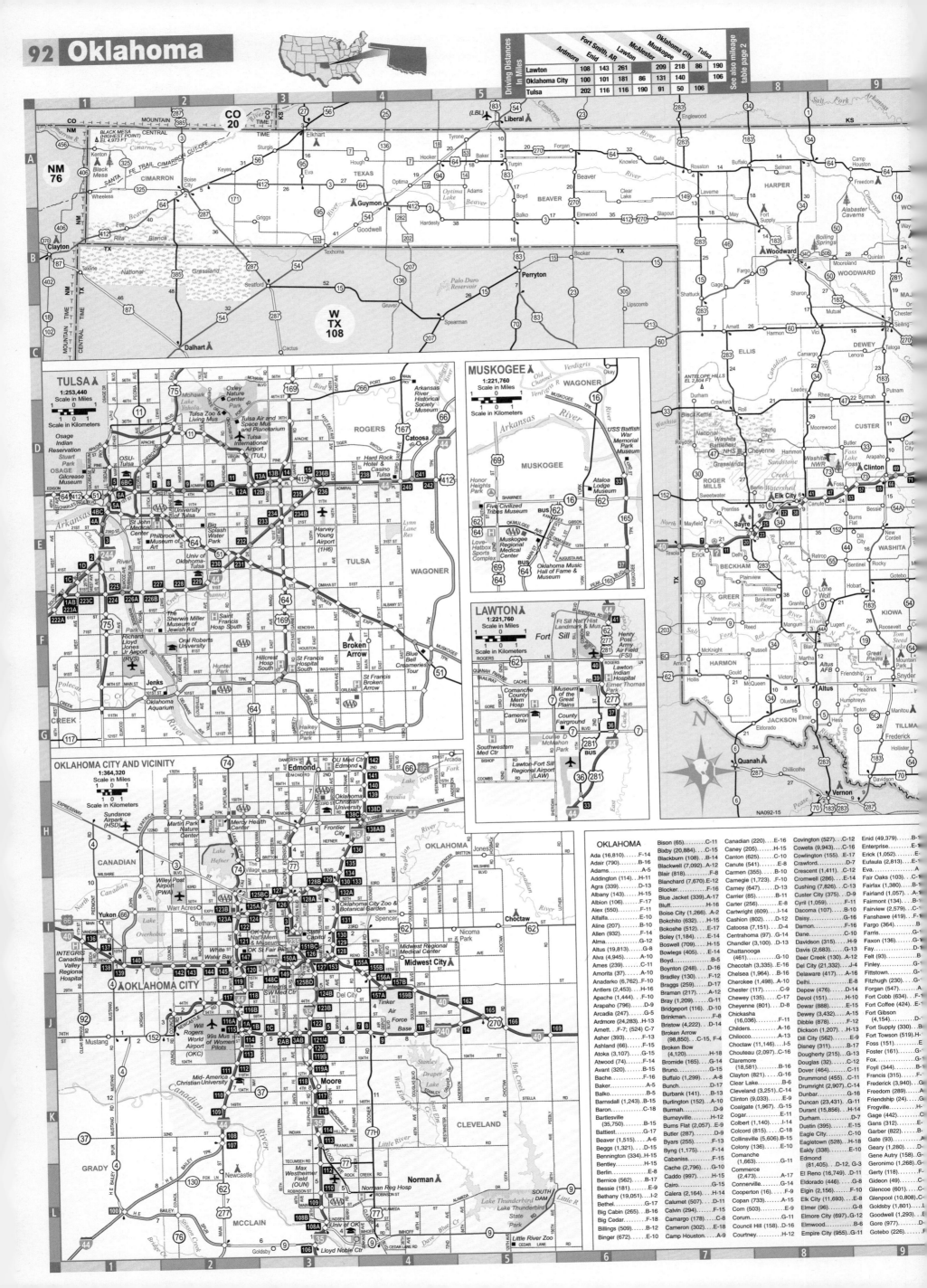

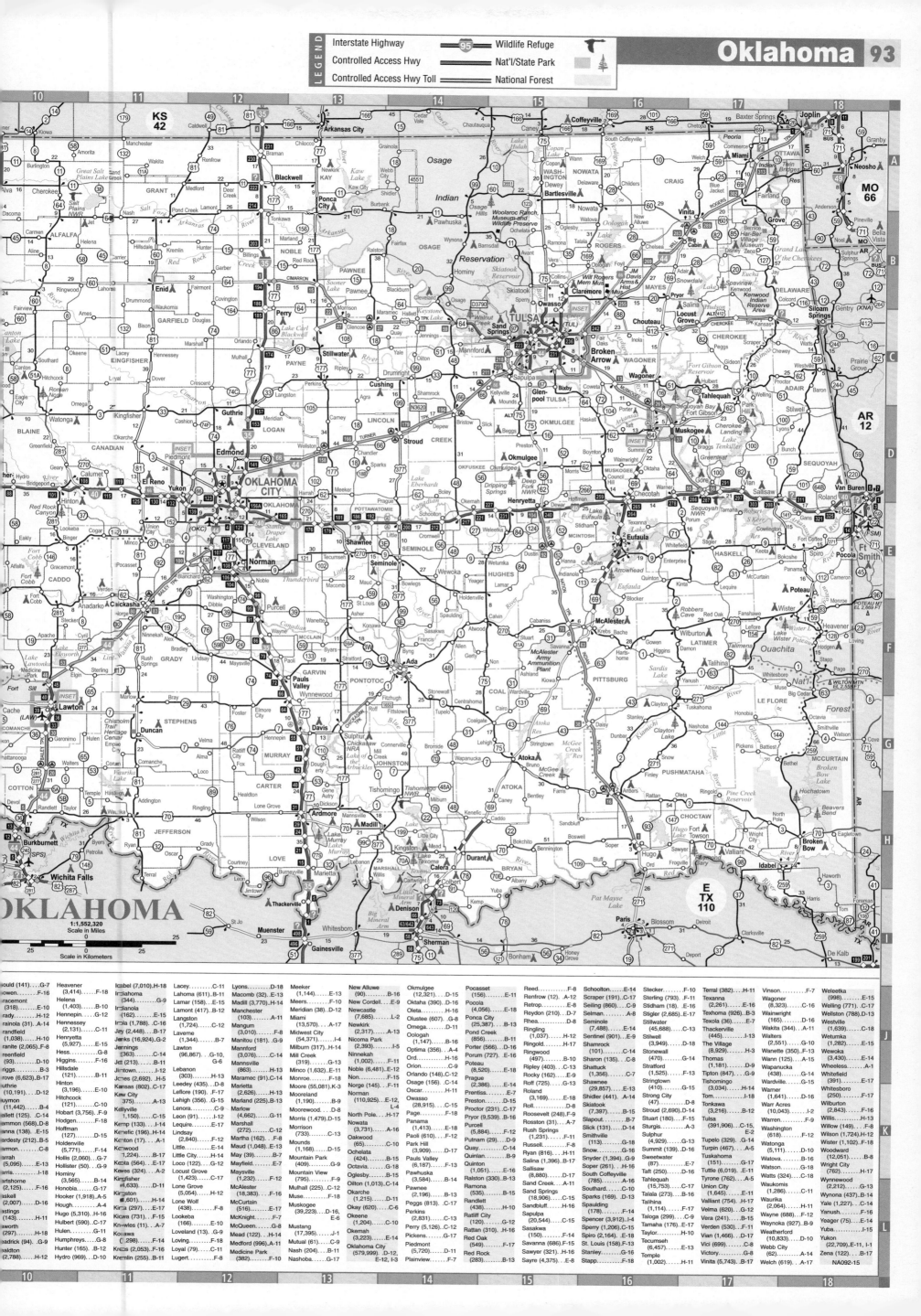

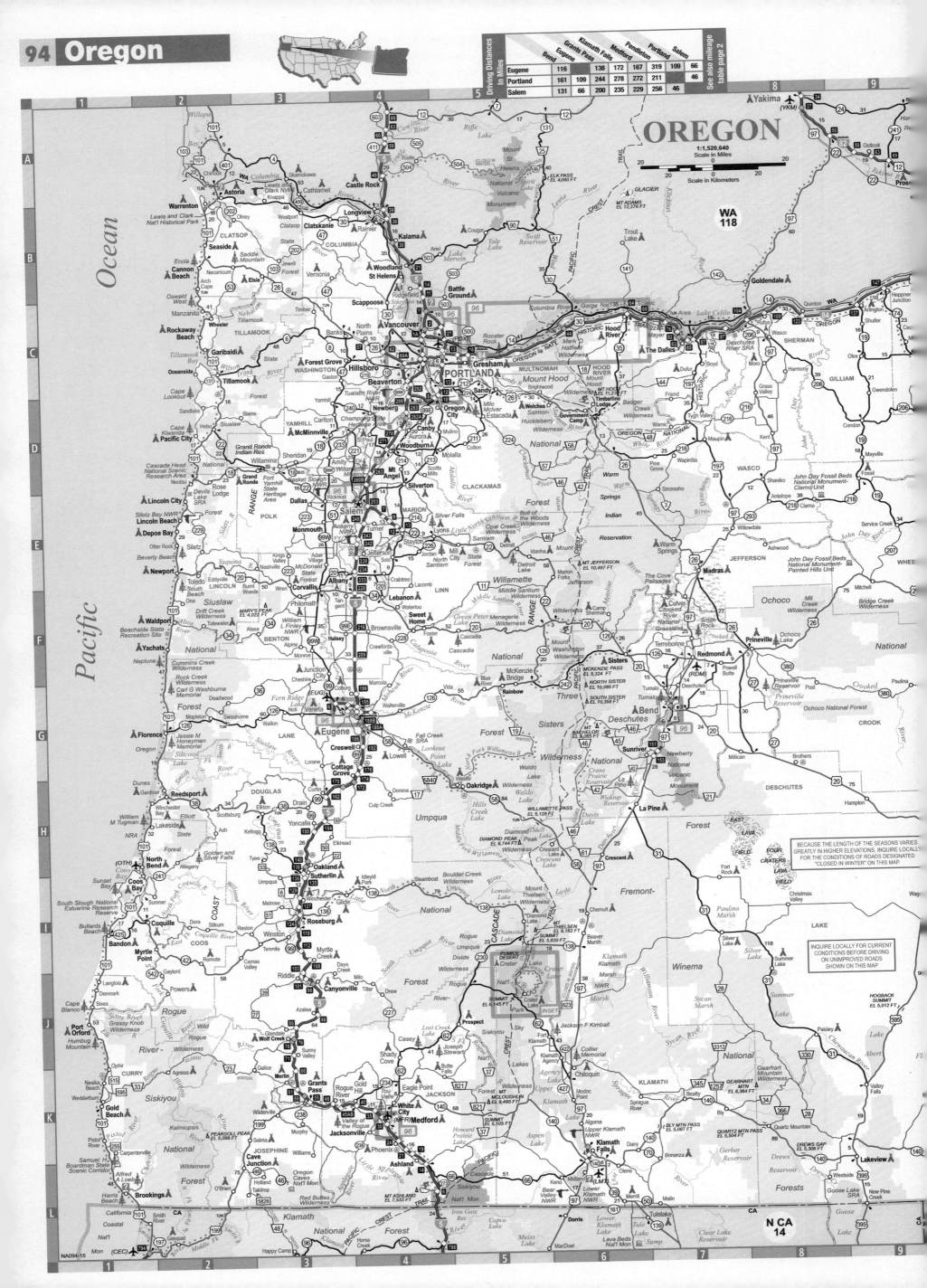

OREGON

1:1,520,640
Scale in Miles

Scale in Kilometers

See also mileage table page 2

Driving Distances In Miles	Bend	Eugene	Grants Pass	Klamath Falls	Medford	Pendleton	Portland	Salem
Eugene	116		138	172	167	319	109	66
Portland	161	109	244	278	272	211		46
Salem	131	66	200	235	229	256	46	

BECAUSE THE LENGTH OF THE SEASONS VARIES GREATLY IN HIGHER ELEVATIONS, INQUIRE LOCALLY FOR THE CONDITIONS OF ROADS DESIGNATED "CLOSED IN WINTER" ON THIS MAP.

INQUIRE LOCALLY FOR CURRENT CONDITIONS BEFORE DRIVING ON UNIMPROVED ROADS SHOWN ON THIS MAP

WA 118

N CA 14

NA094-15

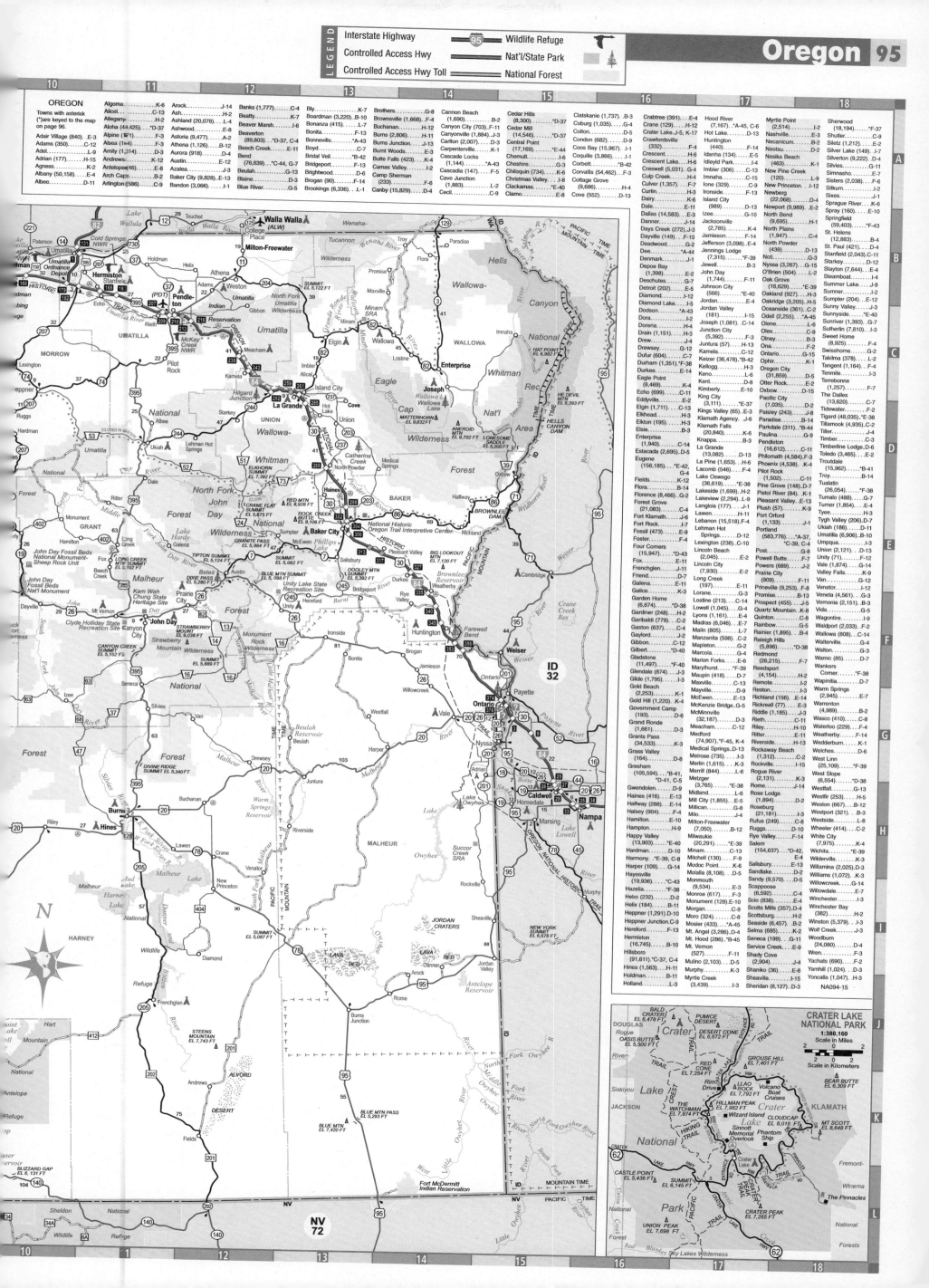

DOWNTOWN PORTLAND
1:63,360
Scale in Miles
0.2   0   0.2
Scale in Kilometers

COLUMBIA RIVER AREA OR / WA
1:633,600
Scale in Miles
4   0   4
Scale in Kilometers

SALEM OR
1:190,080
Scale in Miles
1   0   1
Scale in Kilometers

BEND OR
1:190,080
Scale in Miles
1   0   1
Scale in Kilometers

EUGENE OR
1:196,416
Scale in Miles
1   0   1
Scale in Kilometers

MEDFORD OR
1:190,080
Scale in Miles
0.8   0   0.8
Scale in Kilometers

PORTLAND, OR & VICINITY
1:253,440
Scale in Miles
2   0   2
Scale in Kilometers

WILKES-BARRE PA
1:158,400
Scale in Miles
0.6   0   0.6
Scale in Kilometers

SCRANTON PA
1:253,440
Scale in Miles
0.6   0   0.6
Scale in Kilometers

ALLENTOWN / BETHLEHEM, PA
1:237,600
Scale in Miles
1   0   1
Scale in Kilometers

HARRISBURG, PA
1:139,392
Scale in Miles
0.6   0   0.6
Scale in Kilometers

HERSHEY, PA
1:110,880
Scale in Miles
0.5   0   0.5
Scale in Kilometers

YORK, PA
1:174,240
Scale in Miles
0.7   0   0.7
Scale in Kilometers

LANCASTER PA

PA DUTCH COUNTRY
1:174,240
Scale in Miles
1   0   1
Scale in Kilometers

NA096-15

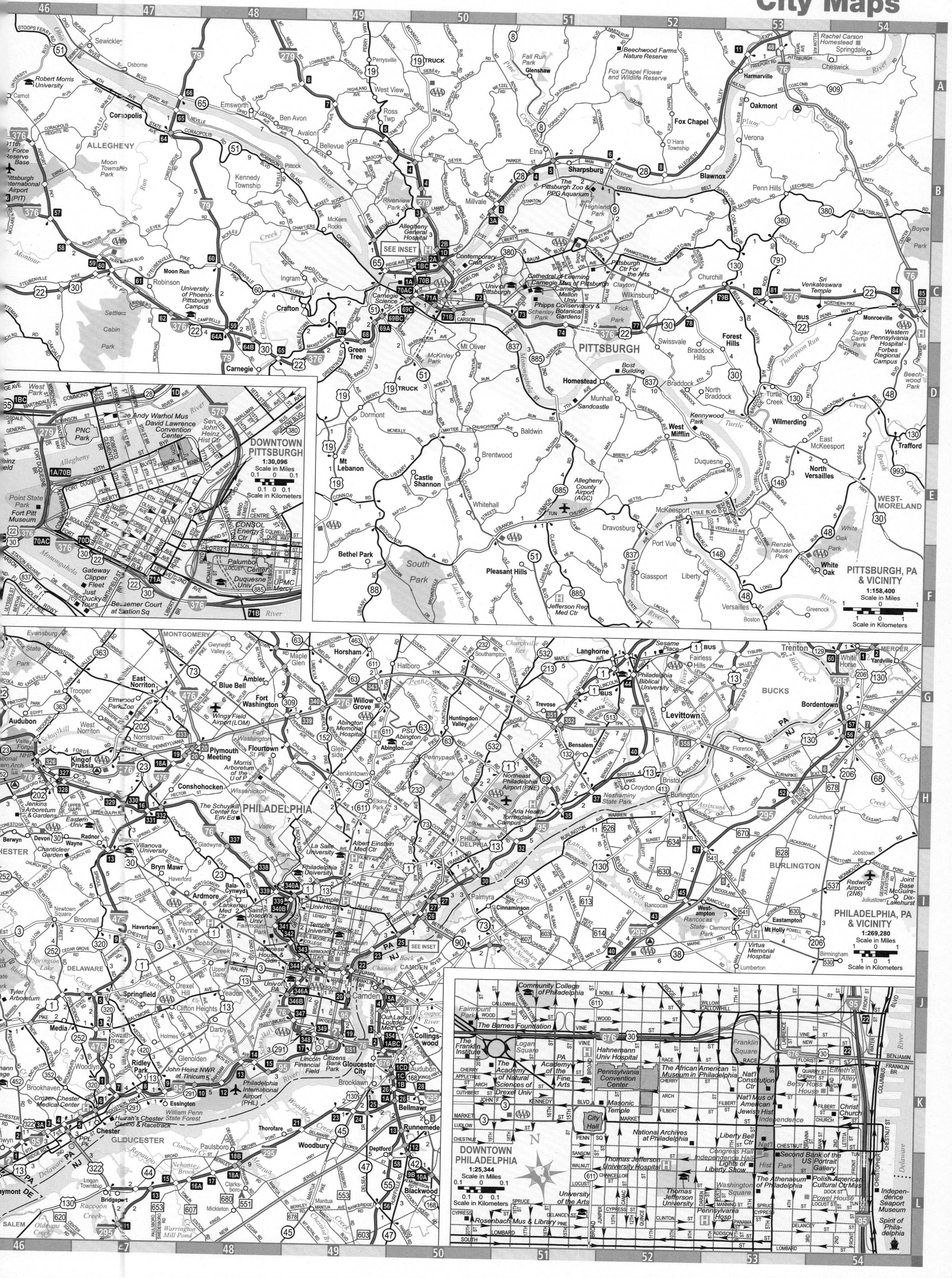

DOWNTOWN PITTSBURGH
1:30,096
Scale in Miles
Scale in Kilometers

PITTSBURGH, PA & VICINITY
1:158,400
Scale in Miles
Scale in Kilometers

PHILADELPHIA, PA & VICINITY
1:269,280
Scale in Miles
Scale in Kilometers

DOWNTOWN PHILADELPHIA
1:25,344
Scale in Miles
Scale in Kilometers

Driving Distances in Miles

	Allentown	Altoona	Erie	Gettysburg	Harrisburg	Johnstown	Lancaster	Philadelphia	Pittsburgh	Reading	Scranton	York
Erie	372	205		307	297	178	335	420	128	353	322	327
Harrisburg	84	135	297	38		135	40	112	204	63	124	24
Philadelphia	63	236	420	140	112	237	71		305	59	125	102
Pittsburgh	284	97	128	185	204	67	238	305		262	282	221
Scranton	76	189	322	160	124	233	132	125	282	101		147

See also mileage table page 2

Western PENNSYLVANIA

Scale 1:792,000

STATE COLLEGE
Scale 1:158,400

ALTOONA
Scale 1:190,080

ERIE
Scale 1:221,760

WESTERN PENNSYLVANIA

Towns with an asterisk (*) are keyed to the maps on pages 96–97.

LEGEND

Interstate Highway	Wildlife Refuge
Controlled Access Hwy	Nat'l/State Park
Controlled Access Hwy Toll	National Forest

FOR ADJOINING AREA SEE PAGES 100-101

Driving Distances In Miles

	Allentown	Altoona	Gettysburg / Erie	Harrisburg	Johnstown	Lancaster	Philadelphia	Pittsburgh	Reading	Scranton	York
Erie	372	205	307	297	178	335	420	128	353	322	327
Harrisburg	84	135	297	38	135	40	112	204	63	124	24
Philadelphia	63	236	420	140	112	237	71	305	59	125	221
Pittsburgh	284	97	128	185	204	67	238	305	262	282	221
Scranton	76	189	322	160	124	233	132	125	282	101	147

See also mileage table page 2

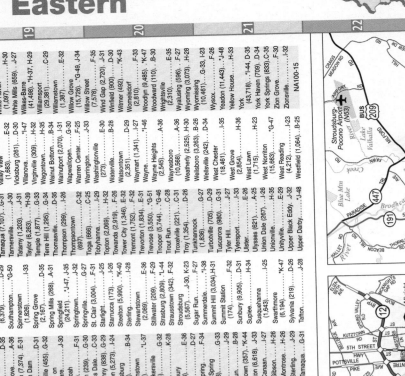

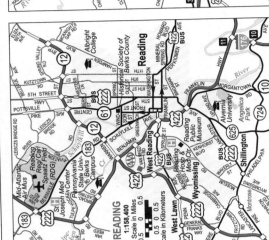

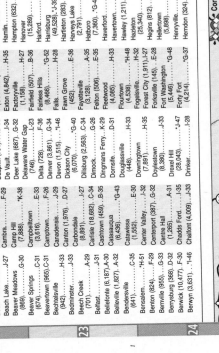

Eastern PENNSYLVANIA

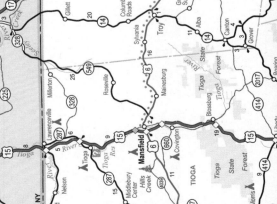
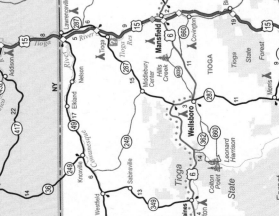

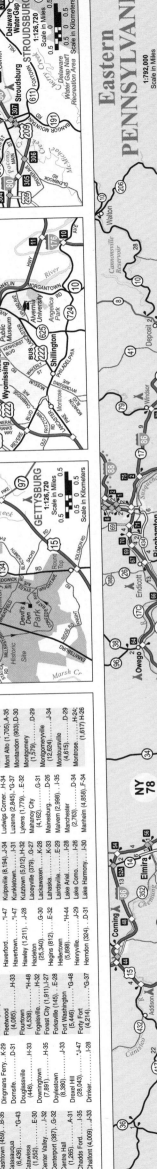

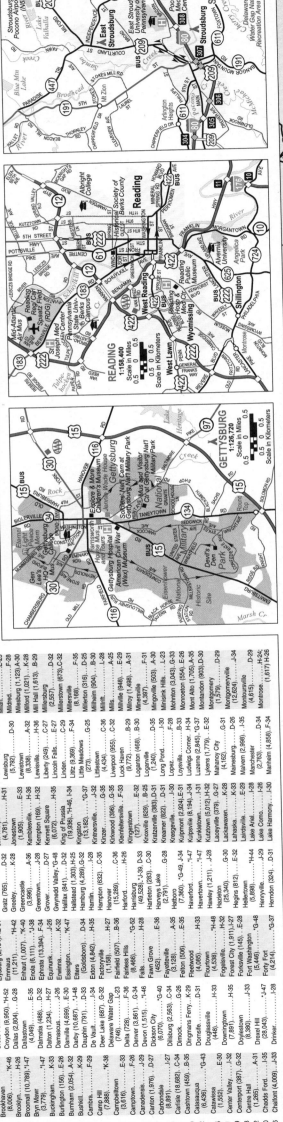

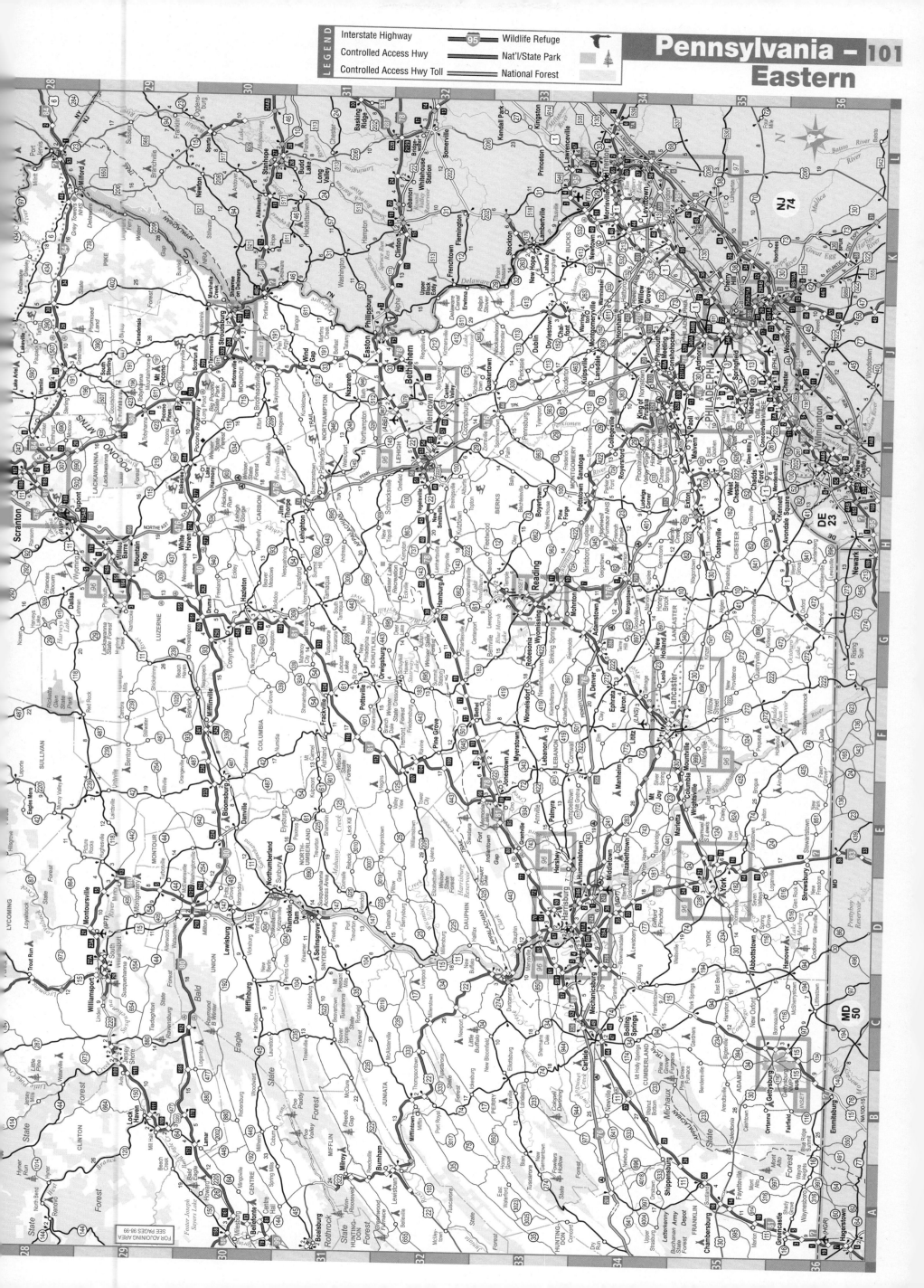

LEGEND

Interstate Highway	95 Wildlife Refuge
Controlled Access Hwy	Nat'l/State Park
Controlled Access Hwy Toll	National Forest

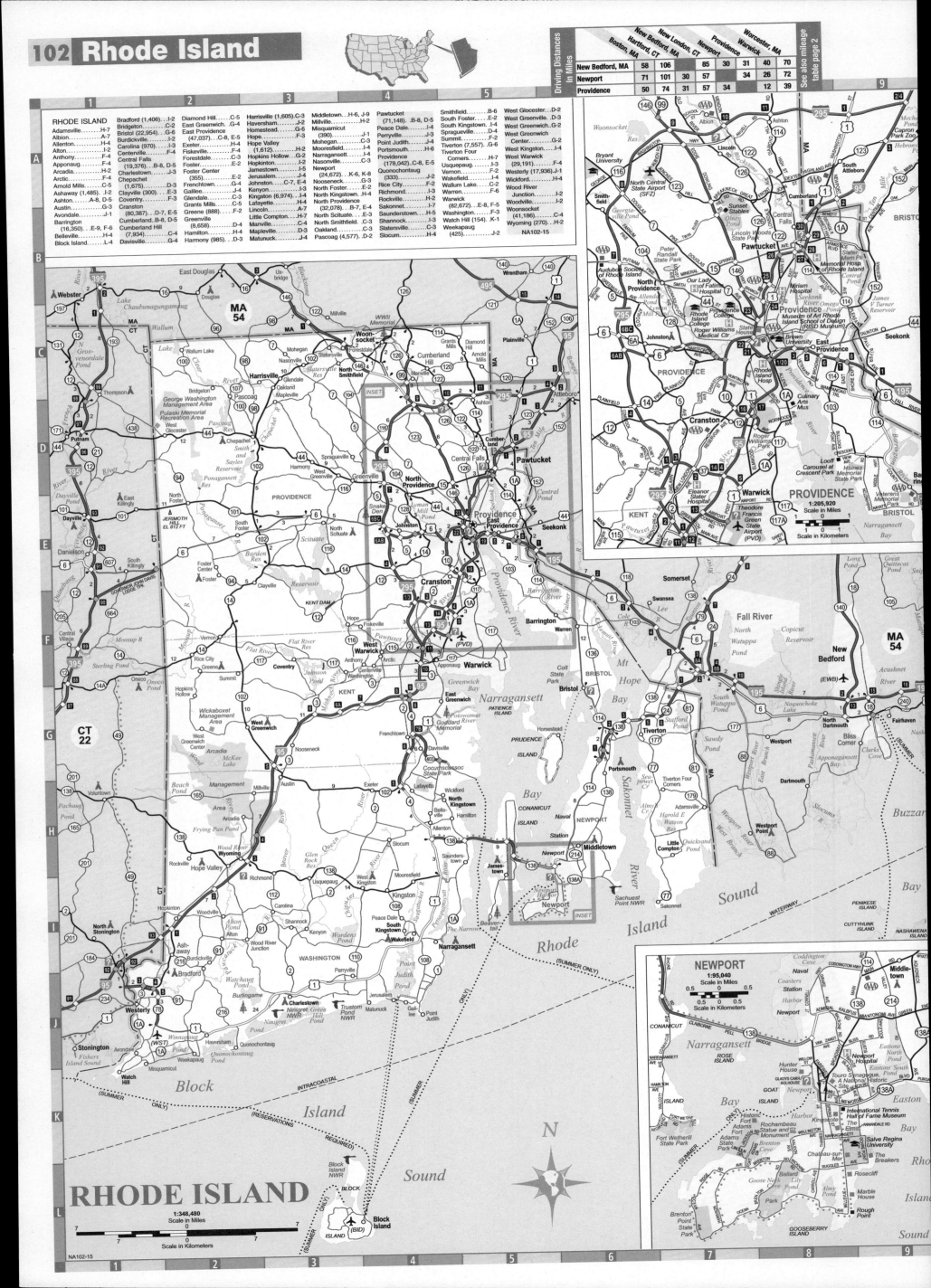

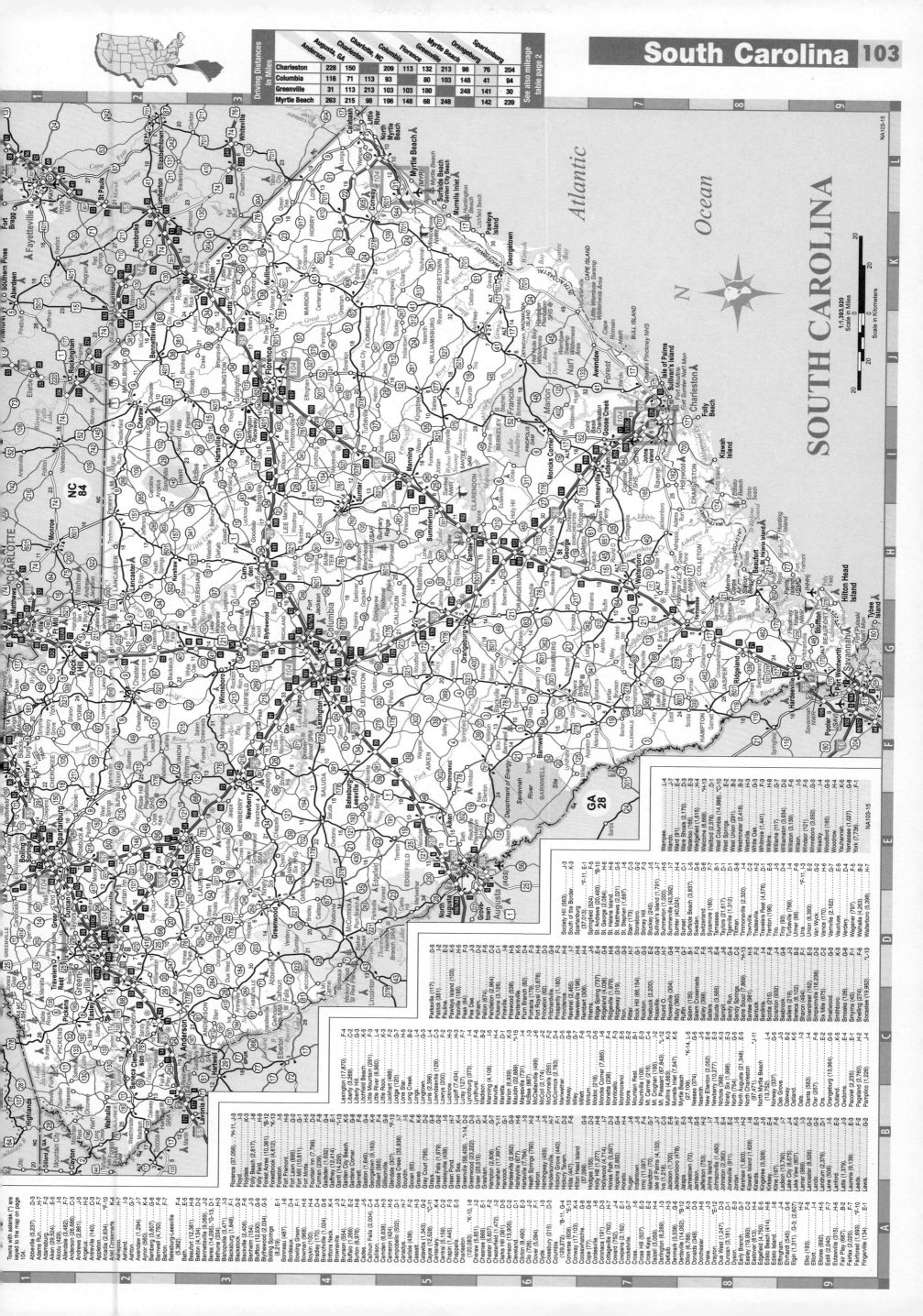

COLUMBIA, SC
1:190,080
Scale in Miles
Scale in Kilometers

SPARTANBURG, SC
1:190,080
Scale in Miles
Scale in Kilometers

FLORENCE, SC
1:221,760
Scale in Miles
Scale in Kilometers

GREENVILLE, SC
1:253,440
Scale in Miles
Scale in Kilometers

CHARLESTON, SC
1:174,240
Scale in Miles
Scale in Kilometers

MYRTLE BEACH, SC
1:190,080
Scale in Miles
Scale in Kilometers

PIERRE, SD
1:158,400
Scale in Miles
Scale in Kilometers

BLACK HILLS AREA, SD
1:633,600
Scale in Miles
Scale in Kilometers

RAPID CITY, SD
1:158,400
Scale in Miles
Scale in Kilometers

SIOUX FALLS, SD
1:158,400
Scale in Miles
Scale in Kilometers

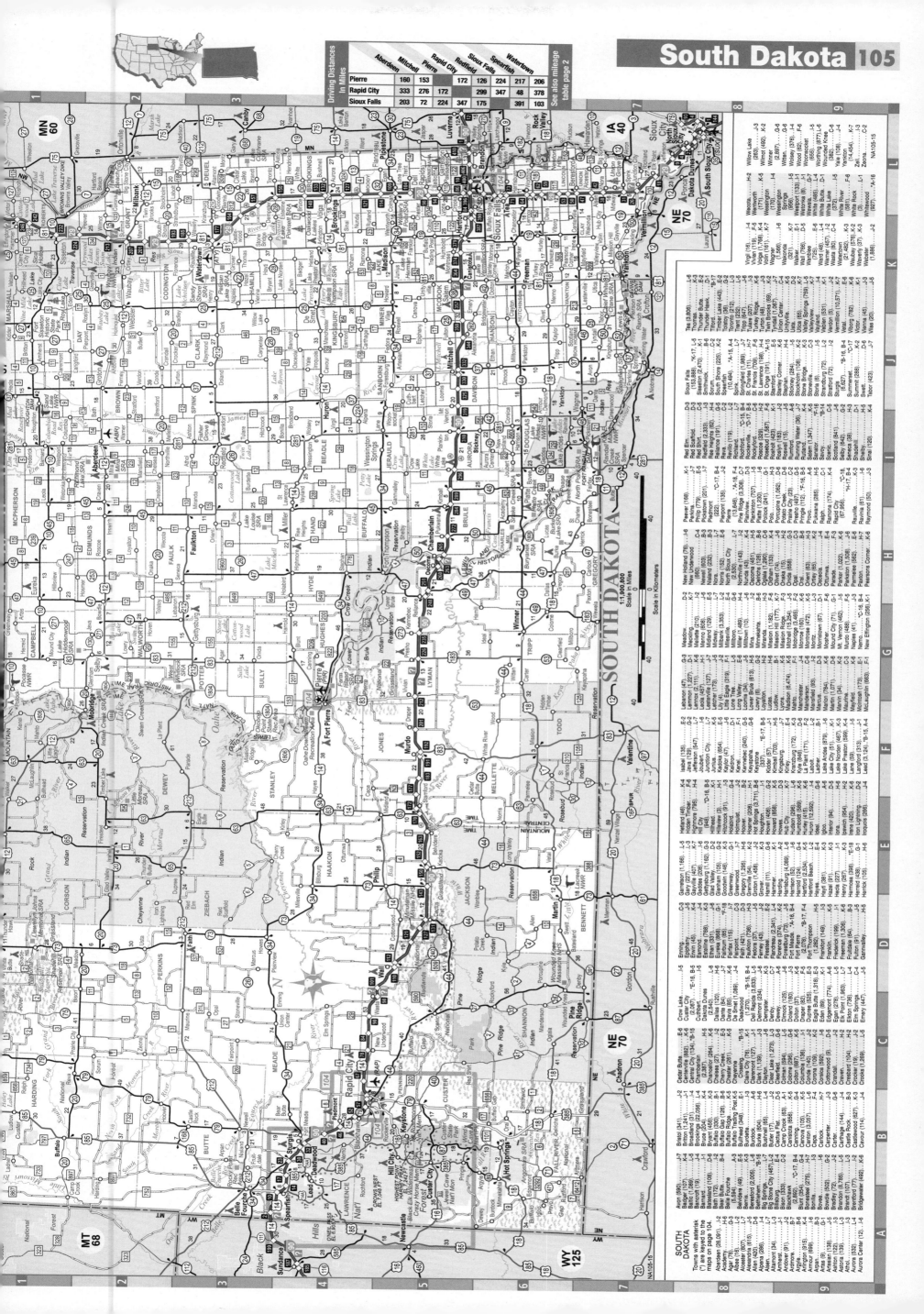

Driving Distances in Miles	Bristol	Chattanooga	Clarksville	Cleveland	Jackson	Johnson City	Kingsport	Knoxville	Memphis	Morristown	Murfreesboro	Nashville
Chattanooga	222		179	32	263	216	210	112	316	158	102	134
Knoxville	112	112	225	84	309	106	99		391	48	175	179
Memphis	501	316	209	346	88	495	489	391		437	245	212
Nashville	290	134	49	163	130	284	277	179	212	226	33	

See also page 2 mileage table on page 2

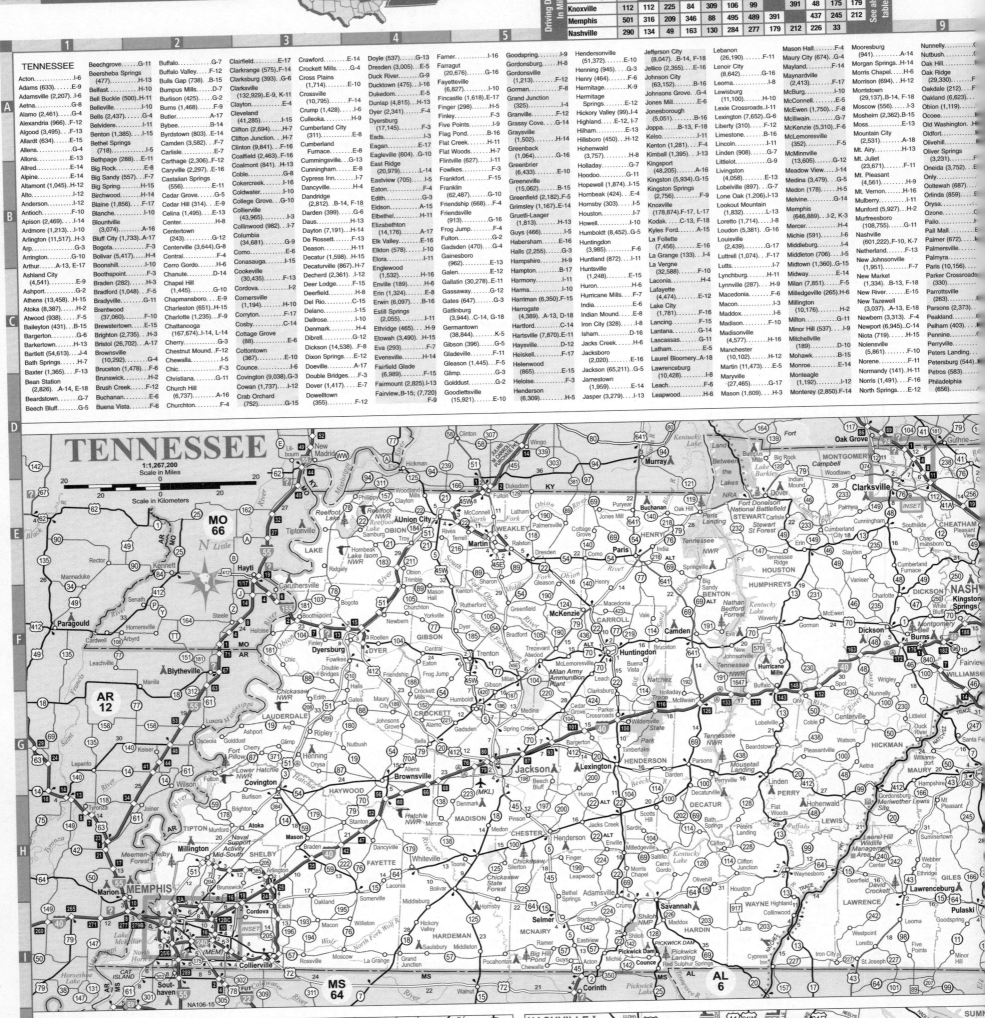

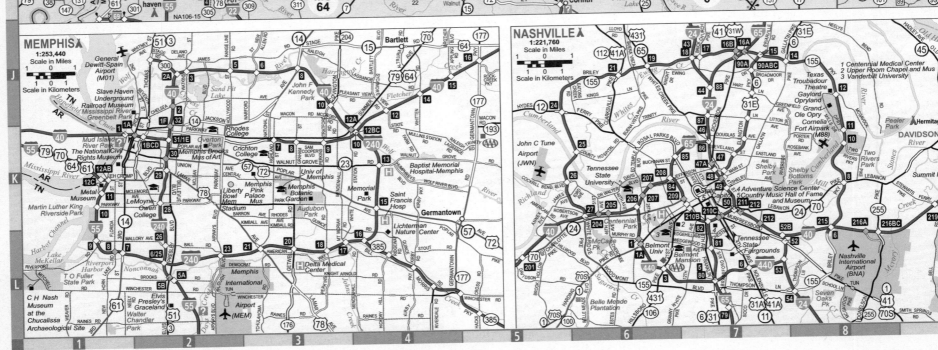

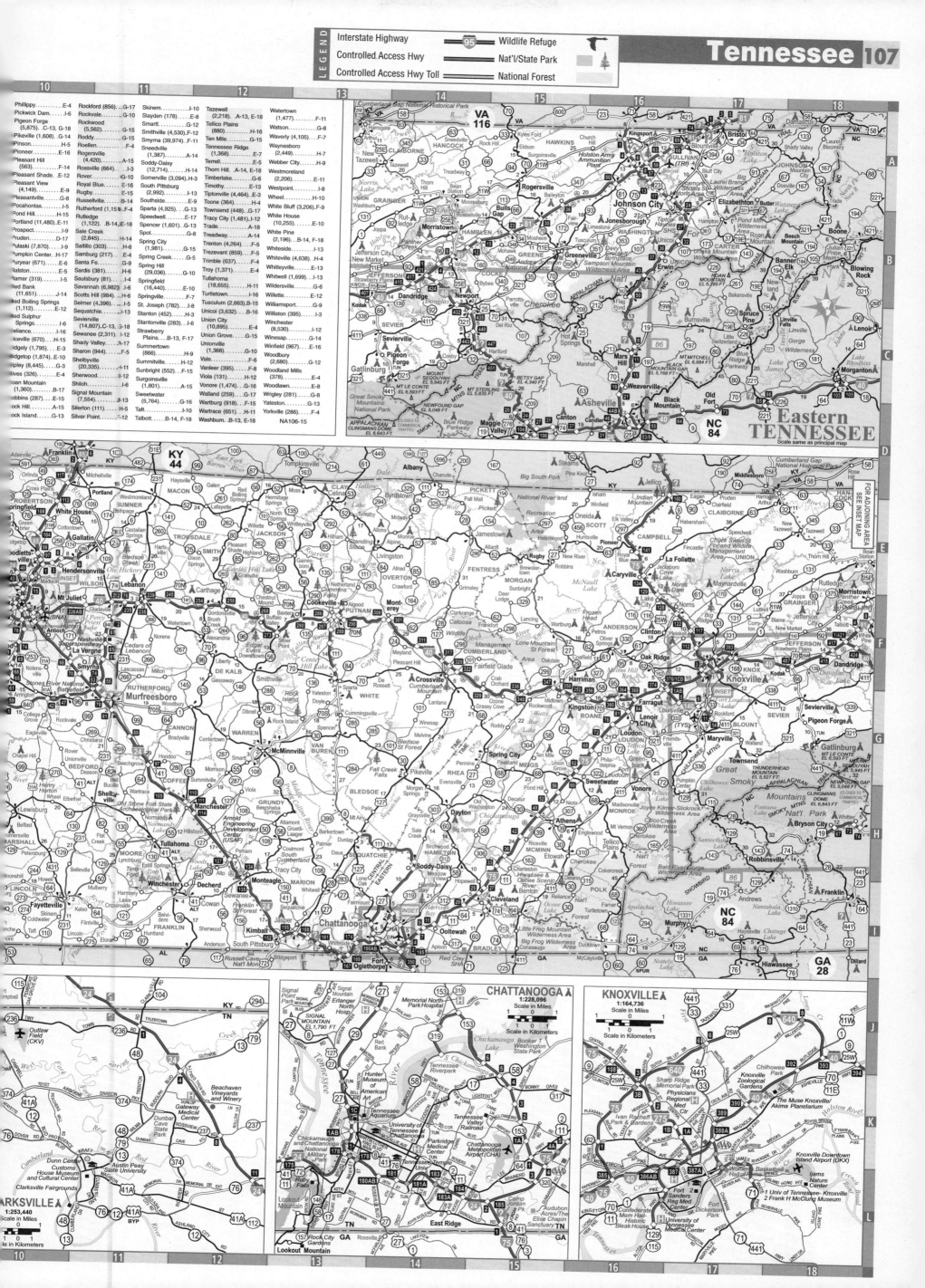

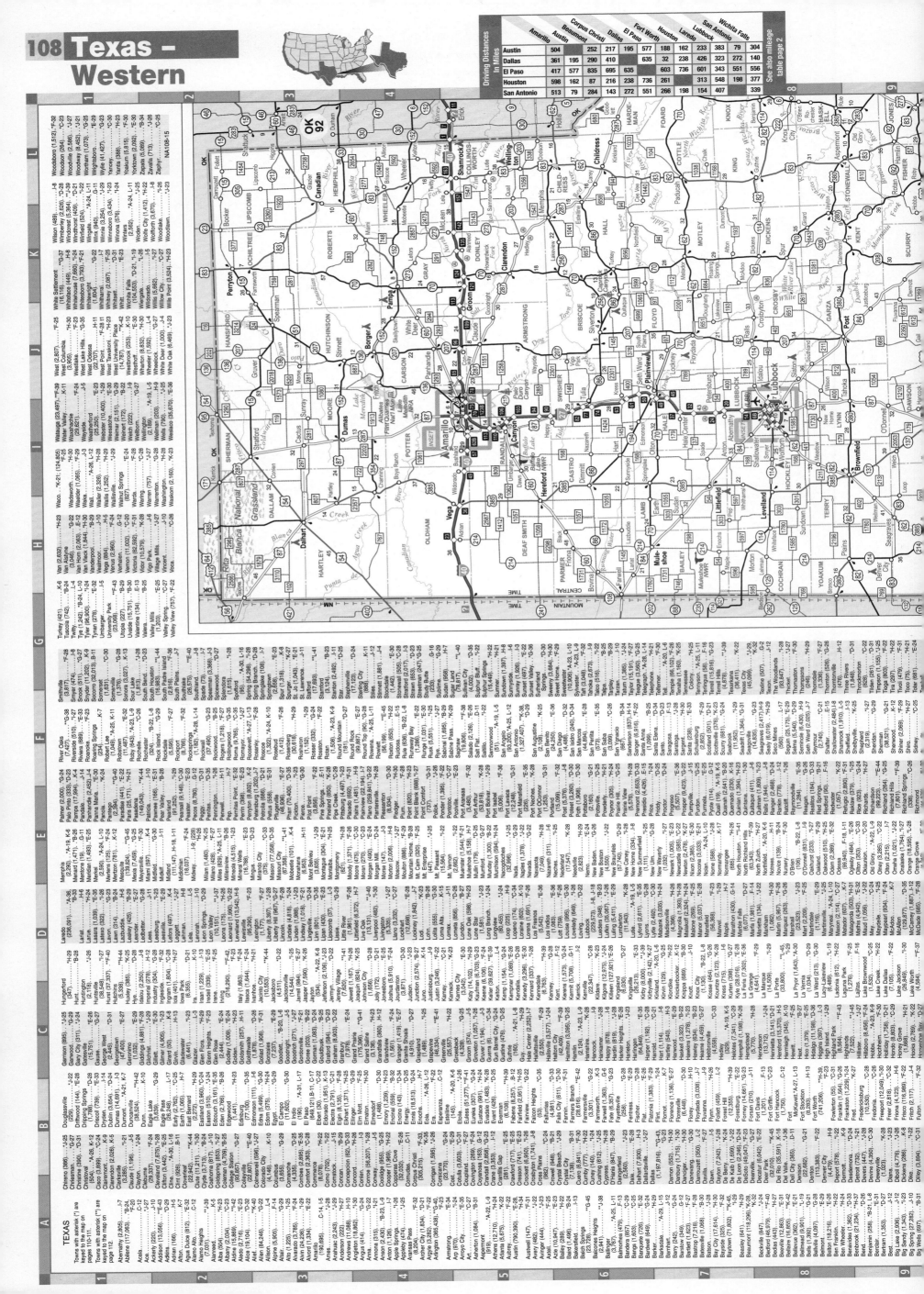

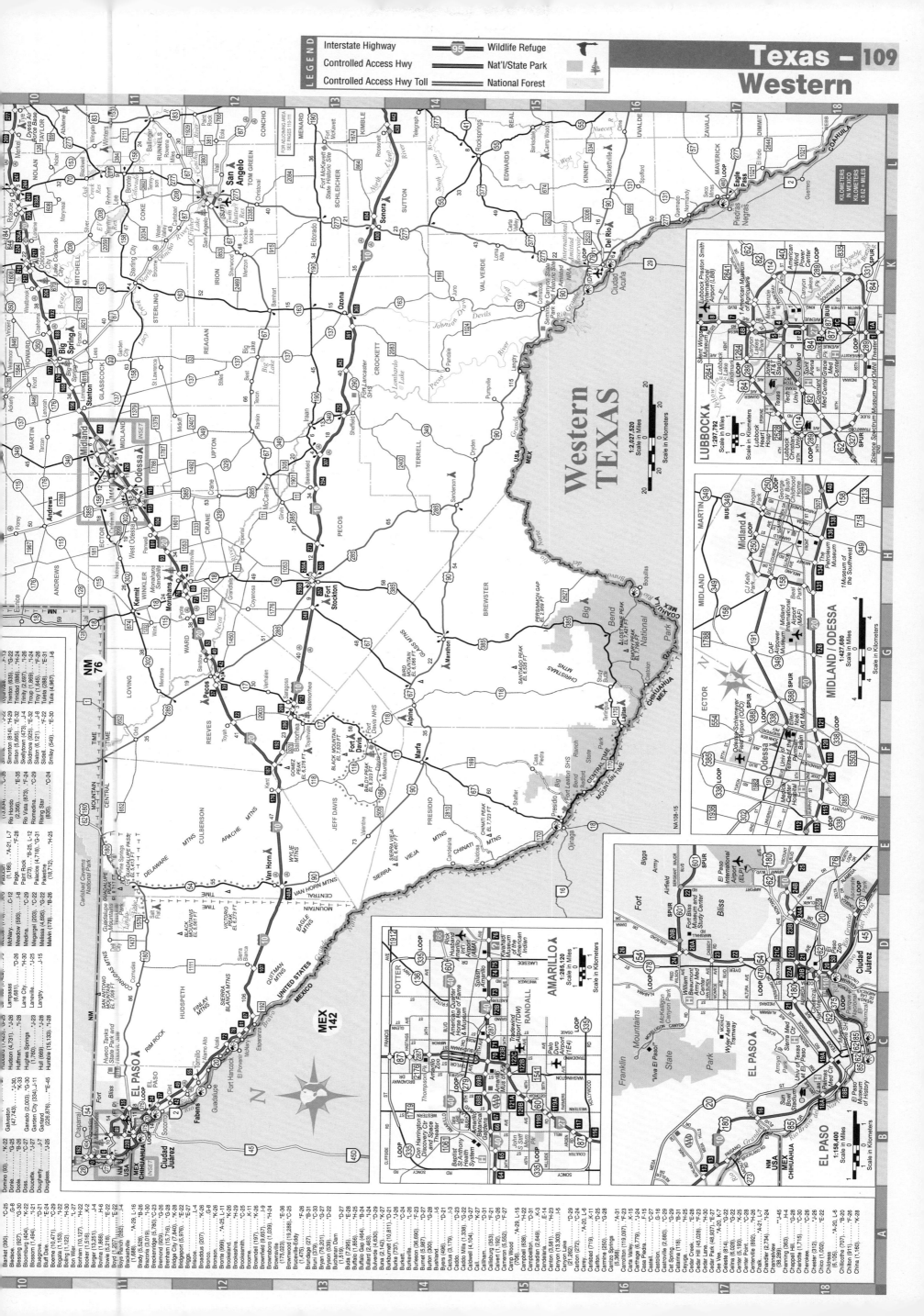

LEGEND
- Interstate Highway
- Controlled Access Hwy
- Controlled Access Hwy Toll
- 95 Wildlife Refuge
- Nat'l/State Park
- National Forest

Western TEXAS

LUBBOCK

MIDLAND / ODESSA

EL PASO

AMARILLO

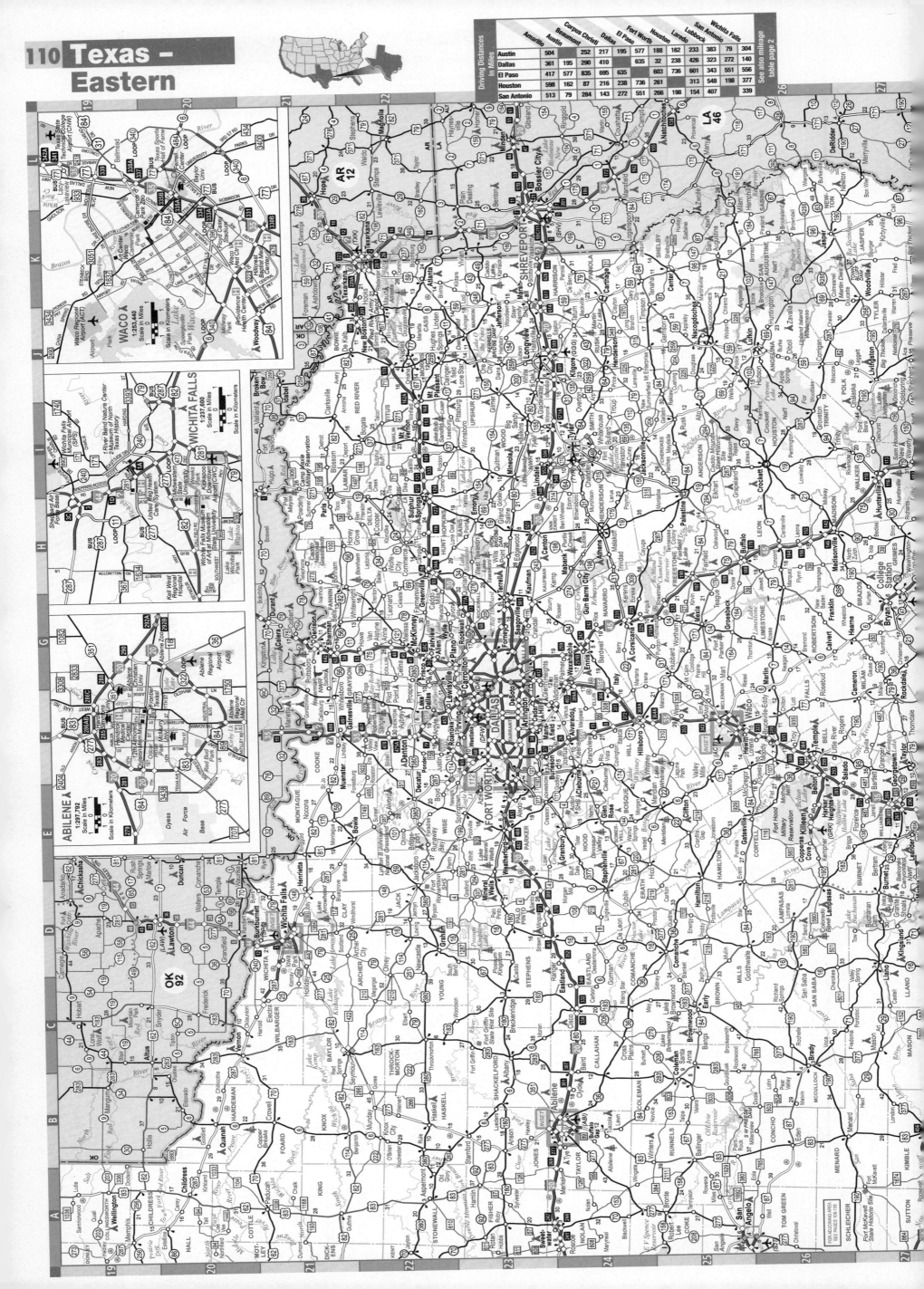

See also mileage table page 2

Driving Distances In Miles	Amarillo	Austin	Beaumont	Corpus Christi	Dallas	El Paso	Fort Worth	Houston	Laredo	Lubbock	San Antonio	Wichita Falls
Austin	504		252	217	195	577	188	162	233	383	79	304
Dallas	361	195	290	410		635	32	238	426	323	272	140
El Paso	417	577	835	695	635		603	736	601	343	551	556
Houston	598	162	87	216	238	736	261		313	548	198	377
San Antonio	513	79	284	143	272	551	266	198	154	407		339

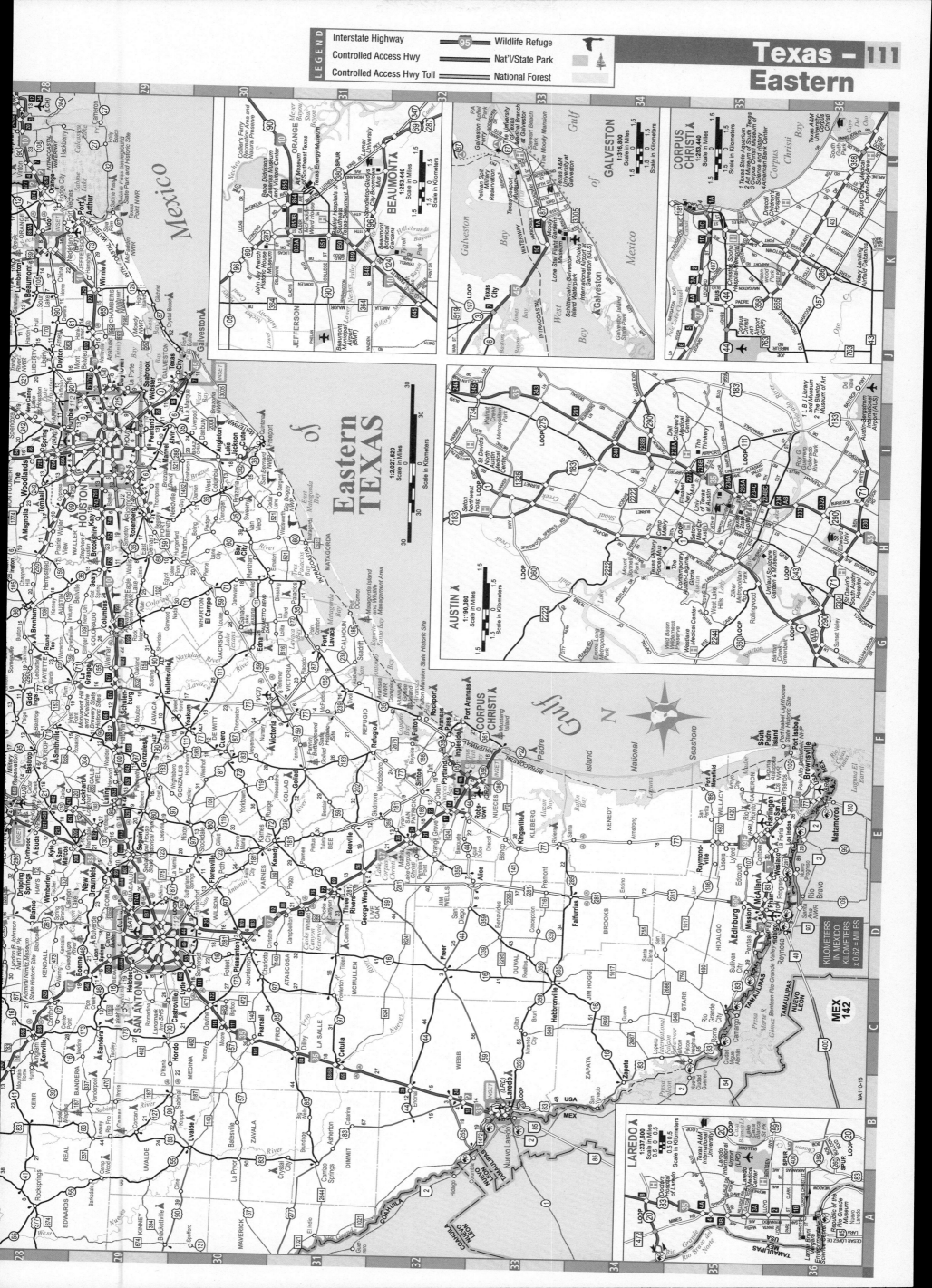

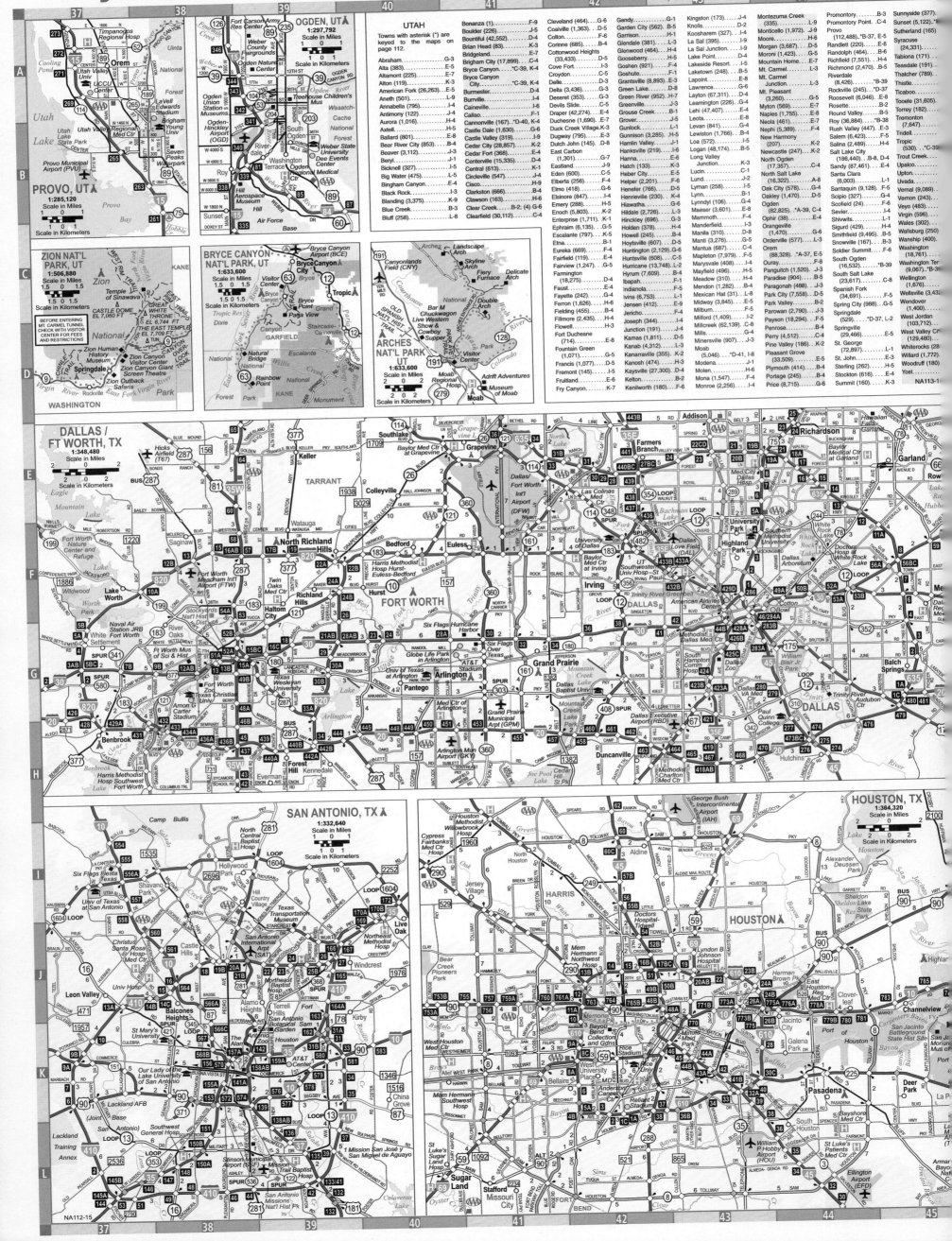

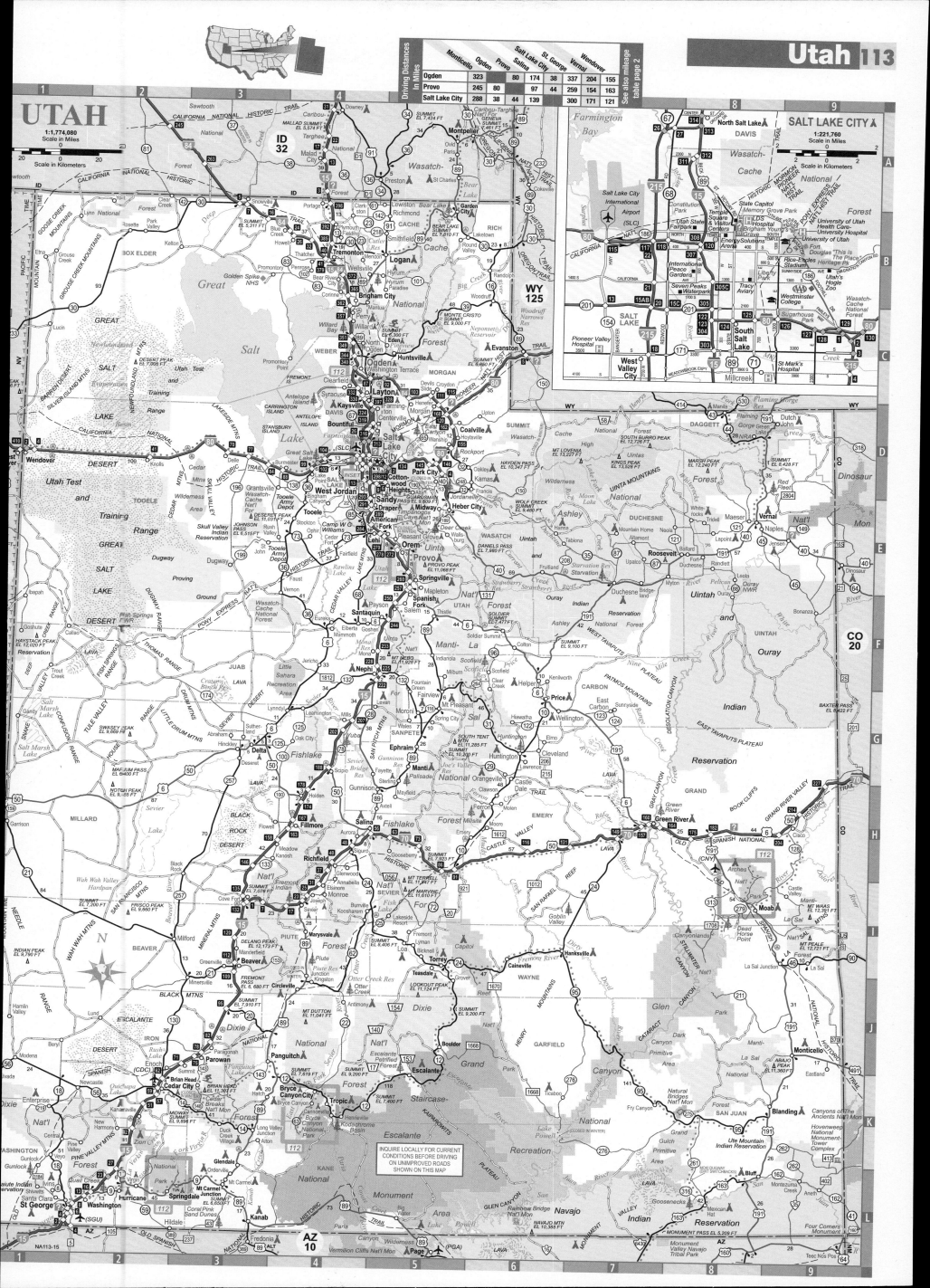

Driving Distances In Miles	Monticello	Ogden	Provo	Salina	Salt Lake City	St George	Vernal	Wendover
Ogden	323		80	174	38	337	204	155
Provo	245	80		97	44	259	154	163
Salt Lake City	288	38	44	139		300	171	121

See also mileage table page 2

SALT LAKE CITY
1:221,760
Scale in Miles
Scale in Kilometers

INQUIRE LOCALLY FOR CURRENT CONDITIONS BEFORE DRIVING ON UNIMPROVED ROADS SHOWN ON THIS MAP

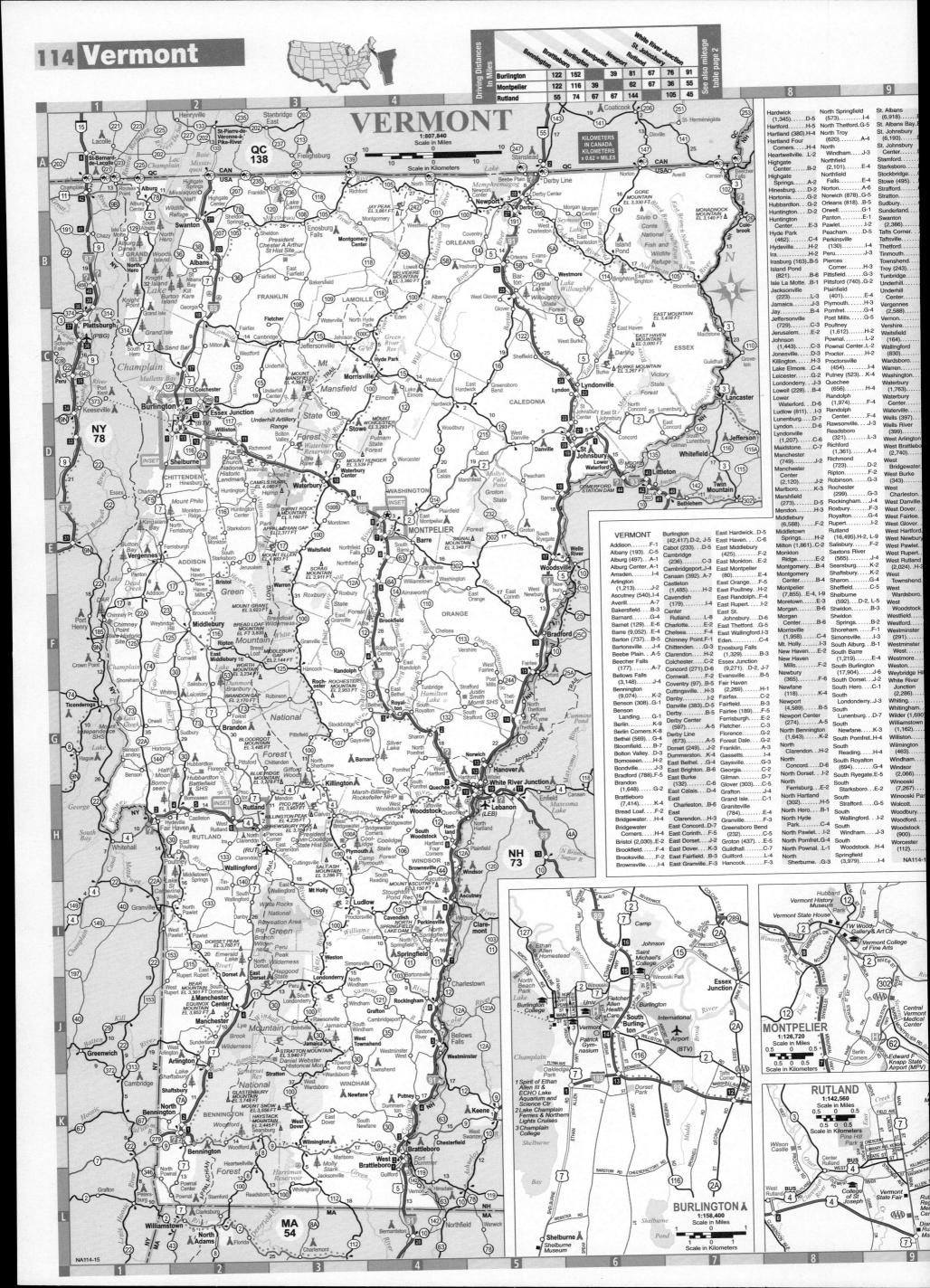

ROANOKE
1:221,760
Scale in Miles
Scale in Kilometers

VIRGINIA'S HISTORIC TRIANGLE
1:269,280
Scale in Miles
Scale in Kilometers

GLOUCESTER

1 Governor's Palace
2 The Original Ghosts of Williamsburg Candlelight Tour
3 The DeWitt Wallace Decorative Arts Mus
4 College of William & Mary

RICHMOND / PETERSBURG AREA
1:269,280
Scale in Miles
Scale in Kilometers

DOWNTOWN RICHMOND
1:38,016
Scale in Miles
Scale in Kilometers

1 The White House of the Confederacy
1 Virginia Mus of Fine Arts
2 Virginia Historical Society
3 Children's Mus of Richmond

6 Virginia Air & Space Center
7 Hampton University
8 Veterans Affairs Med Center

DOWNTOWN NORFOLK
1:38,016
Scale in Miles
Scale in Kilometers

1 St Paul's Episcopal Church
2 US District Court

HAMPTON ROADS AREA
1:253,440
Scale in Miles
Scale in Kilometers

Chesapeake Bay

Atlantic Ocean

ROANOKE · SALEM · VINTON · BOTETOURT · BEDFORD · FRANKLIN · HANOVER · HENRICO · POWHATAN · RICHMOND · MIDLOTHIAN · CHESTERFIELD · CHESTER · COLONIAL HEIGHTS · PETERSBURG · DINWIDDIE · PRINCE GEORGE · HOPEWELL · CHARLES CITY · WILLIAMSBURG · YORKTOWN · JAMESTOWN · NEWPORT NEWS · HAMPTON · NORFOLK · PORTSMOUTH · CHESAPEAKE · VIRGINIA BEACH · ISLE OF WIGHT

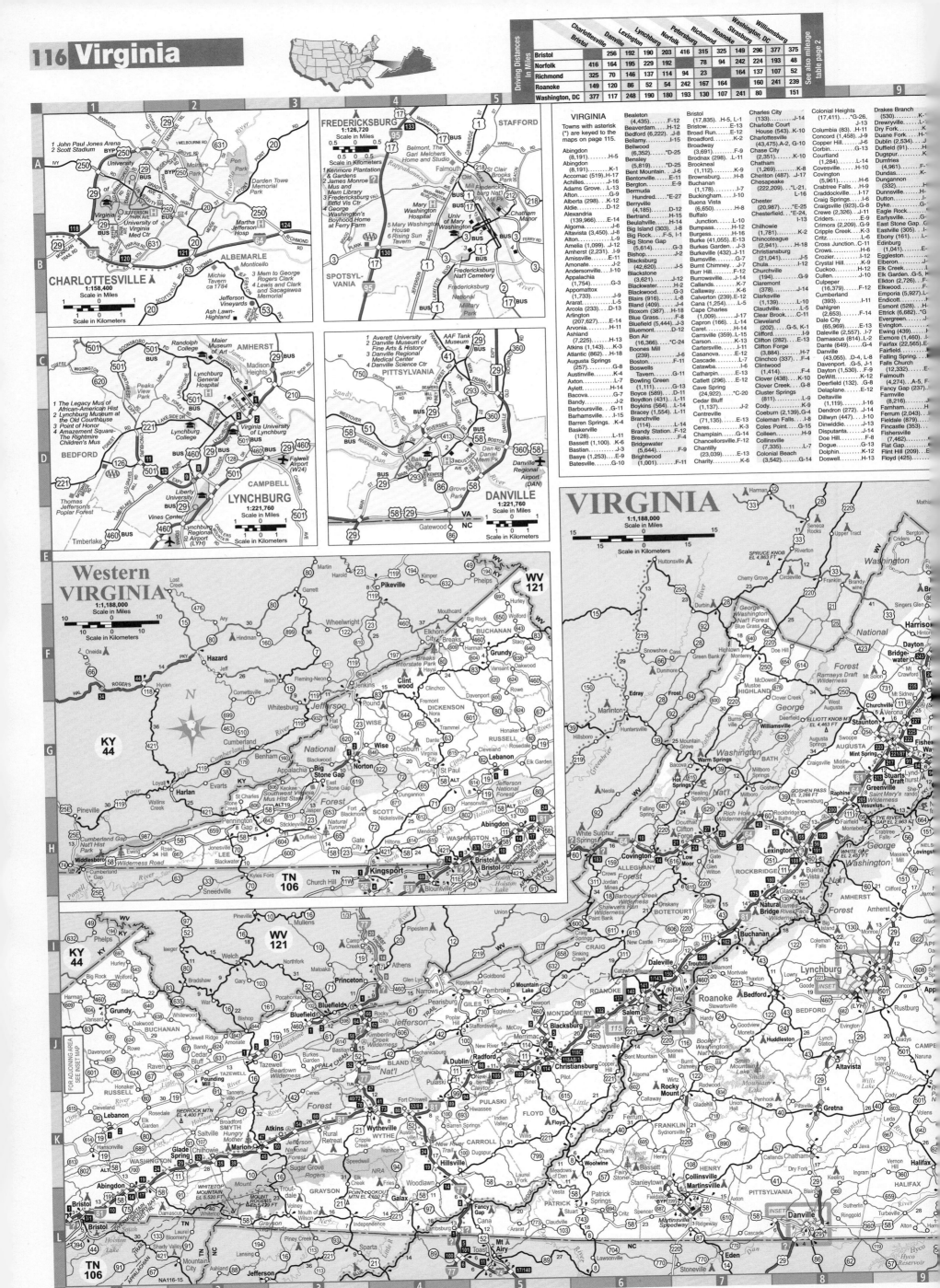

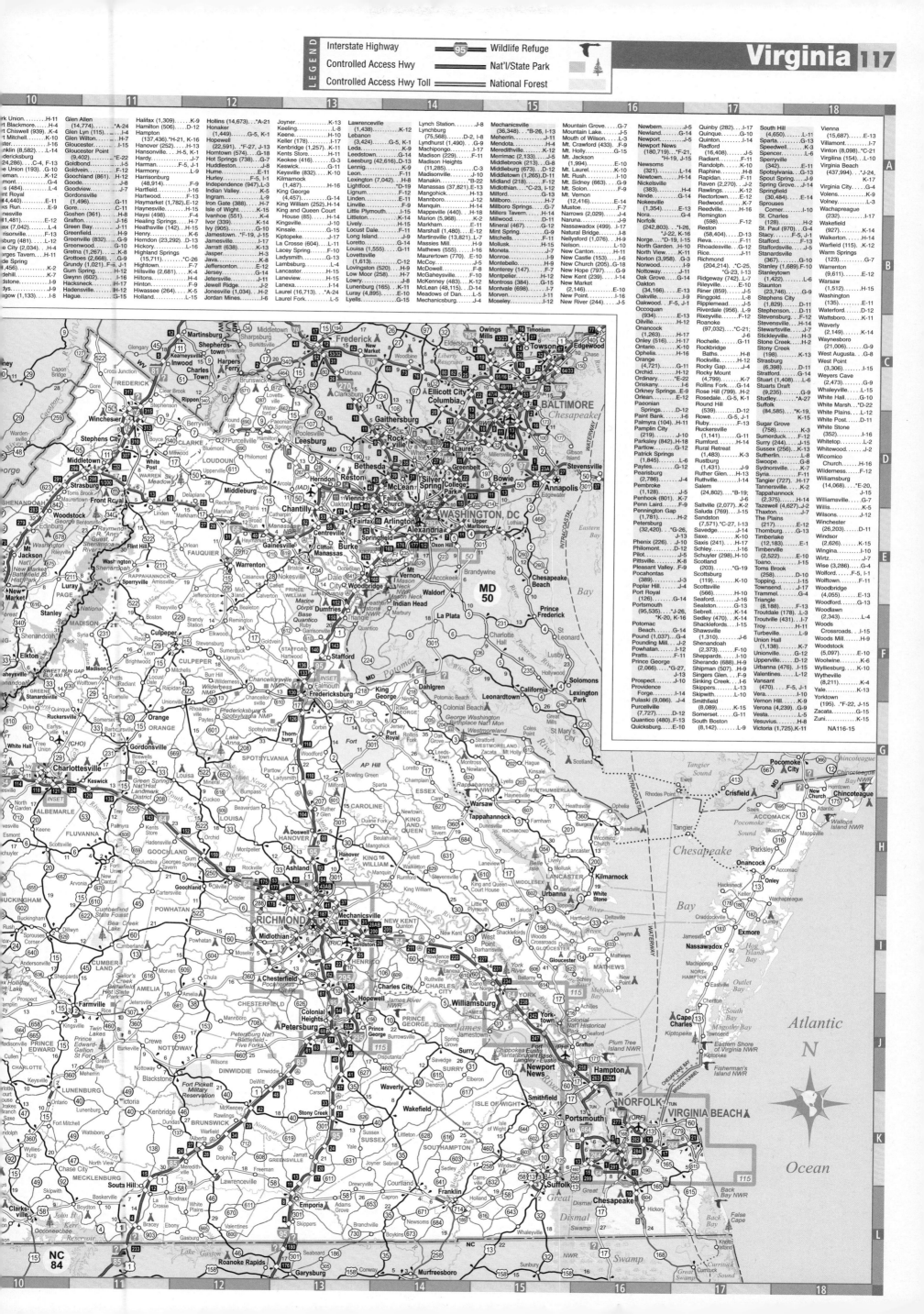

See also mileage table page 2

Driving Distances in Miles

	Aberdeen	Bellingham	Ellensburg	Kelso	Olympia	Omak	Pasco	Port Angeles	Seattle	Spokane	Tacoma	Yakima
Olympia	50	149	148	66		277	267	119	60	320	31	183
Seattle	109	89	107	126	60	237	227	82		279	34	142
Spokane	369	362	173	366	320	140	136	397	279		293	193
Tacoma	79	122	121	96	31	251	241	106	34	293		156
Yakima	204	224	36	166	183	196	85	260	142	193	156	

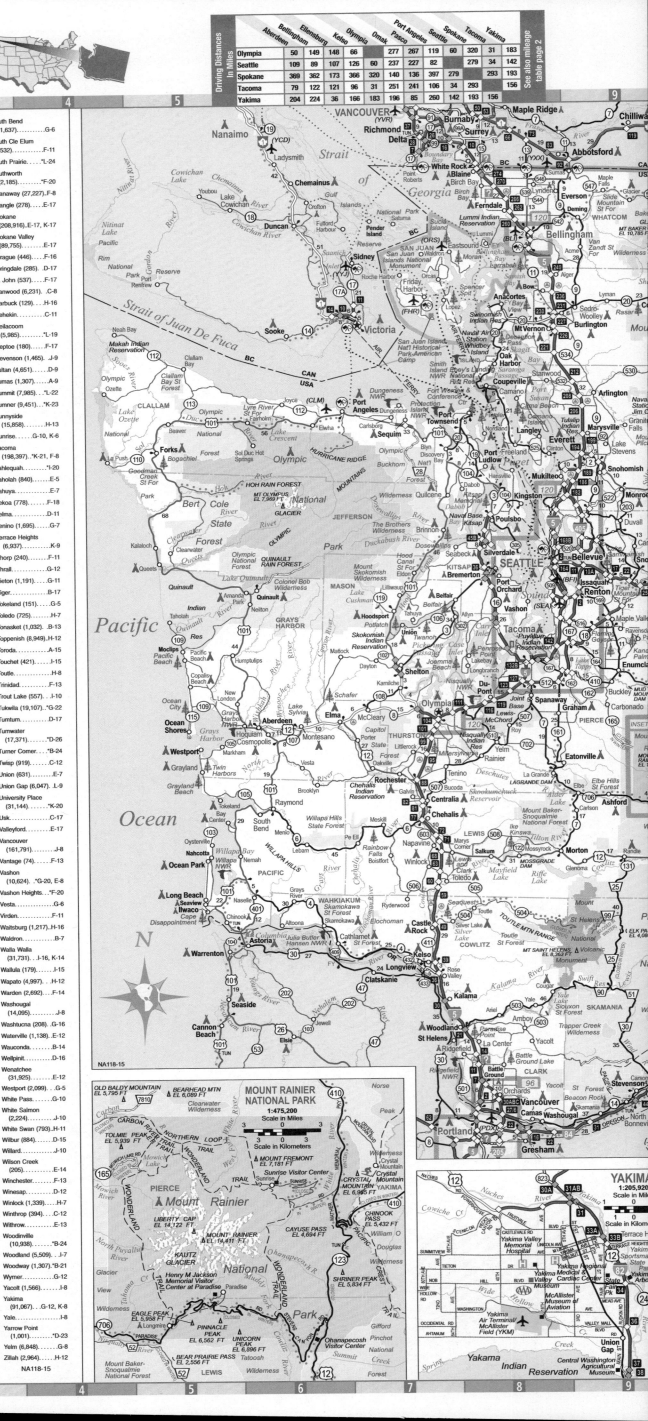

NA118-15

LEGEND

Interstate Highway	Wildlife Refuge
Controlled Access Hwy	Nat'l/State Park
Controlled Access Hwy Toll	National Forest

BC 128

KILOMETERS IN CANADA
KILOMETERS x 0.62 = MILES

CAN / USA
BC / ID
PACIFIC TIME

Idaho

ID 32

WASHINGTON
1:1,457,280
Scale in Miles
Scale in Kilometers

BECAUSE THE LENGTH OF THE SEASONS VARIES GREATLY IN HIGHER ELEVATIONS, INQUIRE LOCALLY FOR THE CONDITIONS OF ROADS DESIGNATED "CLOSED IN WINTER" ON THIS MAP.

Major place names:
Osoyoos, Oroville, Tonasket, Republic, Colville, Kettle Falls, Chewelah, Newport, Priest River, Winthrop, Twisp, Okanogan, Omak, Brewster, Pateros, Chelan, Manson, Coulee Dam, Grand Coulee, Spokane, Airway Heights, Spokane Valley, Liberty Lake, Coeur d'Alene, Hayden, Leavenworth, Cashmere, Wenatchee, East Wenatchee, Waterville, Soap Lake, Ephrata, Quincy, Moses Lake, Davenport, Cheney, Ritzville, Cle Elum, Ellensburg, Kittitas, Royal City, Othello, Connell, Colfax, Pullman, Moscow, Lewiston, Clarkston, Yakima, Zillah, Toppenish, Sunnyside, Granger, Grandview, Prosser, Mabton, Richland, Kennewick, Pasco, Pomeroy, Dayton, Walla Walla, Goldendale, White Salmon, The Dalles, Hood River, Boardman, Hermiston, Umatilla, Pendleton

OR 94

Insets:

TRI-CITIES
Pasco, FRANKLIN, Tri-Cities Airport (PSC), Washington State Railroads Historical Society Museum, Bechtel National Planetarium, KENNEWICK, BENTON, Kennewick General Hospital, Three Rivers Convention Ctr, Benton-Franklin Master Gardener Demonstration Garden
1:253,440
Scale in Miles

WALLA WALLA
Walla Walla Regional Airport (ALW), Whitman College, Kirkman House Museum, Carnegie Art Center, St Mary Medical Center, Jonathan M Wainwright Mem VA Medical Center, Walla Walla Univ, Fort Walla Walla Museum, Walla Walla General Hospital, College Place
1:158,400
Scale in Miles

SPOKANE
Camp Seven Mile Military Res, Spokane VA Medical Center, Providence Holy Family Hospital, Gonzaga University, Northwest Museum of Arts & Culture, John A Finch Arboretum, Manito Park, Providence Sacred Heart Medical Center & Children's Hospital, Deaconess Medical Center-Spokane, Spokane Int'l Airport (GEG), Felts Field Municipal Airport (SFF), Dishman Hills Natural Area
1:190,080
Scale in Miles

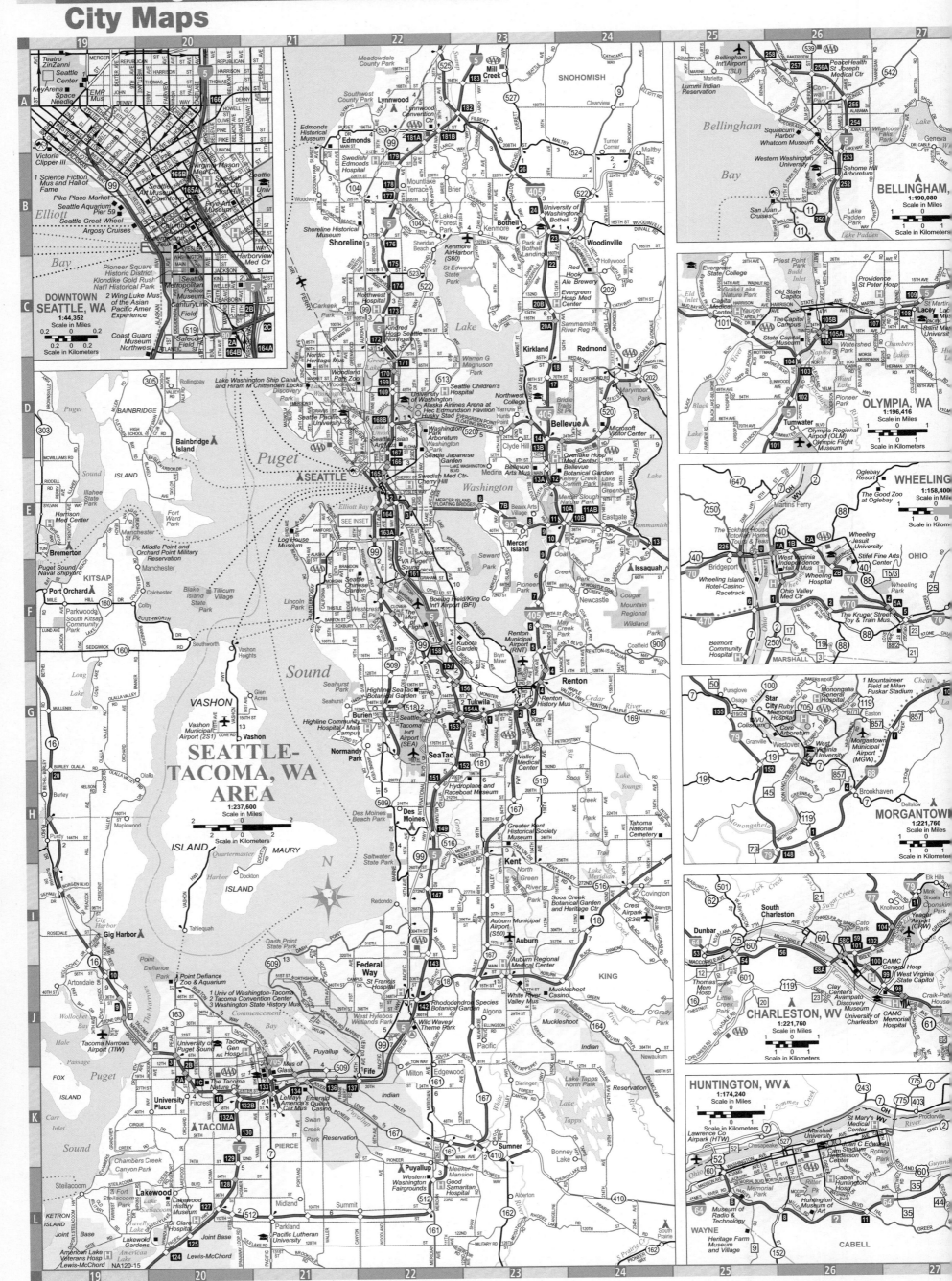

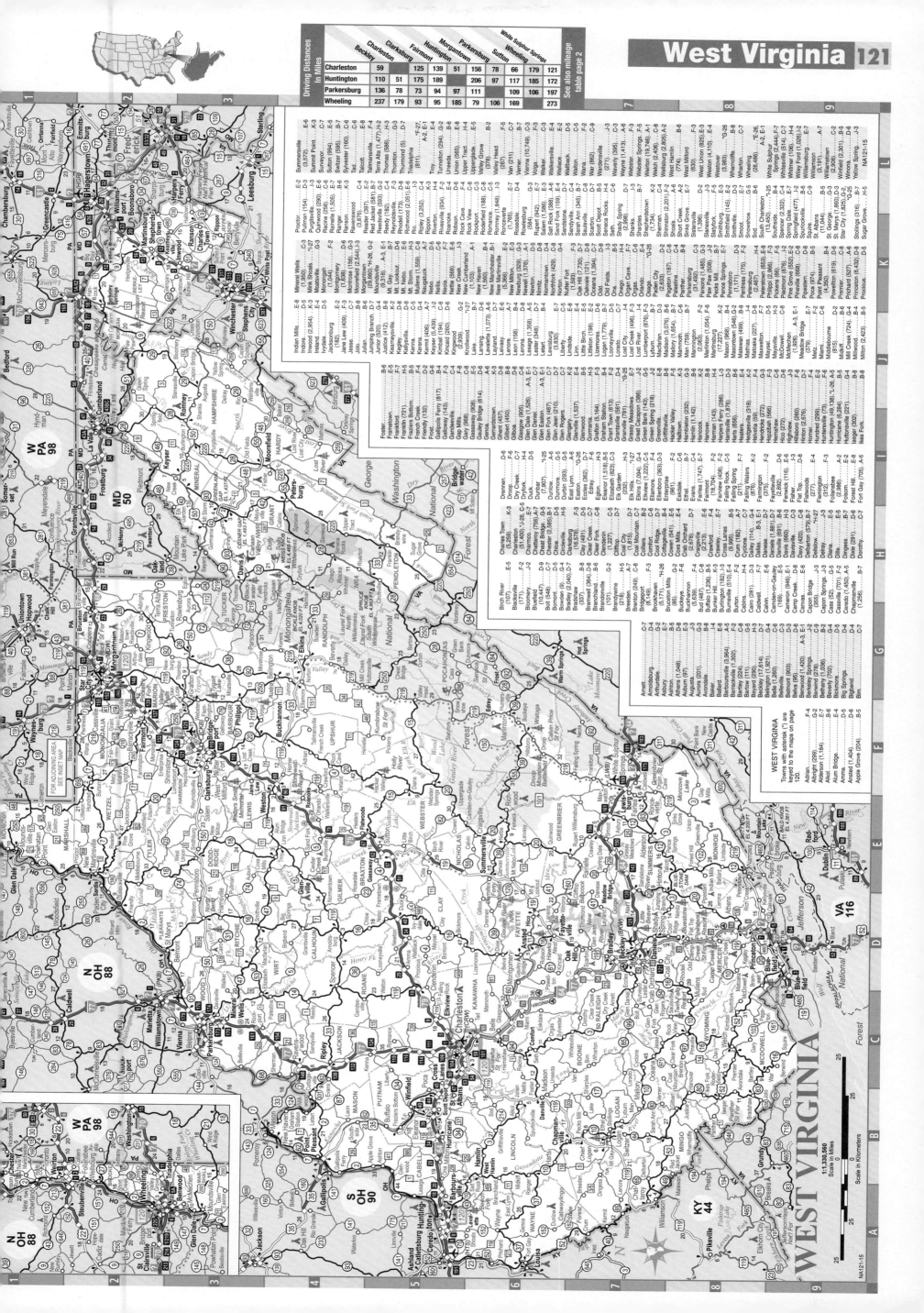

See also page 2 table on page 2

Driving Distances In Miles

	Appleton	Beloit	Eau Claire	Green Bay	Kenosha	La Crosse	Madison	Manitowoc	Milwaukee	Spooner	Tomah	Wausau
Eau Claire	185	225		193	280	90	178	232	246	82	85	101
Green Bay	31	182	193		155	202	135	41	117	257	157	96
La Crosse	172	190	90	202	245		143	212	211	164	44	170
Madison	105	54	178	135	113	143		129	78	253	100	142
Milwaukee	102	76	246	117	39	211	78			324	168	194

GREEN BAY
1:158,400
Scale in Miles
Scale in Kilometers

OSHKOSH
1:221,760
Scale in Miles
Scale in Kilometers

APPLETON
1:221,760
Scale in Miles
Scale in Kilometers

SHEBOYGAN
1:253,440
Scale in Miles
Scale in Kilometers

WISCONSIN

Towns with asterisk
("*") are keyed to
the maps on page 124.

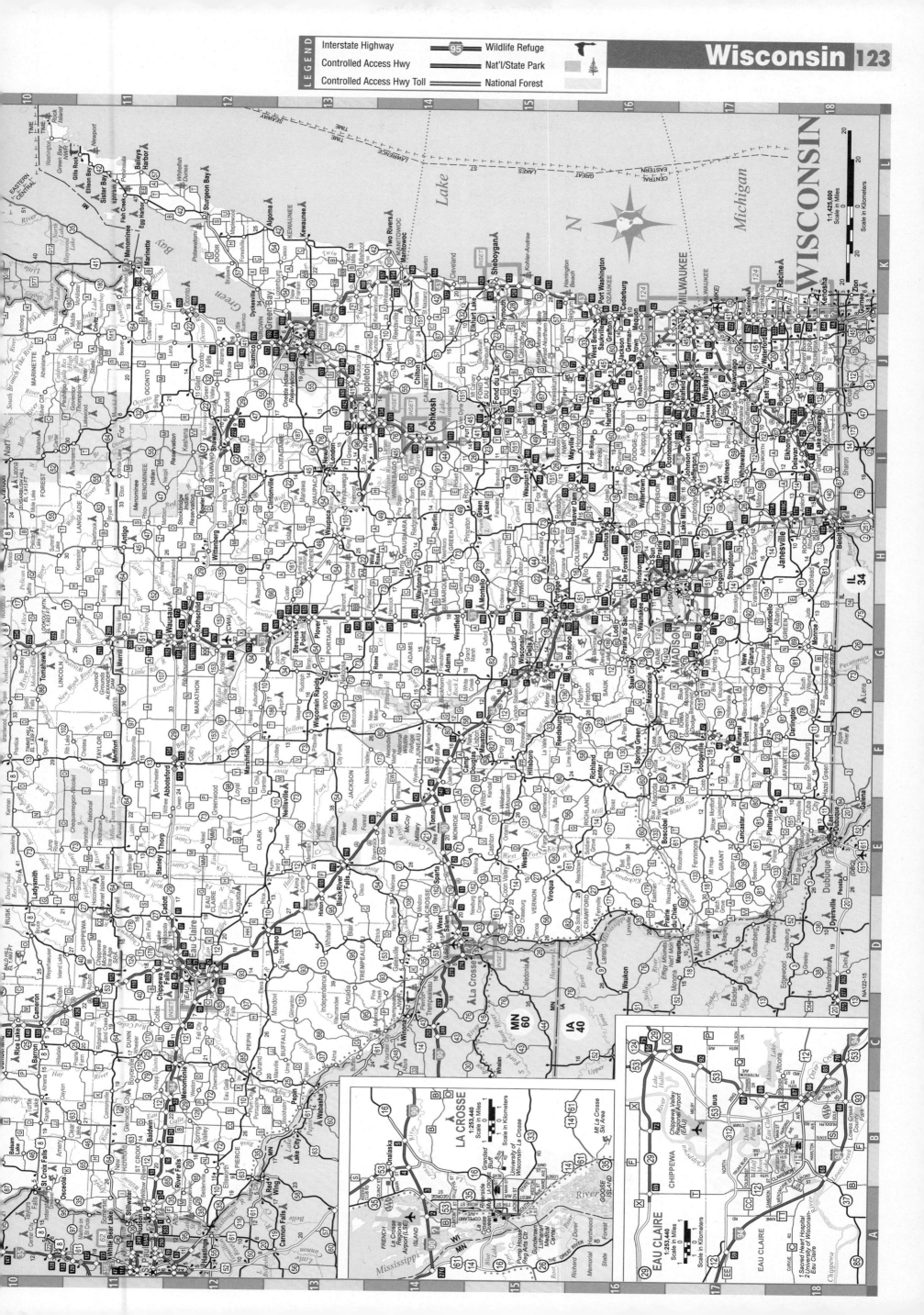

LEGEND

Interstate Highway
Controlled Access Hwy
Controlled Access Hwy Toll

Wildlife Refuge
Nat'l/State Park
National Forest

MILWAUKEE, WI & VICINITY
1:174,240
Scale in Miles
Scale in Kilometers

MADISON, WI
1:190,080
Scale in Miles
Scale in Kilometers

RACINE & KENOSHA WI
1:253,440
Scale in Miles
Scale in Kilometers

YELLOWSTONE NAT'L PARK, WY
1:1,267,200
Scale in Miles

GRAND TETON NATIONAL PARK
1:696,960
Scale in Miles

CASPER
1:158,4
Scale in Kilo

CHEYENNE
1:158
Scale in Kil

NA124-15

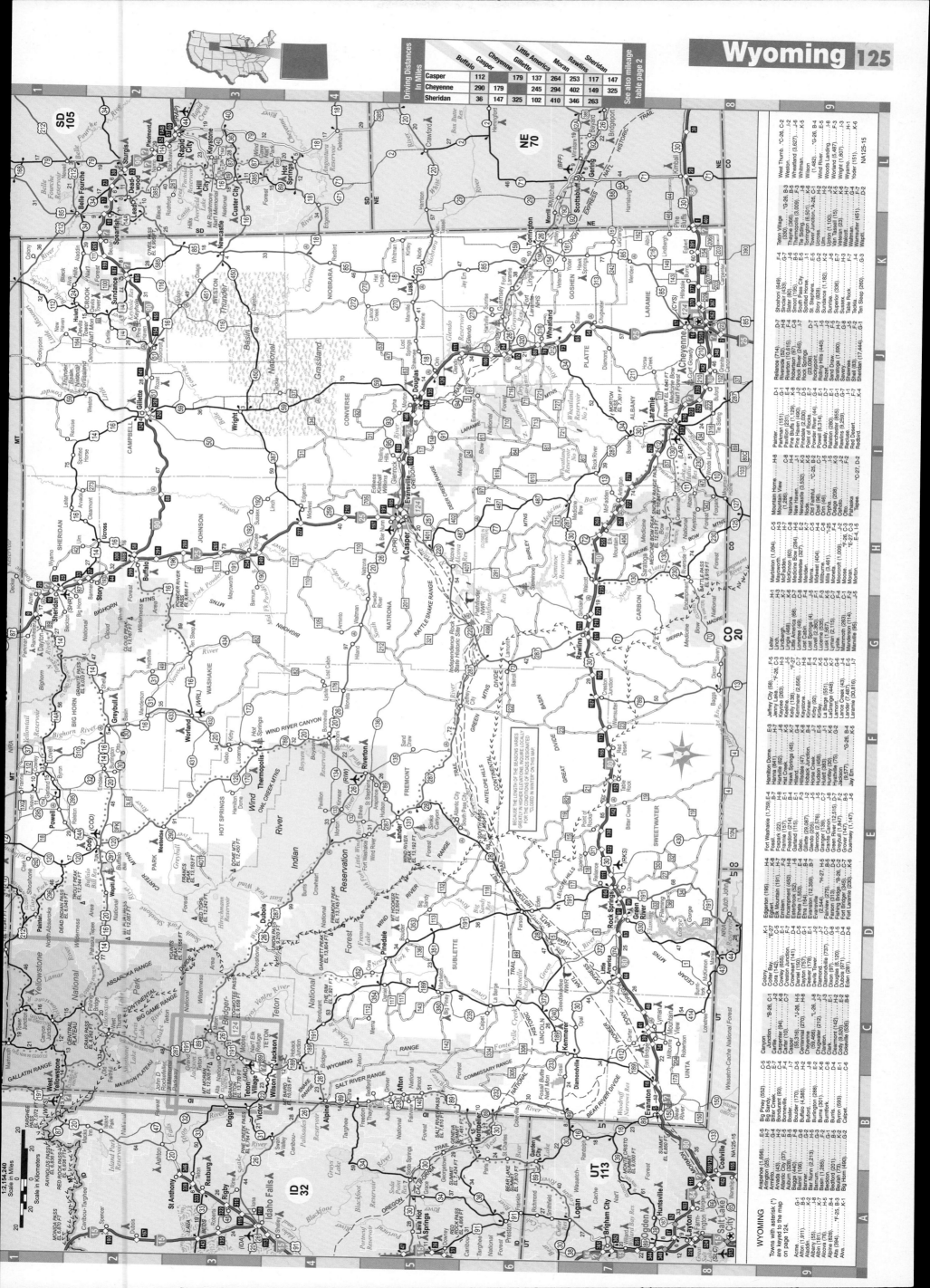

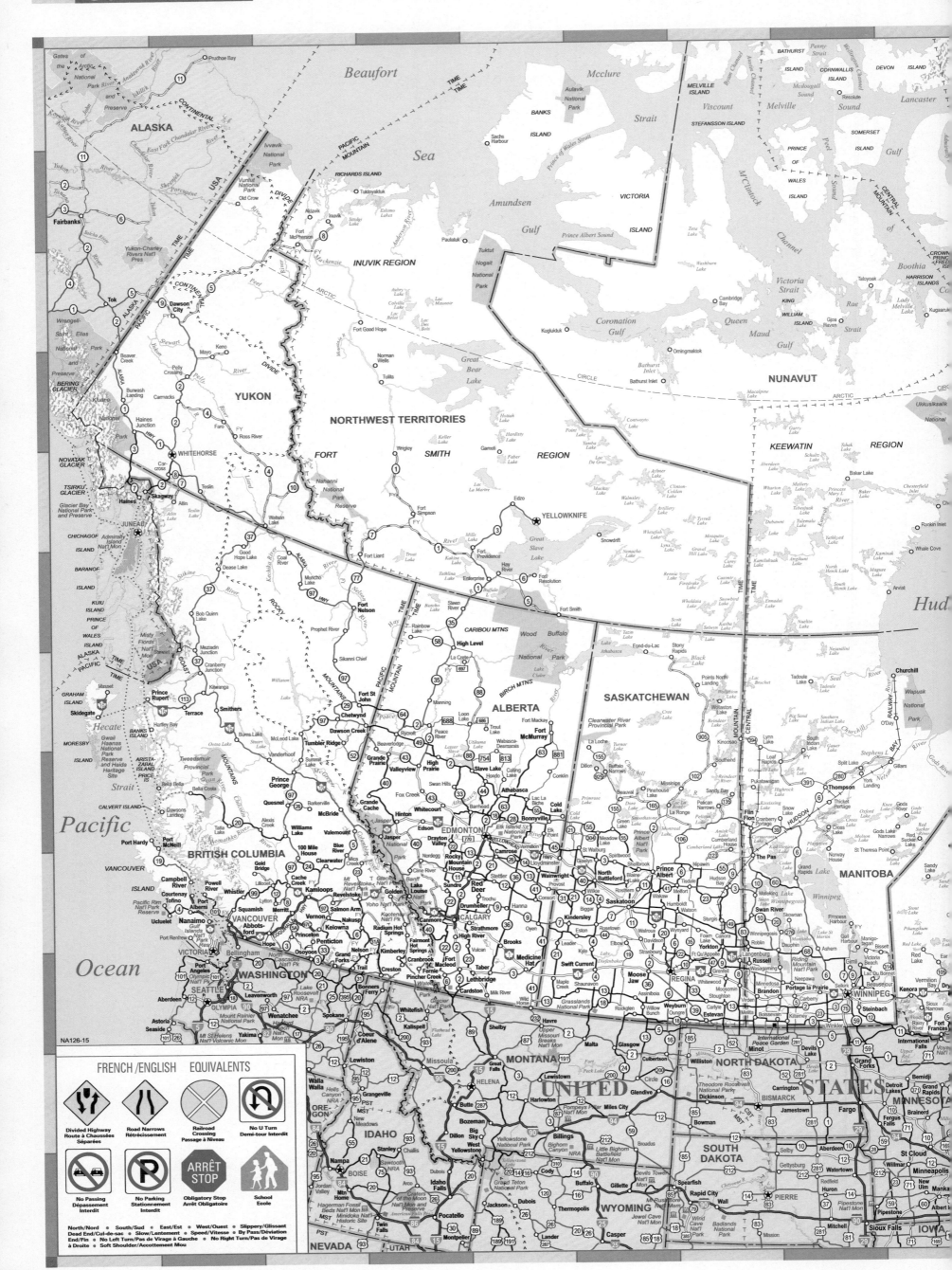

FRENCH / ENGLISH EQUIVALENTS

Divided Highway
Route à Chaussées
Séparées

Road Narrows
Rétrécissement

Railroad
Crossing
Passage à Niveau

No U Turn
Demi-tour Interdit

No Passing
Dépassement
Interdit

No Parking
Stationnement
Interdit

ARRÊT
STOP
Obligatory Stop
Arrêt Obligatoire

School
École

North/Nord • South/Sud • East/Est • West/Ouest • Slippery/Glissant
Dead End/Cul-de-sac • Slow/Lentement • Speed/Vitesse • By Pass/Déviation
End/Fin • No Left Turn/Pas de Virage à Gauche • No Right Turn/Pas de Virage
à Droite • Soft Shoulder/Accotement Mou

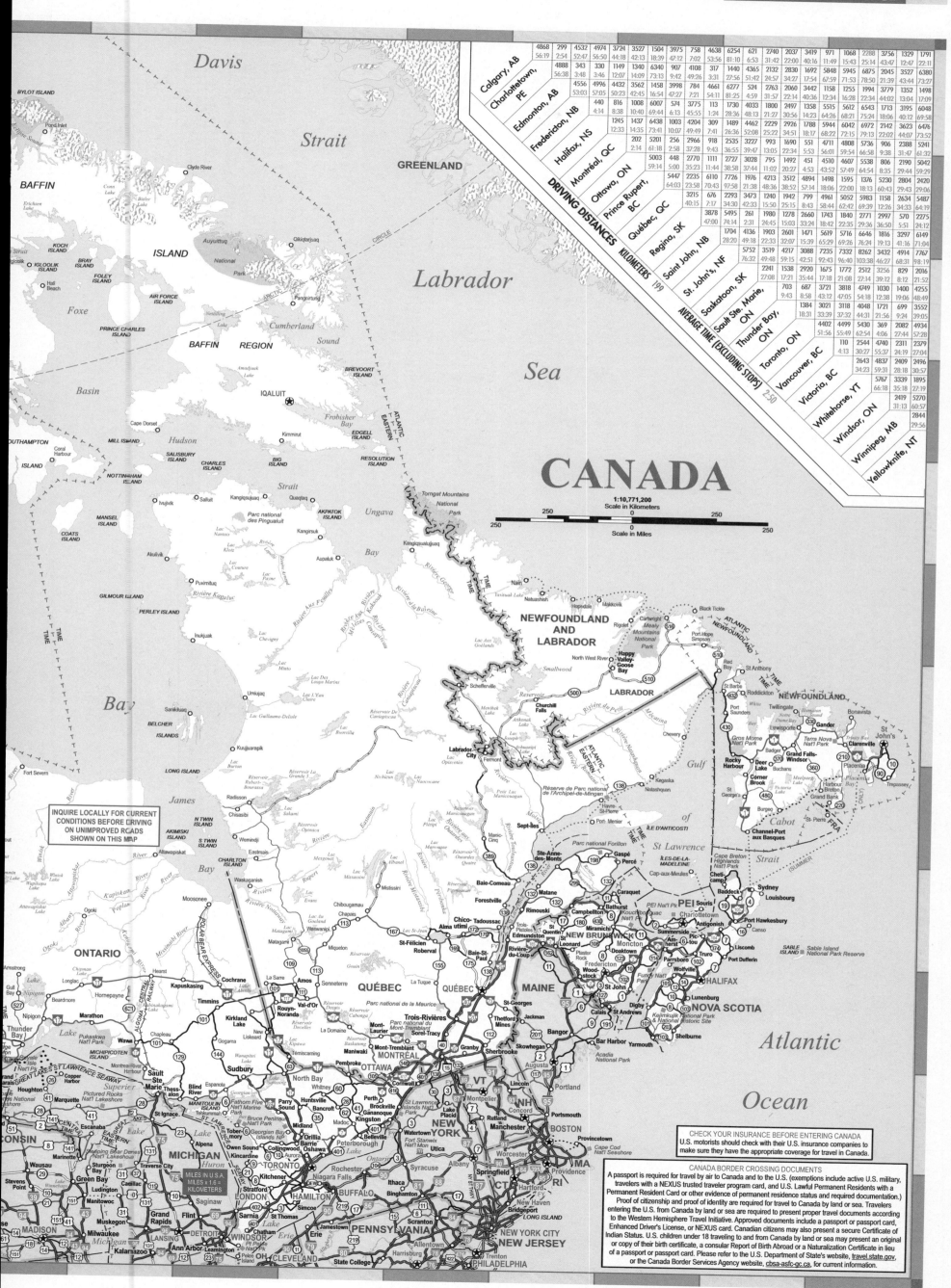

See also mileage table page 2

Driving Distances In Kilometers	Cranbrook	Dawson Creek	Hope	Kamloops	Nanaimo	Osoyoos	Prince George	Prince Rupert	Vancouver	Victoria
Kamloops	608	925	201	431	285	523	1237	349	446	
Prince George	926	405	635	523	867	802		719	785	882
Vancouver	840	1187	150	349	85	396	785	1498		110
Victoria	938	1284	234	446	110	493	882	1595	110	

ALBERTA

Towns with asterisk (*) are keyed to the maps on pages 130-131.

Towns with double asterisk (**) are keyed to the map on page 9.

Acadia Valley (137)...I-36
Acme (653)...I-34
Aden...I-35
Airdrie (42,564)...I-33
Alberta Beach (865)...F-33
Alder Flats (152)...G-32
Alix (830)...H-34
Alliance (174)...H-35
Alsike...G-33
Altario...H-36
Amisk (207)...H-35
Andrew (389)...F-34
Anzac (589)...C-36
Ardmore (333)...F-36
Ashmont (188)...F-35
Athabasca (2,990)...E-34
Atikameg...D-32
Atmore (20)...E-34
Banff (7,584)...I-32, I-32, L-32
Barons (315)...K-34
Barrhead (4,432)...F-33
Bashaw (873)...H-34
Bassano (1,282)...J-34
Bawlf (403)...G-35
Bay Tree...D-29
Beaver Mines (865)...K-33
Beaverlodge (2,365)...D-29
Beiseker (785)...I-34
Bellis...D-34
Bentley (1,073)...H-33
Bezanson (121)...D-30
Big Stone...J-36
Big Valley (364)...H-34
Bindloss...J-36
Bittern Lake (224)...G-34
Blackfoot (266)...F-36
Blue Ridge (239)...F-33
Bluesky (164)...C-30
Bluffton (152)...H-33
Bodo...H-36
Bonnyville (6,216)...F-35
Bow Island (2,025)...K-35
Bowden (1,241)...I-33
Boyle (916)...E-34
Bragg Creek (595)...I-34
Brant...I-34
Breton (496)...G-33
Breynat...E-34
Brocket...K-33
Brooks (13,676)...J-35, L-22
Brosseau...F-35
Brownvale (125)...C-30
Bruce...G-34
Bruderheim (1,155)...F-34
Brule (76)...G-30
Buck Lake (75)...G-33
Buffalo...J-36
Busby (98)...F-33
Cadogan (112)...H-36
Cadomin (32)...G-31
Cadotte Lake (39)...C-32
Calahoo (187)...F-33
Calais...E-31
Calgary (1,096,833)...*C-53, F-53, J-33, L-22
Calling Lake (189)...E-34
Calmar (1,970)...G-33
Camrose (17,286)...G-34
Canmore (12,288)...J-32, L-22
Canyon Creek (259)...D-32
Carbon (592)...I-34
Cardston (3,580)...L-22, L-34
Caroline (501)...H-33
Carseland (568)...J-34
Caslan...E-34
Castle Junction...I-32
Castor (932)...H-35
Cereal (134)...I-36
Champion (378)...K-34
Chard...D-35
Chauvin (334)...G-36
Cherhill...F-33
Cherry Grove...E-36
Chinook...I-36
Chipman (284)...F-34
Clairmont (1,652)...D-30
Claresholm (3,758)...K-34
Cleardale...C-29
Cline River...H-31
Cluny (60)...J-34
Clyde (593)...F-33
Coaldale (7,493)...L-34
Cochrane (17,580)...I-33
Cold Lake (13,839)...E-36, K-22
Coleman...K-33
Colinton (215)...E-34
Compeer...H-36
Conklin (201)...D-35
Consort (689)...H-36
Coronation (947)...H-35
Coutts (277)...L-35
Cowley (236)...K-33
Cranford...K-35
Cremona (457)...I-33
Crooked Creek...E-30
Crossfield (2,853)...I-33

Crowsnest Pass (5,565)...K-33
Cynthia...G-32
Czar (167)...H-36
Dapp (34)...F-33
Daysland (807)...G-35
Dead Man's Flats...
Debolt (133)...D-30
Del Bonita...L-34
Delburne (830)...H-34
Delia (186)...I-34
Demmitt...D-29
Derwent (103)...F-35
Devon (6,510)...G-33
Dewberry (201)...F-36
Dixonville (104)...C-31
Donalda (259)...H-34
Dorothy...I-34
Drayton Valley (7,049)...G-32
Drumheller (8,029)...I-34, L-22
Duchess (992)...J-35
Dunmore (502)...K-36
Dunvegan...D-30
East Coulee (140)...I-34
Eckville (1,125)...H-33
Edberg (317)...G-36
Edmonton (812,201)...*B-48, G-34, K-22
Edson (8,475)...F-31, K-21
Elk Point (1,412)...F-35
Elkwater (50)...K-36
Elnora (313)...H-33
Empress (188)...I-36
Enchant...K-34
Endiang (35)...H-35
Enilda (165)...D-32
Entwistle (43)...F-32
Erskine (290)...H-34
Esther...I-36
Etzikom...K-36
Fairview (3,162)...C-30
Falher (1,075)...D-31
Faust (275)...D-32
Fawcett (73)...E-33
Ferintosh (181)...G-34
Fitzgerald...D-18
Flatbush (30)...E-33
Foisy...F-35
Foremost (526)...K-35
Forestburg (841)...H-35
Fort Assiniboine...E-33
Fort Chipewyan (847)...**E-18, J-22
Fort Macleod (3,117)...K-34, L-22
Fort McMurray (61,374)...D-35, J-22
Fort Saskatchewan (19,051)...F-34
Fort Vermilion (707)...**F-17, J-21
Fox Creek (1,969)...E-31, K-21
Frog Lake (24)...F-36
Gem...I-35
Gibbons (3,030)...F-34
Gift Lake (662)...D-32
Girouxville (266)...D-31
Gleichen (336)...J-34
Glenevis...F-33
Glendon (486)...F-35
Glenwood (287)...L-34
Goodridge...E-35
Gordondale...D-29
Grande Cache (4,319)...F-30
Grande Prairie (55,032)...E-30, K-21
Granum (447)...K-34

Grassland (94)...E-34
Grassy Lake...K-35
Grimshaw (2,515)...C-31, J-21
Grouard Mission (303)...D-32
Grovedale...E-30
Gurneyville...F-35
Guy...D-31
Halkirk (121)...H-35
Hanna (2,673)...I-35
Hardisty (639)...H-35
Hay Lakes (425)...G-34
Hays...K-35
High Level (3,641)...**F-17, J-21
High Prairie (2,600)...D-31, K-21
High River (12,920)...J-33
Hilda (71)...J-35
Hill Spring (186)...L-34
Hines Creek (380)...C-30
Hinton (9,640)...G-31, K-21
Hobbema (2,415)...G-34
Holden (381)...G-34
Hughenden (181)...G-36
Hoselaw...F-35
Hotchkiss...**G-17
Hussar (176)...J-34
Hylo...E-34
Hythe (820)...D-29
Innisfail (7,876)...H-33
Innisfree (220)...G-35
Irma (457)...G-36

Jenner...J-35
Joussard (181)...D-32
Kananaskis Village...J-32
Keg River...**E-16
Kikino (964)...E-35
Killam (981)...G-35
Kinsella...G-35
Kinuso (201)...D-32
Kitscoty (846)...G-36
La Corey...G-35
La Crete (523)...**F-17
La Glace (181)...D-30
Lac La Biche (2,544)...E-35, K-22
Lacombe (11,707)...H-33
Lake Louise (870)...**F-16, J-31
Lamont (1,753)...F-34
Langdon (250)...J-33
Lavoy...G-35
Leduc (24,279)...G-34
Legal (1,225)...F-33
Lethbridge (83,517)...K-34, L-22
Linden (725)...I-34
Little Smoky (36)...E-31
Lodgepole (125)...G-32
Longview (307)...J-33
Lougheed (233)...G-35
Lundbreck (244)...K-33
Magrath (2,217)...L-34
Mallaig (173)...F-35
Manning (1,164)...**G-17, J-21
Mannville (803)...G-35
Manyberries (14)...K-36
Marwayne (612)...F-36

Mayerthorpe (1,398)...F-32
McLennan (809)...D-31
McRae...F-35
Meander River (60,005)...**D-16
Medicine Hat (60,005)...*D-44, K-36, L-23
Metiskow...H-36
Milk River (811)...L-35
Millarville...J-33
Millet (2,092)...G-34
Milo (122)...J-34
Mirror (468)...H-34
Monarch (220)...K-34
Monitor...H-36
Morinville (8,569)...F-33
Morrin (245)...I-34
Mossleigh...J-34
Mountain View (80)...L-34
Mundare (855)...F-34
Myrnam (345)...F-35
Nampa (362)...D-31
Nanton (2,132)...J-33
New Brigden (14)...H-36
New Dayton (41)...L-34
Newbrook (95)...F-34
Niton Junction...F-32
Nojack...F-32
Nordegg (76)...H-32, K-22
North Cooking Lake...**G-18
Okotoks (24,511)...J-33
Olds (8,235)...I-33
Onoway (1,039)...F-33
Orion...K-36
Oyen (993)...I-36
Paddle Prairie (562)...J-21

Paradise Valley (174)...G-36
Parkland...J-34
Patricia (108)...J-35
Peace River (6,744)...C-31, J-21
Peers (108)...F-32
Seven Persons (231)...F-34
Sexsmith (2,418)...D-30
Shepard (10)...*D-54
Sherwood Park (65,475)...**B-50
Sibbald (23)...I-36
Silver Valley...C-29
Slave Lake (6,782)...D-33, K-22
Smith (218)...E-33
Smoky Lake (1,022)...F-34
Spedden...F-35
Spirit River (1,025)...C-30
Spring Coulee...L-34
Spruce View (163)...H-33
St Albert (61,466)...F-33
St Isidore (218)...C-31
St Paul (5,400)...F-35
St Vincent...F-34
Stand Off...K-34
Standard (379)...J-34
Stavely (505)...K-34
Steen River...**E-16, J-21
Stettler (5,748)...H-34
Stony Plain (15,051)...G-33
Strathmore (12,305)...J-34

Saskatchewan River Crossing...H-31
Scandia (154)...J-35
Sunset House...E-31
Swan Hills (1,465)...E-32
Sylvan Lake (12,327)...H-33
Taber (8,104)...K-35
Tangent...D-31
Thorhild (434)...F-34
Thorsby (797)...G-33
Three Hills (3,198)...I-34
Tiger Lily...E-33
Tilley (352)...J-35
Tofield (2,182)...G-34
Tomahawk (79)...G-32
Trochu (1,072)...I-34
Trout Lake (344)...C-33, J-22
Tulliby Lake (24)...F-36
Turin (106)...K-34
Turner Valley (2,167)...J-33
Twin Butte (10)...L-33
Twin Lakes...J-21
Two Hills (1,379)...F-35
Valhalla Centre (45)...D-29
Valleyview (1,761)...E-31, K-21
Vauxhall (1,288)...K-35
Vega...F-33
Vegreville (5,717)...G-35
Vermilion (3,930)...G-35
Veteran (249)...H-35
Vilna (276)...F-34
Vulcan (1,836)...J-34
Wabamun (661)...G-33
Wabasca-Desmarais (1,440)...D-33

Sundre (2,610)...I-33
Walsh (58)...K-36
Wandering River (45)...D-34
Wanham (331)...D-30
Wardlow...J-35
Warner (331)...L-35
Waskatenau (265)...F-34
Water Valley (133)...I-33
Waterton Park (65)...L-33
Watino...D-31
Wembley (1,383)...E-30
Westerose...G-33
Westlock (4,823)...F-33, K-22
Wetaskiwin (11,525)...G-34
Whitecourt (9,605)...F-32, K-22
Widewater (351)...D-32
Wildwood (294)...G-32
Willingdon (275)...F-35
Winfield (224)...G-33
Woking (106)...D-30
Worsley...C-30
Wrentham...K-35
Youngstown (178)...I-35
Zama City (93)...**F-16

Wainwright (5,925)...G-35
Seba Beach (143)...G-33
Sedgewick (857)...G-35

BRITISH COLUMBIA

100 Mile House (1,886)...I-28
100 Mile House (1,886)...I-28
108 Mile Ranch...L-21
150 Mile House (1,172)...H-27

70 Mile House...I-28
Abbotsford (133,497)...L-27
Ahousat...K-25
Ainsworth Hot Springs...K-31
Alert Bay (641)...J-25
Alexis Creek (73)...H-26
Alkali Lake...J-29
Anglemont (410)...J-29
Arras...D-29
Armstrong (4,815)...J-29
Arrow...C-29
Ashcroft (1,628)...J-28
Atlin...**H-11, J-19
Avola...J-30
Balfour (477)...K-31
Bamfield (155)...L-24
Barkerville...H-28
Barriere (1,326)...J-29, L-21
Bear Lake (159)...E-27
Beatton River (41)...J-31
Beaverdell (121)...K-29
Bell II...**I-13
Bella Bella (1,341)...G-23
Bella Coola (95)...G-24, K-20
Big Lake Ranch...H-27
Big White (109)...K-29
Black Creek...J-25
Blubber Bay...J-25
Blue River (196)...H-29, K-21
Bob Quinn Lake...**I-13, J-20
Boston Bar (206)...K-27
Boswell...K-31
Bowen Island (3,402)...L-26
Bowser (1,613)...K-25
Brackendale...L-26
Brentwood Bay...L-26
Bridal Falls...L-27
Bridesville...L-29
Bridge Lake...J-28
Britannia Beach (254)...L-26
Burnaby (223,218)...**I-41
Burns Lake (2,029)...E-25, K-20
Burton (176)...K-30
Cache Creek (1,040)...J-28, L-21
Campbell River (31,186)...J-25, L-20
Canal Flats (685)...K-32
Canim Lake...J-28
Cassiar...**G-13
Castlegar (7,816)...L-30
Cedar (2,830)...K-25
Cedarvale...D-23
Chase (2,495)...J-29
Chemainus...K-26
Chetwynd (2,635)...D-28, K-21
Chilanko Forks...H-26
Chilliwack (77,936)...L-27
Christina Lake (1,168)...L-30
Clearwater (2,331)...I-29
Clinton (636)...I-27
Coal Harbour (160)...J-23
Coalmont...K-28
Bowser Island...K-25

100 Mile House...L-21

Coquitlam (126,456)...**I-43
Courtenay (40,099)...K-25
Cowichan Bay (203)...L-26
Cranberry Junction...**I-14, K-20
Crawford Bay (321)...K-31, L-21
Crescent Spur...F-28
Creston (5,306)...L-31
Cultus Lake (15)...L-27
D'Arcy...J-27
Darfield...I-29
Dawson Creek (11,583)...D-29, K-21
Dawsons Landing...H-23, J-24
Dease Lake (303)...**H-13, J-20
Deer Park (98,863)...**K-40
Dog Creek...J-27
Dome Creek...F-28
Douglas Lake...J-28
Duncan (4,932)...L-26
Dunster...F-28
Edgewater (413)...J-32
Egmont...K-25
Elkford (2,463)...K-32
Elko (523)...K-32
Elko...L-32
Enderby (2,932)...J-29
Fairmont Hot Springs...J-32
Falkland (805)...J-29
Fanny Bay (815)...K-25
Farmington...D-29
Fauquier (170)...K-30

FOR CONTINUING COVERAGE SEE PAGES 8-9

ALBERTA BRITISH COLUMBIA ORIENTATION

1:15,840,000
Scale in Kilometers
100   0   100
Scale in Miles
100   0   100

1:3,168,000
Scale in Kilometers
50   0   50
Scale in Miles
50   0   50

N

ALBERTA
BRITISH COLUMBIA

Pacific Ocean
Hecate Strait
Queen Charlotte Strait
Pacific Strait

Driving Distances in Kilometers	Calgary	Edmonton	Fort Macleod	Jasper	Lake Louise	Medicine Hat	Peace River	Valleyview
Calgary		299	171	413	182	292	781	643
Edmonton	299		465	365	470	577	487	349
Medicine Hat	292	577	215	721	488		1062	921

See also mileage table page 2

VICTORIA, BC
1:69,696
Scale in Kilometers
0.5 0 0.5
Scale in Miles

Strait of Juan De Fuca

Gorge Road Hospital
Point Ellice House
Royal Jubilee Hospital
Victoria Harbour
SpringTide Whale Watching
Miniature World
Pacific Undersea Gardens
Christ Church Cathedral
Legislative Assembly of British Columbia
Emily Carr House
Royal BC Mus
Beacon Hill Park
Art Gallery of Greater Victoria
Craigdarroch Castle
Government House and Gardens
Oak Bay
Ross Bay

PRINCE GEORGE, BC
1:158,400
Scale in Kilometers
0.5 0 0.5
Scale in Miles

Prince George Regional Hospital
Exhibition Park
University of Northern British Columbia
Carrie Jane Gray Park
Cottonwood Island Park
The Exploration Place Museum & Science Center
Prince George Railway & Forestry Mus
Prince George Airport (YXS)

RED DEER, AB
1:158,400
Scale in Kilometers
0.5 0 0.5
Scale in Miles

Cash Casino
Gaetz Lakes Sanctuary
Alberta Sports Hall of Fame & Museum
Red Deer Regional Hosp Ctr
Red Deer Museum and Interpretive Centre
St Mary's Church
Sunnybrook Farm Museum
Red Deer Coll
Collicutt Centre
Westerner Park

DOWNTOWN VANCOUVER
1:44,352
Scale in Kilometers
0.2 0 0.2
Scale in Miles

Stanley Park
Lost Lagoon
Coal Harbour
DEADMAN'S ISLAND
Burrard Inlet
Harbour Cruises
Vancouver Convention Centre
Canada Place
English Bay
Christ Church Cathedral
Vancouver Art Gallery
Holy Rosary Cathedral
St Paul's Hospital
Vancouver Lookout at Harbour Centre Tower
Dr Sun Yat-Sen Classical Chinese Garden
Vancouver Maritime Museum
HR MacMillan Space Centre
Rogers Arena
BC Place Stadium
Edgewater Casino
Science World at TELUS World of Science
Vanier Park
False Creek

KAMLOOPS, BC
1:126,720
Scale in Kilometers
0.5 0 0.5
Scale in Miles

Kamloops Indian Reserve 1
McArthur Island Park
St Joseph's Church
Secwepemc Museum and Heritage Park
Lake City Casino
Thompson Rivers University
Kamloops Art Gallery
Kamloops Mus & Archives
Royal Inland Hospital
Peterson Creek Park

MEDICINE HAT, AB
1:110,880
Scale in Kilometers
0.5 0 0.5
Scale in Miles

The Butterfly House
Medicine Hat Regional Hospital
Medicine Hat Industries Natl Historic District
Esplanade Arts & Heritage Ctr
Police Point Park
Medicine Hat Municipal Airport (YXH)
Saamis Teepee
Medicine Hat College
Casino by Vanshaw

KELOWNA, BC
1:142,560
Scale in Kilometers
0.5 0 0.5
Scale in Miles

Bear Creek Provincial Park
Okanagan
Knox Mountain Park
Geert Maas Sculpture Gardens and Gallery
Lake City Casino
BC Orchard Industry Museum
Kelowna General Hospital
Kelowna Land and Orchard Co
Okanagan College

LETHBRIDGE, AB
1:126,720
Scale in Kilometers
0.5 0 0.5
Scale in Miles

Peenaquim Park
Indian Battle Park
Southern Alberta Art Gallery
Galt Mus & Archives
Nikka Yuko Japanese Garden
Casino Lethbridge
Henderson Lake Park
University of Lethbridge
Chinook Regional Hospital
Nicholas Sheran Lake

VANCOUVER, BC
1:190,080
Scale in Kilometers
0 3
Scale in Miles

Sewell's Marina
Horseshoe Bay
Cypress Provincial Park
Capilano Lake
Grouse Mountain
Lynn Headwaters Regional Park
Nelson Canyon Park
Capilano River Regional Park
Lighthouse Park
West Vancouver
Capilano Suspension Bridge Park
North Vancouver
Capilano Indian Reserve 5
Lions Gate Hosp
North Vancouver Museum and Archives
Maplewood Farm
Seymour Creek Indian Reserve 2
Burrard Inlet
University of British Columbia
UBC Botanical Garden
Old Hastings Mill Store Museum
Jericho Beach Park
Pacific Spirit Regional Park
Vancouver Aquarium Marine Science Centre
VANCOUVER
Pacific National Exhibition
Playland Amusement Park
Deeley Motorcycle Exhibition
Confederation Park
Burnaby Mountain Park
Simon Fraser Univ
Port Moody Station Museum
Port Moody
Eagle Ridge Hosp
Belcarra Regional Park
Minnekhada Regional Park
Musqueam Indian Reserve 2
Vancouver General Hospital
Langara College
VanDusen Botanical Garden
Bloedel Conservatory
Queen Elizabeth Pk
Burnaby Hospital
Burnaby
Burnaby Lake Regional Park
Deer Lake Park
Robert Burnaby Park
British Columbia Open University
Burnaby College
Coquitlam College
Coquitlam
Pinnacle Park
Coquitlam River Regional Park
Mundy Park
Coquitlam Indian Reserve 2
Port Coquitlam
Iona Island Regional Park
McDonald Slough
Vancouver International Airport (YVR)
SEA ISLAND
River Rock Casino Resort
MITCHELL IS
Everett Crowley Park
Central Park
New Westminster Museum and Archives
Royal Columbian Hospital
New Westminster
Queens Park
Douglas Island
Pitt Meadows
Pitt Meadows Airport (YPK)
Katzie Indian Reserve
Maple Ridge
Strait of Georgia
LULU ISLAND
Richmond Nature Park
Richmond Nature Park East
Richmond
Richmond Cultural Centre
Gulf of Georgia Cannery National Historic Site
International Buddhist Temple
London Heritage Farm
Britannia Heritage Shipyard
George C Reifel Migratory Bird Sanctuary
DEAS ISLAND
Deas Island Regional Park
Delta
Delta Hospital
Delta Museum and Archives
Musqueam Indian Reserve 4
WESTHAM ISLAND
Boundary Bay Airport (ZBB)
Delta Heritage Air Park (CAK3)
Mud Bay
Annacis Island
Tilbury Island
TULUS
Green Timbers Urban Forest
BARNSTON ISLAND
Barnston Indian Reserve 3
Tynehead Regional Park
Surrey
Fleetwood Park
Surrey Museum
Kwantlen University College-Surrey
Newton Wave Pool
Bear Creek Park
Serpentine Fen Wildlife Area
Kwantlen University College
Historic Stewart Farm
Langley
Langley Municipal Airport
Nicomekl Flood Plain Pk

NA130-15

EDMONTON, AB
1:158,400
Scale in Kilometers
Scale in Miles

EDMONTON

CALGARY, AB
1:253,440
Scale in Kilometers
Scale in Miles

Tsuu T'ina Indian Reserve 145

SEE INSET

DOWNTOWN CALGARY
1:44,352
Scale in Kilometers
Scale in Miles

THE BATTLEFORDS, SK
1:126,720
Scale in Kilometers
Scale in Miles

North Battleford

FINLAYSON ISLAND

Battleford

SWIFT CURRENT, SK
1:95,040
Scale in Kilometers
Scale in Miles

SASKATOON, SK
1:158,400
Scale in Kilometers
Scale in Miles

Saskatoon John G Diefenbaker International Airport (YXE)

University of Saskatchewan

MOOSE JAW, SK
1:126,720
Scale in Kilometers
Scale in Miles

REGINA, SK
1:126,720
Scale in Kilometers
Scale in Miles

Regina International Airport (YQR)

University of Regina

Wascana Lake

WINNIPEG, MB
1:269,280
Scale in Kilometers
Scale in Miles

SEE INSET

Univ of Manitoba

BANFF, AB
1:63,360
Scale in Kilometers
Scale in Miles

Banff

Bow River

BRANDON, MB
1:126,720
Scale in Kilometers
Scale in Miles

Assiniboine River

PORTAGE LA PRAIRIE, MB
1:126,720
Scale in Kilometers
Scale in Miles

Crescent Lake

Island Park

DOWNTOWN WINNIPEG
1:38,016
Scale in Kilometers
Scale in Miles

The Forks

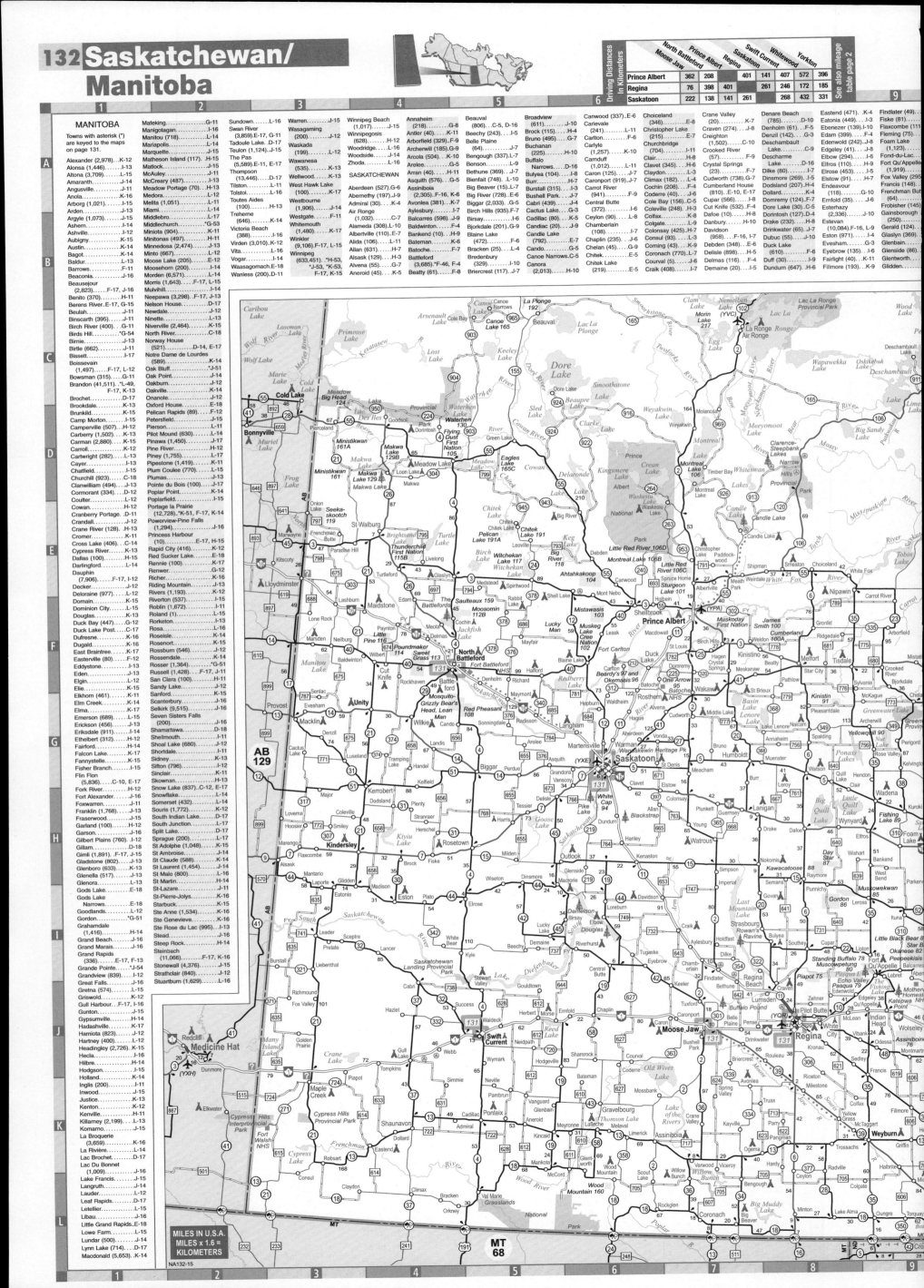

Driving Distances in Kilometers	Moose Jaw	North Battleford	Prince Albert	Regina	Saskatoon	Swift Current	Whitewood	Yorkton
Prince Albert	362	208		401	141	407	572	396
Regina	76	398	401		261	246	172	185
Saskatoon	222	138	141	261		268	432	331

See also mileage table page 2

MANITOBA

Towns with asterisk (*) are keyed to the maps on page 131.

Alexander (2,978)....K-12
Alonsa (1,446)....I-13
Altona (3,709)....L-15
Amaranth....I-14
Angusville....J-11
Anola....K-16
Arborg (1,021)....I-15
Arden....I-13
Argyle (1,073)....J-13
Ashern....I-13
Ashville....I-12
Aubigny....K-15
Austin....K-14
Bagot....K-14
Baldur....L-13
Barrows....F-11
Beaconia....I-16
Beausejour (2,823)....F-17, J-16
Benito (370)....H-11
Berens River....E-17, G-15
Beulah....J-11
Binscarth (395)....J-11
Birch River (400)....G-11
Birds Hill....*G-54
Birnie....I-13
Birtle (662)....J-11
Bissett....I-17
Boissevain (1,497)....F-17, L-12
Bowsman (315)....G-11
Brandon (41,511)....*L-49, F-17, K-13
Brochet....D-17
Brookdale....K-13
Brunkild....K-15
Camp Morton....I-15
Camperville (507)....H-12
Carberry (1,502)....K-13
Carman (2,880)....K-15
Carroll....K-12
Cartwright (282)....L-13
Cayer....I-13
Chatfield....I-15
Churchill (923)....C-18
Clanwilliam (494)....J-13
Cormorant (334)....D-12
Coulter....L-12
Cowan....H-12
Cranberry Portage....D-11
Crandall....J-12
Crane River (128)....H-13
Cromer....K-11
Cross Lake (406)....C-14
Cypress River....K-13
Dallas (100)....I-15
Darlingford....L-14
Dauphin (7,906)....F-17, I-12
Decker....J-12
Deloraine (977)....L-12
Dominion City....L-15
Domain....K-15
Douglas....K-13
Duck Bay (447)....G-12
Duck Lake Post....C-17
Dufresne....K-16
Dugald....K-16
East Braintree....K-17
Easterville (80)....F-12
Eddystone....I-13
Eden....I-13
Elgin....L-12
Elie....K-15
Elkhorn (461)....K-11
Elm Creek....K-14
Elma....K-16
Emerson (689)....L-15
Erickson (456)....I-13
Eriksdale (911)....I-14
Ethelbert (312)....H-12
Fairford....H-14
Falcon Lake....K-17
Fannystelle....K-15
Fisher Branch....I-15
Flin Flon (5,836)....C-10, E-17
Fork River....H-12
Fort Alexander....J-16
Foxwarren....J-11
Franklin (1,768)....J-13
Fraserwood....I-15
Garland (100)....H-12
Garson....K-16
Gilbert Plains (760)....I-12
Gillam....C-17
Gimli (1,891)....F-17, I-15
Gladstone (902)....J-13
Glenboro (633)....J-13
Glenella (517)....I-13
Glenora....I-13
Gods Lake....E-18
Gods Lake Narrows....E-18
Goodlands....L-12
Gordon....*G-51
Grahamdale (1,416)....H-14
Grand Beach....J-16
Grand Marais....I-16
Grand Rapids (336)....E-17, F-13
Grande Pointe....*J-54
Grandview (839)....I-12
Great Falls....J-16
Gretna (574)....L-15
Griswold....K-12
Gull Harbour....F-17, I-15
Gunton....J-15
Gypsumville....H-14
Hadashville....K-17
Hamiota (823)....J-12
Hartney (400)....L-12
Headingley (2,726)....K-15
Hecla....H-15
Hilbre....H-14
Hodgson....I-15
Holland (200)....K-14
Inglis (200)....I-11
Inwood....J-15
Justice....K-13
Kenton....J-12
Kenville....H-11
Killarney (2,199)....L-13
Komarno....I-15
La Broquerie (3,659)....K-16
La Rivière....L-14
Lac Brochet....D-17
Lac Du Bonnet (1,009)....J-16
Lake Francis....J-15
Langruth....I-14
Lauder....L-12
Leaf Rapids....D-17
Letellier....L-15
Libau....J-16
Little Grand Rapids....E-18
Lowe Farm....L-15
Lundar (500)....I-14
Lynn Lake (714)....D-17
Macdonald (5,653)....K-14

Mafeking....G-11
Manigotagan....I-16
Manitou (718)....L-14
Mariapolis....L-13
Marquette....J-15
Matheson Island (117)....H-15
Matlock....I-15
McAuley....J-11
McCreary (487)....I-13
Meadow Portage (70)....H-13
Medora....L-12
Melita (1,051)....L-11
Miami....L-14
Middlebro....L-17
Middlechurch....*G-53
Miniota (904)....J-11
Minitonas (497)....H-11
Minnedosa (2,474)....J-13
Minto (667)....L-12
Moose Lake (205)....E-12
Moosehorn (200)....I-14
Morden (6,571)....F-17, L-14
Morris (1,643)....F-17, L-15
Mulvihill....I-14
Neepawa (3,298)....F-17, J-13
Nelson House....D-17
Newdale....J-12
Ninette....L-13
Niverville (2,464)....K-15
North River....C-18
Norway House (521)....D-14, E-17
Notre Dame de Lourdes (589)....K-14
Oak Bluff....*J-51
Oak Point....J-51
Oakburn....J-12
Oakville....K-14
Onanole....J-12
Oxford House....E-18
Pelican Rapids (89)....F-12
Petersfield....J-15
Pierson....L-11
Pilot Mound (630)....L-14
Pinawa (1,450)....J-17
Pine River....H-12
Piney....L-17
Pipestone (1,419)....K-11
Plum Coulee (770)....L-15
Plumas....J-13
Pointe du Bois (100)....J-17
Poplar Point....K-14
Poplarfield....I-15
Portage la Prairie (12,728)....*K-51, F-17, K-14
Powerview-Pine Falls (1,294)....J-16
Princess Harbour (10)....E-17, H-15
Rapid City (416)....K-12
Red Sucker Lake....E-18
Rennie (100)....K-17
Renwer....G-12
Richer....K-16
Riding Mountain....J-13
Rivers (1,193)....K-12
Riverton (537)....I-15
Roblin (1,672)....I-11
Roland (1)....L-15
Rorketon....I-13
Ross....J-14
Roseisle....K-14
Rosenort....K-15
Rossburn (546)....J-12
Rossendale....K-14
Rosser (1,364)....*G-51
Russell (1,428)....F-17, J-11
San Clara (100)....H-11
Sandy Lake....J-12
Sanford....K-15
Scanterbury....J-16
Selkirk (9,515)....J-16
Seven Sisters Falls (200)....K-17
Shamattawa....D-18
Shellmouth....J-11
Shoal Lake (680)....J-12
Shortdale....J-11
Sidney....K-13
Sifton (796)....I-12
Sinclair....K-11
Skowan....H-13
Snow Lake (837)....C-12, E-17
Snowflake....L-14
Somerset (432)....L-14
Souris (1,772)....L-12
South Indian Lake....D-17
South Junction....L-17
Split Lake....D-17
Sprague (200)....L-17
St Adolphe (1,268)....K-15
St Ambroise....J-14
St Claude (588)....K-14
St Laurent (1,454)....J-15
St Malo (800)....L-16
St Martin....H-14
St-Lazare....J-11
St-Pierre-Jolys....K-16
Starbuck....K-15
Ste Anne (1,534)....K-16
Ste Genevieve....K-16
Ste Rose du Lac (995)....I-13
Stead....J-16
Steep Rock....H-14
Steinbach (11,066)....F-17, K-16
Stonewall (4,376)....J-15
Strathclair (840)....J-12
Stuartburn (1,629)....L-16

Sundown....L-16
Swan River (3,859)....E-17, G-11
Tadoule Lake....D-17
Teulon (1,124)....J-15
The Pas (5,589)....E-11, E-17
Thompson (13,446)....D-17
Tilston....L-11
Tolstoi....L-16
Toutes Aides (100)....H-13
Treherne (646)....K-14
Victoria Beach (388)....I-16
Virden (3,010)....K-12
Vita....L-16
Vogar....I-14
Waasagomach....E-18
Wanless (200)....D-11

Warren....J-15
Wasagaming (200)....J-12
Waskada (199)....L-12
Wawanesa (535)....K-13
Wellwood....K-13
West Hawk Lake (100)....K-17
Westbourne....J-14
Westgate....F-11
Whitemouth (1,480)....K-17
Winkler (9,106)....F-17, L-15
Winnipeg (633,451)....*H-53, *J-53, *K-53, F-17, K-15
Winnipeg Beach (1,017)....J-15
Winnipegosis (628)....H-12
Woodridge....L-16
Woodside....J-14
Zhoda....L-16

SASKATCHEWAN

Aberdeen (527)....G-6
Abernethy (197)....J-9
Admiral (30)....K-4
Air Ronge (1,032)....C-7
Alameda (308)....L-10
Albertville (110)....E-7
Alida (106)....L-11
Allan (631)....H-7
Alsask (234)....H-3
Alvena (55)....G-7
Aneroid (45)....K-5

Annaheim (218)....G-8
Antler (40)....H-4
Arborfield (329)....F-9
Archerwill (185)....G-9
Arcola (504)....K-10
Arelee....L-9
Arran (40)....H-11
Asquith (576)....G-7
Assiniboia (2,305)....F-16, K-6
Avonlea (381)....K-7
Aylesbury....J-7
Balcarres (598)....J-9
Baldwinton....H-4
Bankend (10)....H-9
Bateman....K-6
Batoche....F-7
Battleford (3,685)....*F-46, F-17
Beatty (61)....F-8

Beauval (806)....C-5, D-16
Beechy (243)....I-5
Belle Plaine (64)....J-7
Bengough (337)....L-7
Benson....H-9
Bethune (369)....J-7
Bienfait (748)....L-10
Big Beaver (15)....L-7
Big River (728)....E-6
Biggar (2,033)....G-5
Birch Hills (935)....F-7
Birsay....I-6
Bjorkdale (201)....G-9
Blaine Lake (472)....E-7
Bracken (25)....L-4
Bredenbury (329)....I-10
Briercrest (117)....J-7

Broadview (611)....J-10
Brock (115)....H-4
Bruno (495)....G-7
Buchanan (225)....H-10
Buffalo Narrows....D-16
Bulyea (104)....J-8
Burr....H-7
Burstall (315)....I-3
Cabri (439)....J-4
Cactus Lake....G-3
Cadillac (80)....K-5
Candiac (90)....J-9
Candle Lake (472)....E-7
Cando (43)....G-5
Canoe Narrows....C-5
Canora (2,013)....H-10

Canwood (337)....E-6
Carievale....L-10
Carlyle (1,257)....K-10
Carnduff (1,012)....L-11
Carlton....F-6
Caron (125)....J-7
Caronport (919)....J-7
Carrot River (941)....F-9
Central Butte (372)....J-6
Ceylon (90)....L-7
Chamberlain (108)....J-7
Chaplin (235)....J-6
Chelan (35)....G-9
Chitek Lake....E-5

Choiceland (346)....E-8
Christopher Lake (215)....E-7
Churchbridge (704)....I-10
Clair....H-8
Clavet (345)....H-6
Claydon....L-3
Climax (182)....L-4
Cochin (208)....F-4
Coderre (40)....J-6
Cole Bay (156)....C-5
Coleville (248)....H-3
Colfax....K-8
Colgate....L-9
Colonsay (425)....H-7
Consul (93)....L-3
Corning (43)....K-9
Coronach (770)....L-7
Courval (5)....J-6
Craik (408)....J-7

Crane Valley (20)....K-7
Craven (274)....J-8
Creighton (1,502)....C-10
Crooked River (57)....F-9
Crystal Springs (23)....F-7
Cudworth (738)....G-7
Cumberland House (810)....E-10, E-17
Cupar (566)....J-8
Cut Knife (532)....F-4
Dafoe (10)....H-8
Danbury (71)....H-10
Davidson (958)....F-16, I-7
Debden (348)....E-6
Delisle (898)....G-6
Delmas (116)....F-4
Demaine (20)....I-5

Denare Beach (785)....D-10
Denholm (61)....F-5
Deschambault Lake....C-9
Descharme Lake....D-16
Dilke (80)....I-7
Dinsmore (269)....I-5
Dodsland (207)....H-4
Dollard....K-4
Domremy (124)....F-7
Dore Lake (35)....D-5
Drake (232)....H-8
Drinkwater (65)....J-7
Dubuc (55)....J-10
Duck Lake (610)....F-6
Duff (30)....J-9
Dundurn (647)....H-6

Eastend (471)....K-4
Eatonia (449)....I-3
Ebenezer (139)....I-10
Edam (399)....F-5
Edenwold (242)....J-8
Edgeley (41)....J-8
Elbow (294)....I-6
Elfros (110)....H-9
Elrose (453)....I-5
Elstow (91)....H-7
Endeavour (118)....G-10
Emfold (35)....J-6
Esterhazy (2,336)....J-10
Eston (971)....I-4
Estevan (10,084)....F-16, L-9
Eyebrow (135)....J-6

Findlater (49)....J-8
Fiske (81)....H-5
Flaxcombe (111)....H-3
Fleming (75)....J-11
Foam Lake (1,123)....H-9
Fond-du-Lac....
Fort Qu'Appelle (1,919)....J-9
Fox Valley (295)....I-3
Francis (148)....K-8
Frenchman Butte (64)....F-4
Frobisher (145)....L-10
Gainsborough (250)....L-11
Gerald (41)....J-11
Glaslyn (369)....F-5
Glenbain....J-5
Glenside (56)....I-6
Glentworth....L-5
Glidden....H-4

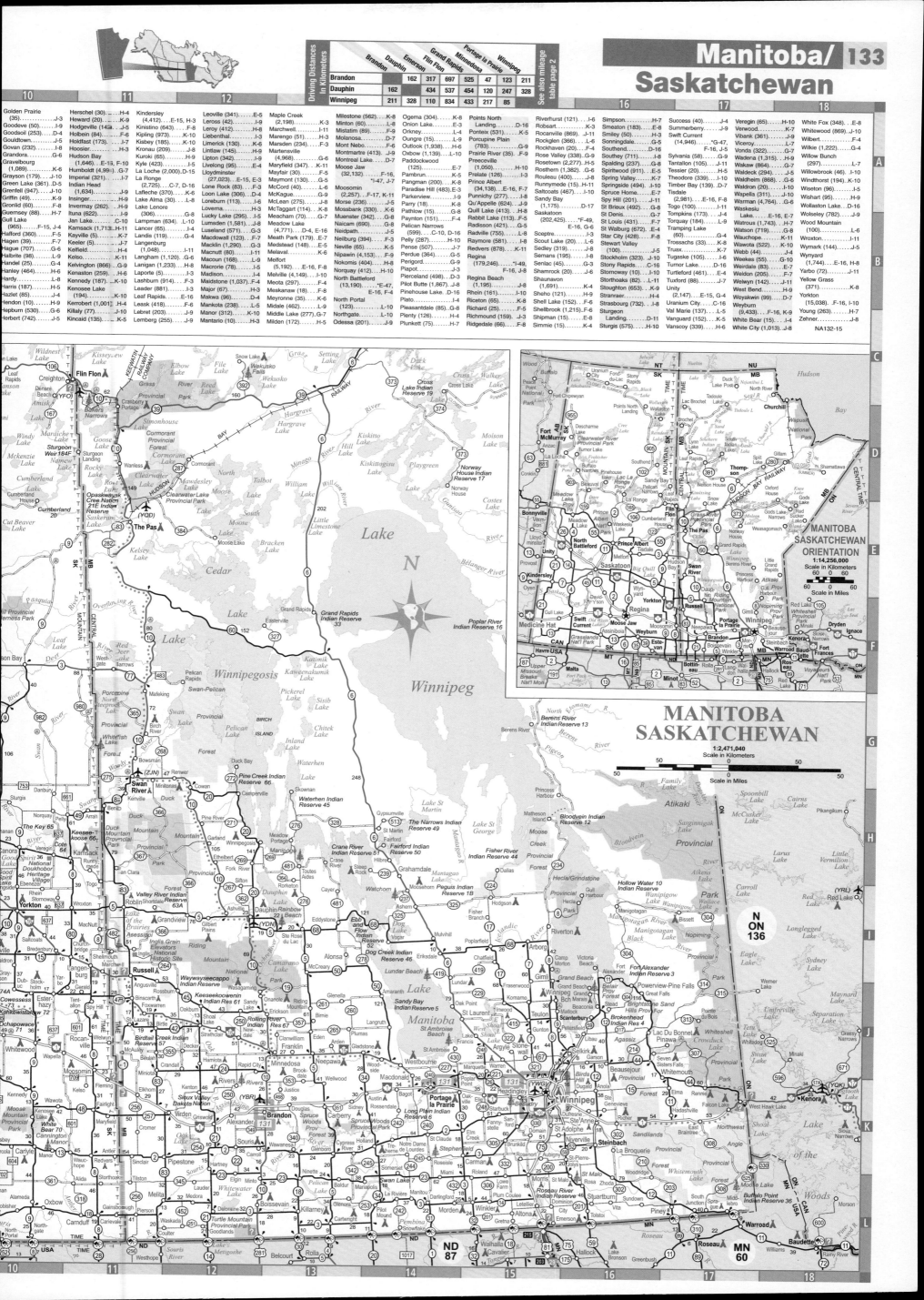

Driving Distances in Kilometers

See also mileage table page 2

	Brandon	Dauphin	Emerson	Flin Flon	Grand Rapids	Minnedosa	Portage la Prairie	Winnipeg
Brandon		162	317	697	525	47	123	211
Dauphin	162		434	537	454	120	247	328
Winnipeg	211	328	110	834	433	217	85	

Index

Golden Prairie (35)....J-3
Goodeve (50)....I-9
Goodsoil (253)....D-4
Gouldtown....J-5
Govan (232)....I-8
Grandora....G-6
Gravelbourg (1,089)....K-6
Grayson (179)....J-10
Green Lake (361)....D-5
Grenfell (947)....J-10
Griffin (49)....K-9
Gronlid (60)....F-8
Gull Lake (965)....F-15, J-4
Hafford (360)....F-5
Hagen (39)....F-7
Hague (707)....G-6
Halbrite (98)....K-9
Handel (25)....G-4
Hanley (464)....H-6
Harris (187)....H-5
Hazlet (85)....J-4
Hendon (110)....F-9
Hepburn (530)....G-6
Herbert (742)....J-5

Herschel (30)....H-4
Heward (35)....K-9
Hodgeville (143)....J-5
Holbein (84)....F-6
Holdfast (173)....I-7
Hoosier....H-3
Hudson Bay (1,646)....E-13, F-10
Humboldt (4,998)....G-7
Imperial (321)....I-7
Indian Head (1,634)....J-9
Insinger....I-9
Invermay (282)....H-9
Ituna (622)....I-9
Jan Lake....C-10
Kamsack (1,713)....H-10
Kayville (5)....K-7
Keeler (5)....I-7
Kelfield....H-4
Kelso....H-11
Kelvington (866)....G-9
Kenaston (259)....H-6
Kennedy (187)....K-10
Kenosee Lake (194)....K-10
Kerrobert (1,001)....H-4
Killaly (77)....J-10
Kincaid (135)....K-5

Kindersley (4,412)....E-15, H-3
Kinistino (643)....F-8
Kipling (973)....K-10
Kisbey (185)....K-10
Kronau (29)....J-8
Kuroki (65)....H-9
Kyle (423)....I-5
La Loche (2,000)....D-15
La Ronge (2,725)....C-7, D-16
Lafleche (370)....K-6
Lake Alma (30)....L-8
Lake Lenore (306)....G-8
Lampman (634)....L-10
Lancer (85)....I-4
Landis (119)....G-4
Langenburg (1,048)....I-11
Langham (1,120)....G-6
Lanigan (1,233)....H-8
Laporte (5)....I-3
Lashburn (914)....G-3
Leader (881)....I-3
Leask (418)....F-6
Lebret (203)....J-9
Lemberg (255)....J-9

Leoville (341)....E-5
Leross (42)....I-9
Leroy (412)....H-8
Liebenthal....H-3
Limerick (130)....K-6
Lintlaw (145)....H-9
Lipton (342)....I-9
Livelong (95)....E-4
Lloydminster (27,023)....E-15, E-3
Lone Rock (83)....E-3
Loon Lake (306)....D-4
Loreburn (113)....I-6
Loverna....H-3
Lucky Lake (295)....I-5
Lumsden (1,581)....J-8
Luseland (571)....G-3
Macdonald (123)....F-7
Macklin (1,290)....G-3
Macnutt (80)....I-11
Macoun (169)....L-9
Macrorie (78)....I-5
Madison....H-4
Maidstone (1,037)....F-4
Major (45)....H-3
Makwa (96)....D-4
Mankota (283)....L-5
Manor (312)....K-10
Mantario (10)....H-3

Maple Creek (2,198)....K-3
Marchwell....I-11
Marengo (51)....H-3
Marsden (234)....F-3
Martensville (4,968)....G-6
Maryfield (347)....K-11
Mayfair (30)....F-5
Maymont (130)....G-5
McCord (40)....L-6
McKague....G-9
McLean (275)....J-8
McTaggart (114)....K-8
Meacham (70)....G-7
Meadow Lake (4,771)....D-4, B-16
Meath Park (179)....E-7
Medstead (148)....E-5
Melaval....K-6
Melfort (5,192)....E-16, F-8
Melville (4,149)....I-10
Meota (297)....F-4
Meskanaw (18)....F-8
Meyronne (35)....K-6
Midale (462)....L-9
Middle Lake (277)....G-7

Milestone (562)....K-8
Minton (60)....L-8
Mistatim (89)....F-9
Molanosa....D-7
Mont Nebo....F-6
Montmartre (413)....J-9
Montreal Lake....D-7
Moose Jaw (32,132)....*I-47, J-7
Moosomin (2,257)....*I-17, K-11
Morse (236)....J-5
Mossbank (330)....K-6
Muenster (342)....G-8
Naicam (690)....G-8
Neidpath....J-5
Neilburg (394)....F-3
Neville (65)....K-5
Nipawin (4,153)....F-9
Nokomis (404)....H-8
Norquay (412)....H-10
North Battleford (13,190)....*E-47, F-4
North Portal (123)....L-10
Northgate....L-10
Odessa (201)....J-9

Ogema (304)....K-8
Onion Lake....E-3
Orkney....L-4
Oungre (15)....L-9
Outlook (1,938)....I-6
Oxbow (1,139)....L-10
Paddockwood....E-7
Pambrun....K-5
Pangman (200)....K-8
Paradise Hill (483)....E-3
Parkerview....I-9
Parry (18)....K-8
Pathlow (15)....F-8
Paynton (151)....F-4
Pelican Narrows (599)....C-10, D-16
Pelly (287)....H-10
Pense (507)....J-7
Perdue (498)....G-5
Perigord....J-9
Piapot....J-3
Pierceland (482)....D-3
Pilot Butte (1,867)....J-8
Pinehouse Lake....D-16
Plato....H-4
Pleasantdale (85)....G-8
Plenty (126)....H-4
Plunkett (75)....H-7

Points North Landing....D-16
Ponteix (531)....K-5
Porcupine Plain (783)....F-10
Prairie River (35)....F-9
Preeceville (1,050)....H-10
Prelate (126)....I-3
Prince Albert (34,138)....*E-16, E-7, F-7
Punnichy (277)....I-8
Qu'Appelle (624)....J-9
Quill Lake (413)....H-8
Rabbit Lake (113)....F-5
Radisson (421)....G-6
Radville (755)....L-8
Raymore (581)....I-8
Redvers (878)....K-11
Regina (179,246)....*F-16, I-8
Regina Beach (1,195)....J-8
Rhein (161)....I-10
Riceton (65)....J-8
Richard (25)....F-5
Richmound (159)....J-3
Ridgedale (66)....F-8

Riverhurst (121)....I-6
Robsart....K-3
Rocanville (869)....J-11
Rockglen (366)....L-6
Rockhaven (20)....F-4
Rose Valley (338)....G-9
Rosetown (2,277)....H-5
Rosthern (1,382)....G-6
Rouleau (400)....J-8
Runnymede (15)....H-11
Saltcoats (467)....I-10
Sandy Bay....D-17
Saskatoon (202,425)....*F-49, E-16, G-6
Sceptre....J-3
Scout Lake (20)....L-6
Sedley (319)....J-8
Semans (190)....I-8
Senlac (45)....G-3
Sheho (153)....H-9
Shell Lake (152)....F-6
Shellbrook (1,215)....F-6
Shipman (15)....E-7
Simmie (15)....K-4

Simpson (15)....H-7
Smeaton (183)....E-8
Smiley (50)....H-3
Sonningdale....G-5
Southend....D-16
Southey (711)....I-8
Spalding (237)....G-8
Spiritwood (911)....E-5
Springside (494)....I-10
Spruce Home....E-7
Spy Hill (201)....I-11
St Brieux (492)....G-8
St Denis....G-7
St Louis (431)....F-7
St Walburg (672)....E-4
Star City (428)....F-8
Stewart Valley (100)....J-5
Stockholm (323)....I-10
Stony Rapids....C-16
Stornoway (10)....I-10
Storthoaks (82)....L-11
Stoughton (653)....K-9
Stranraer....H-4
Strasbourg (732)....I-8
Sturgeon Landing....D-11

Success (40)....J-4
Summerberry....J-9
Swift Current (14,946)....*G-47, J-5
Sylvania (58)....G-9
Tantallon (105)....J-11
Tessier (20)....H-5
Theodore (398)....I-10
Timber Bay (139)....D-7
Tisdale (2,981)....F-9
Togo (100)....I-11
Tompkins (173)....J-4
Torquay (184)....L-9
Tramping Lake (60)....G-4
Trossachs (33)....K-8
Truax....K-7
Tugaske (105)....I-6
Turnor Lake....D-16
Turtleford (461)....E-4
Tuxford (88)....J-7
Unity (2,147)....E-15, G-4
Uranium City....C-16
Val Marie (137)....L-5
Vanguard (152)....K-5
Vanscoy (339)....H-6

Veregin (65)....H-10
Verwood....K-7
Vibank (361)....J-9
Viceroy....L-7
Vonda (322)....G-7
Wadena (1,315)....H-9
Wakaw (864)....G-7
Waldeck (294)....J-5
Waldheim (868)....G-6
Waldron (20)....I-10
Wapella (311)....J-10
Warman (4,764)....G-6
Waskesiu Lake....E-16, E-7
Watrous (1,743)....H-7
Watson (719)....G-8
Wawota (522)....K-10
Webb (44)....J-4
Weekes (55)....G-10
Weirdale (83)....E-7
Weldon (205)....F-7
Welwyn (142)....J-11
West Bend....H-8
Weyakwin (99)....D-7
Weyburn (9,433)....*F-16, K-9
White Bear (35)....J-4
White City (1,013)....J-8

White Fox (348)....E-8
Whitewood (869)....J-10
Wilbert....F-4
Wilkie (1,222)....G-4
Willow Bunch (297)....L-7
Willowbrook (46)....I-10
Windthorst (194)....K-10
Wiseton (96)....I-5
Wishart (95)....I-8
Wolseley (782)....J-9
Wollaston Lake....D-16
Wood Mountain (100)....L-6
Wroxton....I-10
Wymark (144)....J-5
Wynyard (1,744)....E-16, H-8
Yarbo (72)....J-11
Yellow Grass (371)....K-8
Yorkton (15,038)....F-16, I-10
Young (263)....H-7
Zehner....J-8

NA132-15

Manitoba Saskatchewan Orientation

1:14,256,000
Scale in Kilometers
Scale in Miles

MANITOBA SASKATCHEWAN

1:2,471,040
Scale in Kilometers
Scale in Miles

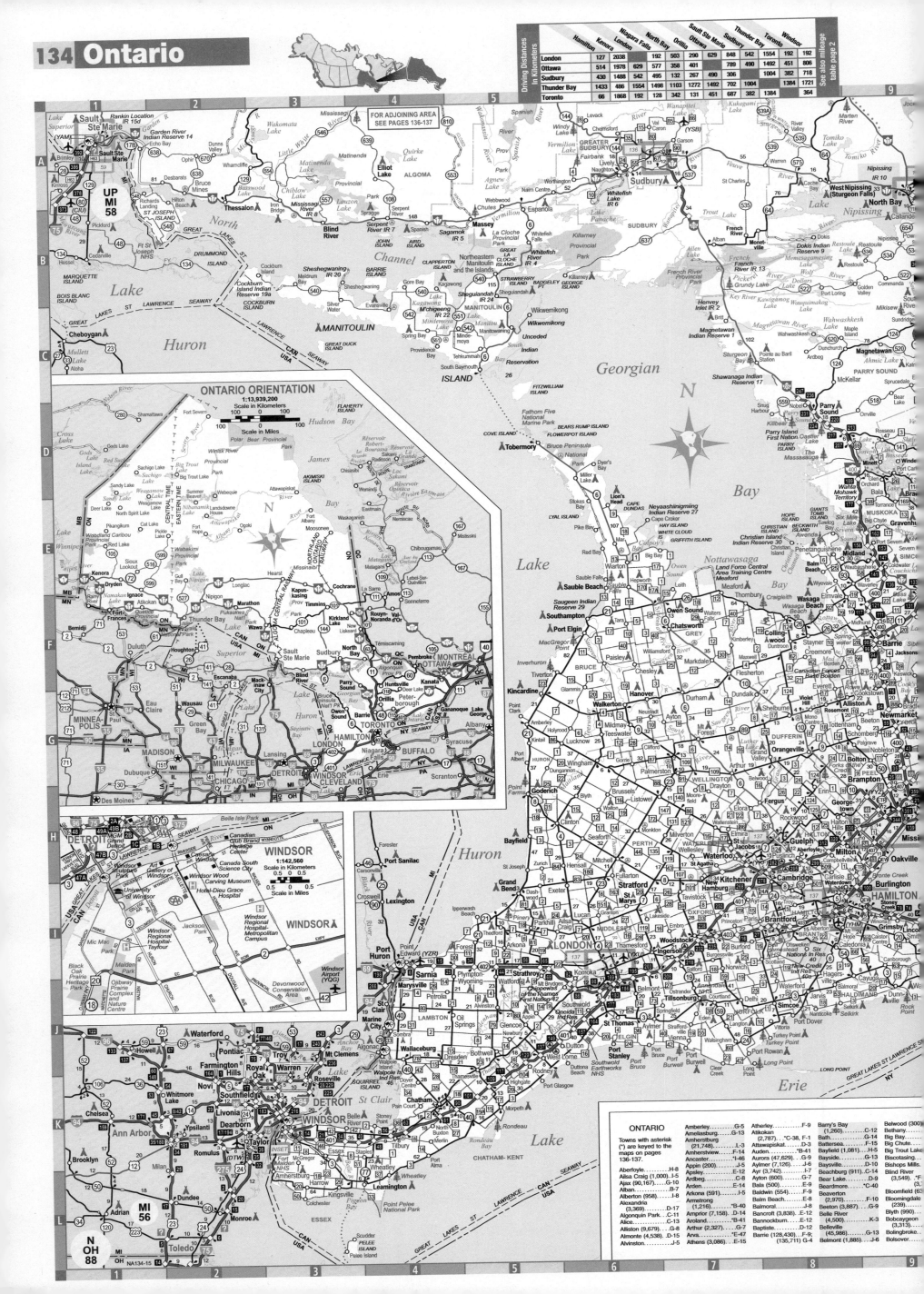

Driving Distances In Kilometers

	Hamilton	Kenora	London	Niagara Falls	North Bay	Orillia	Ottawa	Sault Ste Marie	Sudbury	Thunder Bay	Toronto	Windsor
London	127	2038		192	503	290	629	848	542	1554	192	192
Ottawa	514	1978	629	577	358	401		789	490	1492	451	806
Sudbury	430	1488	542	495	132	267	490	306		1004	382	718
Thunder Bay	1433	486	1554	1498	1103	1272	1492	702	1004		1384	1721
Toronto	66	1868	192	128	342	131	451	687	382	1384		364

See also page 2 table mileage

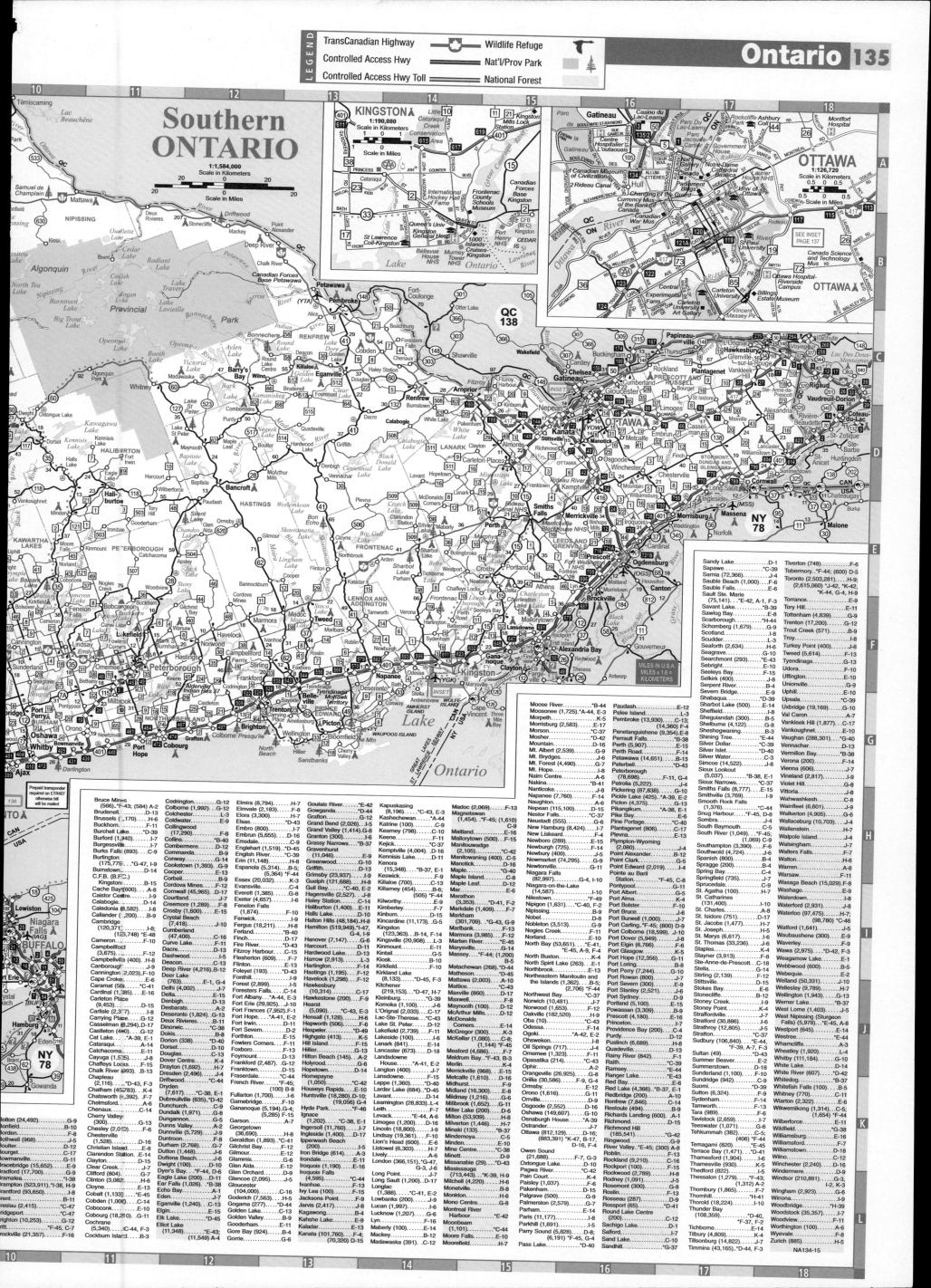

Northern ONTARIO
1:4,672,800
Scale in Kilometers
Scale in Miles

THUNDER BAY, ON
1:300,960
Scale in Kilometers
Scale in Miles

SUDBURY, ON
1:174,240
Scale in Kilometers
Scale in Miles

NORTH BAY, ON
1:205,920
Scale in Kilometers
Scale in Miles

TORONTO, ON AREA
1:221,760
Scale in Kilometers
Scale in Miles

TORONTO, ON
1:47,520
Scale in Kilometers
Scale in Miles

MILES IN U.S.A.
MILES x 1.6 = KILOMETERS

James Bay

Lake Superior

Lake Huron

Lake Ontario

Lake Nipigon

Lake Nipissing

THUNDER BAY

COCHRANE

KENORA

RAINY RIVER

TIMISKAMING

ALGOMA

PEEL

YORK

DURHAM

HALTON

Kenora · Dryden · Ignace · Baudette · Kapuskasing · Cochrane · Timmins · Kirkland Lake · Sudbury · Wawa · Marathon · Thunder Bay · Sault Ste Marie · North Bay · Sturgeon Falls · Parry Sound

Brampton · Mississauga · Vaughan · Richmond Hill · Markham · Toronto · Woodbridge · Kleinburg · Thornhill

Red Lake · Sioux Lookout · Longlac · Geraldton · Nipigon · Hearst · Fort Albany · Moosonee · Moose Factory

QUÉBEC, QC
1:19,008
Scale in Kilometers
0.1   0   0.1
Scale in Miles
0.1   0   0.1

Port of Québec

Museum of Civilization
L'Hôtel-Dieu Le Québec (Chuq)
Hôtel Dieu Augustines Museum
Museum of Francophone America
Our Lady of Victories Church
Fortifications of Québec National Historic Site
Québec City Cruises
The Ursulines Museum
Place Royale
Dufferin Terrace
Maillou House Nat'l Hist Site
The Citadel
Artillery Park Heritage Site
Parc de L'Esplanade
Parliament Building

QUÉBEC, QC AREA
1:190,080
Scale in Kilometers
1.5   0   1.5
Scale in Miles
1.5   0   1.5

QUÉBEC
Ice Hotel
Wendake Réserve Indienne
Hôpital Chauveau
Hôpital De L'enfant-Jésus
L'Ancienne-Lorette
Lorette
Québec City
Jean Lesage International Airport (YQB)
Hôpital Laval
Université Laval
Jesuit House of Sillery
Montmartre Canadien
National Museum of Fine Arts of Québec
Cartier Brébeuf NHS
SEE INSET
Hôtel-Dieu de Lévis
Lévis Forts NHS
Québec Aquarium
LÉVIS
Parc de la Rivière Etchemin
CH Paul-Gilbert
Parc des Chutes-de-la-Chaudière
BELLECHASSE
DORLÉANS
ÎLE-D'ORLÉANS
Ste-Pétronille
LA CÔTE-DE-BEAUPRÉ
Montmorency Falls Park
Fleuve Saint-Laurent
Seaway

KITCHENER / CAMBRIDGE, ON
1:269,280
Scale in Kilometers
1   0   1
Scale in Miles
1   0   1

Waterloo
Bloomingdale
Bechtel Park
Brubacher House Mus
RIM Park
Waterloo International Airport (YKF)
Waterloo Park
University of Waterloo
Canadian Clay & Glass Gallery
Grand River Hospital
Kitchener
Waterloo Region Mus
Homer Watson House and Gallery
Cambridge Butterfly Conservatory
Riverside Park
WELLINGTON
Hespeler
Shade's Mill Conservation Area
Cambridge
Dumfries Conservation Area
Cambridge Memorial Hosp
Shade's Mill Conservation Area
WATERLOO

LONDON, ON
1:253,440
Scale in Kilometers
1   0   1
Scale in Miles
1   0   1

Arva
Kilally West Northside Park
Fanshawe Lake
Fanshawe Conservation Area
London International Airport (YXU)
Kilally Valley Pk
LHSC-Univ
Univ of Western Ontario
The Royal Canadian Regiment Museum
London Museum of Archaeology
Hyde Park
Kiwanis Park
Clark Road Park
London Reg Children's Museum
Banting NHS
Labatt Brewery Tour
Greenway Park
LHSC-Victoria Hospital
Storybook Gardens
Byron Baseline Park
Thames River
North Branch
Dingman Creek

HAMILTON, ON
1:228,096
Scale in Kilometers
1   0   1
Scale in Miles
1   0   1

Burlington
Borer's Falls Conservation Area
Royal Botanical Gardens
HMCS Haida National Historic Site
Burlington Bay
Duncurn NHS
McMaster Univ
Cootes Paradise
Wild Waterworks
Confederation Park
HAMILTON
Lake Ontario
Tim Hortons
St Joseph's Healthcare Charlton Campus
Chedoke Golf Course
Redeemer University College
Mohawk Sports
King's Forest Park
Upper King's Forest Park
Battlefield House Museum NHS
Stoney Creek
CITY OF HAMILTON

MONTRÉAL, QC AREA
1:190,080
Scale in Kilometers
1   0   1
Scale in Miles
1   0   1

LAVAL
Hôpital Cité de la Santé
Parc Naturel du Bois Papineau
Parc Central de la Nature
St-Léonard
Anjou
Boucherville
Cosmodome/Canada Space Camp
ÎLE VERTE
BFC Montréal
Parc Maisonneuve
Hôpital Santa Cabrini
Hôpital du Sacré-Cœur de Montréal
Parc Régional du-Bois-de-Saraguay
Montréal Botanical Garden
Montréal Biodôme
Parc Olympique
Stade Saputo
MONTRÉAL
Parc Jarry
Parc Régional du-Bois-de-Liesse
Marcel-Laurin
St-Laurent
The Museum of Québec Masters & Artisans
Mont-Royal
Parc La Fontaine
Outremont
Université de Montréal
Stewart Museum
St Joseph's Oratory
Montréal Casino
Old Montréal
St-Lambert
St Hubert Airport (YHU)
Longueuil
LONGUEUIL
Greenfield Park
CH Pierre-Boucher
Parc Régional de Longueuil
Shaar Hashomayim Synagogue
The Montreal Holocaust Memorial Centre
Hampstead
Côte-St-Luc
Westmount
St Gabriel House
Pont Champlain
Montréal-Pierre Elliott Trudeau International Airport (YUL)
Pointe-Claire
Dorval
Montréal-Ouest
Verdun
Parc Adrien D Archambault
ÎLE DES SŒURS
ÎLE DORVAL
Lachine
The Fur Trade at Lachine NHS
Lachine Museum
St Francis Xavier Mission and Shrine of Kateri Tekakwitha
Parc Angrignon
Parc Honorable George-O'Reilly
Brossard
Centre de Plein Air de Brossard
La Prairie
ROUSSILLON
Récréo-Parc Ste-Catherine
Kahnawake 14 Réserve Indienne
Fleuve Saint-Laurent (St Lawrence River)

OTTAWA, ON
1:44,352
Scale in Kilometers
0.2   0   0.2
Scale in Miles
0.2   0   0.2

Ottawa River
Gatineau
Jacques-Cartier
Canadian Mus of Civilization
National Gallery of Canada
Notre-Dame Cathedral Basilica
Laurier House Nat'l Hist Site
Parliament Buildings
Currency Mus of the Bank of Canada
Bytown Mus
Changing of the Guard
Univ of Ottawa
Rideau Canal
The Supreme Court of Canada
Canadian Mus of Nature
Collège Universitaire Dominicain
St Paul University
OTTAWA

HALIFAX, NS
1:101,376
Scale in Kilometers
0.5   0   0.5
Scale in Miles
0.5   0   0.5

Spectacle Lake
Frenchman Lake
Lake Micmac
Penhorn Lake
Cyril Smith Golden Acres Park
Oat Hill Lake
Dartmouth
Dartmouth Heritage Museum, Evergreen Historic House
Lake Banook
Royal Canadian Legion Military Museum
Dartmouth General Hospital
CFB Halifax-Shannon Park
Halifax
CFB Halifax-Stadacona
Casino Nova Scotia
Maritime Museum of the Atlantic
Halifax Citadel NHS
Maritime Command Museum
Province House
Canadian Mus of Immigration at Pier 21
Canadian Forces Base Willow Pk
Public Gardens
Dalhousie University
Iwk Health Centre
Chapel of Our Lady of Sorrows
The Thomas McCulloch Museum
Dingle Tower
Point Pleasant Park
Prince of Wales Tower NHS
HALIFAX
Harbour
Georges Island NHS
Bedford Basin
Northwest Arm

MONTRÉAL, QC
1:41,184
Scale in Kilometers
0.1   0   0.1
Scale in Miles
0.1   0   0.1

Mont-Royal
Sir George-Étienne Cartier National Historic Site
Parc Jeanne-Mance
Museum of Hospitallers of the Hospital of Montréal
Percival Molson Mem Stad
McGill Univ
McCord Museum of Canadian History
Lachine Rapids Jet Boat Tours
Château Ramezay-Historic Site & Mus of Montréal
King Edward Quay
St Patrick's Basilica
Basilica de Notre-Dame
Pointe-à-Callière, Montréal Museum of Archaeology & History
Hôpital Général de Montréal
Montréal Museum of Fine Arts
Bell Centre
Temple Emanu-El Beth Sholom
Canadian Centre for Architecture
Lachine Canal Nat'l Hist Site
WESTMOUNT
MONTRÉAL

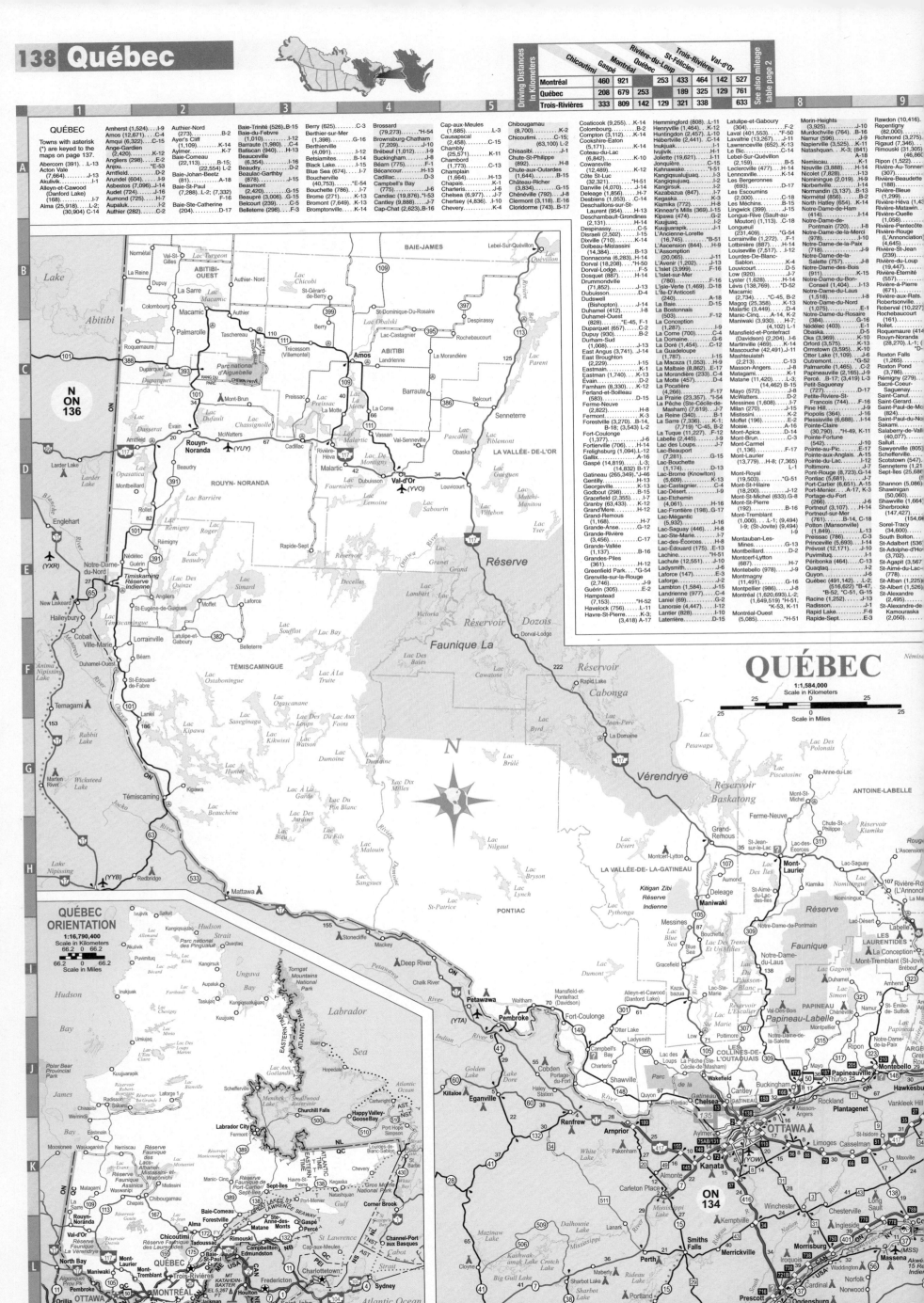

See also mileage table page 2

Driving Distances In Kilometers	Chicoutimi	Gaspé	Montréal	Rivière-du-Loup Québec	St-Félicien Trois-Rivières	Val-d'Or	
Montréal	460	921		253	433	464	142	527
Québec	208	679	253		189	325	129	761
Trois-Rivières	333	809	142	129	321	338		633

QUÉBEC

Towns with asterisk (*) are keyed to the maps on page 137.

Abercorn (391)..I-9
Acton Vale (7,664)..J-13
Akulivik..I-1
Alleyn-et-Cawood (Danford Lake)..F-8
Alma (25,918)..L-2; (30,904) C-14

Amherst (1,524)..I-9
Amos (12,671)..C-4
Amqui (6,322)..C-15
Ange-Gardien (2,420)..
Angliers (298)..E-2
Anjou..*E-53
Arntfield..D-2
Arundel (604)..I-9
Asbestos (7,096)..J-14
Audet (724)..J-16
Aumond (725)..H-7
Aupaluk..I-2
Authier (282)..C-2

Authier-Nord (273)..B-2
Ayer's Cliff (1,109)..K-14
Aylmer..I-12
Baie-Comeau (22,113)..B-15; (22,554) L-2
Baie-Johan-Beetz (81)..A-18
Baie-St-Paul (7,288)..L-2; (7,332) I-16
Baie-Ste-Catherine (204)..D-17

Baie-Trinité (526)..B-15
Baie-du-Febvre (1,010)..I-12
Barraute (1,980)..C-4
Batiscan (940)..H-13
Beauceville (6,354)..I-16
Beaudry..D-2
Beaulac-Garthby (878)..
Beaumont (2,420)..G-15
Beaupré (3,006)..G-15
Belcourt (239)..C-5
Belleterre (298)..F-3

Berry (625)..C-3
Berthier-sur-Mer (1,398)..G-16
Berthierville (4,091)..I-12
Betsiamites..B-14
Béarn (775)..F-1
Bécancour (12,489)..
Bécancour (1,773)..
Bégin..
Belœil (19,621)..I-11

Brossard..*H-54
Brownsburg-Chatham (7,209)..I-10
Buckingham..F-1
Cadillac..D-3
Campbell's Bay..
Cantley (9,888)..J-7
Cap-Chat (2,623)..B-16

Cap-aux-Meules (1,685)..L-3
Causapscai (2,458)..C-15
Chambly (25,571)..K-11
Chambord (1,664)..H-13
Champlain (1,664)..H-13
Chapais (2,131)..H-13
Charteris..
Chartierville (736)..I-16
Châteauguay (45,904)..

Chibougamau (8,700)..K-2
Chicoutimi (63,100) L-2
Chisasibi..J-1
Chute-St-Philippe (892)..I-9
Chute-aux-Outardes (1,644)..B-15
Château-Richer (3,834)..G-15
Chénéville (792)..J-8
Chertsey (4,836)..I-10
Chevery..K-4

Coaticook (9,255)..K-14
Colombourg..B-2
Compton (3,112)..K-14
Cookshire-Eaton (5,171)..
Coteau-du-Lac (6,842)..K-10
Cowansville (12,489)..K-13
Côte-St-Luc..*H-51
Danville (4,070)..J-14
Deleage (1,856)..H-7
Desbiens (1,185)..
Clermont (3,118)..E-16
Cloridorme (743)..B-17

Hemmingford (808)..L-11
Henryville (1,464)..K-12
Huntingdon (2,457)..L-10
Hébertville (2,441)..C-14
Inukjuak..*I-1
Ivujivik..I-1
Joliette (19,621)..I-11
Jonquière..C-15
Kahnawake..*I-51
Kangiqsualujjuaq..I-3
Kangiqsujuaq..I-2
Kangirsuk..I-2
Kazabazua (847)..I-7
Kegaska..K-4
Kiamika (757)..I-7
Kinnear's Mills (369)..I-15
Kipawa (474)..G-2
Kuujjuaq..I-2
Kuujjuarapik..I-1

L'Ancienne-Lorette (16,745)..*B-51
L'Ascension (844)..H-9
L'Assomption (20,065)..I-11
L'Avenir (1,202)..J-13
L'Islet (3,999)..F-16
L'Islet-sur-Mer..F-16
L'Isle-Verte (1,469)..D-18
L'Île-D'Anticosti (240)..A-18
La Baie..D-15
La Bostonnais (503)..F-12
La Conception (1,287)..
La Corne (700)..C-4
La Doré (1,454)..C-12
La Guadeloupe (1,787)..
La Macaza (1,053)..H-9
La Malbaie (8,862)..E-17
La Morandière (233)..C-4
La Motte (457)..D-4
La Pocatière (4,266)..F-17
La Prairie (23,357)..*I-54
La Pêche (Ste-Cécile-de-Masham) (7,619)..J-7
La Reine (340)..B-1
La Sarre (7,336)..*C-45, B-2
La Tuque (11,227)..F-12
Labelle (2,445)..I-9
Lac des Loups..J-6
Lac-Beauport (7,281)..G-15
Lac-Bouchette (1,174)..C-13
Lac-Brome (Knowlton) (5,609)..K-13
Lac-Castagnier (8)..
Lac-Désert..H-6
Lac-Drolet (1,454)..
Lac-Etchemin (4,061)..H-15
Lac-Frontière (198)..G-17
Lac-Mégantic (5,932)..J-16
Lac-Saguay (446)..H-8
Lac-Ste-Marie (446)..J-7
Lac-des-Écorces..H-8
Lac-Édouard (175)..E-13
Lachine..*H-51
Lachute (12,551)..J-10
Ladysmith..J-7
Laforce (147)..
Laforge..J-2
Lambton (1,584)..J-15
Landrienne (977)..C-4
Laniel (69)..G-1
Lanoraie (4,447)..I-12
Lantier (828)..I-10
Laterrière..D-15

Latulipe-et-Gaboury (304)..F-2
Laval (401,553)..*F-50
Lavaltrie (13,267)..I-11
Lawrenceville (652)..K-13
Le Bic..
Lebel-Sur-Quévillon (3,925)..B-5
Leclercville (477)..H-14
Lennoxville..K-14
Les Bergeronnes (693)..D-17
Les Escoumins (2,000)..C-18
Les Méchins..B-15
Lingwick (399)..J-15
Longue-Rive (Sault-au-Mouton) (1,113)..C-18
Longueuil (231,409)..*I-54
Lorrainville (1,272)..F-1
Lotbinière (887)..H-14
Louiseville (7,517)..I-12
Lourdes-de-Blanc-Sablon..K-4
Low (920)..J-7
Lyster (1,828)..H-14
Lévis (138,769)..*G-52
Macamic (2,734)..*C-45, B-2
Magog (25,358)..K-13
Malartic (3,449)..D-4
Manic-Cinq..A-14, K-2
Maniwaki (3,930)..H-7
Mansfield-et-Pontefract (Davidson) (2,204)..I-6
Mansonville (2,004)..K-13
Martinville (480)..K-14
Mascouche (42,491)..I-11
Mashteuiatsh (2,213)..C-13
Masson-Angers (8)..J-8
Matagami..K-1
Matane (11,420)..C-15
Mayo (572)..J-8
McWatters..D-2
Messines (1,608)..I-7
Milan (270)..J-15
Mistissini..K-2
Moffet (196)..F-2
Moisie..A-16
Mont-Apica..D-14
Mont-Brun..C-3
Mont-Carmel (542)..
Mont-Joli (6,568)..*I-7
Mont-Laurier (13,779)..H-8; (7,365) I-9
Mont-Royal (19,503)..*G-51
Mont-St-Hilaire (18,200)..J-12
Mont-St-Michel (633)..G-8
Mont-St-Pierre (192)..B-16
Mont-Tremblant (1,000)..L-1; (9,494) I-9; (St-Jovite) (9,494)
Montauban-les-Mines..
Montbeillard..D-2
Montcerf-Lytton (687)..
Montebello (978)..J-9
Montmagny (11,491)..G-16
Montpellier (986)..I-9
Montréal (491,142)..L-2; (516,622) *B-47, *B-52, *G-51, G-15; (1,649,519) *H-51
Montréal-Ouest (5,085)..*H-51

Morin-Heights (3,925)..J-10
Murdochville (1,739)..
Namur (596)..I-9
Napierville (3,525)..K-11
Natashquan.. K-3; (841) K-4
Nemiscau..A-18
Neuville (3,888)..G-14
Nicolet (7,828)..I-13
Nominingue (2,019)..H-9
Norbertville..B-14
Normandin (3,137)..B-13
Normétal (856)..B-2
North Hatley (654)..K-14
Notre-Dame-de-Ham (414)..
Notre-Dame-de-Pontmain (720)..I-8
Notre-Dame-de-la-Paix (718)..J-8
Notre-Dame-de-la-Salette (757)..J-8
Notre-Dame-des-Bois (911)..J-16
Notre-Dame-du-Bon-Conseil (1,404)..I-13
Notre-Dame-du-Laus (1,518)..I-8
Notre-Dame-du-Nord (1,075)..E-1
Notre-Dame-du-Rosaire (384)..G-16
Nédélec (403)..E-1
Obaska..D-5
Oka (3,575)..
Orford (3,955)..K-13
Ormstown (3,595)..K-10
Otter Lake (1,109)..J-6
Outremont..*G-52
Pabok (571)..
Papineauville (2,165)..J-9
Percé (3,419) L-3..
Petit-Saguenay (727)..D-17
Petite-Rivière-St-François (744)..F-16
Pine Hill..J-7
Piopolis (364)..J-16
Plessisville (6,688)..I-14
Pohénégamook (2,990)..
Pointe-Claire (30,790)..*H-49, K-11
Pointe-Fortune (542)..J-10
Pointe-au-Pic..E-17
Pointe-aux-Anglais (8)..B-15
Pointe-au-Père..
Pont-Rouge (8,723)..G-14
Pontiac (5,681)..J-7
Port-Cartier (6,651)..A-15
Port-Menier..A-17, K-3
Portage-du-Fort (291)..J-6
Portneuf (3,107)..H-14
Portneuf-sur-Mer (761)..B-14, C-18
Potton (Mansonville) (1,849)..L-13
Princeville (5,693)..I-14
Prévost (12,171)..I-10
Puvirnituq..I-1
Quaqtaq..I-2
Québec (491,142)..L-2
Racine (1,252)..J-13
Radisson..J-1
Rapid Lake..F-6
Rapide-Sept..E-3

Rawdon (10,416)..I-10
Repentigny (82,000)..
Richmond (3,275)..J-14
Rigaud (7,346)..
Rimouski (31,305)..K-16
Ripon (1,522)..J-9
Rivière-Beaudette (188)..
Rivière-Bleue (1,058)..
Rivière-Héva (1,491)..D-4
Rivière-Matawin..C-13
Rivière-Ouelle (1,058)..
Rivière-Pentecôte (720)..I-8
Rivière-Rouge (L'Annonciation) (4,645)..I-9
Rivière-du-Loup (19,447)..
Rivière-Éternité (557)..D-15
Rivière-à-Pierre (671)..
Rivière-aux-Rats (1,518)..
Robertsonville..
Roberval (10,227)..B-13
Rochebaucourt (161)..
Rollet..
Roquemaure (114)..B-1
Rouyn-Noranda (28,270)..L-1; (3,786)
Roxton Falls (1,265)..
Roxton Pond (3,786)..
Sacré-Cœur-Saguenay (542)..
Saguenay..C-15
Saint-Canut..
Saint-Gérard..
Saint-Paul-de-Mo (824)..
Saint-Paul-du-Nord..
Sakami..
Salaberry-de-Valleyfield (40,077)..
Salluit..I-1
Sawyerville (805)..
Schefferville (230)..
Scotstown (547)..
Senneterre (1,121)..D-5
Sept-Îles (25,588)..A-16
Shannon (5,060)..
Shawinigan (50,060)..
Sherbrooke (147,427)..J-15
Sorel-Tracy (34,600)..
South Bolton..
St-Adalbert (526)..
St-Adolphe-d'Howard (3,702)..
St-Agapit (3,567)..
St-Aimé-du-Lac-des-Îles (307)..
St-Alban (1,225)..
St-Albert (1,526)..
St-Alexandre (2,495)..
St-Alexandre-de-Kamouraska (2,050)..

Chibougamau (14,384)..K-2
Dégelis (2,502)..I-15
Disraeli (2,502)..J-15
Dixville (710)..K-14
Dolbeau-Mistassini (14,384)..
Donnacona (6,283)..H-14
Dorval (18,208)..*H-50
Dorval-Lodge..F-5
Dosquet (887)..H-14
Drummondville (71,852)..J-13
Dubuisson..D-4
Dudswell (Bishopton)..J-14
Duhamel (412)..I-8
Duhamel-Ouest (828)..*E-45, F-1
Dupont (657)..J-12
Dupuy (930)..B-1
Durham-Sud (1,008)..J-13
East Angus (3,741)..J-14
East Broughton (2,229)..I-15
Eastmain..K-1
Eastman (1,740)..K-13
Évain..D-2
Farnham (8,330)..K-12
Ferland-et-Boilleau (583)..D-15
Ferme-Neuve (2,822)..H-8
Fermont..K-2
Forestville (3,270)..B-14, B-18; (3,543) L-2
Fort-Coulonge (1,377)..J-6
Fortierville (706)..H-14
Frelighsburg (1,094)..L-12
Gallix..A-16
Gaspé (14,819)..L-3
Gatineau (265,349)..*J-46
Gentilly..H-13
Georgeville..K-13
Godbout (298)..B-15
Gracefield (2,355)..I-7
Grand'Mère (14,832) B-17..
Grand-Remous (1,168)..H-7
Grande-Anse..G-12
Grande-Rivière (3,456)..C-17
Grande-Vallée (1,137)..B-16
Grandes-Piles (361)..H-12
Greenfield Park (16,735)..*G-54
Grenville-sur-la-Rouge (2,748)..
Guérin (305)..E-2
Hampstead (7,153)..*H-52
Havelock (756)..L-11
Havre-St-Pierre (3,418) A-17..K-3

QUÉBEC
1:1,584,000

Scale in Kilometers
25 0 25
Scale in Miles
25

QUÉBEC ORIENTATION
1:16,790,400
Scale in Kilometers
66.2 0 66.2
Scale in Miles
66.2 0 66.2

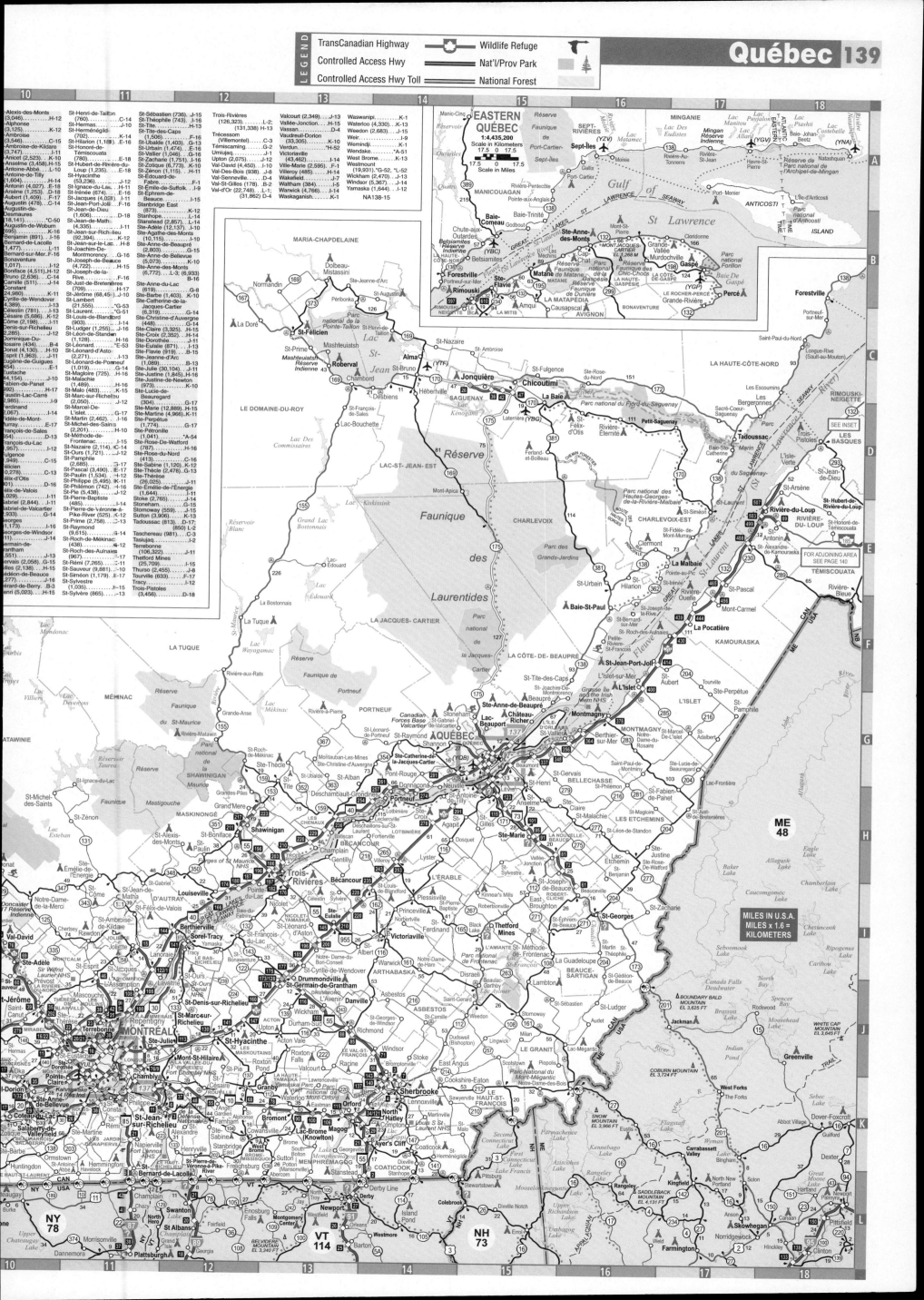

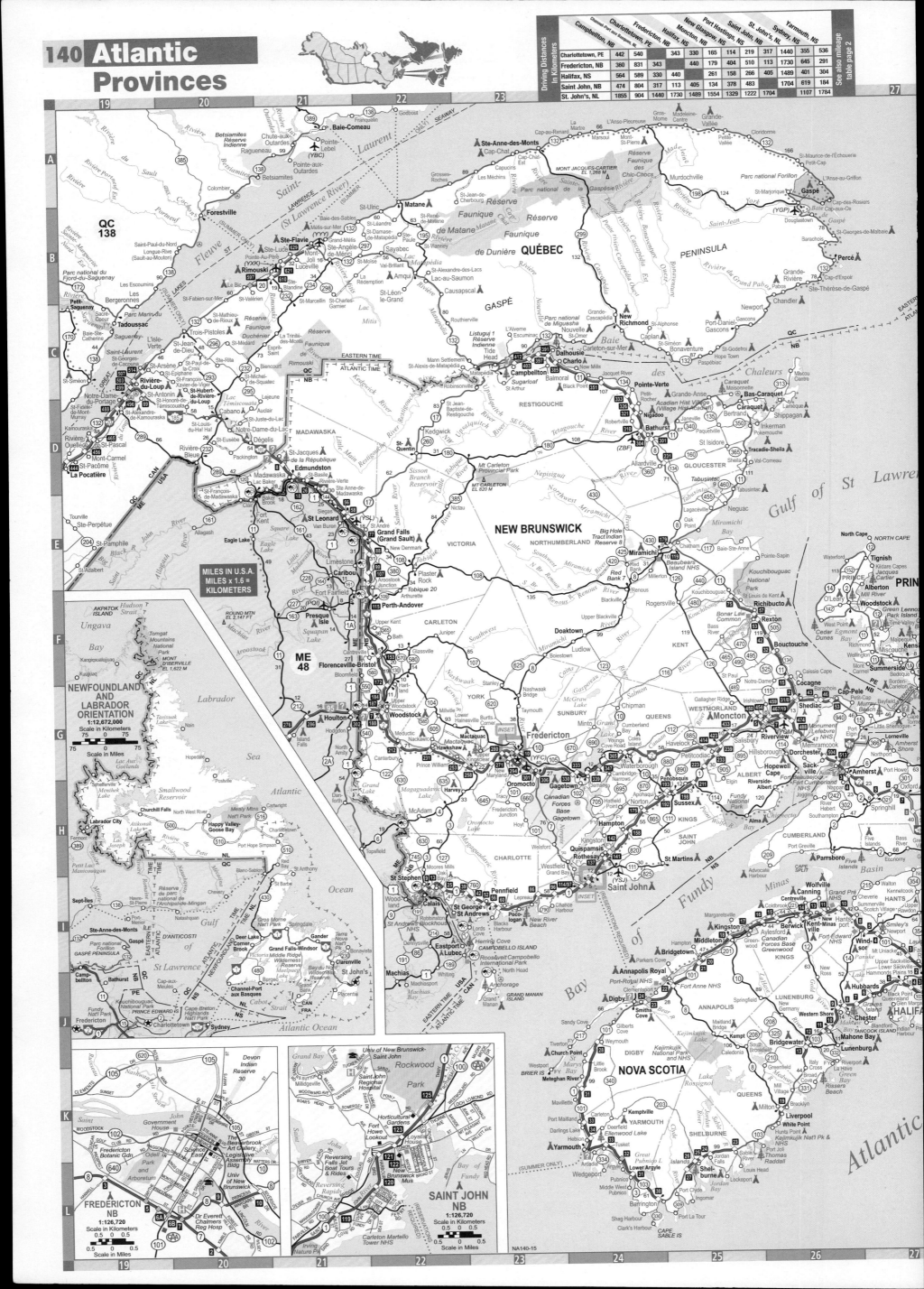

Driving Distances In Kilometers	Channel-Port aux Basques, NL	Campbellton, NB	Charlottetown, PE	Fredericton, NB	Halifax, NS	Moncton, NB	New Glasgow, NS	Port Hastings, NS	Saint John, NB	St. John's, NL	Sydney, NS	Yarmouth, NS
Charlottetown, PE		442	540	343	330	165	114	219	317	1440	355	536
Fredericton, NB		360	831	343	440	179	404	521	113	1730	645	304
Halifax, NS		564	589	330	440		261	158	266	405	1489	401	304
Saint John, NB		474	840	317	113	405	134	378	483		1704	619	184
St. John's, NL		1855	904	1440	1730	1489	1554	1329	1222	1704		1107	1784

See also page 2 table on page 2

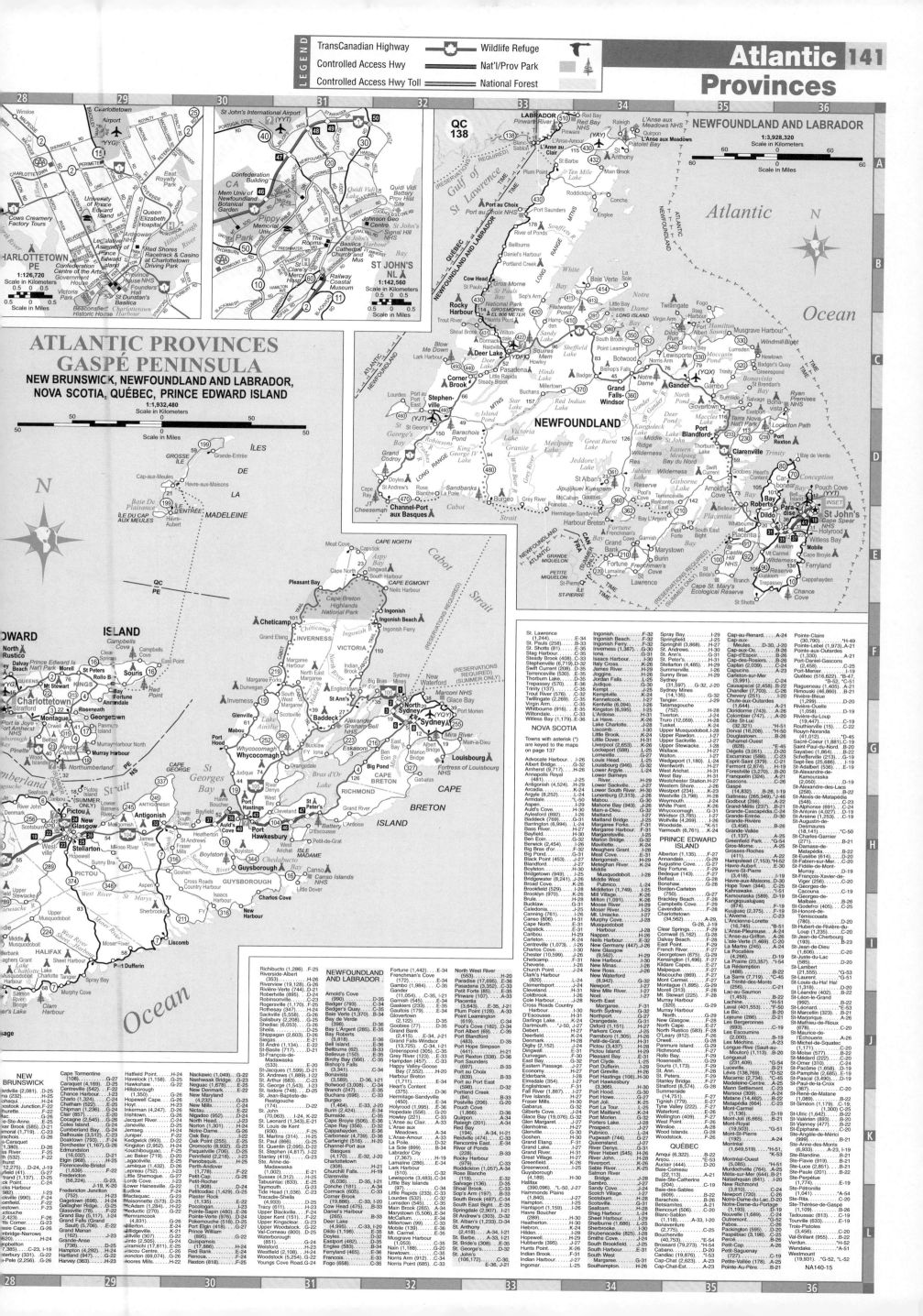

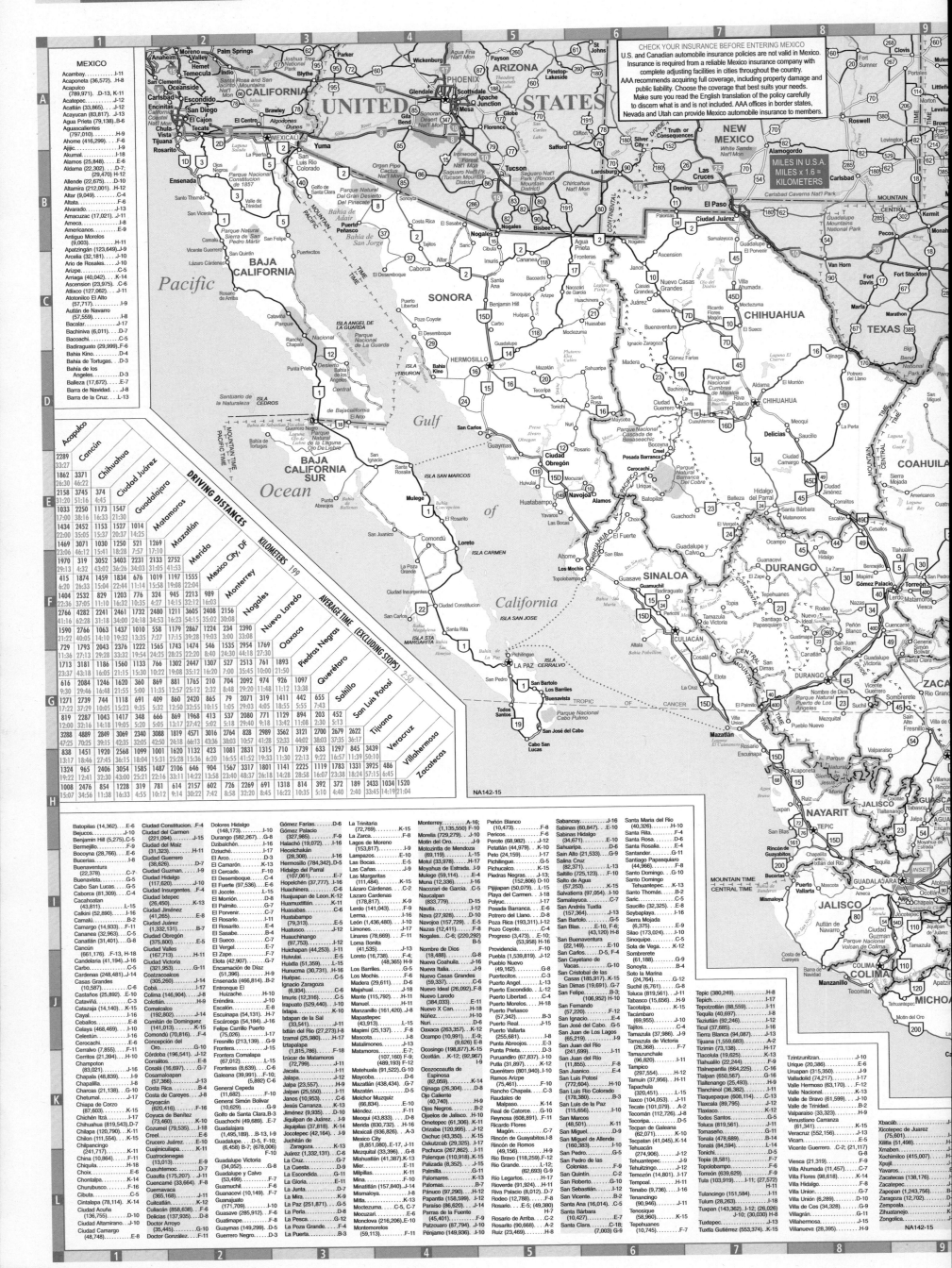

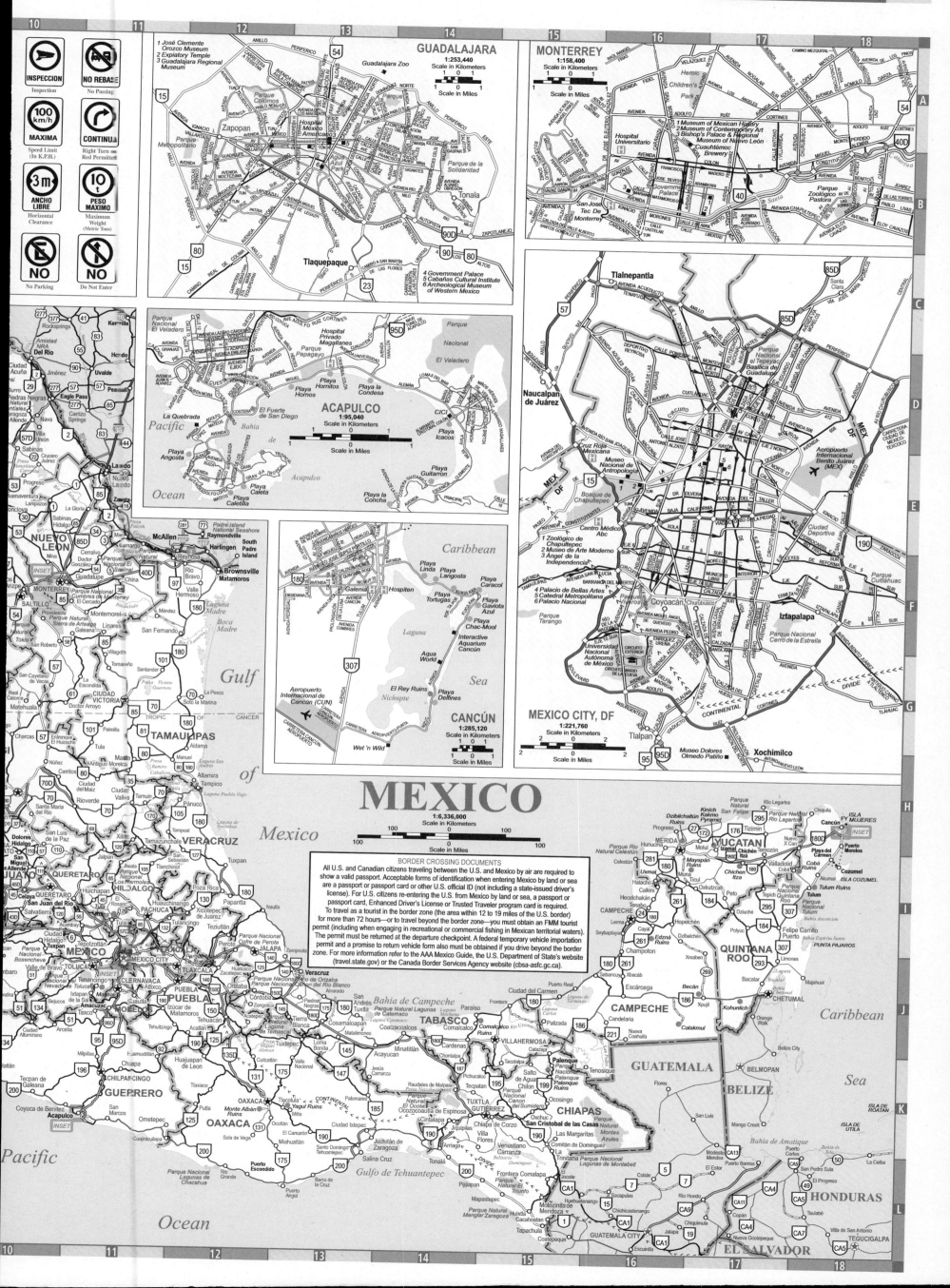

GUADALAJARA
1:253,440
Scale in Kilometers
Scale in Miles

MONTERREY
1:158,400
Scale in Kilometers
Scale in Miles

1 José Clemente Orozco Museum
2 Expiatory Temple
3 Guadalajara Regional Museum
4 Government Palace
5 Cabañas Cultural Institute
6 Archeological Museum of Western Mexico

1 Museum of Mexican History
2 Museum of Contemporary Art
3 Bishop's Palace & Regional Museum of Nuevo León

ACAPULCO
1:95,040
Scale in Kilometers
Scale in Miles

CANCÚN
1:285,120
Scale in Kilometers
Scale in Miles

MEXICO CITY, DF
1:221,760
Scale in Kilometers
Scale in Miles

1 Zoológico de Chapultepec
2 Museo de Arte Moderno
3 Angel de la Independencia
4 Palacio de Bellas Artes
5 Catedral Metropolitana
6 Palacio Nacional

MEXICO
1:6,336,000
Scale in Kilometers
Scale in Miles

BORDER CROSSING DOCUMENTS
All U.S. and Canadian citizens traveling between the U.S. and Mexico by air are required to show a valid passport. Acceptable forms of identification when entering Mexico by land or sea are a passport or passport card or other U.S. official ID (not including a state-issued driver's license). For U.S. citizens re-entering the U.S. from Mexico by land or sea, a passport or passport card, Enhanced Driver's License or Trusted Traveler program card is required.

To travel as a tourist in the border zone (the area within 12 to 19 miles of the U.S. border) for more than 72 hours—or to travel beyond the border zone—you must obtain an FMM tourist permit (including when engaging in recreational or commercial fishing in Mexican territorial waters). The permit must be returned at the departure checkpoint. A federal temporary vehicle importation permit and a promise to return vehicle form also must be obtained if you drive beyond the border zone. For more information refer to the AAA Mexico Guide, the U.S. Department of State's website (travel.state.gov) or the Canada Border Services Agency website (cbsa-asfc.gc.ca).

INSPECCION
Inspection

NO REBASE
No Passing

100 km/h
MAXIMA
Speed Limit (In K.P.H.)

CONTINUA
Right Turn on Red Permitted

3 m
ANCHO LIBRE
Horizontal Clearance

10 t
PESO MAXIMO
Maximum Weight (Metric Tons)

NO
No Parking

NO
Do Not Enter

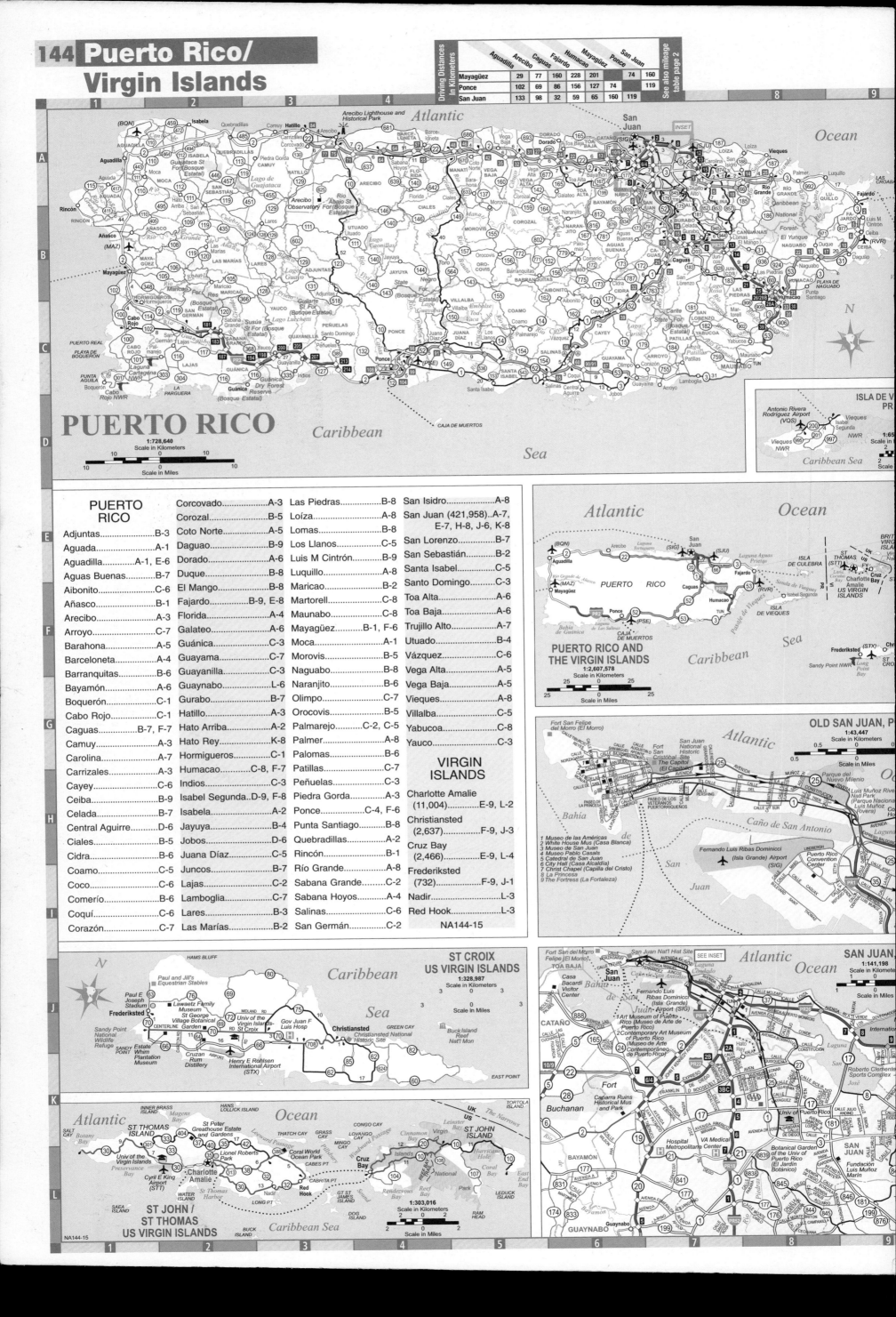

Driving Distances In Kilometers (See also mileage table page 2)

	Aguadilla	Caguas	Fajardo	Humacao	Mayagüez	Ponce	San Juan
Mayagüez	29	77	160	228	201	74	160
Ponce	102	69	86	156	127	74	119
San Juan	133	98	32	59	65	160	119

PUERTO RICO

VIRGIN ISLANDS

PUERTO RICO
1:728,640
Scale in Kilometers
Scale in Miles

PUERTO RICO AND THE VIRGIN ISLANDS
1:2,607,578
Scale in Kilometers
Scale in Miles

OLD SAN JUAN, P
1:43,447

1 Museo de las Américas
2 White House Mus (Casa Blanca)
3 Museo de San Juan
4 Museo Pablo Casals
5 Catedral de San Juan
6 City Hall (Casa Alcaldía)
7 Christ Chapel (Capilla del Cristo)
8 La Princesa
9 The Fortress (La Fortaleza)

ST CROIX US VIRGIN ISLANDS
1:328,987

ST JOHN / ST THOMAS US VIRGIN ISLANDS
1:303,016

SAN JUAN
1:141,198

1 Art Museum of Puerto Rico (Museo de Arte de Puerto Rico)
2 Contemporary Art Museum of Puerto Rico (Museo de Arte Contemporáneo de Puerto Rico)

NA144-15